TRAFFIC-FREE CYCLE TRAILS

Nick Cotton

CYCLECITY

GUIDES

Publisher: CycleCity Guides
Author: Nick Cotton
Production Editor: Julia Gray
Mapping: Mark Fordham

Printed by Butler and Tanner,
Caxton Road, Frome, Somerset

Maps in this publication are based upon Ordnance
Survey Mapping with permission of the Controller
of Her Majesty's Stationery Office © Crown
Copyright. CycleCity Guides, Licence No: 43472U

ISBN 1 900623 17 X

CycleCity Guides, Wallbridge Mill, The Retreat,
Frome, Somerset, BA11 5JU
T: +44 (0)1373 453 533
info@cyclecityguides.co.uk
www.cyclecityguides.co.uk

Acknowledgements and thanks
Photographs: The Forestry Commission for use of
its images, which appear in the Scotland and North-
East sections. Andy McCandish for permission to
use his images on this page, and pages 328, 334
and 339. Sustrans for permission to use various
images throughout the book (photographers:
Alexandra Allen, Julia Bayne, Jonathan Bewley,
John Grimshaw, David Hall, Andy Hazell, Tim
Snowdon and Andy Syme). Martin Whitfield for
permission to use his images in the North-East
section. All other photographs by Nick Cotton.
Cover image: Jason Patient, jason@cycling-
images.co.uk **Design and production:** Lynne
Curry, Charlie Dewey, Caroline Pomeroy

While every attempt has been made to include
the vast majority of traffic-free cycle trails in
mainland Britain, there will inevitably be
omissions. We apologise if we have missed your
favourite ride. Please tell us if this is the case,
letting us know details of start and finish and
cafes and pubs along the way, and we'll try to
include it next time.

Likewise, if you know of any other routes not
listed in this first edition of Traffic-Free Cycle
Trails please contact CycleCity Guides at the
address on the left.

Contents

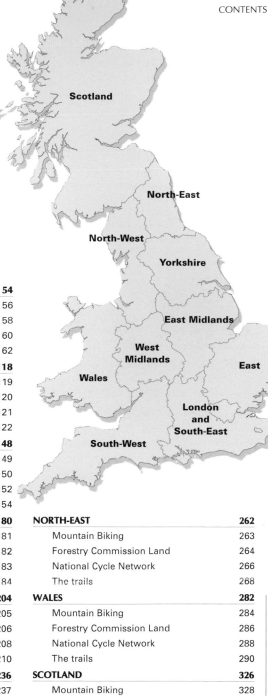

How to use this guide

In this book, you will find more than 400 traffic-free trails from Cornwall to the Scottish Highlands, including railway paths, forestry routes, canal towpaths, round-reservoir routes, purpose-built cyclepaths and some easier ridge rides on byways and bridleways.

How do I find a trail near me?

The country has been divided into ten regions, each with a map showing all the trails in the area. So simply look at the map then look up the numbers of the trails nearest to you. Under the entry for each route number, you will find details of starting point, distance, refreshments and useful publications such as leaflets and maps. The nearest Tourist Information Centre is also mentioned, enabling you to find out about nearby bike shops, bike hire or accommodation.

What if I know the name of a trail but don't know where it is?

The index at the back will help you to find the Granite Way, the Phoenix Trail or the Innocent Railway, for example. Then look up the entry.

How do I get to the start of the ride?

We have included details of the closest railway station and of convenient car parking places (including grid references). A grid reference pinpoints on an Ordnance Survey map exactly where a trail starts. To find out how to use these, see page 6.

What sort of bike should I use?

Few of the trails have sealed surfaces so it is best to use mountain or hybrid bikes. Children's bikes are normally built to withstand knocks and will cope with all of the easier trails. A small number of the trails are out-and-out mountain bike rides and may get quite muddy in winter. Be prepared for this, or enjoy them after a dry spell in summer.

Do I need special clothes?

Ordinary clothes are fine for all the easier rides. Waterproofs are always useful, and gloves and a hat will stop your hands and ears getting cold (a common problem on a bike). If you discover you really love cycling, it is worth investing in cycling shorts and padded gloves, which make riding more comfortable. A top made of 'wicking' fabric stops you getting too clammy.

How long will each trail take to ride?

We have deliberately avoided giving a time as there are so many variables, the most important of which is YOU! A ride that takes a fit cyclist half an hour could take all day with a group of children. Other variables are the quality of the surface, hills, wind and type of bike. These rides are for enjoyment! Indeed, many of the trails are shared with walkers and horseriders, and you should slow down when there are other users around. Most people of average fitness should cover 5 - 9 miles in an hour, discounting any stops (this type of cycling is two or three times as fast as walking).

Are all the rides 100 per cent traffic-free?

Most of the trails have long sections of traffic-free cycling but inevitably, many have to cross roads, and some routes also use quiet lanes. You are given a warning if there are any busier roads to cross.

Will I find somewhere to eat?

If there is a convenient pub, teashop or cafe along the trail then we have mentioned it. This is more likely on canal towpath rides and round-reservoir routes. Forestry routes are the least likely to have refreshments along the way, but many start from visitor centres where you can buy a snack. It is always worth carrying a bar of something and a bottle of water .

What if I break down?

None of these rides is so long or remote that you couldn't walk back to the start or somewhere where your bike can be fixed. The usual problem is a puncture, so carry a spare tube and a pump. Multitools, with screwdrivers, allen keys and spanners can be used to tighten up nuts, bolts and screws that rattle loose and can adjust saddle height.

Does the book include trails on the National Cycle Network?

The National Cycle Network is a mixture of cycle lanes, quiet streets, country lanes and traffic-free trails. Traffic-free sections over 3 miles are included. You will know you are on the National Cycle Network by the red and white route number signs. You will find a section on the National Cycle Network in each region, listing the maps that cover the area. These maps highlight all traffic-free sections and - who knows? - you may be tempted to do an entire long-distance route, such as the famous Sea to Sea (C2C) from Cumbria to the North Sea coast.

What about mountain biking?

Most of the Forestry Commission rides are tougher than railway paths and some areas have purpose-built single track mountain bike trails, particularly in Wales and Southern Scotland. There are also long distance trails such as the Ridgeway, South Downs Way or Peddars Way which are more of a challenge. At the beginning of each section there is a map with details of good mountain biking areas or centres. Most good book shops stock a range of bike guides, including ones covering mountain biking.

Where else can I ride, traffic-free and legally?

You have a right to ride on bridleways and byways, all shown on Ordnance Survey maps, but these are a bit hit-and-miss in terms of quality. You are **NOT** allowed to ride on footpaths. The majority of canal towpaths are too narrow, rough, muddy or overgrown to be much fun. The best option is to go to the nearest Forestry Commission holding where you can explore the broad stone tracks (forestry operations permitting). There is a map of the Forestry Commission holdings at the start of each regional chapter.

What about riding on lanes?

After you have built up your confidence there is no reason why you should not explore Britain's fantastic network of quiet country lanes by bike. At the start of each region there are details of good areas, with suggested bases from which to start. Many of the waymarked long distance routes on the National Cycle Network are also good options for longer rides.

Useful Information

FINDING A GRID REFERENCE

What is a Grid Reference?

A number that allows you to pinpoint a place on a map. It looks and sounds technical, but is easy to learn. Grid references can be enormously helpful, saving the need for heaps of directions you would otherwise need.

Why is it called a Grid Reference?

If you look at any Ordnance Survey map there are numbered blue lines running across and down the map - these form a grid. In the case of the Landranger maps, which we refer to a lot in this book, there are 40 vertical and 40 horizontal lines, creating 1600 squares on each map, each of which represents one square kilometre (just over half a mile by half a mile).

So how does it work?

There are times when you want to direct people to a point in one of the squares formed by the grid to find a feature (a pub, a train station etc) contained in that square. Within the six figure grid reference, the first set of three numbers gives you an imaginary line running up and down the map (north-south), the last set of three numbers gives you a line running across the map (east-west). Where these imaginary lines cross is the place on the map you want to pinpoint.

How do you work out the first three figures of a Grid Reference?

The first two numbers of the six figure grid reference refer to the vertical line on the left of the chosen square. These double-digit numbers can be found along the top and bottom edges of the map. For the third number in the series, imagine the chosen square, the one to the right of the vertical line, divided into ten vertical strips, numbered from '1' on the left to '9' on the right. The third number locates one of these strips so for example '2' would be towards the left of the square and '8' would be towards the right.

What about the last three numbers?

These refer to the horiztonal lines. Instead of starting at the left of the chosen square, start from the bottom and work towards the top. (To find the numbers, look at the left-or right-hand edges of the map.) The line at the bottom of the chosen square gives you the fourth and fifth numbers in the six figure grid reference.

To calculate the sixth number, imagine the chosen square above the horizontal line divided into ten horizontal strips, numbered from '1' at the bottom to '9' at the top. The sixth and final number of the six figure grid reference locates one of these strips. For example, '2' would be towards the bottom of the square and '8' would be towards the top.

Put the vertical numbers together with the horizontal and you have a six-figure grid reference and can locate a point on the map to a high degree of accuracy. To help you remember which set of numbers go first, always remember the saying 'Along the corridor and up the stairs' - ie work along the map from left to right, then up the map from bottom to top.

TOWPATH CYCLISTS' SAFETY CODE

- Give way to other people on the towpath and warn them politely of your approach.
  A 'hello' and a 'thank you' mean a lot.

- Access paths can be steep and slippery - join the towpath with care.

- Dismount if the towpath is busy with walkers or anglers.

- Get off and push your bike:
  - if the path gets very narrow
  - beneath low bridges
  - alongside locks
  - if you encounter any other danger.

- Ride at a gentle pace, in single file and do not bunch. Never race - remember you have water on one side of you.

- If you are a young or inexperienced cyclist, always go with a responsible adult.

- Watch out for hidden mooring spikes or ropes across the path beside moored boats.

- Take particular care on wet or uneven surfaces, and don't worsen them by skidding.

- Never cycle along the towpath in the dark.

- You are responsible for your own and others' safety.

- Your bike should have a bell or hooter.

- Watch for trimmings which can cause a puncture.

For more information about towpath cycling visit:

www.waterscape.com

FORESTRY CODE

The Forestry Commission has, by and large, adopted an enlightened approach to cycling in its woodlands. The broad rule of thumb is that you are welcome to use the hard, stone-based forestry roads that provide excellent opportunities for safe, traffic-free cycling. In certain woodlands there are also waymarked trails on 'single track' paths, which are often more testing. You should pay attention to any signs that may indicate a temporary or permanent restriction on cycling (usually on walkers' trails or where forestry operations are in progress).

The best maps to use for exploring Forestry Commission woodland are the most up-to-date Ordnance Survey Explorer maps, which are at 1:25,000 scale with an orange cover. Alternatively, use the Outdoor Leisure maps, at the same scale but with a yellow cover.

NB It must be stressed that many people use the woodlands for different purposes, so courtesy and consideration should be shown at all times to walkers and horse riders. The fact that a bike can travel faster than a pedestrian does not give it priority - indeed, priority usually lies with the walker or the horse rider. Use a bell or say 'hello' to give warning of your presence, and thank people who step aside for you.

www.forestry.gov.uk/recreation

South-West

SOUTH-WEST TRAILS

1   Cornish Mineral Tramways
    Coast to Coast Trail
2   Camel Trail - Padstow to Wadebridge
    and Bodmin
3   Pentewan Valley, St Austell
4   Cardinham Woods, Bodmin
5   Tarka Trail - Braunton to Barnstaple
6   Tarka Trail - Barnstaple to Bideford
7   Tarka Trail - Bideford to Meeth
8   Okehampton to Meldon Viaduct and
    Lake Viaduct (Granite Way)
9   Plym Valley Trail, north of Plymouth
10 Okehampton Military Loop Road,
    Dartmoor

11 Princetown Tramway, Dartmoor
12 Eggesford Wood, northwest of
    Exeter
13 Dunster Woods, south of Minehead,
    Exmoor (3 routes)
14 Exeter along the River Exe
15 Grand Western Canal, east of
    Tiverton
16 Exmouth to Budleigh Salterton
17 Quantocks Ridge, west of Bridgwater
18 Bridgwater & Taunton Canal
19 The Willow Walk, west of
    Glastonbury
20 Severn Bridge Cyclepath

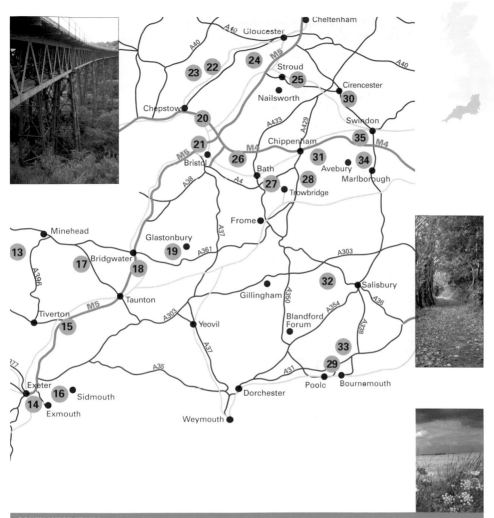

South-West Mountain Biking

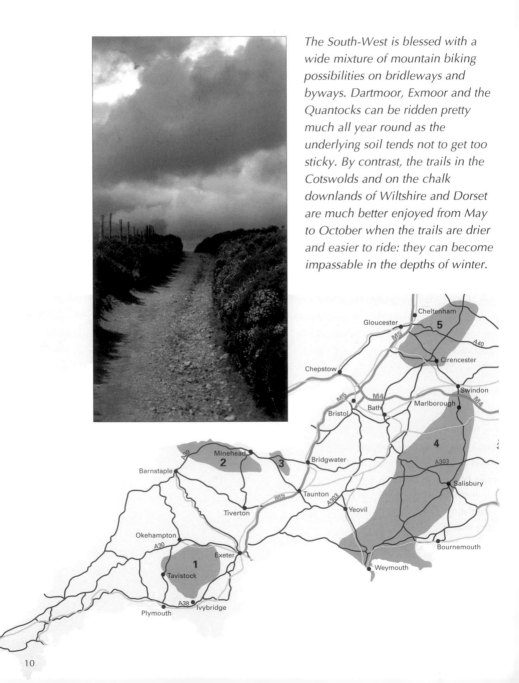

The South-West is blessed with a wide mixture of mountain biking possibilities on bridleways and byways. Dartmoor, Exmoor and the Quantocks can be ridden pretty much all year round as the underlying soil tends not to get too sticky. By contrast, the trails in the Cotswolds and on the chalk downlands of Wiltshire and Dorset are much better enjoyed from May to October when the trails are drier and easier to ride: they can become impassable in the depths of winter.

1 Dartmoor

Although Dartmoor is much larger than Exmoor, it is not nearly so well provided with legal, rideable tracks. Some of the bridleways shown on Ordnance Survey maps run across the open moorland and are barely visible on the ground. The best areas for mountain biking are around Princetown in the centre of the moor and on the east of the moor around Lustleigh.

2 Exmoor

Despite being the UK's smallest National Park, Exmoor is one of the best in the country for mountain biking with a plethora of well-waymarked and generally well-maintained trails. For a taster try the 11-mile descent from Dunkery Beacon down to Winsford via the Exe Valley. Most of the best tracks lie within a circle drawn 10 miles around Exford.

3 The Quantock Hills
   (west of Bridgwater)

For a range of hills which is only 10 miles long by 5 miles wide the Quantock Hills boast an astonishing range of mountain bike rides, from the broad, undulating track along the ridge to some very testing single track down through the combes.

4 The chalk downlands of
   Wiltshire, Salisbury Plain
   and Dorset

Wiltshire and Dorset have a higher proportion of bridleways and byways than anywhere else in the country. The most well known of all is the Ridgeway, the easier sections of which are covered in this guide. It can be ridden along its whole length from West Kennett (near Avebury) to Goring on Thames, a distance of 43 miles. Further south in Wiltshire the village of Wilton, to the west of Salisbury, is a good base from which several excellent ridge tracks can be followed for many miles. In Dorset the finest tracks are found in the triangle formed by Bridport, Blandford Forum and Weymouth.

5 Cotswolds

There is a surprising quantity of rideable tracks in among the picturesque honey-coloured villages of the Cotswolds. The best riding lies in a 20-mile arc to the northeast, east and south of Cheltenham.

Mountain Biking Information

These are possible sources:
- leaflets produced by local authorities, normally available in Tourist Information Centres
- guidebooks which can usually be found in larger, better stocked bookshops
- the staff in bike shops can often put you in contact with local riders or clubs who are sure to have done some of this research already, saving you many hours of trial and error.

South-West Forestry

The South-West of England is not nearly as forested as Wales or Scotland or even the South-East of England: the Forest of Dean is the only large forestry holding in the region (the New Forest is described in the South-East section). However, there are some smaller holdings which have waymarked trails and others where it is possible to devise your own route.

In some forests and woods there are no waymarked routes but you are free to explore the tracks. The relevant Ordnance Survey map is mentioned. It is highly recommended that you take a map for the larger woods where it is very easy to get lost!

Forests and woods with waymarked trails

They are shown with a corresponding trail number and page reference.

6   Eggesford Woods, 20 miles northwest of Exeter
See Trail 12, page 27

7   Dunster Woods, south of Minehead
See Trail 13, page 28

12   Moors Valley Country Park near Ringwood
See Trail 33, page 51

14   The Forest of Dean, Gloucestershire
See Trail 22, page 39

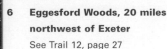

The trails below correspond with the numbers on the map on the right.

1   Idless Woods, north of Truro
OS Explorer Map 105

2   Dunmere, Grogley and Hustyn Woods, northwest of Bodmin
OS Explorer Map 106 /109

3   Abbeyford Woods, north of Okehampton
OS Explorer Map 113

4   Soussons, Bellever and Fernworthy Forests, northeast of Princetown
OS Outdoor Leisure Map 28

5   Haldon Forest, southwest of Exeter
OS Explorer Map 110

8   Great Woods (Quantocks) southwest of Nether Stowey
OS Explorer Map 140

9   Puddletown Forest, east of Dorchester
OS Explorer Map 117

10   Affpuddle Heath, east of Dorchester
OS Outdoor Leisure Map 15

11   Isle of Purbeck, northeast of Corfe Castle
OS Outdoor Leisure Map 15

13   Wye Valley woodland between Chepstow and Monmouth
OS Outdoor Leisure Map 14

15   West Woods, southwest of Marlborough
OS Explorer Map 157

The Forestry Commission's website is a good source of information with details of 1600 miles of waymarked cycling trails throughout the UK. Search by forest name or by the nearest town or city and the search will tell you the grade, length and waymarking details of the trails.

www.forestry.gov.uk/recreation

Further Information

Forest of Dean
Bank House, Bank Street, Coleford, Gloucestershire GL16 8BA.
Tel: 01594 833057

Peninsula Forest District (Devon & Cornwall)
Bullers Hill, Kennford, Exeter, Devon EX6 7XR.
Tel: 01392 832262

New Forest
The Queen's House, Lyndhurst, Hampshire SO43 7NH.
Tel: 02380 283141

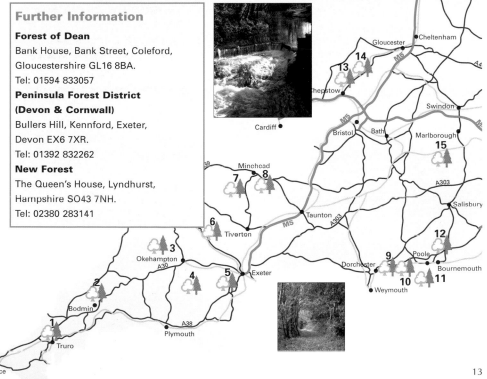

South-West National Cycle Network

Cornish Way

123 miles from Land's End to Bude (with two options between Truro and Bodmin). Highlights include: Land's End, Lamorna Cove, the traffic-free coastal route through Penzance, Cornish Mineral Tramways, the Camel Trail, King Harry Ferry from Falmouth, the Lost Gardens of Heligan and the Eden Project.

Traffic-free sections over 3 miles:
- Crofthandy to Devoran, east of Redruth (NCN 3)
- The Camel Trail from Padstow to Bodmin (NCN 32)

West Country Way

240 miles from Padstow to Bristol (or Bath). Highlights include the Camel Trail, the Tarka Trail, Exmoor, Knighthayes Court, the Grand Western Canal, the

Bridgwater & Taunton Canal, Glastonbury, Wells, the Mendips and the Bristol & Bath Railway Path.

Traffic-free sections over 3 miles:
- The Camel Trail from Padstow to Blisland (NCN 32)
- The Tarka Trail from Petrockstowe to Barnstaple (NCN 3)
- Grand Western Canal east of Tiverton (NCN 3)
- Bridgwater & Taunton Canal (NCN 3)
- Bristol & Bath Railway Path (NCN 4)

Devon Coast to Coast

102 miles from Ilfracombe to Plymouth via Barnstaple, Bideford, Okehampton

Sustrans

Listed below are the Sustrans maps that cover the National Cycle Network within the region. Some of the maps may describe routes that continue on into adjacent regions: these maps are mentioned in both chapters. The maps are not only useful for people wishing to ride the the whole route over several days; they also show all the traffic-free sections which make good day rides. The maps cost £5.99 each and are available from Sustrans.

Sustrans Order Line:
Call **0845 113 0065** or visit their website at
www.sustrans.org.uk

and Tavistock. Highlights include the North Devon Coast at Ilfracombe, the Tarka Trail, Meldon Viaduct and the Granite Way, Dartmoor views, the handsome town of Tavistock, the Plym Valley Trail and Plymouth.

Traffic-free sections over 3 miles:

- The Tarka Trail from Barnstaple to Meeth (NCN 3 & 27)
- The Granite Way from Okehampton to Lake Viaduct (NCN 27)
- The Plym Valley Trail from Clearbrook to Plymouth (NCN 27)

Severn & Thames Cycle Route

141 miles from Gloucester to Newbury via Bristol. Highlights include Gloucester Cathedral, the Severn Vale, the Gloucester & Sharpness Canal, Avon Gorge, Clifton Suspension Bridge, Bristol & Bath Railway Path, Bath, the Kennet & Avon Canal, Avebury and Marlborough.

Traffic-free sections over 3 miles:

- Gloucester & Sharpness Canal (NCN 41)
- Riverside path from Pill to Bristol (NCN 41)
- Bristol & Bath Railway Path (NCN 4)
- Kennet & Avon Canal from Bath to Devizes (NCN 4)
- Marlborough to Chiseldon Railway Path (NCN 45)

Other areas for lane cycling

For such popular tourist areas, there is very little good, easy cycling on the lane networks of Cornwall, Devon and Dorset: the narrow, hilly lanes are often set between high hedgerows with poor visibility. The exceptions are those right on the top of **Exmoor** and **Dartmoor**. By contrast the **Somerset Levels** offer some very easy cycling alongside the rhynes (drainage ditches) bordered by weeping willows. There are good bases at Somerton, Glastonbury and Mark. The **Severn Vale** is bypassed by both the A38 and the M5 and there is a gentle charm to the network of quiet lanes that run north from Thornbury to Gloucester, linked at times by the Gloucester & Sharpness Canal towpath. Try starting from Berkeley or Frampton on Severn. As for the **Cotswolds**, think of them like a wedge of cake on its side: the edge of the cake represents the steep escarpment overlooking the Severn Vale where the cycling is strenuous; east from here (the flatter part of the cake!), the land slopes gently down towards the Thames and there is a wonderful network of quiet lanes linking together the honey-coloured stone villages and towns. Northleach, Malmesbury, Bourton on the Water and Burford are all good starting points.

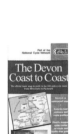

South-West Trails

1 Cornish Mineral Tramways Coast to Coast Trail

CATEGORY

Railway path, mineral tramways and quiet lanes.

DISTANCE

Up to 12 miles each way.

The Mineral Tramways route from the north coast of Cornwall at Portreath to the south coast at Devoran is destined to become Cornwall's second most popular cycle trail after the Camel Trail. The result of many years of patient negotiation and engineering, the trail uses several sections of old tramroad that used to serve the mines scattered around this part of Cornwall, with old ruins and chimneys still visible. The route climbs gradually from the attractive seaside resort of Portreath through Cambrose to Wheal Rose and Scorrier. From this highpoint the trail drops down into the Poldice Valley and along the Carnon River down to Devoran, passing beneath the soaring railway viaduct. The route is generally well waymarked with handsome granite stones, but there are a couple of places (particularly in Scorrier) where you should keep a sharp eye out for signposts.

STARTING POINTS & PARKING

→ The car park by the beach in **Portreath**, on the B3300 to the north of Camborne / Redruth (grid reference 693480).

→ The car park by Bissoe Cycle Hire Centre, about 5 miles southwest of **Truro** (grid reference 772415).

→ The car park by the village hall on Quay Road in **Devoran**, just south of the A39 between Truro and Falmouth (grid reference 792393).

NB There is one very busy road (the A39) to cross if you want to go into the village of Devoran (to visit the pub and Restronguet Creek) or if you start from here.

ON YOUR BIKES!

Leave the car park by the beach in Portreath and follow the B3300 towards Redruth. At the Portreath Arms bear left onto Sunnyvale Road, signposted 'Portreath Tramroad'. After 1/2 mile, just before rejoining the B3300, bear left uphill on to the start of the traffic-free trail. Continue in the same direction on a generally level track at several minor junctions.

OTHER INFORMATION

Station: Perranwell Station.
TIC: Falmouth, 01326 312300.
Useful publications: OS Landranger Maps 203 & 204. A leaflet is available from Falmouth TIC.
Refreshments: Pubs in Devoran, Scorrier and Portreath.

2   Camel Trail, Wadebridge, Cornwall

CATEGORY
Railway path.

DISTANCE
Poley's Bridge to Bodmin - 6 miles each way.
Bodmin to Wadebridge - 5 miles each way.
Wadebridge to Padstow - 6 miles each way.

The most popular recreational ride in the country, visited by over 300,000 people a year, the Camel Trail runs from Poley's Bridge and the wooded countryside of the upper Camel Valley past Bodmin to Wadebridge, then alongside the picturesque Camel Estuary as far as Padstow. The route is very busy in July and August. There are many cycle hire centres in Padstow, Wadebridge and Bodmin, with a huge variety of bikes, many of which you will see along the ride!

STARTING POINTS & PARKING
→ There are several possible starting points and car parks - **Poley's Bridge, Bodmin, Wadebridge** and **Padstow.**

Station: Bodmin Parkway Station, 6 miles southeast of the trail.

TIC: Padstow, 01841 533449; Wadebridge, 01208 813725; Bodmin, 01208 76616.

Other nearby trails: The Camel Trail forms the start of Sustrans West Country Way (NCN Route 32), which runs 250 miles from Padstow to Bristol. There is a waymarked forest trail in Cardinham Woods, northeast of Bodmin.

Useful publications: OS Landranger Map 200. A leaflet about the Camel Trail is available from TICs.

Refreshments: Lots of choice in Bodmin, Wadebridge and Padstow.

3   Pentewan Valley, St Austell

CATEGORY
Railway path and specially-built cyclepath.

DISTANCE
4 miles each way.

This route forms part of the Cornish Way (NCN Route 3), the 180-mile cycle route from Land's End to Bude. The traffic-free section starts in the woodland just south of St Austell and follows the river valley down towards seaside village of Pentewan. After about one mile you have the choice of continuing on the flat down towards the beach or climbing for 300 ft up past the Lost Gardens of Heligan and down the other side of

3

the hill to the popular fishing village of Mevagissey. The descent to Mevagissey is quite steep so you may well prefer to walk up the hill on the way back. As you are surrounded by wild flowers and fine views, this hardly constitutes hardship!

NB If you wish to go into the heart of Mevagissey, or visit the Lost Gardens of Heligan, you will need to use roads for about 1/2 mile.

STARTING POINTS & PARKING

→ **London Apprentice.** The car park in Shepherdshill Woods about 2 miles south of St Austell (grid reference 008498). Follow the B3273 towards Mevagissey. Just after London Apprentice turn left, signposted 'Retail Leisure Warehouse'. Follow the lane round to the right and park in the woods.

→ **Mevagissey.** Park in the main car park on the B3273 just north of Mevagissey then follow the road towards St Austell. Shortly after passing a petrol station on the left turn left by a 'Heligan Bike Trail' signpost. The gradient steepens soon after the start of the traffic-free section.

ON YOUR BIKES!

1. From the Retail Leisure Warehouse follow the tarmac lane through the woods. As the road swings left uphill, bear right onto the lower, broad woodland track soon running alongside the river. After 1 mile, at a bridge and a Millennium Milepost, you have a choice: straight on for Pentewan (1 mile) or turn right across the bridge for Mevagissey (3 miles).

2. (Towards Mevagissey) After crossing the bridge, turn left at the B3273 along the shared-use pavement, cross the road via the traffic island and continue until the track swings right away from the road and begins to climb. At a junction of tracks shortly after a zig-zag, turn right for Mevagissey (or go straight ahead for the Lost Gardens of Heligan).

3. (Mevagissey) Descend, climb, then descend again. At the T-junction (with a footpath to the left) turn right. Steep descent to the road on the edge of Mevagissey. Turn right for the village. Retrace your steps.

Station: St Austell.
TIC: St Austell, 01726 879500.
Other nearby trails: The Camel Trail runs from Padstow through Wadebridge to Bodmin.
Useful publications: OS Landranger Map 204. *The Cornish Way Cycle Route Map* produced by Sustrans (£5.99) shows this and several other traffic-free routes in Cornwall, including the Camel Trail, the Mineral Tramways from Bissoe to Devoran and the route through Penzance from Mousehole to Marazion.
Sustrans Order Line: Call 0845 113 0065 or visit their website at www.sustrans.org.uk
Refreshments: Lots of choice in Mevagissey and in Pentewan.

4 Cardinham Woods, Bodmin, Cornwall

CATEGORY
Forest trails.

DISTANCE
3-mile circuit (with plenty of opportunities to extend).

There are few Forestry Commission holdings of any real size in Cornwall. With the exception of Idless Woods, to the north of Truro, there is only a scattering of small holdings along the A389 and A38 between Wadebridge, Bodmin and Liskeard. Of these, Cardinham Woods is the largest (650 acres) and it is possible to devise several short rides within the woodland, of which this is just one. The Forestry Commission bought Cardinham Woods in 1922. Today their fertile soils produce fine timber, saw logs for house building from the impressive old Douglas

firs, and pulp for newsprint from the younger thinnings. Nearly 80 years of careful management have created a varied and attractive forest. Each age of tree is home to a different range of wildlife. Look out for ravens and buzzards soaring above the forest. Catch the occasional glimpse of grey squirrels, rabbits or foxes. Red and roe-deer are here but melt away into the forest at the first hint of danger.

STARTING POINT & PARKING

→ The car park in **Cardinham Woods** at grid reference 100666. From Bodmin take the A38 towards Liskeard for 2 miles. Cross the bridge over the A30 dual carriageway then, after 1/4 mile, turn left along a road signposted 'Cardinham, Fletchersbridge'. Shortly after a sharp right-hand bend, turn left and follow signs for the Cardinham Woods car park.

ON YOUR BIKES!

1. At the end of the car park, cross the bridge and turn right by a black and white wooden barrier and signpost marked 'All walks begin here'. Take the right-hand of the three tracks, signposted 'All ability route. Ladyvale Bridge'.
2. Climb steadily. At the T-junction turn left,

signposted 'Lidcutt Valley 2kms'. At the next major junction of tracks, at the bottom of a short descent, turn right, again signposted 'Lidcutt Valley' and cross a small stream.
3. At the bottom of a fast descent take the second track on the right, ie cross a second bridge over the stream (this bridge has low wooden barriers on either side). Shortly turn right again, signposted 'Car park'. Go round a black and white barrier to join a tarmac lane and return to the car park.

Station: Bodmin.
TIC: Bodmin, 01208 76616.
Other nearby trails: The Camel Trail starts west of Bodmin.
Useful publications: OS Landranger Map 200. For further information contact Forest Enterprise, Peninsula Forest District, Bullers Hill, Kennford, Exeter, Devon EX6 7XR (01392 832262).
Refreshments: None on the route, the nearest are in Bodmin.

5   Tarka Trail from Braunton to Barnstaple

CATEGORY
Railway path.
DISTANCE
6 miles each way.

Forming part of Sustrans West Country Way (NCN Route 3, Padstow to Bristol), the Tarka Trail is one of the longest railway paths in the country, runnning north from near the edge of Dartmoor down to the coast then following the estuaries of the Rivers Torridge and Taw through Bideford, Barnstaple and Braunton. The trail has been split into three easily-managed sections. The section described below links Braunton to the town of Barnstaple with its famous Pannier Market, passing brightly-painted boats and yellow RAF Rescue helicopters on its way.

5

STARTING POINTS & PARKING

→ **Braunton.** The trail starts by the police
station at the far end of the main car park in the
centre, signposted 'Museum, Tourist Information
Centre, Countryside Centre' (grid reference
487366). Braunton is on the A361 to the west of
Barnstaple. Once on your bikes leave the car
park, following signs for 'The Burrows,
Barnstaple'. Briefly join the road past Otter
Cycle Hire then turn right on to Station Close
and left on to the cyclepath.

→ **Barnstaple.** The railway station in Barnstaple
is a good place to park, but starting here will
involve pushing your bike on the pavement
across the main river bridge, as you need to get
from south to north and there is no segregated
cycle lane. It is best to use the pavement on the
east side of the bridge as there is an underpass
which takes you on to the start of the trail.

Station: Barnstaple.
TIC: Barnstaple, 01271 375000; Braunton,
01271 816400.
Other nearby trails: The Tarka Trail continues
from Barnstaple to Bideford and south to Great
Torrington and Meeth.
Useful publications: OS Landranger Map 180.

The *West Country Way* map produced by
Sustrans (£5.99) shows this and several other
traffic-free trails in Cornwall, Devon and
Somerset, including the Camel Trail, the Grand
Western Canal, the Bridgwater & Taunton
Canal, the Willow Walk (Glastonbury) and the
Bristol & Bath Railway Path.
Refreshments: Lots of choice in Braunton and
Barnstaple.

6   Tarka Trail from Barnstaple to Bideford

CATEGORY
Railway path.
DISTANCE
9 miles each way.

This ride forms part of the longest railway path
in the South West, running almost 30 miles from
Braunton to Meeth. In its entirety the trail
encompasses a range of vistas from the broad
flat expanses of the Taw / Torridge estuary to
the intimacies of wooded riverbanks. The trail
threads its way down the River Torridge, passing
the port of Instow where there is a fine sandy

6

beach and a ferry across to Appledore on the western banks of the Torridge and on to East-the-Water, the settlement opposite Bideford. There is plenty of wildlife along the route and a good cafe at the cycle hire centre at Fremington Quay. Barnstaple is famous for its Pannier Market, held on Tuesdays and Fridays. It would be easy to extend this ride in both directions, ie to continue west from Barnstaple to Braunton on the north side of the River Taw, or south from Bideford towards Meeth.

NB Care should be taken crossing busy road bridges, over the River Torridge into Bideford, and if you go north from Barnstaple station into Barnstaple itself.

STARTING POINTS & PARKING
→ The railway station in **Barnstaple**.
→ The Old Bideford Station on the north side of the River Torridge in **East-the-Water** (just east of the A386 bridge, grid reference 456264).

Station: Barnstaple.
TIC: Barnstaple, 01271 375000; Bideford, 01237 477676.
Other nearby trails: The Tarka Trail continues south from Bideford to Great Torrington and Meeth and west from Barnstaple to Braunton.
Useful publications: OS Landranger Map 180. A leaflet is available from TICs.
Refreshments: Lots of choice in Barnstaple, Instow and Bideford. Cafe at Fremington Quay, next to the cycle hire centre.

7 Tarka Trail from Bideford to Meeth

CATEGORY
Railway path.
DISTANCE
Up to 15 miles each way.

The final ride on the Tarka Trail runs south from Bideford to Meeth, on the A386 near Hatherleigh. There is a steady 350ft climb on the stone and gravel railway path over 4 miles from the Puffing Billy pub (west of Great Torrington) to the highpoint near to East Yarde. The railway used to carry clay from the quarries at Petrockstowe to the ships at Bideford. The trail runs past the pretty village of Weare Giffard, where Tarka the Otter was born and fought his last battle, and on to Meeth. There is a very different feel to the ride compared with the other two sections described, as it is largely wooded with several river crossings.

NB Care should be taken if you cross the busy road bridge over the River Torridge from East-the-Water into Bideford.

STARTING POINTS & PARKING
→ The Old Bideford Station in **East-the-Water** (Bideford, grid reference 456264).
→ The Puffing Billy on the A386 to the west of **Great Torrington** (grid reference 480197).
→ In **Meeth**, on the A386 to the north of Hatherleigh (grid reference 547079).
Station: Barnstaple or Eggesford.
TIC: Bideford, 01237 477676.
Other nearby trails: The Tarka Trail continues from Bideford to Barnstaple and Braunton.
Useful publications: OS Landranger Maps 180 & 191. A leaflet is available from TICs.
Refreshments: Lots of choice in Bideford. Puffing Billy pub to the west of Great Torrington. Bull & Dragon pub in Meeth.

8   Okehampton to Meldon and Lake Viaduct - The Granite Way

CATEGORY
Railway path

DISTANCE
6 1/2 miles each way.

The Devon Coast to Coast Route (NCN Route 27) will within a few years offer a largely traffic-free route all the way from Ilfracombe on the north coast down to Plymouth on the south. The ride described here forms part the middle section, along the course of an old dismantled railway linking Okehampton station via the magnificent Meldon Viaduct to a picnic spot beyond Lake Viaduct. There are superb views into the heart of Dartmoor and across to the west over typical the rolling patchwork of fields and hedgerows of Devon. A steam engine runs between Okehampton station and Meldon Viaduct, so it would be easy to combine the

bike ride with a trip on the wonderfully-restored old train. Another short section of railway line has been converted to recreational use closer to Lydford, but you will need to use some steep lanes to connect the two sections.

STARTING POINT & PARKING
→ **Okehampton** Station car park. Follow signs for the station from the traffic lights at the crossroads in the centre of Okehampton (grid reference 593944).

ON YOUR BIKES!
Exit Okehampton Station car park and cross on to the minor road opposite, signposted 'National Cycle Network Route 27. Tavistock'. Shortly, turn sharp left to join the path running alongside the railway line. Follow this for 6 1/2 miles to the picnic spot (some granite slabs) about 3/4 mile beyond Lake Viaduct (the second viaduct).

Station: Okehampton (seasonal).
TIC: Okehampton, 01837 53020.

Other nearby trails: The Tarka Trail starts from Meeth, a few miles to the north on the A386 (north of Hatherleigh). There is a mountain bike trail on the old tramway at Princetown.

Useful publications: OS Landranger Map 191. The *Devon Coast to Coast* map produced by Sustrans (£5.99) shows this and several other traffic-free trails in Devon including the Ilfracombe Railway Path, the Tarka Trail, the Okehampton Military Loop Road, the Princetown Tramway and the Plym Valley Path. There is also an excellent free leaflet, The *Granite Way*, available from the TIC.

Sustrans Order Line: Call 0845 113 0065 or visit their website at www.sustrans.org.uk

Refreshments: Cafe at Okehampton railway station. The Buffet Car at the station at Meldon Viaduct. The Bottle Neck Inn, Sourton Down (just off the route). The Highwayman Inn, Sourton (just off the route). The Bearslake Inn, Lake (just off the route)

9 Plym Valley Trail, Plymouth

CATEGORY
Railway path.

DISTANCE
9 miles each way.

This popular railway path climbs steadily as it runs north from Plymouth (Laira Bridge) over a series of spectacular stone viaducts, and through the Plym Valley to Clearbrook. There is one much steeper (but short) section on road in Bickleigh. The ride follows the course of the old Great Western Railway which started its life as the South Devon & Tavistock Railway. In addition to the magnificent viaducts mentioned, there is also the 300yd Shaugh Tunnel towards the northern end of the ride and it is the southern start of Sustrans Devon Coast to Coast Cycle Route (NCN Route 27).

9

STARTING POINT & PARKING

→ The ride starts at Laira Bridge, **Plymouth** (where the A379 crosses the River Plym). There are car parks at Point Cottage, at the entrance to Saltram House grounds, at Plym Bridge and at Clearbrook.

Station: Plymouth.
TIC: Plymouth, 01752 264859.
Other nearby trails: A trail runs along the old mineral tramway from Princetown.
Useful publications: OS Landranger Map 201. A leaflet is available from the TIC.
Refreshments: Pub in Clearbrook.

10   Okehampton Firing Ranges, Dartmoor

CATEGORY

Little-used loop road climbing on to Dartmoor.

DISTANCE

10-mile circuit.

This ride offers the chance to climb right into the heart of Dartmoor on a little-used public road that forms a loop, so carries no through traffic. The drawbacks are that you have a climb of 550ft and that you will be sharing the route with the odd vehicle. On the plus side are some of the best views from all Dartmoor, a sense of

achievement when you get to the highest point and one of the most wonderful descents in the whole book! This is definitely a ride to leave for a day of good visibility as you deserve to be rewarded for your efforts with the panorama from the top. If several of you have arrived in the same vehicle, why not persuade the driver to let the others continue downhill on bikes from the start point all the way into Okehampton, a drop of a further 700ft!

WARNING The road is occasionally closed when ranges are being used for firing. Details of the firing programme are obtainable from Okehampton Tourist Information, 01837 53020.

STARTING POINT & PARKING

→ At the fork of roads at grid reference 597922, to the south of **Okehampton**. From the centre of Okehampton follow signs for 'Station' and 'Okehampton Camp'. Follow the road over the A30 bypass and past Okehampton Camp. Cross the cattle grid, continue straight ahead then at the first major fork of tarmac roads park in the car parking area.

ON YOUR BIKES!

From the car parking area take the left-hand fork. Descend to cross Black-a-ven Brook then climb steadily. The gradient steepens near the top of the climb, reached when you pass a

drystone wall shelter / lookout post. Enjoy the fabulous descent back to the start.

Station: Okehampton (seasonal).
TIC: Okehampton, 01837 53020.
Other nearby trails: Okehampton to Meldon Viaduct and Lake Viaduct. The Tarka Trail starts from Meeth, a few miles to the north on the A386 (north of Hatherleigh). There is a trail on the old tramway at Princetown.
Useful publications: OS Landranger Map 191 or Outdoor Leisure Map 28 are highly recommended as this is not a waymarked cycle trail and there are several tracks in the area.
Refreshments: Lots of choice in Okehampton.

11   Princetown, Dartmoor

CATEGORY
Railway path (suitable for mountain bikes only).
DISTANCE
6 miles each way.

The trail uses a remote stretch of dismantled railway (formerly part of the Yelverton to Princetown line) in the heart of Dartmoor, running around King's Tor and past old granite quarries. Vast granite blocks went to build bridges, including the widening of London Bridge in 1903. The ride starts from near the infamous Dartmoor Prison, originally built to house French prisoners of war in Napoleonic times. The trail is also known as the Tyrwhitt Trail, after Thomas Tyrwhitt, who founded Princetown and built the prison. The stone and gravel path drops 500ft as it meanders west and southwest from Princetown to the suggested turnaround point at the stile just before junction of the railway with the B3212 (just east of Dousland), so be aware that the return part of the journey will take far longer than the first half. As the going is fairly rough and because of

12

the drop this is a not a ride for the unfit or for young children. Princetown is also one of the best bases for mountain biking on Dartmoor, with a wide variety of bridleways in all directions. These tend to be strenuous and should not be undertaken by the inexperienced, particularly if visibility is poor.

STARTING POINT & PARKING

→ **Princetown** lies at the heart of Dartmoor, at the junction of the B3357 and the B3212. The ride starts from the main car park (with an honesty box) in the centre of Princetown and leaves the car park by the fire station, signposted 'Disused Railway'.

ON YOUR BIKES!

1. At a three-way fork of tracks after about 1 1/2 miles, take the left-hand of the three tracks to go around King's Tor.
2. After a further 4 1/2 miles of gentle downhill you will come to a stile. It is suggested you turn round here. The alternative is to go over the stile and follow the ever-rougher tramway to the B3212 and turn left, climbing back to Princetown. This road can be busy.

Station: None nearby.
TIC: Tavistock, 01822 612938.
Other nearby trails: The Plym Valley Trail from Plymouth.
Useful publications: OS Outdoor Leisure Map 28 or OS Landranger Maps 191, 201 & 202.
Refreshments: Several options in Princetown.

12 Eggesford (Heywood) Wood, northwest of Exeter

CATEGORY
Forestry trail (mountain bikes essential).
DISTANCE
3 miles.

There are very few Forestry Commission holdings in the Southwest peninsula and even fewer waymarked routes. This short circuit in Heywood Wood is waymarked with round wooden posts with a red band at the top. The only cycle signs you are likely to see are those telling you where you cannot go! Mountain bikes are essential for this undulating route with steeper sections as there are occasional rough bits. There is another nearby Forestry Commission holding called Flashdown Wood, which you are welcome to explore, although some of the tracks seem to go from stone to grass then earth so be prepared for mud! The trail through Heywood Wood goes past the remains of a motte and bailey which can be accessed via steps.

STARTING POINT & PARKING

→ The small car park on the eastern edge of **Heywood Wood** at grid reference 672119. From Eggesford Station (on the A377 halfway between Exeter and Barnstaple) take the road, signposted 'Wembworthy, Winkleigh' and shortly turn right (same sign). After climbing for 1 mile, on a sharp left-hand bend, turn right signposted 'Bridge Reeve'. Go past the Wembworthy Outdoor Centre then after 1/2 mile you will come to a small car parking area, off the road to the left.

ON YOUR BIKES!

1. From the car park, return to the minor lane, turn right then shortly after passing Eggesford Farm on your left, turn right downhill on to a wide forestry track, signposted 'Footpath', then

shortly bear left on to a narrower track, marked with a red-banded round wooden post.

2. At a T-junction by a wooden barrier with a wider track turn right. Follow this main track in the same direction, crossing a minor road on to the wide stone track opposite.

3. Follow the main track as it curves around the humped remains of the motte and bailey to return to the car park.

Station: Eggesford.
TIC: Exeter, 01392 265700.
Other nearby trails: The Tarka Trail starts in Meeth, 12 miles to the west. There are trails south and west from Okehampton.
Useful publications: OS Landranger Maps 180 & 191.
Refreshments: At Eggesford Garden Centre.

13 Dunster Woods, Exmoor (south of Minehead)

CATEGORY
Woodland trails. 3 routes.

DISTANCE
From 1 to 9-mile circuits.

There are three waymarked trails in the forestry to the south of Dunster. One is described as a Family Route and is a relatively flat circuit, a second involves a lot more climbing but is on good broad stone-based forest roads which will not deteriorate in the winter months. The third is a tougher challenge. It would be easy to combine Dunster Woods with a trip to Dunster Castle or a journey on the steam railway that runs between Minehead and Bishops Lydeard.

13

Grade	Distance	Waymarks
Family	1 mile	Green
Intermediate	6 miles	Orange
Explorer	9 miles	Brown

STARTING POINT & PARKING

→ Family and Explorer Routes. From **Dunster** take the A396 towards Tiverton. Less than a mile after the end of the village (and shortly after crossing a bridge over the River Avill) take the next lane to the left. Nutcombe Bottom Car Park is on the left, about 3/4 mile up this steep and narrow lane (grid reference 978424).

→ Intermediate Route. The Upper Car Park (grid reference 974420) is about 3/4 mile up the hill, on the right, from **Nutcombe Bottom** car park. Just as the gradient starts to ease, opposite a 'Dunster Woods Mountain Biking' signpost, turn sharp right on to a broad track into the car park.

ON YOUR BIKES!

The Family Route. Leave Nutcombe Bottom car park, cross the road on to the track opposite and turn right following the green arrows, climbing steadily. Ignore the first major track to the left. Continue straight ahead at this point but keep bearing left look out for the green arrow pointing you left on to a grassier track. Rejoin the outward route and return to the car park.

Station: Taunton or Tiverton Parkway.
TIC: Minehead, 01643 702624.
Other nearby trails: The ridge ride along the Quantocks. The towpath of the Grand Western Canal, near Tiverton.
Useful publications: OS Landranger Map 181 or Outdoor Leisure 9. Leaflet called *'Exmoor: Bike it / Dunster Woods'* can be bought from Minehead TIC.
Refreshments: Lots of choice in Dunster.

14 Exeter - along the River Exe

CATEGORY
Riverside path and specially-built cyclepath.
DISTANCE
9 miles each way.

A traffic-free route starts in the heart of Exeter and follows a combination of the River Exe and the Exe Canal down past the Double Locks Inn to the wide expanse of the Exe estuary at Turf Locks. The River Exe and its tributary the River Culm drain much of Exmoor and the Blackdown Hills, making Exeter prone to flooding. Weirs and defence works have reduced the risk, creating at times a bewildering amount of water channels and possible paths to follow. All paths lead south to Turf Locks! The section through the town centre passes the attractive marina, where brightly-coloured dinghies tack and jibe. Further south there is an option of following the river or the canal, the

14

Exeter Cycle Guide & Map

14

latter passing the popular Double Locks Inn.
Beyond the major road bridge, the towpath
becomes narrower and at times a little
overgrown although the surface is very good by
general canal towpath standards.

STARTING POINT & PARKING

→ Station Road car park, across the river from
St David's railway station, off the Cowley Bridge
Road (the A377 on the northwest side of **Exeter**).

ON YOUR BIKES!

1. From the car park off Station Road, follow
signs for 'Exe Bridges, City Centre'. The route
passes beneath a railway bridge then rejoins the
river.
2. At the start of the canal (just past the
Maritime Museum) you have a choice of
following a route through the Riverside Valley
Park or alongside the canal. The canal route
will take you past the Double Locks Inn.
3. Both routes rejoin at Bridge Road (A379)

where there is a pelican crossing to enable you
to follow the canal towpath further south.
4. The path narrows and may be overgrown.
Please show consideration to other users.
Continue on under the M5 bridge to the Turf
Inn. Retrace your steps.

Station: Exeter St David's.
TIC: Exeter, 01392 265700.
Other nearby trails: Exmouth to Budleigh
Salterton. There are many miles of forest roads
in Haldon Forest, although no waymarked trails.
Useful publications: OS Landranger Map 192.
A leaflet, *Exeter Cycle Guide and Map* is
available from the Tourist Information Centre
(01392 265700).
Refreshments: Lots of choice in Exeter. The
Double Locks Inn, halfway between the city
centre and Bridge Road (the A379). Turf Inn, at
the end of the canal where it joins the Exe
estuary (southeast of Exminster).

15 Grand Western Canal, Tiverton

CATEGORY

Canal towpath (with a 3-mile minor road connecting section through Halberton and Sampford Peverell).

DISTANCE

Up to 10 miles each way.

Built in 1810-1814, the Grand Western Canal was part of a grand coast-to-coast scheme to link Exeter (and the River Exe) to Bridgwater (and the River Parrett) thus enabling ships and their cargoes to avoid the treacherous Cornish coast. The scheme was never fully realised and this is one of the fragments that remain. It runs between Tiverton and Whipcott in Mid Devon. There are two sections of the towpath that are used on National Cycle Network Route 3 (the West Country Way), connected by 3 miles of quiet lanes through Halberton and Sampford Peverell. The 3-mile stretch near Tiverton is the best-maintained part of the towpath. In the distance the views of patchwork red earth fields and green pastures is so characteristic of Devon.

STARTING POINT & PARKING

→ The Grand Western Canal Visitor Centre, **Tiverton.** (grid reference 963124) From the A361 (North Devon Link Road) follow the A396 towards the centre of Tiverton for 1 1/2 miles. At a sign for 'Police Station, Butterleigh, Grand Western Canal' turn left on to Old Road (leading to Canal Hill). Keep following the brown signs for 'Grand Western Canal'. Start climbing the hill, ignore 'The Avenue' to the left and take the next left signposted 'Grand Western Canal'. Park here and go to the end of the car park to join the towpath.

ON YOUR BIKES!

1. From the end of the Grand Western Canal car park bear right on to the towpath. Follow for 3

miles, passing under Tidcombe and Warnicombe Bridges.

2. The well-made trail ends at Crown Hill Bridge, made of grey stone. At this point you can return or continue onwards, following National Cycle Network Route 3 (the West Country Way) on lanes through Halberton and Sampford Peverell to regain the towpath further east. There are a further 4 miles along the towpath, of varying quality, ending at Whipcott.

Station: Tiverton.
TIC: Tiverton, 01884 255827.
Other nearby trails: The Bridgwater & Taunton Canal on the West Country Way. The Quantocks Ridge is a good challenge for mountain bikes.
Useful publications: OS Landranger Map 181. *The West Country Way* map produced by Sustrans (£5.99) shows this and several other traffic-free trails in Cornwall, Devon and Somerset including the Camel Trail, the Tarka

Trail, the Bridgwater & Taunton Canal, the Willow Walk (Glastonbury) and the Bristol & Bath Railway Path. It costs £5.99 from Sustrans. **Sustrans Order Line:** Call 0845 113 0065 or visit their website at www.sustrans.org.uk **Refreshments:** Lots of choice in Tiverton. Tea shop at the start of the ride (at the end of the car park). Pubs in Halberton and Sampford Peverell if you choose to follow the West Country Way (National Cycle Network Route 3).

16 Exmouth to Budleigh Salterton

CATEGORY
Railway path.
DISTANCE
4 miles each way.

Starting conveniently from Phear Park in the centre of the seaside town of Exmouth, this ride heads east along the course of a recently-improved railway path towards Budleigh Salterton. The trail climbs gradually up through woodland on a good quality path then drops down towards Knowle. If you wish to visit the attractive seaside town of Budleigh Salterton you will need to use a map to work out the combination of quiet lanes and residential streets to reach shops, cafes and pubs. If it is a hot summer's day and a swim in the sea beckons, there is an excellent beach at Sandy Bay, to the southeast of Exmouth.

STARTING POINT & PARKING
→ The free car park in Phear Park to the northeast of the centre of **Exmouth** (grid reference 007816). If approaching from the north on the A376, you should turn left off the Exeter Road on to Gipsy Lane, just after Hulham Road, before reaching the town centre.

ON YOUR BIKES!
1. Return past the cafe in Phear Park, go over the bumps and leave the park through the opening with bollards and eagle-topped stone pillars. Turn left on the pavement up Marlpool Hill and shortly first left, signposted 'Littleham Cycle Route', then follow signs for Budleigh

16

Salterton for 4 miles.

2. (On to Budleigh Salterton by road) At the T-junction with the minor lane (Bear Lane), at the end of the traffic-free trail, turn right. Then, at the next T-junction (with the busier B3178) turn left then right on to Bedlands Lane. At the T-junction at the end of Bedlands Lane turn right and follow the road around to the left.

3. At the T-junction at the end of Moor Lane turn right and follow this downhill into the centre of Budleigh Salterton. If you wish to visit the beach turn left at the traffic lights along the High Street for 1/4 mile. From wherever you choose to finish the outward ride, retrace your steps back to Exmouth via Station Road - Moor Lane - Bedlands Lane - Bear Lane - cyclepath - Phear Park.

Station: Exmouth.
TIC: Exmouth, 01395 222299.
Other nearby trails: Exe Valley through Exeter.
Useful publications: OS Landranger Map 192.
Refreshments: There is a cafe in Phear Park in Exmouth. There is plenty of choice in Budleigh Salterton beyond the end of the railway path.

17 Quantocks Ridge, West of Bridgwater

CATEGORY
Bridleway ride along fine ridge.

DISTANCE
7 miles each way (mountain bikes essential). The car park at Crowcombe Gate is half way along so you have the option of two 7-mile round trips: northwest to the trig point at Beacon Hill above West Quantoxhead or southeast to the car park above West Bagborough at grid reference 181338.

This ride on byways and bridleways along the top of the Quantocks ridge offers a real 'roof-of the-world' experience. It is best left for a day of excellent visibility as the views are potentially magnificent, looking north across the expanse of the Bristol Channel to Wales and west towards the hills of Exmoor. The route undulates between a height of 300 and 350m (about 1,000ft) above sea level along its length so there are plenty of short climbs, but few of them are very steep or prolonged. It runs along broad, stone-based tracks through carpets of heather and gorse at the western end and between avenues of beech trees and high earth banks at the eastern end. If you feel fairly confident with a map it would be possible to put together any number of loops using the ridge as just one part of a spectacular circuit with thrilling descents and steep climbs.

WARNING
Although the route is along the ridge there are hills to climb and there will be mud after rain and in the winter, so this ride can only be undertaken on mountain bikes and it is not suitable for young children.

Strangely for a ridge ride, there is room for confusion at some of the junctions of tracks as there are few signposts. A good tip is to stop

17

and have a look round at each major junction in order to remember it for the return trip. A compass is also useful. If you find yourself dropping hundreds of feet, STOP! You have come off the ridge and face a long climb back up to the top!

STARTING POINT & PARKING

This is a little difficult to find! It lies at a crossroads of broad tracks near the cattle grid at the top of the hill on the minor road **between Crowcombe and Nether Stowey** (grid reference 150375). To get there:

→ From Taunton follow the A358 northwest towards Minehead. About 4 miles after passing Bishops Lydeard turn right to **Crowcombe**. Shortly after the start of the village turn right, signposted 'Nether Stowey'. Climb steeply to the top of the hill, following signs for Nether Stowey. There is a stone parking area on the left about 400yds after the cattle grid and the brow of the hill.

→ From Bridgwater follow the A39 towards Minehead for about 7 miles then turn left into **Nether Stowey**. From the clocktower / Post Office / pubs in the centre of the village go up Castle Street, signposted 'Crowcombe'. At the end of the village, at the T-junction turn left (no signpost). Following signs for Crowcombe, bear right at the fork then, at the crossroads soon afterwards go straight ahead. Climb up out of the woodland. About 3/4 mile after passing a right turn to Holford and Dodington, park in the stone parking area to the right. Once on your bikes, continue along the road for about 1/4 mile to reach the starting point (about 100yds before the cattle grid).

*There is also a car park above and east of **West Bagborough**, off the A358 between Taunton and Minehead (grid reference 181338).*

Station: Taunton or Bridgwater.
TIC: Taunton, 01823 336344.

Other nearby trails: The Bridgwater & Taunton Canal lies to the southeast.

Useful publications: Best is OS Explorer 22 or alternatively OS Landranger Map 181.

Refreshments: Nothing on the ridge. Lots of choice in Nether Stowey. There are pubs in most of the villages just below the ridge.

18 Bridgwater & Taunton Canal

CATEGORY
Canal towpath.

DISTANCE
Up to 15 miles each way.

Part of the West Country Way (NCN Route 3, Padstow to Bristol), the fine stone and gravel towpath of the Bridgwater & Taunton Canal runs along the western edge of the Somerset Levels and links the two historic Somerset towns of Bridgwater and Taunton. There is plenty of wildfowl to be seen on the water and there is also a series of stone sculptures of the planets set back in the hedgerows. The route starts from Binford Place / Town Bridge, Bridgwater and passes through Huntworth, North Newton, Creech St Michael and Bathpool to reach the county cricket ground in Taunton. There are short road sections from the centres of Bridgwater and Taunton to the start of the towpath and a short stretch on quiet minor lanes in the middle of the ride.

STARTING POINTS & PARKING
→ From **Bridgwater**, the West Country Way (NCN Route 3), is signposted from Town Bridge in the centre of town. You may prefer to join the towpath on the outskirts of town at the Boat & Anchor, Huntworth, just north of the M5 Jct 24 (grid reference 313350).

→ From **Taunton**, the ride starts from Coal Orchard car park, right next to Somerset county

cricket ground in the centre of town.

Station: Taunton or Bridgwater.

TIC: Taunton, 01823 336344; Bridgwater, 01278 427652.

Other nearby trails: The Quantocks Ridge is an undulating track along the top of the ridge, suitable for mountain bikes.

Useful publications: OS Landranger Maps 182 & 193. This ride and the Camel Trail, the Tarka Trail, the Grand Western Canal and the Bristol & Bath Railway Path are included in Sustrans *West Country Way* map (£5.99).

Sustrans Order Line: Call 0845 113 0065 or visit their website at www.sustrans.org.uk

Refreshments: Lots of choice in Taunton and Bridgwater. There are pubs at Huntworth, Creech St Michael and North Newton.

19

19 The Willow Walk, west of Glastonbury

CATEGORY

Railway path.

DISTANCE

5 miles each way.

This ride runs through a lovely nature reserve full of swans and other wildfowl. There are glimpses of fields of dark, rich peat characteristic of the Somerset Levels, the wildflowers are prolific and there is a real indication of how the area would return to dense and impenetrable vegetation if left to its own devices for a few decades. The ride starts from the Willows Visitor Centre which has recreated some of the wooden huts that people used to live in thousands of years ago. The craft centre is full of interesting sculptures, carvings and other artistic creations (not to mention the

tea shop!). At the other end of the ride it is easy to go into the heart of the mystical town of Glastonbury on relatively quiet roads. There is a short road section at the start from the visitor centre to the start of the trail. There are two 1/2-mile road sections close to Glastonbury. These can be avoided if you turn around at the end of the traffic-free section.

STARTING POINT & PARKING

→ The Willows Visitor Centre, west of **Glastonbury**. This is located on the minor road between the B3151 at Westhay and the A39 near to Ashcott (grid reference 426415). The owners of the cafe / craft centre are happy for you to leave your car here provided you park at the end of the car park furthest from the entrance to the cafe, as this is needed for disabled parking. It is well worth having a look at the variety of crafts on display (or stopping for some tea and cakes after the ride).

ON YOUR BIKES!

1. Leave the Willows Visitor Centre car park and turn left along the lane. Ignore the first track to the left. Cross the bridge over the drainage channel and turn immediately left into Shapwick Heath Nature Reserve. The trail, signposted NCN Route 3, runs for 5 miles to the outskirts of Glastonbury.

2. (From the centre of Glastonbury). Follow Benedict Street, a continuation of the High Street, to cross the A39 bypass via the pelican crossing. Go past Bradfords Building Suppliers and take the first lane to the right after Snows

Timber Yard. Shortly turn left following signs for the Peat Moors Visitor Centre.

Station: Castle Cary.

TIC: Glastonbury, 01458 832954.

Other nearby trails: Bridgwater & Taunton Canal.

Useful publications: OS Landranger Map 182. The *West Country Way* map produced by Sustrans (£5.99) shows this and several other traffic-free trails in Cornwall, Devon and Somerset including the Camel Trail, the Tarka Trail, the Grand Western Canal, the Bridgwater & Taunton Canal and the Bristol & Bath Railway Path.

Sustrans Order Line: Call 0845 113 0065 or visit their website at www.sustrans.org.uk

Refreshments: Cafe in the craft shop. The Railway Inn, about halfway along the route. Lots of choice in Glastonbury.

20 Severn Bridge Cyclepath

CATEGORY

Cyclepath on motorway bridge.

DISTANCE

3 miles each way.

The first Severn Bridge, opened in 1967, has seen its traffic flows slashed with the opening of the Second Severn Crossing, a few miles further south. As a result, as you cycle high above the swirling brown waters of the River Severn, you are more aware of a sense of space and height than noise and traffic fumes. There are cycleways on both the north and south sides of the bridge, climbing to a highpoint in the middle. At the Chepstow end these are connected via a conveniently located subway. At the Gloucestershire end it is a bit more complicated! This is a ride best undertaken on a bright sunny day when the wind is not too strong: what may be a gentle breeze elsewhere

can be funnelled by the shape of the Severn estuary into a strong and gusty crosswind.

STARTING POINTS & PARKING

→ **English side.** Follow the M4 / M48 towards Chepstow. At Junction 1, just before the old Severn Bridge, turn left on the A403 towards Avonmouth then first right towards 'St Augustine's Vineyard, Severn Bridge Maintenance Department'. Park along this minor road.

→ **Welsh side.** From the roundabout at the junction of the A466 and the A48 (on the western edge of Chepstow) take the unsigned minor road running southeast parallel with the A466. At the offset crossroads turn right then left. Park along this road. You can join the cyclepath alongside the A466 which links to the Severn Bridge.

ON YOUR BIKES!

1. **(Aust)** Climb the minor road that leads towards Old Passage and take the first right, signposted 'No entry except access. Bridge Maintenance Unit'. After 200 yds take the first left, signposted 'National Cycle Network Route 4'.
2. Cross the bridge and follow the track downhill away from the motorway. At the T-junction turn right through the subway under the M48 signposted 'Caldicot, Usk' then at the end of the tunnel turn left uphill and sharp left at the top to recross the bridge on the cyclepath along the north side.
3. Descend to the roundabout by Aust Services then turn sharp left uphill (use the pavement / concrete track parallel to the road). Go past the petrol station then turn left down the steps that lead to the bridge running across the top of the toll booths, signposted 'Aust, Chepstow'. At the other side of the bridge turn left, signposted 'Aust', then shortly at the T-junction turn right to return to the start.

Station: Chepstow or Severn Beach (via Bristol).
TIC: Chepstow, 01291 623772.

Other nearby trails: Forest of Dean. Gloucester & Sharpness Canal.
Useful publications: OS Landranger Map 172 .
Refreshments: Aust Services. Lots of choice in Chepstow.

21 Bristol to Pill Riverside Path

CATEGORY
Riverside path.

DISTANCE
5 miles each way.

Explore the broad riverside path running beneath the Clifton Suspension Bridge, one of Isambard Kingdom Brunel's finest creations. The path runs for 5 miles along the bottom of the gorge. The tidal rise and fall of the Bristol

Channel is one of the highest in the world, so do not be surprised to see the river flowing strongly in the wrong direction! The path can easily be linked to the trails in Leigh Woods above the gorge or via quiet lanes to form a circuit returning to Bristol via Ashton Court.

STARTING POINTS & PARKING

→ Starting from opposite house no. 78 Cumberland Road in **Bristol city centre**, the ride follows a cobbled riverside path to the CREATE Centre, crosses the grey steel bridge over the river then runs along the stone and gravel riverside path for a further 4 miles to Ham Green (Pill).

→ If you wish to start from **Leigh Woods**, cross Clifton Suspension Bridge away from Clifton then take the first right on to North Road. Follow this for 3/4 mile then just after the third turning on the left, you will see wooden gates on your right, marking the start of the waymarked cycle track through the woods to join the Avon Gorge path. There is parking for a few cars near here. You will have a steep hill to climb on your way back to this point.

Station: Temple Meads, Bristol.
TIC: Bristol, 0117 926 0767.
Other nearby trails: The Bristol & Bath Railway Path starts from the other side of the city from Midland Road. The Kennet & Avon Canal runs from Bath east towards Hungerford. There is a waymarked trail in the Forest of Dean.
Useful publications: OS Landranger Map 172. CycleCity Guides *Bristol & Bath cycle map*. The ride is also included in Sustrans *Severn & Thames Cycle Route* map (£5.99) This map also shows the Bristol & Bath Railway Path, the Kennet & Avon Canal Towpath and the Marlborough to Chiseldon Railway Path.
Sustrans Order Line: Call 0845 113 0065 or visit their website at www.sustrans.org.uk
Refreshments: At the CREATE Centre. Pubs in Pill, 1 mile beyond the end of the path.

22

22 Forest of Dean Family Trail, Gloucestershire

CATEGORY
Railway path and forestry tracks.
DISTANCE
11-miles circuit.

The Forest of Dean lies on an area of higher land between the River Severn and River Wye and provides spectacular views of the borderland of England and Wales. It represents one of the brightest stars in the firmament of recreational cycling in the whole of southern England. A combination of enlightened thinking by the Forestry Commission in their largest holding in the West Country and co-operation with local authorities and Sustrans has created an integrated recreational cycling network linking towns with woodland over a large area. The flagship route is the 11-mile Family Cycling Trail, which follows disused railway lines for much of its course, providing mostly shallow gradients that are ideal for family cycling. There are challenges at all levels in other parts of the forest.

STARTING POINT & PARKING

→ Pedalabikeaway Cycle Hire Centre **near Cannop Ponds**, in the centre of the Forest of Dean. This is just north of the crossroads of the B4226 and B4234 between Cinderford and Coleford (15 miles southwest of Gloucester, grid reference 609125).

ON YOUR BIKES!

1. Facing the Pedalabikeaway Cycle Centre go to the right past the 'Cannop Colliery' signpost to join the yellow 'tyre track' bike trail waymarks. Descend, cross the road with care on to the path opposite, go up a short steep climb and turn left. Shortly, at a T-junction by a tall wooden signpost, turn left again, signposted 'Drybrook Road Station'.

2. Keep following the yellow tyre track signs in the direction of Drybrook. At a fork, with Lydbrook signposted left, bear right to Drybrook. Long steady climb up to Drybrook Road Station. Shortly after passing Foxes Bridge there is a steep climb then a long descent, steep at the start. Go past Spruce Ride and Central Bridge.

3. Follow signs for 'Cannop Wharf' and 'Cycle Centre', at one point turning right where 'Mallards Pike' is signposted straight ahead. Descend steeply from Three Brothers to Cannop Wharf. At the T-junction at the bottom turn right for the cycle centre. The route runs briefly along a road near to Cannop Ponds then bears off right, soon returning to the cycle centre.

Station: Lydney.
TIC: Coleford, 01594 812388.
Other nearby trails: The Stroud Valleys Cycle Trail, the Sharpness & Gloucester Canal and the Severn Bridge Cyclepath.
Useful publications: OS Landranger Map 162 or, better still, Outdoor Leisure Sheet 14. The Forestry Commission produces a fold-out leaflet, *Cycling in the Forest of Dean*, available from Forest Enterprise, Crown Offices, Bank Street,

Coleford, Gloucestershire, GL16 8BA (01594 833057) or from Coleford TIC.
Refreshments: At the cycle centre. Otherwise you will need to use an Ordnance Survey map to find your way to the various pubs in the villages nearest to the cycle trail. There is an ice cream van near Cannop Ponds at busy times.

23 Coleford to Parkend and Cannop Wharf

CATEGORY
Railway path.
DISTANCE
5 miles each way.

From Coleford this trail joins the Forest of Dean Family Cycle Trail, running through woodland, between rock cuttings and past the ruins of Darkhill Ironworks, a reminder of the industrial past of the area. Be warned that it is almost all downhill from Coleford to Parkend so almost all uphill on the way back. Starting and finishing at Coleford, together with the Family Trail, would form a 'balloon with a string' shaped ride, 21 miles in length.

23

STARTING POINT & PARKING

➜ The Railway Museum in the main central car park in **Coleford**, 15 miles southwest of Gloucester (grid reference 577104).

ON YOUR BIKES!

1. From the Railway Museum you will see a bike route signpost with 'Milkwall 1' on it. Cross the road with care and follow the obvious cyclepath, now signposted 'Parkend'.

2. After a short climb, descend to cross the road then continue downhill past the ruins of Darkhill Ironworks. At the next road, go straight ahead and continue in the same direction through a rocky cutting, following signs for 'Parkend' then 'Cannop Wharf'.

3. The track runs parallel to the road then along Hughes Terrace for a brief lane section. Cross the main road, go past Coleford Junction and, if you wish, join the Family Trail at Cannop Wharf. Remember this point if you do the Family Circuit for your return to Coleford.

Station: Lydney
TIC: Coleford, 01594 812388.
Other nearby trails: Forest of Dean Family Trail, Severn Bridge Cyclepath.
Useful publications: OS Landranger Map 162 or, better still, Outdoor Leisure Sheet 14. The Forestry Commission produces a fold-out leaflet,

Cycling in the Forest of Dean, available from Forest Enterprise, Crown Offices, Bank Street, Coleford, Gloucestershire GL16 8BA (01594 833057) or from Coleford TIC.

Refreshments: Lots of choice in Coleford. Otherwise you will need to use an Ordnance Survey map to find your way to the various pubs located in the villages nearest to the cycle trail. There is an ice cream van near Cannop Ponds at busy times.

24 Gloucester & Sharpness Canal

CATEGORY

Canal towpath (mountain bikes recommended).

DISTANCE

Up to 15 miles each way.

The Gloucester & Sharpness Canal performs the curious function of joining the River Severn to... the River Severn! The tidal rise and fall in the Bristol Channel and the Severn Estuary is one of the highest in the world and makes navigation up the River Severn to Gloucester very tricky. The canal was opened in 1817 and at the time it was the broadest and deepest canal in the world. The towpath is of varying standard: the section which is undoubtedly the jewel in the

crown is the 2-mile stretch south of Frampton on Severn to Shepherd's Patch (near Slimbridge) which forms part of National Cycle Network Route 41, from Gloucester to the old Severn Bridge. Here, the surface is excellent. Either side of this section the towpath is more grass and earth. Mountain bikes with wide tyres to absorb the bumps are highly recommended. There are long term plans to improve the quality of the whole towpath. The route runs from Sharpness Docks through Purton, Frampton on Severn and Quedgeley to Hempsted Bridge (southwest edge of Gloucester).

STARTING POINT & PARKING

➔ The car park by Wycliffe College Rowing Club in **Saul**, on the Gloucester & Sharpness Canal, about 7 miles southwest of Gloucester. Leave the M5 at Jct 13, follow the A419 / A38 / B4071 into Frampton on Severn. Just before the Bell pub turn right on to Whitminster Lane, signposted 'Whitminster'. At the end of the houses turn left, signposted 'Bike Route 41',

then immediately after crossing the canal, turn right. Park in the large car park by the rowing club (grid reference 754091).

ON YOUR BIKES!

1. From the car park by Wycliffe College Rowing Club follow the tarmac lane alongside the canal (with the water to your left). Cross the road at Sandfield Bridge on to the towpath straight ahead. The track is good as far as Fretherne Bridge then soon becomes grassy for less than a mile.

2. At Splatt Bridge (at the southern end of Frampton on Severn) the quality of the towpath improves dramatically: the next 2 miles (as far as Patch Bridge) forms part of the National Cycle Network.

3. At Patch Bridge you may wish to retrace your steps, as the track becomes grassy once again as it heads west to Sharpness. The Tudor Arms pub is located on the other side of the bridge. You have two other options:

(a) continue along the towpath through Purton

as far as the marina in Sharpness (the most interesting section is the 2-mile stretch from Purton to Sharpness with wide views of the Severn Estuary)

(b) return to the start by following the quiet road through the attractive village of Frampton on Severn. To do this, leave the canal towpath at Splatt Bridge.

From the start you can also follow the towpath northeast for 7 miles towards Hempsted Bridge and Gloucester. There are several rough sections on this stretch.

Station: Cam & Dursley.
TIC: Gloucester, 01452 421188.
Other nearby trails: The Stroud Valleys Cycle Trail, Bristol & Bath Railway Path.
Useful publications: OS Landranger Map 162.
Refreshments: The Bell Inn and the Three Horseshoes pub in Frampton on Severn and the Tudor Arms pub at Shepherd's Patch.

25 Stroud Valleys Cycle Trail (Dudbridge / Stroud to Nailsworth), south of Gloucester

CATEGORY
Railway path.
DISTANCE
5 miles each way.

This attractive, largely wooded ride follows a disused railway along the bottom of the Stroud Valley, passing close to many of the settlements that grew up in the late Middle Ages as the valley became the centre of a flourishing cloth trade. Although the path extends further west, from Dudbridge to Stonehouse, it runs at this stage alongside the busy and noisy new bypass and can hardly be deemed a recreational route. By contrast, the course of the route from

Nailsworth west to Dudbridge appears to be one of those secret hidden passages tucked between the edge of the built-up area and the surrounding countryside.

STARTING POINTS & PARKING
→ Egypt Mill, **Nailsworth.** From the roundabout by the clocktower in the centre of Nailsworth, take Bridge Street (the A46) towards Stroud and Woodchester. Shortly, turn first right, signposted

25

'Egypt Mill', then immediately turn left and park at the far end of the car park at the start of the trail (grid reference 849000).

→ The Bell Hotel in the centre of **Stroud,** near the railway station and the roundabout at the junction of the A46 and the A419 (grid reference 849051). Once on your bike, go downhill from The Bell through the subway then uphill past Kwik Fit and the Vet Hospital, following cycle signs for Woodchester.

→ **Dudbridge**, at the roundabout at the junction of the B4066 and the A419 to the southwest of Stroud, near to the new Sainsburys store (grid reference 834045).

ON YOUR BIKES!

From the far end of the Egypt Mill car park in the centre of Nailsworth follow the railway path towards Stonehouse and Stroud for almost 4 miles, crossing several minor roads. You arrive in Dudbridge immediately after passing through a round concrete tunnel about 20yds long. At this point you have a choice of turning around and returning to Nailsworth or going into Stroud. For the Stroud option, come back through the tunnel and at the Millennium Milepost turn left downhill through the housing estate, crossing a bridge over a stream. Continue in the same direction, cross the A46 using the traffic island, climb the steps opposite (use the wheeling ramp) and follow the railway path to its end.

Station: Stonehouse.
TIC: Stroud, 01453 760960.
Other nearby trails: The Gloucester & Sharpness Canal starts at Sharpness, west of Stroud.
Useful publications: OS Landranger Map 162. A leaflet, *Stroud Valleys Pedestrian / Cycle Trail* (75p) is available from Stroud Tourist Information Centre (01453 765768).
Refreshments: Lots of choice in Stroud and Nailsworth. The Egypt Mill at the Nailsworth end of the ride serves coffees, lunches and teas.

26 Bristol & Bath Railway Path

CATEGORY
Railway path.
DISTANCE
Up to 13 miles each way.

One of Sustrans first railway path trails, the route now carries over a million visits a year. The flat, tarmac path runs from the centre of Bristol to the outskirts of Bath, running through the (lit) tunnel at Staple Hill, passing old steam trains at Bitton Station and crossing the River Avon on a series of bridges as you approach Bath. In springtime the broadleaf woodland of Kelston Woods is carpeted with bluebells. There are many remarkable sculptures along the way, such as a fish standing on its head and a drinking giant.

26

STARTING POINTS & PARKING

→ Starting in **Bristol**, there is a signposted link route from Bristol Bridge / Castle Green via Gardiner Haskins to St Philips Road (off Midland Road, near Old Market) where the railway path starts. The route runs from here to Brassmill Lane Trading Estate on the western edge of Bath, passing through Fishponds, Staple Hill, Warmley, Bitton and Saltford.

→ Starting in **Bath**, there is a waymarked link along the riverside path from the centre of Bath to the start of the railway path in Brassmills Lane Trading Estate (grid reference 722653).

→ Another popular starting point is the car park at **Bitton steam railway station** on the A431 to the east of Bristol (grid reference 670704).

Station: Bristol Temple Meads or Bath.
TIC: Bristol, 0117 926 0767, Bath, 01225 477101.
Other nearby trails: Bristol to Pill Riverside Path can be picked up from the CREATE centre on Cumberland Road, Bristol. The Kennet & Avon Canal Towpath starts in Bath and runs east towards Reading.
Useful publications: OS Landranger Map 172. A free leaflet, *Bristol & Bath Railway Path* is

available from Bristol or Bath Tourist Information Centres. The ride is also included in Sustrans *West Country Way* map (£5.99). This map also shows the Camel Trail, the Tarka Trail, the Grand Western Canal and the Bridgwater & Taunton Canal Towpath.
Sustrans Order Line: Call 0845 113 0065 or visit their website at www.sustrans.org.uk
Refreshments: Pubs at Saltford and Warmley. Refreshments in summer at Bitton steam railway station.

27 Kennet & Avon Canal, Bath to Bradford-on-Avon

CATEGORY
Canal towpath.
DISTANCE
9 miles each way.

Linking Bath to Reading (and ultimately, via the River Avon and Thames, linking Bristol to London) the Kennet & Avon Canal was completed in 1810. It has been much restored in the last 30 years and large parts of it are used in National Cycle Network Route 4. There are spectacular viaducts at Avoncliff and Dundas.

27

28

STARTING POINT & PARKING

→ From the **centre of Bath** the canal towpath is reached at Beckford Road by following Sustrans National Cycle Network Route 4, signposted along streets from Pulteney Bridge. It is also possible (just!) to follow the river from the back of the railway station to the start of the canal, although this is a fairly bitty route and involves steps. If coming by car from outside Bath it is better to avoid driving into Bath and start either from the George pub in Bathampton (grid reference 777665) or from the Pound Lane car park in Bradford-on-Avon, off the B3109 Frome Road (grid reference 826604).

Station: Bath or Bradford-on-Avon.
TIC: Bath, 01225 477101.
Other nearby trails: The towpath continues east from Bradford-on-Avon to Devizes. The Bristol & Bath Railway Path runs from the west side of Bath to the east side of Bristol.
Useful publications: OS Landranger Map 172 & 173. Sustrans *Severn & Thames Cycle Route map.*
Sustrans Order Line: Call 0845 113 0065 or visit their website at www.sustrans.org.uk
Refreshments: Lots of choice in Bath and Bradford-on-Avon. The George pub at Bathampton. Pub and teashop at Avoncliff.

28 Kennet & Avon Canal, Bradford-on-Avon to Devizes

CATEGORY
Canal towpath.

DISTANCE
Up to 12 miles each way.

One of the most extraordinary sights on this section of the towpath is the Caen Hill flight of locks: 29 locks in 2 miles make it look like a veritable hill of water, lifting boats up on to the higher section across the chalk downland before the canal drops down to the east to Hungerford and Newbury. The completion of the locks in 1810 signalled the end of the canal project, which started in Bradford-on-Avon and Newbury in 1794. This is a pleasant, open stretch of the canal, far less busy than the Bath to Bradford-on-Avon section. There are pubs conveniently situated every few miles along the towpath. Beyond Devizes, National Cycle Network Route 4 follows lanes almost to Newbury, where it rejoins the canal towpath.

STARTING POINT & PARKING
→ The Pound Lane car park in **Bradford-on-Avon,** off the B3109 Frome Road (grid reference

29

826604) or the Canal Centre in Devizes (grid reference 005618).

Station: Bradford-on-Avon.
TIC: Bradford-on-Avon, 01225 865797.
Other nearby trails: The Kennet & Avon Canal can also be followed west to Bath from Bradford-on-Avon.
Useful publications: OS Landranger Map 173.
Refreshments: Lots of choice in Bradford-on-Avon and Devizes. Canalside pubs at Semington, Seend Cleeve and Sells Green.

29 Castleman Trail, Wimborne Minster

CATEGORY
Railway path.

DISTANCE
West Moors to Ashley Heath - 4.5 miles each way. Wimborne Minster to Upton Country Park - 4 miles each way.

This woodland railway path runs between Ringwood and Poole on the course of the old Dorchester to Southampton railway. Due to its twists and turns it was nicknamed 'Castleman's

Corkscrew' after Charles Castleman, who was chiefly responsible for the building of the line. The route is broken into two sections, as parts of the old railway track between West Moors and Wimborne Minster have been lost to development. The first part runs from Moors Valley Country Park (Ashley Heath) to West Moors and the second part from Merley (south of Wimborne Minster) to Upton Country Park.

STARTING POINTS & PARKING
→ The Pay & Display car park at **Moors Valley Country Park,** located off the minor road leading west from the A338 / A31 roundabout to the west of Ringwood (grid reference 106056). It is best to pick up a leaflet called '*Moors Valley Country Park & Forest*' to see how to link with the Castleman Trail from the visitor centre.

→ At the eastern end of Moorlands Road, **West Moors,** at the start of West Moors Plantation woodland (grid reference 087033). Follow signs for 'Trailway', 'Moors Valley Country Park' and 'Ashley Heath'. The trail ends at the junction with the B3081, west of Ringwood. There is no parking at this point.

→ The Willet Arms pub, **Merley** lies south of Wimborne Minster (grid reference 017984), just off the more southerly of the two roundabouts near the junction of the A31 and A349. If you wish to use the Willet Arms pub car park you must ask permission.

→ **Upton Country Park,** off the A35 just east of Upton, near Poole (grid reference 992931). Exit the country park and turn left onto the waymarked route along the pavement to the start of the trail, marked with a train logo. Once on the Roman Road, keep an eye out for the path up to the right to join the railway path by the bridge (grid reference 992943).

Station: Upton.
TIC: Wimborne Minster, 01202 886116.
Other nearby trails: There are waymarked trails in the Moors Valley Country Park itself and lots

more in the New Forest.

Useful publications: OS Landranger Map 195. A leaflet covering this and several other trails in Dorset is available from Wimborne TIC.

Refreshments: The visitor centres at Moors Valley Country Park and Upton Country Park.

30 Cotswold Water Park, south of Cirencester

CATEGORY

Railway path, bridleways and minor roads (mountain bikes recommended).

DISTANCE

7-mile circuit.

This route has largely been created by the wardens at the Cotswold Water Park who have done an excellent job managing an ever-changing asset (new gravel pits are constantly being excavated and the course of rights of way diverted). The circular route takes you among some of the many lakes formed by gravel

extraction and along the course of a dismantled railway. Certain sections will be muddy from late autumn to spring and prolonged rain. If you explore the village of South Cerney in search of refreshments, keep an eye out for a street called 'Bow Wow'! Although waymarked, a map and /or the *Cotswold Water Park Leisure Guide* (see below) are highly recommended. The bridleway sections are only suitable for mountain bikes.

STARTING POINT & PARKING

→ Start from Clayhill car park / picnic site on Spine Road East (the B4696) south of **South Cerney**, about 4 miles south of Cirencester. The car park is about 2 1/2 miles southwest of the junction of the B4696 with the A419 on the way towards Ashton Keynes (grid reference 052953).

ON YOUR BIKES!

1. From the car park follow signs for 'Bridlepath Circuit. South Cerney, Cricklade'. (This is the corner furthest from the entrance to the car park.) Cross the motorcycle barrier (made of

30

railway sleepers) and follow the blue arrows to the right on the narrow, stone-based track around the edge of the field.

2. At the end of the first field turn right (blue arrow) along the edge of a second field. Cross a concrete track, turn right then left to continue in the same direction on the bridleway to Waterhay. Keep following signs for Waterhay, Thames Path and South Cerney.

Station: Kemble.

TIC: Cirencester, 01285 654180.

Other nearby trails: The Stroud Valleys Trail and the River Ray Parkway (Swindon).

Useful publications: OS Landranger Map 163. A brochure with a fold-out map, the *Cotswold Water Park Leisure Guide* shows all the footpaths and bridleways in the water park. It can be obtained by sending a SAE to Park Office, Keynes Country Park, Spratsgate Lane, Shorncote, Cirencester, Glos GL7 6DF (01285 861459). Website: www.waterpark.org. E-mail: info@waterpark.org

Refreshments: Three pubs in South Cerney.

31 Chippenham to Calne Railway Path

CATEGORY
Railway path.

DISTANCE
6 miles each way.

The ride links the two handsome Wiltshire towns of Chippenham and Calne via a dismantled railway, neatly avoiding both the busy A4 and the hills either side of the valley formed by the River Marden. The attractive exit from Chippenham runs by the river and through parkland, with a brief zig-zag climb up on to the railway path. A wonderful, new, eccentric-looking bridge carries you safely over the A4 and through a wooded corridor to the outskirts of Calne. There are traces of the old Wiltshire & Berkshire Canal (now disused) alongside the path which leads right into the heart of Calne, once an important staging post on the A4 from Bristol to London.

31

STARTING POINT & PARKING

→ The Olympiad Leisure Centre car park, **Chippenham**. From the centre of town follow signs for the railway station up Station Hill. Go past the station and turn right opposite the car park on to Sadlers Mead (by Wiltshire College), signposted 'Olympiad, Golf Course' (grid reference 922735).

ON YOUR BIKES!

1. From the far left-hand end of the Olympiad car park (ie the corner furthest away from the entrance to the Olympiad) go downhill to the river and turn left.

2. Keep the river to your right and golf course to the left. At a crossroads of paths (with a blue bridge to your right) turn left, for 100 yds then right, around the edge of the housing estate.

3. Join Riverside Drive and turn right, keeping the parkland to your right. Follow the road to the end and climb up the zig zag path on to the railway path. Remember this point for the return trip. Turn right to cross the bridge.

4. Follow the railway path for 2 miles. Join the lane for 1/2 mile (at Pound Farm) then, 300 yds after passing Rose Cottage on your left, turn left by a Millennium Milepost through a small parking area to rejoin the railway path.

5. Follow the path to its end, go though an ornate metalwork arch, cross the river and the canal, turn right then keep bearing left to emerge on Patford Street in the centre of Calne (the Lansdowne Strand Hotel is just to your left).

Station: Chippenham.
TIC: Chippenham, 01249 706333.
Other nearby trails: Marlborough to Chiseldon Railway Path, Kennet & Avon Canal Towpath (Bath to Devizes), the Ridgeway near Avebury.
Useful publications: OS Landranger Map 173.
Refreshments: Loads in Chippenham and Calne.

32 Wilton Old Roman Road, west of Salisbury

CATEGORY
Old Roman Road.

DISTANCE
7 miles each way.

Wilton is a superb base for both road rides and offroad rides. The lanes tend to follow the valley bottoms (along the Rivers Wylye and Ebble) whereas the offroad rides use the ridges. Most of the offroad rides are only suitable for mountain bikes in summer after a dry spell. This is the easiest of the ridge rides and after a steep 350ft

climb up from Wilton, offers a lovely trip through the beech trees of Grovely Wood. There is a stone and gravel path at the start, but this turns to chalk in parts so the ride is best done in summer. It is suggested you turn around and retrace your steps when you get to the minor road linking Dinton and Wylye (grid reference 007350).

STARTING POINT & PARKING

→ At the top of a lane called Hollows in **Ditchampton**, on the northwest edge of Wilton, west of Salisbury (grid reference 088318). To get there from the traffic lights in the centre of Wilton, follow West Street / A30 towards Shaftesbury. Turn right by The Bell pub on to Water Ditchampton. Pass beneath a railway bridge, turn immediately left into Hollows which is a no-through-road. Park at the top, beyond the houses, where the tarmac turns to track.

ON YOUR BIKES!

1. Follow the broad chalk and stone track west. After 1/2 mile take the right-hand track at a 3-way junction of tracks.

2. After a further 3 miles, the broad stone track swings right to a T-junction with tarmac. Turn left here (remember this point for the return trip) then keep bearing right, leaving the buildings of Grovely Lodge to your left and rejoining the main broad track to continue in the same direction.

3. It is suggested you turn round at the next tarmac road at grid reference 007350 (the Dinton to Wylye road).

Station: Salisbury.
TIC: Salisbury, 01722 334956.
Other nearby trails: Several other rougher bridleways and byways start at Wilton (mountain bikes preferable). The best of these runs westwards from the Race Course towards Donhead St Andrew, parallel with the A30.
Useful publication: OS Landranger Map 184.
Refreshments: Lots of choice in Wilton.

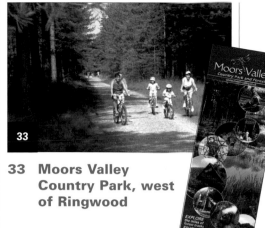

33 Moors Valley Country Park, west of Ringwood

CATEGORY
Forest tracks.

DISTANCE
Four circuits of between 2 and 6 miles.

This is an absolute model of how recreational cycling for families should be developed in Forestry Commission holdings. The routes start from an excellent visitor centre with a good cafe attached, there are plenty of other activities for children of all ages and the routes themselves are well laid out so that at almost any point you have the option of extending the ride or following a more direct route back to the start. The broad stone and gravel tracks through tall pines and heather heathland are gently undulating so you have a few climbs and descents. If only it were all this simple..! The only drawback is the steep cost of the Pay & Display Car Park but when you realise that you have the potential of a full day's entertainment in addition to the cycling it puts the cost into context.

STARTING POINT & PARKING

→ The Moors Valley Country Park Visitor Centre, signposted off the A31 to the west of Ringwood is located just north of **Ashley Heath** at grid reference 106057.
Station: Christchurch.

34

TIC: Ringwood, 01425 470896.

Other nearby trails: New Forest, Castleman Trail

Useful publications: OS Landranger Map 195. A much more useful map, *Moors Valley Country Park & Forest*, is produced by the visitor centre. This shows all the waymarked routes and how they connect to each other.

Refreshments: Good cafe at the visitor centre.

34 Ridgeway from West Kennett / Avebury to Barbury Castle, near Swindon

CATEGORY

Long distance byway / bridle trail.

DISTANCE

7 miles each way (mountain bikes essential).

The Ridgeway is claimed to be the oldest road in Europe, dating back more than 5,000 years. It would have been a useful trading route when the valleys and plains below were thickly wooded and still populated by wolves and bears. The surrounding rolling countryside undulates in soft rounded hills, mainly with a patchwork of arable crops interspersed with copses of deciduous trees. The Ridgeway itself is a broad track, the surface of which varies from chalk and gravel to earth and grass. It is best to do the ride (mountain bikes essential) in the summer months after several hot, dry days: in the winter the track will become muddy with large puddles. The track climbs gently, past fields bordered with poppy, vetch and willowherb to a plateau of around 800ft. Barbury Castle, an Iron Age hillfort is the suggested turnaround point as there happens to be a cafe. However there is nothing to stop you carrying on further along the Ridgeway or even devising a circular route using the amazing network of bridleways and byways that criss-cross the area. See also pages 108-110 for more sections of the Ridgeway.

NB The trail is NOT suitable for young children.

STARTING POINTS & PARKING

➜ The layby on the A4 at the **West Kennett / Overton** start of the Ridgeway (between Calne and Marlborough). This is easy to sail past, but if you slow down at the brow of the hill between West Kennett and West Overton you should find the layby without too much problem (grid reference 119681).

➜ The parking area on **Hackpen Hill** on the minor road between Marlborough and Broad Hinton (grid reference 129747).

➜ **Barbury Castle Country Park**, at the end of the minor road to the south of Swindon and Wroughton (grid reference 158760).

Station: Swindon.
TIC: Marlborough, 01672 513989.
Other nearby trails: The Ridgeway can be followed further east. The Marlborough to Chiseldon Railway Path. The Chippenham to Calne Railway Path. The Kennet & Avon Canal Towpath.
Useful publications: OS Landranger Map 173.
Refreshments: A cafe at Barbury Castle and pubs near Avebury or West Overton.

35

35 Marlborough to Chiseldon, south of Swindon

CATEGORY
Railway path.
DISTANCE
7 1/2 miles each way.

The ride starts a mile east of the town centre, on the A4 towards Hungerford and runs through Ogbourne St Andrew and Ogbourne St George (where there is a short section on lanes) to Chiseldon. The railway path uses the course of the old Midland & Southwest Junction Railway that ran between Cheltenham and Southampton. There are fine views of the rolling Marlborough Downs either side of the path.

STARTING POINTS & PARKING

➜ (South end of ride) From the (long stay) car parks in the centre of **Marlborough**, follow the pavement alongside the A4 towards Hungerford. Immediately after crossing the old railway bridge turn left into a road called Barnfield (grid reference 202689).

➜ (North end of ride) The car park just off the A346 to the south of **Chiseldon**, near M4 Jct 15 (grid reference 193793).

Station: Great Bedwyn, 7 miles to the southeast.
TIC: Marlborough, 01672 513989.
Other nearby trails: The trail crosses The Ridgeway. The Kennet & Avon Canal towpath can be ridden to the west of Devizes.
Useful publications: OS Landranger Maps 173 & 174. The ride is also included in Sustrans *Severn & Thames Cycle Route* map (£5.99). This map also shows the Bristol to Pill Riverside Path, the Bristol & Bath Railway Path and the Kennet & Avon Canal Towpath.
Sustrans Order Line: Call 0845 113 0065 or visit their website at www.sustrans.org.uk
Refreshments: Lots of choice in Marlborough. Old Crown Inn, Ogbourne St George.

South-East

Milton Keynes

47
48

A421

M1

Bicester
A41
Aylesbury

A40
Oxford
Thame
46
45
M40
A4010
A413

44
A34
A4074

A420
A338

43
Didcot
42
A4130
High Wycombe
Slough
41
Maidenhead
M4
Windsor
39
London
40

Reading
28
29 30
M4
37
38
Staines

Hungerford
Newbury
33
36
M25
Leatherhead
M25
Sevenoaks

A33
Bracknell
31
Woking
A3
34
Redhill
A26

M3
32
Guildford
20
Dorking
35
Tonbridge
23
Tunbridge Wells

Basingstoke
Farnham
19
21
A24
Crawley
22
A26
A261

A34
A303
Andover
A3
Horsham
A23
M23
24
25

17
A281
18
A272
A272
A265

Winchester
6
Petersfield
A272
A22

Eastleigh
A32
A24
12
A22

4
5
7
8
9
11 10
13
14
A27
16

3
Southampton
M27
A27
Brighton
15
Eastbourne

Gosport
Chichester
Worthing

Cowes
Portsmouth
Bognor Regis

1
2

Isle of Wight

SOUTH-EAST TRAILS

1   The Tennyson Trail, Isle of Wight
2   Cowes to Newport Cycleway, Isle of Wight
3   New Forest, Hampshire
4   Meon Valley Trail, northwest of Fareham
5   West Walk Forest, northwest of Portsmouth
6   Queen Elizabeth Country Park, Petersfield
7   Centurion Way, Chichester
8   Houghton Forest, north of Arundel
9   South Downs Way: Rackham Hill, Storrington, north of Worthing
10 Downs Link: Bramber to Old Shoreham
11 South Downs Way: near Worthing
12 South Downs Way: Ditchling Beacon, north of Brighton
13 Dyke Railway Trail, Hove
14 South Downs Way: Firle Beacon, east of Lewes
15 Friston Forest, west of Eastbourne
16 Cuckoo Trail, Hailsham
17 Test Way, Stockbridge, northwest of Winchester
18 Downs Link: Southwater to Steyning and Bramber

19 Alice Holt Forest, southwest of Farnham
20 Downs Link: Bramley to Cranleigh, south of Guildford
21 Downs Link: Cranleigh south to Slinfold
22 Worth Way, west of East Grinstead
23 Forest Way, east of East Grinstead
24 Bewl Water, Lamberhurst
25 Bedgebury Forest, Hawkhurst
26 North Downs Way - see also Reigate Hill
27 Canterbury to Whitstable - the Crab & Winkle Way
28 Kennet & Avon Canal through Newbury
29 Kennet & Avon Canal from Reading to Thatcham
30 Reading - along the Thames to Sonning
31 The Lookout, Bracknell
32 Basingstoke Canal
33 Wey Navigation, from Weybridge to Pyrford Lock
34 Norbury Park, Leatherhead
35 Reigate Hill (along the North Downs Way)
36 Horton Park, northeast of Epsom
37 Windsor Great Park, west of London
38 Thames Towpath between Putney Bridge and Weybridge
39 Richmond Park (the Tamsin Trail), southwest London
40 Greenwich and the Thames Barrier to Erith
41 Slough Arm of the Grand Union Canal, east of Slough
42 The Ridgeway from Streatley west to East Ilsley, south of Oxford
43 The Ridgeway east and west from Uffington White Horse, near Wantage
44 Oxford waterways north and south
45 The Phoenix Trail between Thame and Princes Risborough
46 Wendover Woods, Chilterns, southeast of Aylesbury
47 Ouse Valley Trail, Milton Keynes
48 Milton Keynes Redway

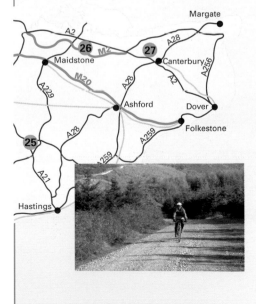

South-East Mountain Biking

Mountain biking in the South-East is almost exclusively on the chalk and flint tracks that abound in the area. These are best enjoyed in the summer months from May to October when the trails are drier and easier to ride: they can become impassable in the depths of winter. The main exception to the chalk is the area lying just south of the North Downs where there are many sandy tracks, often easier when they are wet and harder-packed (imagine riding on a wet beach or a dry beach!) This sandy area extends east from Alton in Hampshire across towards Dorking, Reigate and Oxted in Surrey and on to Maidstone and Ashford in Kent.

1 Isle of Wight

There are many miles of excellent tracks on the Isle of Wight, particularly the Tennyson Trail on the western half of the island between Freshwater Bay and Newport. The council has produced a series of leaflets covering mountain biking on the island, available from: Isle of Wight Tourism, Westridge Centre, Brading Road, Ryde, Isle of Wight PO33 1QS (01983 813800) or visit www.cyclewight.gov.uk

2 Hampshire Downs

As with Wiltshire and Dorset, Hampshire is blessed with many hundreds of miles of chalk and flint byways and bridleways. Some of the waymarked long distance trails such as the Wayfarer's Walk and the Test Way, both of which start on Inkpen Hill to the south of Hungerford, have long bridleway and byway sections. This bridlepath/footpath mixture is also true to a lesser extent of other waymarked trails such as the Clarendon Way, King's Way, Three Castles Path and Monarch's Way. Please remember that you are **not** allowed to ride on the footpath sections of these trails. Winchester is also the start of the South Downs Way, one of the premier long distance bridleways in the country that runs east for 100 miles to Eastbourne. Hampshire County Council publishes two packs of offroad cycling leaflets, available from: Tourist Information, Guildhall, The Broadway, Winchester, Hampshire SO23 9LJ (01962 840500).

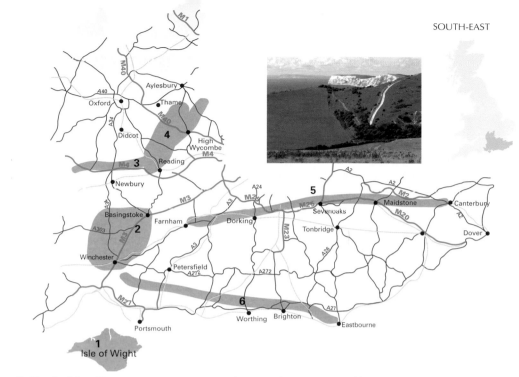

3 Berkshire Downs (Ridgeway)

There is a plethora of fine tracks to the south of the Ridgeway and to the north of the M4 through West Berkshire and South Oxfordshire. Lambourn is an excellent base with tracks radiating off in every direction.

4 Chilterns

The beechwoods of the Chilterns offer splendid woodland rides on well-maintained and well-waymarked bridleways and byways. The best tracks lie to the west and north of Henley.

5 North Downs

Unlike the South Downs Way, or the Ridgeway, where you are allowed to cycle from one end to the other, the North Downs Way, running along the chalk ridge from Farnham to Canterbury and Dover, is mainly a footpath and you are **not** permitted to cycle on footpaths.

There are, however, several long bridleway and byway sections that are open to cyclists, easily found by looking at the relevant Ordnance Survey map. There are many good bases from which to explore the North Downs bridleway and byway network: Gomshall, Peaslake, Leith Hill, Walton on the Hill, Limpsfield and Wye.

6 South Downs

The South Downs Way is a 100-mile linear bridleway from Winchester to Eastbourne. A few miles either side of the trail there are many other bridleways and byways enabling you to devise all sorts of circular rides. The South Downs tracks are very definitely best ridden in summer, on mountain bikes, after a few dry days; the chalk and clay can be depressingly sticky in the depths of winter. Easier 'plateau' sections of the South Downs Way are described more fully in the main list of routes.

South-East Forestry

The South-East of England is not nearly as forested as Wales or Scotland but surprisingly, for such a densely populated area, has more woodland than either the South-West or the Midlands. The largest forestry holding is the New Forest but there are also large swathes of forestry along the South Downs.

In some forests and woods there are no waymarked routes but you are free to explore the tracks. The relevant Ordnance Survey map is mentioned. It is highly recommended that you take a map for the larger woods where it is very easy to get lost!

The trails below correspond with map numbers

1   Brighstone Forest, Isle of Wight

OS Outdoor Leisure Map 29

3   Farley Mount, west of Winchester

OS Explorer Map 132

6   Rewell Wood, Charlton Forest and Eartham Wood between Arundel and Midhurst

OS Explorer Map 121

9   Wilmington Wood and Abbot's Wood, southwest of Hailsham

The Forestry Commission's website is a good source of information with details of 1600 miles of waymarked cycling trails throughout the UK. Search by forest name or by the nearest town or city and the search will tell you the grade, length and waymarking details of the trails.

www.forestry.gov.uk/recreation

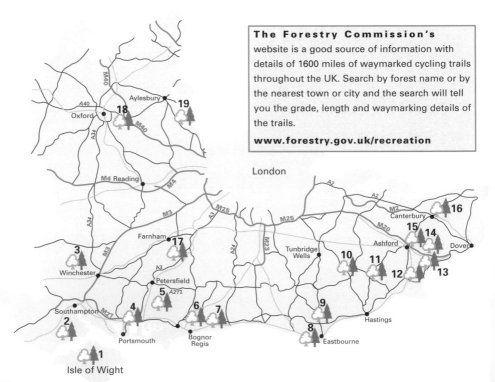

OS Explorer Map 123

11   Hemsted Forest, east of Cranbrook
OS Explorer Maps 125 & 137

12   Longrope Wood, south of Ashford
OS Explorer Map 137

13   West Wood, Elhampark and Covert Wood, east of Ashford
OS Explorer Map 138

14   Denge Wood, northeast of Ashford
OS Explorer Map 137

15   King's Wood, north of Ashford
OS Explorer Map 137

16   Clowes Wood, north of Canterbury
OS Explorer Map 150

18   Shabbington Wood and Waterperry Wood, east of Oxford
OS Explorer Map 180

Forests and woods with waymarked trails

They are shown with a corresponding trail number and page reference.

2   New Forest
See Route 3, page 65

4   West Walk, Wickham
See Route 5, page 67

5   Queen Elizabeth Country Park,
Petersfield - see Route 6, page 68

7   Houghton Forest, north of Arundel
See Route 8, page 71

8   Friston Forest, Eastbourne
See Route 15, page 79

10   Bedgebury Forest, Cranbrook
See Route 25, page 83

17   Alice Holt Woodland Park, Farnham
See Route 19, page 83

19   Wendover Woods, Aylesbury
See Route 46, page 113

Further Information

New Forest
The Queen's House, Lyndhurst, Hampshire SO43 7NH.
Tel: 02380 283141.
www.forestry.gov.uk/newforest
new.forest.rangers@forestry.gsi.gov.uk

Downs and Chilterns Forest District
Bucks Horn Oak, Farnham, Surrey GU10 4LS.
Tel: 01420 23666

Mention should also me made of the waymarked trails from The Lookout near Bracknell (Route 31): these are on Crown Commission land but to you or me they are waymarked woodland trails!

The New Forest

Although this is by far the largest forest in the South-East, there is no set list of waymarked circular rides; instead you will find a large network of excellent, broad, gravel-based trails waymarked with green and white disks that enable you to make up your own rides. Key to this is the map produced by the Forestry Commission called *Cycling in the New Forest - The Network Map*. See Route 3, page 65 for further details.

South-East National Cycle Network

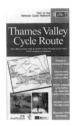

Thames Valley Cycle Route

97 miles from Oxford to London via Reading and Windsor. Highlights include Oxford, the Chiltern Hills, Windsor Castle and Great Park, the Thames Towpath east of Weybridge, Hampton Court, Richmond Park and Barnes Wildfowl & Wetlands Centre.

Traffic-free sections over 3 miles:

- Teddington to Weybridge along the Thames (NCN 4)
- Windsor Great Park (NCN 4)
- Kennington to Oxford along the Thames (NCN 5)

Downs & Weald Cycle Route

159 miles from London to Brighton and along the coast to Hastings, with an alternative route from Crawley via East Grinstead and Heathfield to Eastbourne. Highlights include Greenwich, the Waterlink Way through South London, the North Downs, the three traffic-free railway paths - Worth Way and Forest Way near East Grinstead and the Cuckoo Trail south of Heathfield, the South Downs and Brighton.

Traffic-free sections over 3 miles:

- Worth Way from Crawley to East Grinstead (NCN 21)
- Forest Way from East Grinstead to Groombridge (NCN 21)
- Cuckoo Trail from Heathfield to Polegate (NCN 21)

Garden of England Cycle Route

180 miles from London to Canterbury then along the coast to Sandwich, Deal, Dover, Rye and Hastings. Highlights include Greenwich, the traffic-free Thames-side route to Erith, Whitstable, the Crab & Winkle Way railway path south from Whitstable, Canterbury Cathedral, Dover Castle and Rye.

Traffic-free sections over 3 miles:

- Crab & Winkle Way between Canterbury and Whitstable (NCN 1)
- Thames Riverside between Greenwich and Erith (NCN 1)

The London Thames Cycle Route

44 miles from Hampton Court Palace, near Kingston upon Thames, in the west

Sustrans

Listed below are the Sustrans maps that cover the National Cycle Network within the region. Some of the maps may describe routes that continue on into adjacent regions: these maps are mentioned in both chapters. The maps are not only useful for people wishing to ride the the whole route over several days; they also show all the traffic-free sections which make good day rides. The maps cost £5.99 each and are available from Sustrans.

Sustrans Order Line:
Call **0845 113 0065** or visit their website at **www.sustrans.org.uk**

Northampton and Market Harborough, the Grand Union Canal towpath, the traffic-free route through Leicester and the railway path from Worthington into Derby.

Traffic-free sections over 3 miles:
- Route through Milton Keynes (NCN 51)
- Brampton Valley Way from Northampton to Market Harborough (NCN 6)
- Market Harborough to Foxton along the Grand Union Canal (NCN 6)
- Route through Leicester to Birstall (NCN 6)
- Cloud Trail from Derby to Worthington (NCN 6)

Other areas for lane cycling

From a cyclist's point of view, the South-East has a high density of population, high levels of car ownership and high levels of car use, filling the roads with traffic. The concept of 'quiet lane networks' is somewhat alien in this region. The best rule of thumb is that the further you go from London the quieter the roads will become, for example try **west** or **north Oxfordshire**, with good bases at Burford or Hook Norton; **north Buckinghamshire** - start from Winslow or Buckingham; **south Hampshire** try the networks of lanes between the M3 and the A3; and the **eastern half of Kent** ie southwest, south and southeast of Canterbury.

to Dartford in the east. The route is all on the south side of the river with the exception of the section between Putney Bridge and Lambeth Bridge. The longest traffic-free sections are in the west between Hampton Court and Putney, and in the east between Greenwich and Dartford. Quiet streets and cycle lanes are largely used through the central section.

Traffic-free sections over 3 miles:
- Hampton Court to Putney Bridge (NCN 4)
- Greenwich to Erith (NCN 1)

South Midlands Cycle Route

148 miles from Oxford to Derby via Leicester. Highlights include the ancient city of Oxford, the largely traffic-free route from Winslow through Milton Keynes to Wolverton, the Brampton Valley Way railway path between

South-East Trails

1   The Tennyson Trail on the Isle of Wight

CATEGORY

Wide chalk and stone track with fabulous views.

DISTANCE

6 miles from Freshwater Bay to the far end of Brighstone Forest (ie 12 miles return). From this point it is a further 5 miles along the Tennyson Trail to Carisbrooke at the eastern edge of Newport or 2 miles along the Worsley Trail to the B3323 and a chance of refreshment in Shorwell.

This is without doubt one of the finest chalk ridges in the country, equal to anything along the Ridgeway or South Downs and in many ways better in that the views from high up on the island enable you to see far out across the English Channel, to the far ends of the island and north across the Solent to Hampshire. Starting from the charms of Freshwater Bay you are faced with a very steep climb, parts of which you may well wish to walk. Beyond the Golf Clubhouse the views just get better and

better and there is a succession of thrilling grassy descents and steep climbs to regain height. At the edge of Brighstone Forest you have a choice of continuing along the Tennyson Trail into Newport or of following the more open chalk ridge along the Worsley Trail. In either case there are plenty of hills and thrills to look forward to on your return to Freshwater Bay. As the ride uses trails over chalk, stone and grass, it is only suitable for mountain bikes and is best ridden in the summer months after a few hot, dry days. This ride is not suitable for very young children or the very unfit! Try the Newport to Cowes railway path instead!

STARTING POINT & PARKING

→The car park by the beach in **Freshwater Bay**, near the western tip of the Isle of Wight, south of Yarmouth (grid reference 347857).

ON YOUR BIKES!

1. Facing the sea in Freshwater Bay turn left uphill on the A3055, climbing steeply. (Push your bike along the pavement). Take the second

left onto Southdown Road signposted 'Freshwater Bay Golf Club' then first right signposted 'Tennyson Way' to pass straight through the golf club.

2. Climb with ever better views behind you. Descend. At the road go straight ahead onto a tougher climb.

3. Fine grassy descent. At the next road turn right then left.

4. Midway up the third climb you have a choice:

(a) follow the Tennyson Trail, bearing left into the woodland on a broad stone track signposted 'Old Highway, Tennyson Trail, Carisbrooke'. Once out of the woodland the track becomes a bit rougher then more enclosed. Follow for 5 miles, emerging opposite the lion-topped brick wall of Park House. Turn left downhill then right for the Waverley pub.

(b) continue straight ahead on the Worsley Trail for 2 miles, enjoying the open views to the right. It is suggested you go as far as the B3323 then turn right for 3/4 mile to the pub in Shorwell before retracing your steps.

(c) do neither of the above but turn around at this point and go back to Freshwater Bay.

Nearest Ferry: Yarmouth (from Lymington).

TIC: Yarmouth, 01983 760015.

Other nearby trails: There are three railway paths on the Isle of Wight - Yarmouth to Freshwater Bay, Cowes to Newport and Shanklin to Wroxall.

Useful publications: OS Landranger Map 160. There is an excellent set of leaflets produced by Isle of Wight Council called *Byways & Bridleways by Mountain Bike*. For further details contact: Isle of Wight Council, Highways and Transportation, County Hall, Newport, Isle of Wight PO30 1UD (01983 821000).

Refreshments: Lots of choice in Freshwater Bay. Pubs in Carisbrooke if you choose to follow the Tennyson Trail towards Newport and pubs in Shorwell if you follow the Worsley Trail (this will involve a short road section on the B3323).

2

2 Cowes to Newport Cycleway, Isle of Wight

CATEGORY

Railway path.

DISTANCE

4 miles each way.

The Isle of Wight is a great place to explore by bike and as taking a car on the ferry is so expensive it is well worth leaving the car on the mainland and catching the ferry with just your bikes. In this way you will also avoid adding to the vehicle traffic on the island. This ride from Cowes to Newport is the longest and the best known of the four railway paths on the Isle of Wight. The three others run from Freshwater to Yarmouth, from Shanklin railway station to Wroxall and south from Newport to Blackwater. The Cowes to Newport Cycleway runs for 4 miles alongside the River Medina, a wide expanse of water with hundreds of moored yachts. Cowes is of course a famous yachting centre and during Cowes Week the whole of the Solent is filled with bright sails.

STARTING POINTS & PARKING

→ From the clocktower in the centre of **Newport** follow Quay Street / Little London / Hurstake Road / Manners View and signs for 'Cowes Cycle Route'. There is a small car park on the trading estate on the north side of Newport, just beyond the Royal Mail building (grid reference 501902).

→ The trail starts / ends on the south side of **Cowes** on the Medina Industrial Estate, Arctic Road (grid reference 498948). From the ferry terminal take the first left and keep following 'Cowes to Newport Cycleway' signs.

ON YOUR BIKES!

Starting from the centre of Newport

1. From the Guildhall / Clocktower in the centre of Newport turn along Quay Street. Follow round a sharp left-hand bend then turn second right onto Little London signposted 'Cowes Bike Route'.

2. Follow this road around a left-hand bend. At the T-junction at the end of Hurstake Road turn right signposted 'Cowes'. Continue straight ahead at the roundabout onto Manners View, passing a large Royal Mail building.

3. Join the trail proper, follow for 4 miles alongside the River Medina.

4. The trail ends in Cowes at the Medina Court Industrial Estate, Arctic Road. To continue into the centre of Cowes, at the roundabout by Bernard Road turn left signposted 'Cowes Town Centre' and keep following 'Town Centre' signs.

Nearest Ferry Terminal: Cowes.
TIC: Newport, 01983 525450.
Other nearby trails: There are three other railway paths (all are almost 3 miles long) - Yarmouth to Freshwater lies at the western end of the island, Shanklin to Wroxall at the eastern end and Newport to Blackwater in the centre of the island. The chalk ridge of the Tennyson Trail from Freshwater to Carisbrooke (Newport) is a superb, challenging ridge ride.

Useful publications: OS Landranger Map 196. A guide to Cycling Trails on the Isle of Wight costs £2 from Isle of Wight Tourism, Westridge Centre, Brading Road, Ryde, Isle of Wight PO33 1QS (01983 813800) or visit www.cyclewight.gov.uk

Refreshments: Plenty of choice in Cowes and Newport.

3   New Forest, Hampshire

CATEGORY
Wide, gravel-based forest tracks.

DISTANCE
As short or as long as you want. There are over 100 miles of waymarked routes. You are encouraged to make up your own routes, as long as you stay on the gravel roads waymarked with green and white disks.

The New Forest's gravel forest tracks link villages and the main tourist sites. The vast majority of the tracks and trails lie either side of an imaginary line drawn between Beaulieu in the southeast and Fordingbridge in the northwest, passing through Bolderwood. The A31 can be crossed via an underpass near Bolderwood. Great care should be taken crossing the other A-roads in the New Forest.

STARTING POINTS & PARKING
➔ There are many car parks which are suitable starting points, particularly to the south and west of Lyndhurst.

Station: Brockenhurst.
TIC: Lyndhurst, 023 8028 2269.
Other nearby trails: There are over 100 miles of tracks to explore in the New Forest.
Useful publications: OS Landranger Maps 195 & 196. Much more useful is the excellent leaflet called *Cycling in the New Forest - The Network Map* produced by the Forestry Commission and available from the New Forest Visitor Information Centre in Lyndhurst (023 8028 2269).
Refreshments: Lots of choice in Lyndhurst and Brockenhurst.

4 Meon Valley Trail, north of Fareham

CATEGORY
Railway path.

DISTANCE
Up to 10 miles each way.

A lovely 10-mile wooded trail running through chalk cuttings and on top of high embankments in deepest Hampshire linking the attractive villages and towns of West Meon, Droxford, Soberton and Wickham. Although a stone and gravel path, there are occasionally muddy patches, particularly after rain and in winter so mountain bikes are recommended.

West Meon is an old village with timbered cottages and gabled roofs. It is the burial place of Thomas Lord, founder of Lord's cricket ground in London. The nearby village of Hambledon was the early home of cricket: the cricket club, founded in 1760, evolved the laws of modern cricket.

STARTING POINTS & PARKING
→**West Meon**, on the A32 southwest of Alton. Follow the A32 towards Wickham, passing the Red Lion pub. After 150 yds, on a sharp right-hand bend, turn left onto Station Road then take the first lane / track to the right. **Beware** of the height barrier if you have the bikes on the roof! (grid reference 643237).

→**Droxford**, on the A32 southwest of Alton. Use the car park near the church / bus shelter (grid reference 606183). From the car park, cycle uphill away from the church and take Mill Lane on the right. Go downhill past the house alongside the stream then over the bridge. At the main road turn right then immediately before the bridge turn right again to go up onto the cycle track.

→**Wickham**, north of Fareham. From the main square in Wickham follow 'Free parking' signs out of town towards the A32. After 150 yds turn left onto Mill Lane then first right by the Fire Station onto Station Close and right again to park beneath the trees (grid reference 576117).

Station: Fareham, 4 miles south of Wickham.
TIC: Fareham, 01329 221342.
Other nearby trails: There is a waymarked forestry trail in West Walk Forest, northeast of Wickham and two forest trails in Queen Elizabeth Country Park near Petersfield.
Useful publications: OS Landranger Maps 185 & 196.
Refreshments: Pubs in West Meon, Droxford, Soberton and lots of choice in Wickham.

5   West Walk Forest, northwest of Portsmouth

CATEGORY

Waymarked forest trail.

DISTANCE

3-mile circuit.

The ride described below is a waymarked 3-mile woodland circuit in this 350-hectare forest situated to the north of Fareham. There is also a waymarked mountain biking route with more technical sections (starting on the other side of the road from the car park). The Family Route runs very close to the Meon Valley Trail, a railway path running from Wickham to West Meon, so it would be easy to link the two for a much longer ride.

West Walk is the largest remaining fragment of the former Royal Forest of Bere, which in ancient times used to stretch for over 30 miles from the River Test in the west to Rowland's Castle in the east. The last monarch to hunt here was Charles I in 1628. Like other royal forests its main purpose was to provide hunting but it soon became important for timber. By the 17th century, timber was fast disappearing. To take an example, in 1653, in just three days, 500 trees were felled to repair ships damaged in skirmishes with the Dutch. Only 3% of its timber remained and the land area had been reduced to 25 square miles. Bere suffered from its proximity to the shipbuilding industry and land-hungry farmers. The woodland was eventually taken over by the Forestry Commission in 1919. Much of the old oak remains, protected by a management plan for the next 200 years!

STARTING POINT & PARKING

➔West Walk lies 5 miles north of **Fareham**. The start is from the Forest Enterprise car park on the minor road connecting the B2177 east of

Wickham with Newtown and Soberton Heath (grid reference 597123).

ON YOUR BIKES!

1. From the car park take the left-hand fork, signposted with a red bike on a green square. On a gentle descent take the first broad track to the left (signposted).
2. At a five-way junction of tracks at the bottom of the hill turn right (signposted) then shortly first left. This is the start of the side loop, shaped like a balloon with a string.
3. Descend, climb, go through the car park, cross the road (with care) and continue straight ahead through the barrier.
4. At the crossroads at the bottom turn right and follow the broad gravel track round to the right to complete the loop (the balloon!). Turn left (along the string!), recross the road (take care) and go straight ahead.

5. At the T-junction turn left to rejoin the main loop, then at a crossroads after 1/2 mile turn right (signposted).

6. On a long steady climb keep an eye out for a signpost directing you sharply right by a wooden bench. Descend back to the start.

Station: Fareham or Botley.

TIC: Fareham, 01329 221342.

Other nearby trails: The Meon Valley Trail starts in Wickham. There are many miles of trails in the New Forest and two forest trails in Queen Elizabeth Country Park near Petersfield.

Useful publications: OS Landranger Map 196. A full colour A3 leaflet, *The Forest of Bere* is available from: Forest Enterprise, Downs & Chilterns Forest District Office, Bucks Horn Oak, Farnham, Surrey GU10 4LS (01420 23666).

Refreshments: None on route. The nearest are pubs in Soberton Heath and North Boarhunt or there is plenty of choice in Wickham.

6 Queen Elizabeth Country Park, Petersfield

CATEGORY

Forest trails.

DISTANCE

3.7 miles (family trail) and 3.2 miles (mountain bike trail).

Queen Elizabeth Country Park is certainly not flat but there is an excellent waymarked woodland circuit (purple waymarks) and plenty of other attractions in the park and at the visitor centre. For the more adventurous there is a technically challenging mountain bike circuit (orange waymarks). There are also trails leading out of the park onto the network of bridleways and lanes that criss-cross the South Downs, the great chalk ridge stretching from Winchester to Eastbourne. The park is part of the landscape of the South Downs and is in an Area of Outstanding Natural Beauty. It covers 1400 acres and is dominated by the three hills of Butser, War Down and Holt Down, which provide a contrast between the dramatic downland and beautiful woodland. With 38 species of butterfly and 12 species of wild orchid, it is a naturalist's paradise, a large area of which is designated as a Site of Special Scientific Interest. The many Roman and Iron Age sites in the park are also preserved as Scheduled Ancient Monuments.

STARTING POINT & PARKING

→Queen Elizabeth Country Park is well signposted off the A3 to the southwest of Petersfield, on the way to Portsmouth. There is a Pay & Display car park by the visitor centre.

ON YOUR BIKES!

The routes are well signposted. The trails start from the corner of the car park to the left of the visitor centre by a large colourful wooden signpost, or alternatively go through the first car park and onto the Gravel Hill car park. In general terms the purple (easier) route climbs steadily for the first half of the route and descends for the second half.

Station: Petersfield.
TIC: Petersfield, 01730 268829.
Other nearby trails: The South Downs Way passes through Queen Elizabeth Country Park. The Meon Valley Trail is a few miles to the west.
Useful publications: Ordnance Survey Landranger Map 197. Much better is the excellent A2 full colour *Queen Elizabeth Country Park Trails Guide* produced by Hampshire County Council / Forest Enterprise and available from: Queen Elizabeth Country Park, Gravel Hill, Horndean, Waterlooville, Hampshire PO8 0QE (01705 595040).
Refreshments: Well-stocked cafe at the visitor centre.

7   Centurion Way, Chichester

CATEGORY
Railway path.

DISTANCE
3 miles each way.

A short section of railway path between Chichester and Mid Lavant passing some extraordinary metal sculptures of Roman centurions and 'surveyors'. The route passes through woodland and arable land with a profusion of wildflowers along the verges. The name Centurion Way was suggested by a local schoolboy and is based on the fact that the path crosses the course of a Roman Road. It is hoped that in the future the path will be extended north beyond Lavant. At its southern end the path meets the South Coast Cycle Route (National Cycle Network Route 2) which will eventually run along the length of the South Coast from Kent to Cornwall!

The Chichester to Midhurst Railway was opened in 1881 to improve access to London. The line included three tunnels and eight stations, the most notable of the latter being Singleton, due to its proximity to Goodwood Racecourse. In 1994 the County Council purchased the railway line and with investment and help from English Partnerships, Chichester District Council and Tarmac Quarry Products, the old railway line was converted to recreational use.

STARTING POINTS & PARKING

→There is a car park at the northern end of the railway path, in Mid Lavant (grid reference 856086). Coming from the north, turn left off the A286 in **Mid Lavant** just **before** the wooden-spired church onto St Nicholas Road. Follow the road to the left then turn right onto Springfield Close and right again onto Churchmead Close, now following signs for 'Chichester Cycle Route'. The trail goes beneath the railway bridge.

→The southern end of the path is on the west side of **Chichester** near to the College of Technology. Follow Westgate from the centre of Chichester, straight over a roundabout past the Swan pub signposted '7.5 ton weight limit'. Continue following Westgate until just before the railway lines - bear right onto tarmac path then shortly turn left onto the Centurion Way (grid reference 848047).

Station: Chichester or Fishbourne.
TIC: Chichester, 01243 775888.
Other nearby trails: The South Downs Way is a long distance bridleway between Winchester and Eastbourne. There is a waymarked trail in Houghton Forest, north of Arundel.
Useful publications: OS Landranger Map 197. A leaflet, *Cycle Chichester* is available from Transport Planning Services, West Sussex County Council, The Grange, Tower Street, Chichester, West Sussex PO19 1RH (01243 777100).
Refreshments: Earl of March pub in Mid Lavant. Lots of choice in Chichester.

8 Houghton Forest, north of Arundel

CATEGORY
Forest trail.

DISTANCE
4 mile-circuit.

There are several large Forestry Commission holdings along the South Downs between Petersfield and Arundel, two of which have waymarked trails in them. The first of these is in Queen Elizabeth Park which also has the attraction of a well-laid out visitor centre. The ride described here has an outdoor cafe in a large car park rather than a visitor centre but the waymarked ride is easier, offers superb views from the downland edge section and there are many options for extending the route and taking in more forest tracks or sections of the South Downs Way.

There is plenty else of interest nearby: the old Roman Road of Stane Street passes right by the Roman Villa at Bignor (65 rooms, splendid mosaics) on its way from Chichester to London; Arundel Castle with its Toy and Military Museum stands glorious and intact just 3 miles south of Houghton Forest; Amberley Castle is considerably less intact but set in a delightful village near the River Arun and a little further afield are Petworth Deer Park and Chichester Cathedral.

STARTING POINT & PARKING
→Whiteways roundabout, at the junction of the A29, A284 and the B2139, about 4 miles to the north of **Arundel**.

ON YOUR BIKES!
1. The trail starts opposite the entrance to the car park. Follow the main track directly away from the road signposted 'Public Bridleway to Bike Trail'.

2. Follow the signs showing a white bike on a green background. At a major fork of tracks on the descent bear left.

3. Short descent, long steady climb. **Easy to miss.** Keep an eye out for a bike signs indicating a track to the right. (This is opposite a two way 'Public Bridleway' signpost). Shortly turn right again at the crossroads of tracks.

4. At the T-junction at the bottom of the descent turn right and follow this track back to the car park.

Station: Amberley.
TIC: Arundel, 01903 882268.
Other nearby trails: There are plenty Forestry Commission holdings between Houghton and Petersfield where you can devise your own routes. There are more waymarked trails in Queen Elizabeth Country Park near to Petersfield. The South Downs Way is a long distance bridleway that runs from Winchester to Eastbourne with some easier 'plateau' sections.
Useful publications: OS Landranger Map 197.
Refreshments: Kiosk serving hot drinks and snacks at the roundabout.

9   South Downs Way: Rackham Hill, Storrington, north of Worthing

CATEGORY
Chalk and stone long distance bridleway.

DISTANCE
West to Rackham Hill - 2 miles return. East to Barnsfarm Hill - 5 miles return

The South Downs Way is a long distance bridleway that stretches for 100 miles from Winchester to Eastbourne. It follows the line of chalk hills that rise up to over 800 ft between the Sussex Weald and the English Channel. In its entirety it would be a tough challenge in the summer months for fit mountain bikers. For those who would prefer not to face lung-bursting 600ft climbs but would nevertheless like to enjoy the wonderful views from the ridge and the pleasure of riding along the broad, chalk and flint tracks, there are several short sections which can be easily accessed by road. In addition to the ride described below, the other sections of the South Downs Way worth considering for similar rides are: Chanctonbury Ring from the minor road between Steyning and Sompting, Firle Beacon from West Firle and Ditchling Beacon north of Brighton. There is a gentle 100ft climb to the trig point to the west (Rackham Hill) and a slightly steeper 130ft climb to the east on to Kithurst Hill.

STARTING POINT & PARKING
→The Kithurst Hill car park (grid reference 070124) at the top of the minor road leading up from the B2139 between **Storrington** and Amberley. As you head west from Storrington towards Amberley, the lane you need to take is the first on the left **after** the end of the restricted speed limit. Climb to the car park right at the top.

ON YOUR BIKES!
Go through the car park barrier onto the South Downs Way:

1. *Turn right (west) for 1 mile.* Follow the South Downs Way, taking the right-hand fork soon after a small woodland section, going as far as the trig point (up in the field at the end of the fairly flat section). Beyond the trig point there is

9

a 600ft descent down to Amberley in the valley of the River Arun: great fun going down but not so much fun coming back up!

2. *Turn left (east) for 2 1/2 miles.* Climb, descend then climb again. Go beyond the barn and stop at the brow of the hill at the junction of tracks by a signpost which says 'Safe Road Crossing - South Downs Way'. Beyond here there is a steep descent down to Washington.

NB Don't be tempted to use the B2139 to make this into a circular ride - it is a fast and busy road unsuitable for quiet recreational cycling.

Station: Amberley.
TIC: Arundel, 01903 882268.
Other nearby trails: There is a waymarked forestry trail in Houghton Forest (southwest of Amberley).
Useful publications: OS Landranger Maps 197 & 198.
Refreshments: None on route, lots of choice in Storrington or Amberley.

10   Downs Link: Bramber to Old Shoreham

CATEGORY
Railway path.
DISTANCE
4 miles each way.

The most southerly section of the Downs Link, this part of the trail crosses the South Downs Way and continues south to Old Shoreham. Bramber is a very attractive village at the foot of the South Downs, located on the banks of the tidal River Adur, one of only three rivers that flows south from the Weald, cutting a course through the chalk hills of the South Downs. The ride runs south from Bramber alongside the river to Old Shoreham where there is a choice of refreshment stops. There is plenty of wildlife to

see along the river and fine views of Lancing College from the southern end of the ride.

NB. There is one difficult road crossing near the start of the ride. Please take **EXTREME CARE** crossing the A283 just south of Bramber. Alternatively start from the church in Old Shoreham and ride north as far as the A283.

STARTING POINT & PARKING

→ The car park in **Bramber**, a village signposted off the A283 roundabout at the south end of the Steyning bypass. The ride itself starts at the roundabout with the A283. There is a 'Downs Link' sign at the northeast corner of the roundabout (grid reference 186106).

ON YOUR BIKES!

1. Exit the car park in the centre of Bramber and turn right on the road as far as the roundabout. A 'Downs Link' sign immediately **before** the roundabout directs you onto a track running parallel with the southbound A283.
2. **TAKE EXTREME CARE** crossing the A283 to the other side. Wait patiently until you have gauged the speed of the traffic and there is a clear gap to cross.
3. At the T-junction of tracks turn left signposted 'South Downs Way. Eastbourne'. Cross the river bridge then turn right 'Coastal Link'.
4. Follow the track alongside the river for 3 miles. It is suggested you go as far as the Amsterdam pub / Red Lion Inn in Old Shoreham then return. (Beyond this point the trail soon peters out).

Station: Shoreham-by-Sea.
TIC: Hove, 01273 292589.
Other nearby trails: The Downs Link continues north from Bramber to Henfield and Southwater. There is a traffic-free cyclepath along Brighton & Hove Seafront Promenade. The Dyke Railway Trail runs north from Hove. Nearby ridge sections of the South Downs Way are OK in the summer months on mountain bikes.
Useful publications: OS Landranger Map 198.
Refreshments: Lots of choice in Bramber and Old Shoreham.

11   South Downs Way: Chanctonbury Ring, near Worthing

CATEGORY

Chalk and stone long distance bridleway.

DISTANCE

4 1/2 miles each way.

Chanctonbury Ring is one of the most atmospheric spots along the whole of the South Downs Way. The extensive prehistoric earthworks occupy a 783ft downland summit which affords views over some 30 miles of countryside. The original beeches were planted in 1760 by Charles Goring of Wiston House but were very badly devastated by the Great Storm of 1987 and will probably take a hundred years to recover. The ride suggested here runs from the minor road between Steyning and Sompting and heads northwest to the distinctive clump of beeches on top of Chanctonbury Ring. It uses a chalk and stone track which is only suitable for mountain bikes and best ridden in the summer months after a few hot dry days. There is a steady climb of 550 ft from the car park to Chanctonbury Ring.

NB The climb on the minor road up from the car park to the South Downs Way can be quite busy and is therefore not suitable for young children.

STARTING POINT & PARKING

→ The car park (grid reference 162080) on the minor road leading north from **Sompting** (Worthing) to Steyning (West Sussex). If one of the party is feeling fit and wants to be a hero / heroine, leave the others at the brow of the hill on the minor road, where the South Downs Way crosses (grid reference 163097), drop the car down the hill at the car park and cycle back up to meet them. This will save them almost 300 ft of climbing but give them the chance to enjoy the full descent. Using the map you can also devise an offroad route from the car park, avoiding the road altogether, although this option is steeper and rougher.

Station: East Worthing.
TIC: Worthing, 01903 210022.
Other nearby trails: There are other similar sections of the South Downs Way. The Downs Link from Bramber to Old Shoreham.
Useful publications: OS Landranger Map 198.
Refreshments: None on route. Lots in Steyning.

12 South Downs Way: Ditchling Beacon, north of Brighton

CATEGORY

Chalk and stone long distance bridleway.

DISTANCE

West from Ditchling Beacon to the Jack and Jill windmills - 4 1/2 miles return; east from Ditchling Beacon to Black Cap - 6 miles return.

Stretching west from Beachy Head into Hampshire, the South Downs range is all that remains of a huge chalk backbone that connected England with the continent until about 6000 years ago. Spare a thought for the thousands of people who cycle the London to Brighton Ride every year who have to climb to the top of Ditchling Beacon before their final descent down towards the coast! The ride uses a chalk and stone track which is only suitable for mountain bikes and best ridden in the summer months after a few hot dry days. The ride is generally downhill if you go west to the windmills (ie a climb back to the start). To the east, towards Black Cap, the ride is gently undulating. Jack and Jill Windmills are noted Sussex landmarks: 'Jack' is a brick-built towermill of 1866. 'Jill' is a wooden postmill, built in Brighton in 1821 and dragged to Clayton in about 1850 by a team of oxen.

STARTING POINT & PARKING

➔The car park at the top of the hill, on the minor road leading south from **Ditchling** towards Brighton (grid reference 334130). For the windmills, go to the far end of the car park following 'South Downs Way' signs. For Black Cap you will need to cross the road, again following 'South Downs Way' signs.

Station: Hassocks.
TIC: Brighton, 01273 292599.
Other nearby trails: Other sections of the South Downs Way. Dyke Railway Trail, north of Hove.
Useful publications: OS Landranger Map 198.
Refreshments: None on route. The nearest are in Ditchling.

13 Dyke Railway Trail, Hove

CATEGORY

Railway path and minor lane.

DISTANCE

3 1/2 miles each way.

This short trail climbs 450ft along the course of an old railway line from the outskirts of Hove then follows a quiet lane right up onto the South Downs ridge with magnificent views northwards across the Sussex Weald. It would be possible to make this into a longer ride by turning left along the South Downs Way as far as the masts on Truleigh Hill, although this would involve using some rougher sections of bridleway and quite a few ups and downs! It is worth waiting for a day with good visibility to do this ride as the views from the top are spectacular.

The Dyke Railway opened in 1887 and ran up to the Devil's Dyke Station at an almost continuous gradient of 1 in 40. It was never a very profitable route and finally closed in 1938. The line served the Brighton & Hove Golf Club where a halt was constructed in 1891. In 1895 a bell was installed between the Golf Clubhouse and the Dyke Station which would sound in the Golf Club bar on the departure of a train from the terminus, allowing members time to drink up in the bar and still catch their train home!

It is said that Devil's Dyke was created by the Devil in an attempt to flood the many Wealden churches. It is in fact a natural formation in the chalk hillside rising over 300ft on either side. The Dyke viewpoint was the site of a massive hillfort dating back to the Iron Age and one of the largest of its kind on the South Downs. The highest point is marked by a triangulation pillar.

STARTING POINTS & PARKING

➔The trail starts in the suburb of **Hangleton**, on the northern outskirts of Hove (grid reference 270076). There is a car park at the start of the trail in Hangleton between the Countryman pub and the row of shops. These are located a short distance up the hill from the Church of St Helens.
➔Car park at **Devil's Dyke**, off the A27 / A23 to the north of Hove (grid reference 258111).

ON YOUR BIKES!

1. Climb steadily from the Hangleton car park. Cross the bridge over the A27. Go past the golf course. When you are parallel with the golf clubhouse (to your right) turn left onto a continuation of the railway path.
2. At the road either turn left on tarmac or cross the road and turn left on a track parallel with the road. **Remember** this point for the return trip. Where the road swings right, bear left to continue climbing towards Devil's Dyke.
3. After reaching the top you may wish simply to return. As an option to make the ride longer you could follow the South Downs Way west as far as Truleigh masts. This is a further 6-mile round trip on on a track (at times rough) which undulates between 500 ft and 700 ft above sea level, with wonderful views of the Weald.

Station: Hove.
TIC: Hove, 01273 292589.
Other nearby trails: Sections of the South Downs Way. Friston Forest, west of Eastbourne.
Useful publications: OS Landranger Map 198.
Refreshments: Devil's Dyke pub at Devil's Dyke.

14 South Downs Way: Firle Beacon, east of Lewes.

CATEGORY

Chalk and stone long distance bridleway.

DISTANCE

West to Red Lion Pond - 3 miles return. East to Firle Beacon - 3 miles return.

This is the most easterly of the 'plateau' sections of the South Downs Way described in this guide, sections that enable you to sample the delights and panoramic views of this long distance trail without the need for Tour de France legs to climb 600 ft up from the Sussex Weald to the top of the ridge. The ride uses a chalk and stone track which is only suitable for mountain bikes and best ridden in the summer months after a few hot dry days. There is a gentle 190ft climb to the east to Firle Beacon. To the west, to Red Lion Pond, the ride is more undulating in character. It is worth visiting the lovely village of West Firle and its excellent pub.

STARTING POINT & PARKING

→West Firle lies off the A27 about 5 miles to the west of Lewes. As the road bears left into **Firle** village, bear right / straight ahead following signs for 'Firle Beacon'. Park at the top (grid reference 468059).

ON YOUR BIKES!

1. *East towards Firle Beacon.* Leave the broad stone track, follow the large 'Footpath' sign into the field (it is in fact a bridleway) and aim for the hill ahead. You can either return directly from the beacon or go as far as the next hill. It is suggested you turn around here as beyond this point there is a long steep descent down into Alfriston.

2. *West towards the masts.* The suggested turn around point is at the trig point / Red Lion Pond.

Station: Glynde.

TIC: Lewes, 01273 483448.

Other nearby trails: There are waymarked routes in Friston Forest, to the west of Eastbourne.

Useful publications: OS Landranger Map 198.

Refreshments: None on route. Good pub in West Firle.

14

15   Friston Forest, west of Eastbourne

CATEGORY

Forest trail / stone track through Seven Sisters Country Park.

DISTANCE

Forest circuit - 4.7 miles; to the coast and back - 2.6 miles.

There are two rides starting from Exceat, where the River Cuckmere has cut a course through the chalk ridge of the South Downs. The short ride goes to the coast and back; the longer ride is a waymarked forest route. The Seven Sisters Country Park Visitor Centre is housed in a converted 18th-century barn at Exceat Farm. The Living World is a mini-zoo of small creatures including butterflies, bees, spiders, scorpions and marine life.

STARTING POINT & PARKING

→Forestry Commission car park in **Exceat**, on the minor lane towards Litlington, just off the A259 to the east of Seaford (grid reference 519995).

ON YOUR BIKES!

Route to the sea

Push your bike past the cafe and visitor centre. Cross the busy A259 by the bus stop, signposted 'To the beach, Foxholes'. **TAKE GREAT CARE.** Follow the track through Seven Sisters Country Park for 3/4 mile then as the concrete track swings left towards Foxholes bear right onto a gravel track for fine sea views. Retrace your steps.

Waymarked forest route

1. The forest trail starts from the far end of the bottom car park signposted 'Public Bridleway to West Dean'.
2. Pass to the right of a flint house called Pond Cottage. After a mile go past two more flint buildings on the left. At a crossroads of tracks go straight ahead. Follow the main track around a left-hand bend then shortly turn left uphill on

to an earth track by a metal barrier and soon turn left again on to a grassy track

3. At the junction with a wide stone forest road turn right then, ignoring the grassy track, take the first proper forest road to the left. Climb steeply then half way down the descent turn left on to a grassy track. At a T-junction with a wide stone forestry track turn right to rejoin the outward route back to the start.

Station: Berwick or Polegate (between Lewes and Eastbourne).

TIC: Eastbourne, 01323 411400.

Other nearby trails: The Cuckoo Trail starts at Polegate, 4 miles north of Eastbourne. The South Downs Way is a long distance bridleway that runs from Winchester to Eastbourne with some easier 'plateau' sections.

Useful publications: OS Landranger Map 199.

Refreshments: Cafe at start. Plenty of pubs nearby in Friston, Jevington and Litlington.

16 Cuckoo Trail, Hailsham

CATEGORY
Railway path.
DISTANCE
Up to 11 miles each way.

The Cuckoo Trail is one of the longest and most popular railway paths in the South-East of England. The line gained its name because of a Sussex tradition that the first cuckoo of spring was released each year at Heathfield Fair. It offers superb traffic-free cycling through a mixture of broadleaf woodland, open grassland, arable farmland and pasture. As you head back down towards Polegate there are views of the rolling chalk hills of the South Downs ahead of you. Along the way are metal sculptures, an arch in the form of a Chinese Pagoda roof, a claw-like hand and plenty of carved wooden seats with a variety of motifs, made from local oaks blown down in the Great Gale of 1987. The verges are thick with wildflowers such as willowherb and vetch. There is a gentle climb up from Polegate to Heathfield so that you can look forward to a gravity-assisted return journey! In several places along the way bridges have been dismantled and houses have been built on the the course of the railway requiring you to cross several minor roads and use short sections of estate roads through Hailsham and Horam to regain the railway path.

STARTING POINT & PARKING
→Heathfield, Hailsham, Horam or Polegate. The car parks are all close to the trail. Better to start at the southern end (Polegate) and climb when you are fresh, giving you a downhill for the second half of the ride.

ON YOUR BIKES!
1. From Polegate follow the railway path for 3 miles into Hailsham. At this point the route follows estate roads so look out for 'Cuckoo

Trail (bikes)' signs.

2. Rejoin the railway path and follow for 5 miles through to Horam. There is a second, short section on estate roads.

3. The trail ends after a further 3 miles in Heathfield. In this final section there are several roads to cross, mainly quiet lanes, but care should be taken none the less if you are with young children.

Station: Polegate, less than 1/2 mile from the start of the route.
TIC: Hailsham, 01323 844426.
Other nearby trails: Friston Forest lies 5 miles to the southeast of Polegate. The South Downs Way has some 'plateau' sections.
Useful publications: OS Landranger Map 199. A Cuckoo Trail leaflet is available from Boship Tourist Information Centre, Lower Dicker, Hailsham, East Sussex BN27 4DT (01323 442667).
Refreshments: Lots of choice in each of the towns. Tea shop on the trail at the Old Loom Mill Craft Centre (2 miles north of Polegate, just before crossing the B2104).

17 Test Way, Stockbridge (northwest of Winchester)

CATEGORY
Railway path.
DISTANCE
5 miles each way.

This 5-mile section of the Test Way runs south from the attractive, large village of Stockbridge parallel with and occasionally crossing the delightfully clear, shallow, fast-flowing River Test, one of the best fishing rivers in England. The old railway track has been converted into a good, stone-based trail. There is now a traffic-free connection from the end of the railway path to the lane leading to Mottisfont Abbey, a

National Trust property with a tearoom.

The Test Valley railway line was also known as the 'Sprat & Winkle Line'. It was unusual in that it was built on the bed of an old canal which linked Andover and Southampton. The waterway was first used in 1794 but had fallen into disuse within 50 years. The railway began service in 1865 and was used in both World Wars to move troops and supplies to Southampton Docks. It closed in 1964 and has since become part of the Test Way, a long-distance footpath from Inkpen to Totton. Short sections of it are also open to cyclists.

STARTING POINT & PARKING
→Trafalgar Way, off the roundabout at the eastern end of **Stockbridge** at the junction of the A30 and A3057m by the White Hart pub (grid reference 359350). Stockbridge is about 10 miles northwest of Winchester.

Station: Mottisfont.
TIC: Winchester, 01962 840500.
Other nearby trails: The long distance bridleway, the South Downs Way, starts in

Winchester, 10 miles southeast of Stockbridge.
Useful publications: OS Landranger Map 185.
Refreshments: Lots of choice in Stockbridge.
The John of Gaunt pub by the River Test at
Stockbridge. Tearoom at Mottisfont Abbey, a
National Trust property.

18 Downs Link: Southwater to Steyning & Bramber

CATEGORY

Railway path.

DISTANCE

Up to 12 miles each way.

The Downs Link between Slinfold and
Southwater is the least suitable for traffic-free
cycling with road sections and rough surfaces.
The quality improves south of Southwater
Country Park, the section described here. The
chalk ridge of the South Downs looms as you
head south. The track leaves the bed of the
railway soon after crossing the bridge over the
River Adur and climbs along the edge of a field.
You may wish to follow reasonably quiet roads
into Steyning or Bramber for a choice of pubs
and shops.

Southwater Country Park was opened in 1985
and provides some 54 acres for informal
recreation and conservation. The site used to be
a brickworks, home of the Southwater Red
Engineering Brick. Around 1,000 million of
these bricks were produced during the factory's
working life from 1890 to 1981.

NB The B2135 needs to be used for about 1/2
mile near to Partridge Green and you will need
to use 2 miles of lanes and quiet streets to get to
Bramber or Steyning for refreshments.

STARTING POINT & PARKING

➜ **Southwater Country Park**, just off the A24

about 5 miles south of Horsham (grid reference
161258).

ON YOUR BIKES!

1. Exit the Southwater Country Park car park
and cross the road onto Stakers Lane, signposted
'Copsale, Horsham'.

2. Go under the noisy A24. As the tarmac track
swings left by the red-brick building of the water
treatment works, bear right by a wooden fence,
soon joining a a good broad track. After 1/2 mile
cross a minor lane by the Bridge House pub.

3. About 4 miles after the Bridge House pub, at
a crossroads with a broad tarmac lane, you
should be able to see the yellow-hatted tree
trunk creature in the garden of the Partridge
pub. Go straight ahead for a continuation of the
route or turn left here for the pub.

4. At the T-junction with the B2135 turn right.
You may prefer to walk along the pavement.
Ignore the first left to the Trading Estate. Take
the next tarmac lane to the left signposted
'Downs Link'. At a crossroads of tracks about
200 yds after the end of the tarmac, turn right.
Cross a field on a narrow track.

5. There is a short climb to a gravel car park by
the Old Railway Tavern pub, Henfield. At the road
turn left then first right, opposite the pub. After 200

yds, as the road swings to the left, turn right onto Hollands Lane then left onto the Downs Link.
6. For refreshments in Bramber or Steyning, follow the track for 2 miles, eventually climbing along a field edge. At the T-junction turn left downhill. The track turns to tarmac. For Steyning follow the road around to the right and across the bridge over the A283 into the heart of the town. For Bramber follow 'Downs Link' signs. Both these options involve using roads with traffic.

Station: Horsham.
TIC: Horsham, 01403 211661.
Other nearby trails: Other sections of the Downs Link. 'Plateau' sections of the South Downs Way.
Useful publications: OS Landranger Map 198. A leaflet, *The Downs Link* (cost £2.00) is available from The Planning Department, West Sussex County Council, County Hall, Chichester PO19 1RL (01243 777100).
Refreshments: Cafe in Southwater Country Park. Pubs in Partridge Green and Henfield. Lots of choice in Bramber and Steyning.

19 Alice Holt Forest, southwest of Farnham

CATEGORY
Forestry trail.
DISTANCE
4 mile-circuit.

An easy, well-designed route on the sandy soils south of Farnham, part of the greensand strata that runs east from Alton, between the chalk of the North Downs and the clay of the Weald, providing well-drained, all-year-round tracks. The well-waymarked circular route starts from the visitor centre and uses stone and gravel paths with the occasional gentle hill.

From the Middle Age onwards, timber from Alice Holt was being used to build ships for Britain's navy. Hundreds of mature oaks were needed to build a single ship and the forest was periodically stripped of its large trees to supply the naval shipyards dotted along the south coast. Today, Alice Holt oak is being used to

19

build a replica of Shakespeare's Globe Theatre in London. This ride could easily be combined with a visit to Birdworld which lies less than a mile away and has a fantastic collection of birds from all over the world.

STARTING POINT & PARKING

➔At the visitor centre, 4 miles southwest of **Farnham** just off the A325 Farnham to Petersfield road at Bucks Horn Oak (grid reference 810416). Cycle hire available (01420 476612)

Station: Bentley.
TIC: Farnham, 01252 715109.
Other nearby trails: The Basingstoke Canal runs from Odiham to Weybridge and pases through Fleet, 5 miles north of Farnham. The Downs Link runs from near Guildford south to Shoreham. The Lookout at Bracknell.
Useful publications: OS Landranger Map 186. Further details about forest cycle routes in the area are available from Forest Enterprise, Downs and Chilterns Forest District, Bucks Horn Oak, Farnham, Surrey GU10 4 LS (01420 23666).
Refreshments: At the visitor centre.

20 Downs Link: Bramley to Cranleigh, south of Guildford

CATEGORY
Railway path.
DISTANCE
6 miles each way.

As its name suggests, this railway path route links the North Downs Way, which is part footpath, where you **cannot** cycle and part bridleway / byway, where you **can**, with the South Downs Way which has bridleway status along its entire length and offers good mountain biking. The Downs Link, which is over 30 miles long, has been split into four sections. There is a short 1 mile railway path stretch to the north of Bramley, as far as the A281, but the trail described below heads south from Bramley to Cranleigh. The track is owned and managed by Surrey County Council. Small areas of trees are periodically cut back (coppiced) to diversify the woodland structure and encourage the growth of wildflowers. This also benefits butterflies,

small mammals and bird life. The railway was built in two sections: the southern part, from Christ's Hospital to Shoreham was completed in 1861 and the northern part, from Guildford to Christ's Hospital, was built in 1865. The railways served the local communities and industries like the Southwater Brickworks but were not profitable and were shut in 1966.

STARTING POINTS & PARKING

→ **Bramley** and Wonersh Old Station car park, south of Guildford. At the junction of the A281 and B2128, exit the roundabout towards 'Wonersh, Shamley Green'. After 200 yds turn left signposted 'Bramley Business Centre, Bramley and Wonersh Railway Station' (grid reference 010451).

→ In **Cranleigh**, at the far corner of the main car park, off the High Street, near the NatWest Bank (grid reference 056391).

Station: Shalford.
TIC: Guildford, 01483 444333.
Other nearby trails: The Downs Link can be followed southwards beyond Cranleigh. There is a waymarked trail in Alice Holt Forest, southwest of Farnham. The Worth Way and Forest Way start in East Grinstead.
Useful publications: OS Landranger Maps 186 & 187. A leaflet, *The Downs Link* (cost £2.00) is available from The Planning Department, West Sussex County Council, County Hall, Chichester PO19 1RL (01243 777100).
Refreshments: Pub in Bramley. Pubs and cafes in Cranleigh.

21   Downs Link: Cranleigh south to Slinfold

CATEGORY
Railway path.
DISTANCE
7 miles each way.
It is worth cycling this section in May when the woods south of the Thurlow Arms pub (near Baynards) are carpeted with a magnificent display of bluebells.
The stone-based track will become muddy in winter or after prolonged rain. There is one hill south of the Thurlow Arms pub at Baynards where the trail has to climb up over the blocked tunnel that the railway used to use. There are a couple of minor lanes to cross and one busy road - the A281 south of Rudgwick - where you should take GREAT CARE.

STARTING POINTS & PARKING

→ In **Cranleigh**, at the far corner of the main car park, off the High Street, near the NatWest Bank (grid reference 056391).
→ There is a small car park in **Slinfold** near the trail. Slinfold lies due west of Horsham, just off the A29 (grid reference 114310).

ON YOUR BIKES!

1. Exit at the corner of the main car park in Cranleigh and turn left. After 300 yds cross the road towards the houses then shortly turn right by low wooden posts, signposted 'Downs Link'. Follow the track / lane between playing fields. Continue for 3 1/2 miles to the Thurlow Arms pub.
2. At a tarmac lane just beyond the pub turn left then right, signposted 'Downs Link'. Just beyond the first bridge, turn left uphill onto the road, cross the bridge then go first left through a gate signposted 'Public Bridleway. Downs Link'. In order to avoid the old tunnel you now have a steep climb. After 400 yds, at a crossroads of tracks, turn left and go steeply downhill.

(Remember this point for the return trip.)

3. About 1 mile after rejoining the course of the railway line you have to cross the busy A281. **TAKE EXTREME CARE.**

4. After 2 miles, and about 200 yds after going through a short round tunnel beneath the A29 and past a factory on your right, turn left onto tarmac to go into Slinfold. At the T-junction at the end of the lane turn right for the pub in the village.

Station: Horsham.
TIC: Horsham, 01403 211661.
Other nearby trails: The Downs Link can be followed north from Cranleigh to Bramley. To the south, the next good section of the Downs Link runs from Southwater Country Park. The Worth Way and Forest Way start from East Grinstead.
Useful publications: OS Landranger Map 187. A leaflet, *The Downs Link* (cost £2.00) is available from The Planning Department, West Sussex County Council, County Hall, Chichester PO19 1RL (01243 777100).
Refreshments: Lots of choice in Cranleigh. Thurlow Arms pub at Baynards. King's Head pub just off the route in Slinfold.

22 Worth Way, west of East Grinstead

CATEGORY
Railway path.
DISTANCE
6 1/2 miles each way.

One of two railway paths that start in East Grinstead, the Worth Way whisks you away from commuter land into a wooded landscape in the twinkling of an eye. There is a 1/2-mile section along roads through Crawley Down before you dive back into woodland once again. The route ends at Worth (on the eastern edge of Crawley). As with the Forest Way, this forms part of National Cycle Network Route 21, the Downs & Weald Cycle Route between London and the South Coast.

STARTING POINT & PARKING
→The car park at the back of the railway station in **East Grinstead**. Follow the one-way system out of town on the A22 (A264) towards London and Crawley. After passing the railway station on your left, just before a major junction with the A264 Tunbridge Wells road, turn left on to Park Road, then first left on to Grosvenor Road. Turn right into the station car park. The Worth Way starts by a wooden signpost on the right (grid reference 388383).

ON YOUR BIKES!
1. Follow the Worth Way for 2 1/2 miles at which point the track turns to tarmac. Three T-junctions! At the first, at the end of Cob Close, turn left; at the second, at the end of Hazel Way, turn right then at the third, at the end of Woodland Drive, turn left.

2. At the offset crossroads at the end of Burleigh Way go straight ahead onto Old Station Close. The tarmac turns to track. Continue in the same direction at the next crossroads.

3. At the next road, by a brick and slate

building, turn left then shortly right through Rowfant car park.

4. The railway path ends at the third road (by Keepers Cottage) but it is possible to continue a further mile to the church at Worth on a good, stone-based bridleway. Cross the road and turn left on to the track along the verge. On a sharp left-hand bend after 200 yds turn right and follow this track in the same direction for a mile, past a farm and over the M23 as far as Worth, perhaps visiting its lovely Anglo-Saxon church.

Station: East Grinstead.
TIC: Horsham, 01403 211661.
Other nearby trails: The Forest Way runs southeast from East Grinstead.
Useful publications: OS Landranger Map 187.
Refreshments: Lots of choice in East Grinstead.

23 Forest Way, east of East Grinstead

CATEGORY
Railway path.

DISTANCE
Up to 10 miles one way.

The countryside around Hartfield is the setting of A. A. Milne's *Winnie the Pooh* stories so watch out for Tiggers and Heffalumps! This fine ride passes through woodland and arable land lying between East Grinstead and Groombridge. There are picnic tables along the way and the broad, good quality track makes an ideal ride for exercise and conversation. The railway path forms part of National Cycle Network Route 21, the Downs & Weald Cycle Route between London and the South Coast. The railway line was opened by the London, Brighton & South Coast Railway in 1866 as an extension of the Three Bridges to East Grinstead branch line. Forest Row was the busiest of the intermediate stations, dealing in minerals and general goods. It was finally closed as part of the Beeching cuts in 1966.

STARTING POINT & PARKING
→ The car park on College Lane / De La Warr Road on the east of **East Grinstead**. This is located on the town centre side of the roundabout on the A22 Eastbourne Road (grid reference 399381).

ON YOUR BIKES!
1. From the car park return to De La Warr Road and turn right. At the T-junction with College Lane turn right for 100 yds then turn first left downhill by a stone wall. At the end of Old Road, cross to the opposite pavement, turn left then right through fence onto path. At the next road go straight ahead onto Forest Way.

2. Use the toucan crossing to cross the busy

A22 and continue straight ahead onto a tarmac drive signposted 'Tablehurst Farm'. After 400 yds, shortly after passing Forest Row Pumping Station on your left, near the end of a line of cypress trees, turn right onto a narrow path signposted 'Forest Way Country Park'.

3. After 4 miles, at a T-junction, just after going through a large yellow stone bridge under the B2026, turn left then right past Hartfield Station, which is now a private house.

4. The Forest Way continues for a further 3 1/2 miles to the edge of Groombridge. To visit the pub, shop or bakery turn left at the T-junction with the lane and follow up and down for 1/2 mile.

Station: East Grinstead.
TIC: Tunbridge Wells, 01892 515675.
Other nearby trails: The Worth Way starts from East Grinstead railway station car park.
Useful publications: OS Landranger Maps 187 & 188.
Refreshments: Lots of choice in East Grinstead.

Good pubs just off the route in Hartfield, Withyham and Groombridge.

24 Bewl Water, Lamberhurst

CATEGORY
Round-reservoir route.
DISTANCE
13 mile-circuit.

The only round-reservoir route south of London, Bewl Water offers a magnificent, challenging summer ride through woodland and pasture on a mixture of tracks and quiet lanes. Be warned that there are some steep hills on the lane sections and that on some of the offroad stretches the surface can be rough. The route should be avoided after prolonged rain. It is shut from November to the end of April. As a full 13-mile circuit it is not suitable for young children. The dam is made from local clay and faced with concrete slabs to prevent erosion.

24

Holding back 6,900 million gallons of water, Bewl Water is the largest reservoir in the South-East. Nearby Chingley Wood is a mixed coppice woodland once used for fuelling ironworks in the valley. Several willow plantations around the lake produce timber for the manufacture of cricket bats.

NB This is a very popular route with walkers and horses - please give way to them and ride with consideration for others at all times.

STARTING POINT & PARKING
→Bewl Water Visitor Centre, near **Lamberhurst**, off the A21 between Tunbridge Wells and Hastings (grid reference 676337). There is a charge to use the car park.

ON YOUR BIKES!
With your back to the entrance to the visitor centre bear left towards the low wooden building housing the bike hire centre. Turn sharp left and follow bike signs. The route is waymarked with 'Round Water Route' signs but the waymarking is patchy and it is not sufficient to say 'Follow the edge of the lake' as the route veers away from the water's edge on the southern part of the ride. A map is useful for the first time you ride the circuit. On the tarmac sections, keep an eye out for 'Round Water Route' signs at each junction.

Station: Wadhurst.
TIC: Tunbridge Wells, 01892 515675.
Other nearby trails: There is a waymarked route in Bedgebury Forest, just to the east of the reservoir. The Cuckoo Trail runs from Polegate to Heathfield.
Useful publications: OS Landranger Map 188. A map is available at the visitor centre (01892 890661).
Refreshments: At the visitor centre or The Bull pub at Three Leg Cross about half way around the circuit.

25 Bedgebury Forest, Hawkhurst

CATEGORY
Forest trail.
DISTANCE
5 mile-circuit.

This is the only waymarked forestry route in Kent and probably the hardest thing about it is finding the start! Bedgebury Forest is mixed woodland and in amongst the fir and conifers you will find sweet chestnut, birch, oak and sycamore, not to mention bright yellow ragwort, purple willowherb and foxgloves. The forest lies adjacent to Bedgebury Pinetum which contains a magnificent collection of rare trees and flowering shrubs. There is a lovely picnic spot by the lakes you pass along the route. The trail starts from near Louisa Lodge at the eastern end of the forest and follows a gently undulating stone and gravel path.

STARTING POINT & PARKING
→The start of the cycle trail in Bedgebury Forest lies at the end of a minor road running west from the A229 Cranbrook to Hawkhurst road. This unsigned minor road is difficult to find! Coming south from Cranbrook towards Hawkhurst, it is the first proper road to the right 3/4 mile after passing the B2085 to Goudhurst on the right. (The turn off the A229 is located at grid reference 759335). Follow the minor road to its end. There is parking just after the end of the tarmac.

ON YOUR BIKES!
1. From the car park mentioned above take the left-hand fork signposted 'Forest Cycle Trail. 5 miles'. After 1/2 mile, at the bike signpost, turn right off the main stone track onto a narrower, rougher track. At the first T-junction turn right, at the second T-junction (with a wide stone track) turn left.

2. Go past a lake. Climb then descend. At the next T-junction, with some wooden barns to the left, turn right *(or for the Old Trout pub in Flimwell turn left then left again alongside the A21)*.

3. Go past a second barn (with a corrugated iron roof). At the T-junction after 1 mile turn right *(or to visit the Pinetum turn left)*.

4. At a point after 1/2 mile where a track turns off to the left you have a choice of continuing straight ahead back to the start (signposted 'Short Cut') or of taking this left turn (signposted 'Sugar Loaf Hill') and following the waymarked route which takes a slightly longer course to return to the start.

Station: Etchingham, southwest of Hawkhurst.
TIC: Cranbrook, 01580 712538.
Other nearby trails: Bewl Water lies just to the west.
Useful publications: OS Landranger Map 188. Kent High Weald Project (01580 715918) produces, a pack of four laminated leaflets including an 8-mile circuit of Bedgebury Forest.
Refreshments: At Bedgebury Pinetum or the Old Trout pub, Flimwell, is just off the route.

26 North Downs Way
see also 35 Reigate Hill

CATEGORY
Chalk and stone long distance trail
DISTANCE
Several sections of 5 - 10 miles.

Unlike the South Downs Way, or the Ridgeway, where you are allowed to cycle from one end to the other, the North Downs Way, running along the chalk ridge from Farnham to Canterbury and Dover, is mainly a footpath and you are **not** permitted to cycle on footpaths. There are, however, several bridleway / byway sections that are open to cyclists. There are many good bases from which to explore the North Downs bridleway / byway network: Gomshall, Peaslake, Leith Hill, Walton on the Hill, Limpsfield and Wye.

Bridleway / byway sections
These stretches are almost all on bridleway, byway or minor road. If you take the appropriate Ordnance Survey Landranger maps you will be able to work out the best route for yourself. Lisrted from west to east:

1. Puttenham (west of Guildford) to Dorking (OS maps 186 & 187)
2. Wrotham (M20, Jct 2) - Rochester - Blue Bell Hill (OS maps 178 & 188)
3. Hollingbourne (east of Maidstone) to Dunn Street (north of Ashford) (OS maps 188 & 189)
4. Canterbury to Dover (OS map 179)

Surface & Hills: There are lots of hills and the surface can vary enormously, from a quiet tarmac lane or a fine stone path to a rough, muddy track, particularly in winter. Explore the area nearest to you after a dry spell in summer / early autumn when most tracks will be rideable. Mountain bikes are recommended.

TICs
Guildford, 01483 444333; Maidstone, 01622 602169; Dover, 01304 205108.

27 Canterbury to Whitstable (Crab & Winkle Way)

CATEGORY
Newly-built cycle path and railway path.
DISTANCE
8 miles each way.

The ride, known as the Crab & Winkle Way, starts from the centre of the beautiful, historic city of Canterbury and uses traffic-calmed roads and specially-built cyclepaths to link town to countryside, following the course of a dismantled railway through broadleaf woodland to the attractive seaside town of Whitstable. The streets around Canterbury Cathedral are best explored on foot and there is in any case a restriction on cycling here between 10.30 AM and 4.00 PM. The route climbs steadily out of the city with wonderful views opening up behind you. After passing close to the university the route soon joins a traffic-free section that runs for over four miles past fruit farms and through woodland to South Street on the edge of Whitstable. Cyclepaths and traffic-calmed streets lead right into the heart of this fine coastal town.

STARTING POINTS & PARKING
→Westgate, **Canterbury** or **Whitstable** town centre. Alternatively there is a small car park on the route, located just off the A290 about 1 1/2 miles to the northwest of Canterbury, opposite Kent College (grid reference 131595).

ON YOUR BIKES!
1. From Westgate, at the junction of Pound Lane and St Peter's Street in the centre of Canterbury, use the cycle facility to cross the main road and follow the route waymarked 'Route 1, Whitstable' along Westgate Grove and Whitehall Road.
2. The route runs eastwards, parallel with the A2050 then turns north through a more rural

the new A299 and follow the farm track to the road near Brooklands Farm, South Street.

6. Turn left on the road for 300 yds then immediately **after** passing Millstrood Road to the left bear left onto the red tarmac cyclepath signposted 'Station, Town Centre Cycle Route'. At the end of the cyclepath turn left then right downhill through the residential road with sea views ahead.

7. Follow the waymarked route into the heart of Whitstable. It is well worth visiting the harbour. Follow: All Saints Close, railway station, Stream Walk, Albert Street, town centre and harbour.

Station: Whitstable or Canterbury.

TIC: Canterbury, 01227 766567.

Other nearby trails: A newly-built section of the National Cycle Network leads from the centre of Canterbury out to the east to Fordwich. There are several small Forestry Commission holdings lying within 15 miles of Canterbury where there is an open access policy on the broad stone forest tracks. These include Thornden Wood and Church Wood to the north and northwest of Canterbury and King's Wood and Denge Wood to the southwest. A largely traffic-free National Cycle Network route is being built along the coast from Margate to Sandwich and Deal.

Useful publications: OS Landranger Map 179. *Canterbury Cycle Routes* is an A3 leaflet showing cycle routes in Canterbury, available from Canterbury City Council, Council Offices, Military Road, Canterbury, Kent CT1 1YW (01227 763763). Sustrans *Garden of England Cycle Route* map (£5.99) shows this route and all the rest of the National Cycle Network from London to Sandwich and back west along the coast to Hastings.

Sustrans Order Line: Call 0845 113 0065 or visit their website at www.sustrans.org.uk

Refreshments: Lots of choice in Whitstable and Canterbury.

setting and climbs steadily. Look behind you and to your right for fine views of Canterbury and the cathedral.

3. Go past a tall white water tower. Use the toucan crossing to cross the busy Whitstable Road (A290) onto the shared-use pavement. Opposite Kent College turn right onto a tarmac lane that goes past a car park and turns to track as it continues northwards.

4. Descend to cross a stream, climb again passing fruit orchards and farms. Follow the obvious track into woodland turning right at the first crossroads then left at a T-junction of forestry tracks. To your left is a pond which was used to cool the winding gear on the old Canterbury & Whitstable Line.

5. After 3/4 mile bear left away from the wide forestry track, descend to cross the bridge over

28 Kennet & Avon Canal through Newbury from Hamstead Park to Thatcham railway station

CATEGORY
Canal towpath.

DISTANCE
7 miles each way.

National Cycle Network Route 4 diverges from the canal towpath from Devizes through Hungerford to a few miles west of Newbury: there is an excellent network of quiet lanes which offers safe and attractive cycling. The towpath is rejoined at Hamstead Park, giving the cyclist a fine entry into (or exit from) the centre of Newbury. The orange sandy path passes a series of pill boxes built as a line of defence during the Second World War and runs underneath the new Newbury A34 bypass. The path crosses Bridge Street in the centre of Newbury and continues eastwards alongside the canal to Thatcham. The next section (from Thatcham to Reading) is described in the next ride. Mountain bikes are recommended.

NB Please read *The Waterways Code - Cycling on the towpath* at the front of the book

STARTING POINT & PARKING
→If arriving by bike, the route starts by the Lock, Stock & Barrel pub on Bridge Street in the heart of Newbury. If arriving by car there are no car parks adjacent to the canal in the centre of town and it may be worth starting well to the east of the town centre, for example Thatcham railway station which is right on the towpath, and cycling west through Newbury to the minor road crossing by Hamstead Park. West of this point National Cycle Network Route 4 leaves the canal towpath for the network of quiet lanes and as a result the surface of the towpath is rougher and narrower.

Station: Newbury.
TIC: Newbury, 01635 30267.
Other nearby trails: The Kennet & Avon Canal can be followed into Reading. Sections of the Ridgeway offer good cycling in the summer months (mountain bikes only).
Useful publications: OS Landranger Map 174.
Refreshments: Lots of choice in Newbury.

28

29 Kennet & Avon Canal from Reading to Thatcham

CATEGORY
Canal towpath.

DISTANCE
Up to 16 miles each way.

Forming part of National Cycle Network Route 4 between Bristol and London, the Kennet & Avon Canal towpath between Thatcham and Reading has been improved to a standard suitable for recreational cycling. Although the towpath is predominantly of stone and gravel, there is a 1-mile section that runs along the meadows by the canal, to the east of Aldermaston. There are several pubs along the way and a chance for tea and coffee at the British Waterways Visitor and Information Centre at Aldermaston Wharf. It is in Reading that the canal links up with the Thames.

NB Please read *The Waterways Code - Cycling on the towpath* at the front of the book

STARTING POINTS & PARKING
➜The railway station at **Thatcham** or the centre of **Reading** by the Oracle Centre. You may also choose to start at the car parks at Sheffield Bottom picnic site south of **Theale**, at Tyle Mill, off the A4 towards Sulhamstead, or at the **Aldermaston** Wharf visitor centre.

ON YOUR BIKES!
By bike from the centre of Reading. (If arriving by car it would be better to start at the western end)
1. There are two cycle route options to the south of Reading from the Oracle Centre. Either follow Fobney Street and signs for 'Green Park' and 'Majedski Stadium', soon joining the canal towpath on the west side of the canal **OR** follow National Cycle Network Route 4 signs which link cyclepaths and quiet streets to the towpath

running down the east side of the canal. Both link at the junction of the A33 and Rose Kiln Lane, to the south of Reading (near Whitley) then turn west towards Theale.
2. There is short section near to Burghfield Mill where National Cycle Network Route 4 signs will direct you away from the canal and around the edge of a lake close to the M4. You rejoin the towpath to the east of Theale (just east of where the M4 bridge crosses the canal).

Station: Thatcham, Midgham, Theale or Reading.
TIC: Reading, 0118 956 6226.
Other nearby trails: The Thames towpath can be followed east from Reading to Sonning. The Kennet & Avon Canal towpath can be followed through Newbury west to Marsh Benham.
Useful publications: OS Landranger Maps 174 & 175.
Refreshments: Lots of choice in Reading. Teas and coffees at the visitor centre at Aldermaston Wharf. The Butt Inn, just south of Aldermaston Wharf and the Rowbarge Inn, just south of Woolhampton.

30 Reading - along the Thames to Sonning

CATEGORY
Riverside path.

DISTANCE
4 miles one way, 8 miles return.

Reading is where the Kennet & Avon Canal, which starts in Bath, joins the Thames, linking Bristol, via the River Avon, to London, via the Thames. It is possible to cycle along the towpath of the canal into the centre of Reading and beyond towards Newbury. The town is at an important junction of the National Cycle Network - Route 4 runs through Reading on its way from London to Wales and Route 5 heads north from Reading through the Chiltern Hills to Oxford. You will see one of the attractive Sustrans Millennium Mileposts at the point where Route 4 joins the Thames. Sonning is a fine little village with a good pub and tea shop.

STARTING POINT & PARKING
→Bridge Street (Oracle Centre) in the centre of **Reading**. If arriving by car it is better to park near the Thames Valley Business Park right by the river on the east side of Reading. It lies at the very northern end of the A329(M), just off the roundabout after the A4 junction and the railway bridge (grid reference 736/740).

ON YOUR BIKES!
East to Sonning
1. From the car park at the western end of the A329(M) return to the Business Park road and turn left along the shared-use pavement. At the roundabout bear left through the gate onto a track. Bear right at each fork.
2. After 1 mile emerge at the River Thames by a Sustrans Millennium Milepost. (Remember this point for your return route).
3. Follow the track for 1 1/2 miles. Just **before** Sonning Bridge turn right to go past the church

and the Bull Inn. There is also a tea shop and small village shop in Sonning. Return to the starting point.

West to Reading
1. After about 1 mile you will need to turn right and cross the River Kennet by pushing your bike up and over the stepped bridge by the railway bridge (signposted 'Wallingford, National Cycle Network Route 5). The riverside path can be followed for a further 2 miles west through the centre of Reading, past Caversham Bridge.
2. The River Kennet and the canal towpath can be followed as far as Bridge Street (the Oracle Centre) in the centre of Reading, following NCN Route 4 (and beyond, towards Newbury, if you are feeling fit!)

Station: Reading.
TIC: Reading, 0118 956 6226.
Other nearby trails: The Kennet & Avon Canal can be followed west from Reading towards Newbury.
Useful publications: OS Landranger Map 175. A good leaflet, *Cycling in Reading*, showing all the cycle routes and facilities in Reading, is available from Reading Borough Council, Civic Centre, Reading RG1 7TD (0118 939 0883) or visit their website: www.reading.gov.uk/cycling. Another useful website is at www.readingcyclecampaign.org.uk
Refreshments: Jolly Angler pub, Fisherman's

Cottage pub, on the canal towpath near Reading centre. Lots of choice in Reading itself. The Bull Inn and tea shop in Sonning.

31 Bracknell (The Lookout), east of Reading

CATEGORY
Woodland tracks.

DISTANCE
Several circuits of between 3 and 10 miles.

This area of the Crown Estate, Windsor comprises 2600 acres of predominantly Scots Pine woodland. The current policy is to increase the amount of broadleaf trees where appropriate. Although owned and managed by the Crown Estate Commisioners, The Lookout has been set up in partnership with the Bracknell Forest Borough Council. From The Lookout rides and tracks radiate through the forest. The ride suggested below is just one of many that could be devised along the wide gravel tracks that criss-cross the woodland. There is also a designated mountain bike area with tricky, testing single track should you be looking for something more challenging. The Discovery Outpost at The Lookout is a hands-on science fun with over 70 exhibits including 'Zones' covering Light & Colour, Sound & Communication, Forces & Movement, Woodland & Nature and Body & Perception.

Due to insurance conditions all cyclists should have a permit. These are available from The Lookout reception.

STARTING POINT & PARKING
The Lookout Visitor Centre is located in the woodland just to the south of **Bracknell**, about 3/4 mile west of the roundabout at the junction of the B3430 and the A322 (grid reference 876661).

ON YOUR BIKES!
1. With your back to the entrance to The Lookout Visitor Centre go diagonally right towards the 'Nature Trail' and 'Walks' (brown and yellow arrows), passing to the right of the coach park. Go through the gate.

2. Continue in the same direction. At Signpost Number 1 turn right signposted 'Pudding Hill'. At the crossroads by green Signpost Number 9 turn left.

3. At the junction of many tracks by Signpost Number 5 (the Upper Star Post) turn sharp right, passing to the left of the power lines.

4. At Signpost Number 6 turn left alongside the line of telegraph poles signposted 'Devil's Highway'. After a short descent and climb, at Signpost Number 7 turn right.

5. At Signpost Number 8 turn right sharply back on yourself. Back at Star Post Number 6 turn left signposted 'Lookout, Pudding Hill'.

6. At Signpost Number 9 turn left signposted 'Lookout' to return to the start.

Station: Bracknell.
TIC: At The Lookout, 01344 868196.
Other nearby trails: Windsor Great Park, Kennet & Avon Canal towpath through Reading, Basingstoke Canal between Frimley Green and Woking.
Useful publications: Ordnance Survey Landranger 175. Much more useful is the full colour leaflet, *Walks & Trails in Windsor Forest, Bracknell* which can be purchased at the visitor

centre of from the adjacent bike hire outlet.
Refreshments: Cafe at the visitor centre.

32 Basingstoke Canal, Hampshire and Surrey

CATEGORY

Canal towpath.

DISTANCE

Up to 32 miles each way. The best section
is the 8-mile stretch between Ash and
Brookwood.

The canal towpath runs from near Odiham
in Hampshire to the junction with the Wey
Navigation near West Byfleet (between Woking
and Weybridge) passing through some lovely,
deep, wooded cuttings. The trail can be linked
via the Wey Navigation to the Thames
Towpath, taking you right into London at
Putney Bridge. The Surrey section of the
towpath (northeast of Aldershot) is in better
condition than the Hampshire section.

The Basingstoke Canal was finally completed
in 1794. It was 37 miles long with 29 locks
and a 1230-yd tunnel through Greywell Hill.
The canal was built to boost agricultural trade
in central Hampshire with long boats carrying
coal and fertilizers from London. After delivery
they would return with timber, corn and other
produce to the capital. The canal was never a
commercial success and by the mid-1960s it
was lying semi-derelict. All the locks were
decaying, the towpath was overgrown and
the water channel choked by weed, refuse
and silt. Efforts to stop the rot were made by
the Surrey and Hampshire Canal Society.
Restoration work was completed and the canal
reopened in 1991.

NB Please read *The Waterways Code - Cycling
on the towpath* at the back of the book

STARTING POINTS & PARKING

→Odiham Wharf car park, **Odiham** (grid
reference 747517).

32

→In **Fleet**, just off the B3013 by the traffic lights at the bridge over the canal (grid reference 808537).

→Basingstoke Canal Centre, **Mytchett** (grid reference 894551).

→Brewery Road car park, **Woking** (grid reference 003589).

Station: Hook is the nearest station to the start in Greywell. There are stations all along the route.

TIC: Fleet, 01252 811151.

Other nearby trails: This ride can be linked via the Wey Navigation at Weybridge to the Thames Towpath to take you right into London (Putney Bridge). There are woodland trails from The Lookout, Bracknell.

Useful publications: OS Landranger Maps 176 & 186.

Refreshments: Lots of choice and variety along the way.

33 Wey Navigation, from Weybridge to Pyrford Lock

CATEGORY

Canal towpath.

DISTANCE

5 miles each way.

There are several traffic-free options for escaping from southwest London along the waterways: the Thames Towpath runs from Putney Bridge to Weybridge, the Basingstoke Canal starts south of Weybridge and runs southwest through Woking to Odiham in Hampshire. Connecting the two and taking a more southerly course, the Wey Navigation starts in Weybridge and heads through Byfleet towards Guildford and Godalming. The southern end of the canal towpath is fairly rough but the 5-mile stretch described here is in reasonable condition and offers a chance to

33

enjoy a ride along a green corridor through this built-up area ending at a waterside pub at Pyrford Lock.

The Wey Navigations opened in 1653, making this waterway one of the oldest in the country. It runs for 20 miles from Godalming to Weybridge and is the southernmost link in Britain's 2000-mile canal network. Timber, coal, corn, flour and even gunpowder were regularly moved up and down the waterway. Later, in 1796, the Basingstoke Canal was dug and connected to the Wey and in 1816 the Wey and Arun Junction Canal was opened, connecting with the Wey at Stonebridge.

STARTING POINT & PARKING

→The riverside car park on the sharp bend on Thames Street / Walton Lane to the north of **Weybridge** High Street (grid reference 076658). You can also get to this point by following the minor road to the west of Walton Bridge.

ON YOUR BIKES!

1. Exit the car park and bear right towards the Lincoln Arms pub. Immediately before the Old Crown Inn turn right down Church Walk (by the Public Conveniences).
2. At the end of the path turn right, cross the bridge and bear left, keeping an eye out for a path to the right between wire fences. Emerge at the canal, cross the bridge and turn left.
3. After 3/4 mile, at the T-junction with Addlestone Road turn right then bear left to rejoin the towpath.
4. You will occasionally need to cross roads and the towpath changes sides. It is suggested you continue for 4 miles as far as the Anchor pub at Pyrford Marina then turn back to Weybridge. Beyond this point the towpath becomes rougher.

About 3 miles from the start, immediately after passing under the M25 you have the option of

turning right, away from the Wey Navigation and following the Basingstoke Canal for many miles through Woking, Aldershot and Fleet to Odiham.

Stations: West Byfleet and Brooklands.
TIC: Guildford, 01483 444333.
Other nearby trails: The Wey Navigation joins the Thames Towpath at Weybridge and can be followed to Putney Bridge in London. It joins the Basingstoke Canal at West Byfleet.
Useful publications: OS Landranger Maps 176 & 187. A street atlas of Surrey would be more useful.
Refreshments: Lots of choice in Weybridge. Lincoln Arms pub, Old Crown Inn at the start. The Anchor at Pyrford Lock.

34 Norbury Park, Leatherhead

CATEGORY
Cyclepath through country park.

DISTANCE
4-mile circuit.

Norbury Park offers a short waymarked circuit in amongst woodland and farmland which seems a million miles away from the busy roads in this densely populated part of Surrey. There is a good network of bridleways stretching away to the southeast through Polesden Lacey and Ranmore Common along the North Downs towards Shere and Gomshall, so with an Ordnance Survey map you could easily devise your own offroad routes through the woodland.

Norbury Park was the first area of countryside that Surrey County Council purchased in the 1930s to protect it from development. Lying within the Surrey Hills Area of Outstanding Natural Beauty and covering 1300 acres, Norbury Park is made up of an attractive mix of woodland, farms and grassland. Much of the park lies on chalk and flint with a clay cap on higher ground. These soil types support different woodland communities. Beech, yew, ash and cherry are classic chalk area trees whereas clay supports oak and chestnut. Some of the yews are up to 2000 years old.

STARTING POINT & PARKING
➔Car park off the roundabout at the junction of the A246 and B2122 (southeast of **Leatherhead**), signposted 'Bocketts Farm, Norbury Country Park' (grid reference 152249).

ON YOUR BIKES!
1. Exit the car park, turn sharp right on the tarmac lane leading directly away from the main road. At the major crossroads of stone tracks by a four-way signpost go straight ahead

signposted 'Westhumble'.

2. At the first major fork of stone tracks bear left then at the second fork by a large triangle of grass planted with trees bear right (both forks have a bike route waymark). Go through a barrier with a sign 'Backroad to Westhumble'.

3. Go past the viewpoint. **Easy to miss.** On the descent keep an eye out for a bike route signpost directing you onto a track bearing uphill to the right.

4. Climb then descend. At the end of Crabtree car park turn right uphill on tarmac. Immediately after a tall flint wall to the right bear right onto a track.

5. Long fine descent. At the next major fork bear right staying close to the woodland to the right. Follow this track past a red-brick farm (Roaring House Farm) then at the next crossroads turn left signposted 'Fetcham, car park' and follow the outward route back to the start.

Station: Westhumble.
TIC: Guildford, 01483 444333.
Other nearby trails: Horton Country Park (Epsom), Reigate Hill, Wey Navigation (Weybridge).
Useful publications: OS Landranger Map 187.
Refreshments: The closest are in Leatherhead or Great Bookham.

35 Reigate Hill (along the North Downs Way)

CATEGORY
Chalk and stone-based bridleway with fantastic views.

DISTANCE
3 miles each way.

The chalk slopes of the North Downs, which stretch from Farnham in Surrey to the famous white cliffs of Dover, offer some fine offroad riding. Unlike the South Downs Way, which has bridleway status along its entire length (meaning that you have a right to ride along it), the North Downs Way is a mixture of byway, bridleway and footpath and you are **not** allowed to ride on footpaths. This section runs along a bridleway section high up on the North Downs escarpment with fantastic views down to the wide valley of the River Mole. There are plenty more bridleways nearby criss-crossing Walton Heath, Banstead Heath, Headley Heath and Mickleham Downs.

Reigate, Colley and Juniper Hill lie on the scarp slope of the North Downs and were acquired by the National Trust between 1912 and 1955. The chalk grasslands provide an ideal habitat for a whole range of insects such as the Chalkhill Blue butterfly and the day-flying Burnet moth. The monument was presented to the Corporation of the Borough of Reigate for the benefit of the public by Lt Colonel Robert William Inglis in 1909.

The surface is mixed - some tarmac, some stone and some chalk and gravel tracks likely to be muddy after prolonged rain. There is a climb at the start of the ride up to the monument.

STARTING POINT & PARKING
→ The car park at the top of **Reigate Hill** signposted from the M25, Junction 8. Take the A217 south towards Reigate then shortly turn off left for the car park (grid reference 264524).

ON YOUR BIKES!
1. From the Reigate Hill car park go past the wooden buildings (toilets / cafe), cross the bridge and climb gently on a broad stone track. At a crossroads with tarmac go straight ahead

signposted 'North Downs Way'.

2. Continue in the same direction past the round 'temple' with pillars. At the T-junction with the road turn left signposted 'North Downs Way' then shortly, with Mole Place ahead, turn right alongside a fence signposted 'Bridleway'.

3. It is suggested that you continue as far as the next wide open view then return. If you wish to go on, the track drops steeply and becomes a little rougher. There are several circuits possible if you continue as far as the B2032, cross the M25 then return via Walton Heath, Mogador and Margery Wood. (You will need an Ordnance Survey map to plan your route).

Station: Reigate.
TIC: Guildford, 01483 444333.
Other nearby trails: Norbury Country Park, south of Leatherhead. Horton Country Park, northwest of Epsom. There are plenty of bridleways suitable for mountain bikes in summer in the triangle formed by Reigate, Epsom and Guildford.
Useful publications: OS Landranger Map 187.
Refreshments: Cafe in the car park at the start.

36 Horton Park, northeast of Epsom

CATEGORY
Cycle path through country park.
DISTANCE
3-mile circuit.

This short circuit around Horton Country Park takes you past a mixture of woodland, farmland and through a golf course - as you are not crossing any greens you should be safe from flying golf balls! Part of the route uses the course of the old Horton Light Railway, a branch line that was used to supply coal to the hospital boiler house. In springtime some of the woods are covered with a carpet of bluebells, indicating that the woodlands have grown undisturbed for many years. There is also a circuit around Epsom Common starting from the car park located on the south side of the B280 (Christ Church Road) about 2 miles to the west of Epsom.

Lying to the south of Horton Country Park, Epsom Common covers 435 acres and is a Site of Special Scientific Interest (SSSI). There are rare plants on the open grassland such as the Common Spotted Orchid and the Southern Marsh Orchid. The woodland area of the common consists mainly of oak and birch trees but there are also large areas of hawthorn and willow. There are a few large old oak pollards which provide homes for rare species of beetles and flies.

STARTING POINT & PARKING

→ From the centre of Epsom follow the B280 west towards the A243. Shortly after the start of **Epsom Common** on your left turn right onto Horton Lane. The entrance to Horton Country Park is about 1/2 mile along on the left (grid reference 190618).

ON YOUR BIKES!

1. Exit the car park and turn left to go past the Equestrian Centre. Go straight ahead, following bike route signs. **Easy to miss.** On a gentle descent on this broad stone track take the next broad track to the right. (Bike sign).

2. **Easy to miss.** Ignore two right turns. At a fork of tracks, shortly after passing a 'Footpath to Castle Hill' to the left, bear right for a circuit of the park (the white arrow points left but this track just leads to the road).

3. Pass through the golf course with greens to right and left, ignoring turnings to the left. At the T-junction with a low wooden bench ahead turn left to return to the Equestrian Centre and the car park.

Station: Epsom, Ewell or Chessington.
TIC: Guildford, 01483 444333.
Other nearby trails: Norbury Park (southeast of Leatherhead), Reigate Hill.
Useful publications: OS Landranger 187. Much better is the A2 full colour *Epsom & Ewell Cycle Guide* available from Epsom & Ewell Borough, Planning & Engineering, Town Hall, The Parade, Epsom KT18 5BY.
Refreshments: Lots of choice in Epsom.

37 Windsor Great Park, west of London

CATEGORY

Estate roads through magnificent parkland.

DISTANCE

No specific route - several miles of estate roads to explore

Although there will be occasional vehicles within Windsor Great Park, it is a very cycle-friendly place and an amazing oasis of tranquility set in the heart of such a built-up area (the M3, M4, M25 and Heathrow are all less than 5 miles away). There is an estate village with a village shop, the fields are ploughed, seeded and harvested, there are woods and lakes and a school. The place is free of the creeping urbanisation that blights so much of the area to the west of London. No specific route is described: you are allowed on the tarmac roads (and through the big green gates operated by buttons!). Signs will tell you where you **cannot** go. Polo matches are frequently played here.

Windsor Castle was established by William the Conqueror and it is the largest inhabited castle in the world. The enormous round tower has a view over 12 counties. Savill Garden is famous for its rhododendrons and the Valley Garden is noted for its heathers. Nearby is the 160-acre lake of Virginia Water.

STARTING POINTS & PARKING

➜**Bishop's Gate Entrance** to Windsor Great Park, on the east side of the park, about 2 miles south of Old Windsor (off the A328, which links the A30 and the A308). If all the spaces are taken near to the Fox & Hounds pub follow signs for Savill Garden car park.

➜It would also be possible to start from **Windsor** itself, following the waymarked, traffic-free National Cycle Network Route 4 from the Windsor & Eton Football Club (grid reference 958755). This is located on St Leonard's Road, just off the B3022 Cranbourne and Winkfield road, opposite the Stag & Hounds pub. Parking may be possible here (except on match days). This route crosses the A332 at Ranger's Lodge via a toucan crossing.

Station: Windsor.
TIC: Windsor, 01753 743900.
Other nearby trails: The Thames Towpath and the Basingstoke Canal are nearby. Woodland tracks at Bracknell (The Lookout).
Useful publications: OS Landranger Map 175. Maps of the park from the ticket office at the Savill Gardens, just south of Bishop's Gate.
Refreshments: Pub at Bishop's Gate. Cafe / restaurant at Savill Gardens.

38

38 Thames Towpath between Putney Bridge and Weybridge

CATEGORY
Riverside path.

DISTANCE
Up to 23 miles each way.

The Thames towpath is the best exit for cyclists from southwest London, with plenty of interest to see along this wonderful green and leafy corridor, including Hampton Court Palace. There is a striking contrast between the wide, untamed tidal stretch as far west as Teddington Lock and the highly-managed pleasure boat section which lies beyond. The towpath overlaps entirely with National Cycle Network Route 4 for the second half of the ride for the 11 miles from Teddington Lock through Kingston to Weybridge and it is here that the quality of the towpath is at its very best. For the section between Putney Bridge and Teddington (a section where NCN 4 takes an alternative route across Richmond Park), the quality is variable and mountain bikes are recommended. There is one quite rough patch between Hammersmith Bridge and Barnes Bridge.

NB Please note that the towpath is frequently busy with pedestrians, particularly on summer weekends, so please slow down and show consideration.

STARTING POINTS & PARKING
→Putney Bridge, Kew Gardens, Kingston, Ham Lands (opposite Eel Pie Island), Richmond and Walton Bridge.

ON YOUR BIKES!
The river needs to be crossed twice, in Kingston then after Hampton Court.
1. In Kingston you should follow 'NCN 4' signs, turning left away from the river at a grey metal 'Meccano' bridge with a '12ft 6 ins' height limit sign on it in the direction of 'Kingston Town

Centre'. There is a safe waymarked route through the traffic on green painted cycle lanes signposted 'NCN 4' that will take you across Kingston Bridge.

2. After Hampton Court, cross the road at the toucan crossing, turn left across the bridge and then right at the end of the bridge to continue alongside the river towards Walton-on-Thames.

Station: Several railway stations along the route.
TIC: Richmond, 0208 940 9125.
Other nearby trails: This ride can be linked via the Wey Navigation to the Basingstoke Canal forming a 50-mile route from Putney Bridge almost to Basingstoke in deepest Hampshire. There is a circuit inside the perimeter of Richmond Park.
Useful publications: OS Landranger Map 176. Better to use a coloured A-Z map of London. The route is also covered by Sustrans *Thames Valley Cycle Route* map (£5.99).
Sustrans Order Line: Call 0845 113 0065 or visit their website at www.sustrans.org.uk
Refreshments: All along the way.

39 Richmond Park (the Tamsin Trail), London

CATEGORY
Cycle track around the park.

DISTANCE
8-mile circuit.

Created by the generosity of an anonymous donor who wanted the trail named after his daughter, Tamsin, this 8-mile purpose-built circuit of Richmond Park is one of the best things to have happened to recreational cycling in southwest London. The trail runs along a fine gravel path with several gentle hills. The park lies on the sloping plateau above Richmond. It was enclosed by Charles I in 1637 with an 8-mile wall, enabling him to hunt for deer. From Pembroke Lodge, on the western edge of the park, the views on a clear day extend far into Berkshire. To the north of Pembroke Lodge is King Henry VIII's mound where it is possible to see the dome of St Paul's Cathedral.
NB Several roads are crossed in the park, so take care if you are with young children.

STARTING POINT & PARKING
→ Any of the car parks near the gates / entrances into **Richmond Park**.

Station: Richmond or Kingston.
TIC: Richmond, 0208 940 9125.
Other nearby trails: The Thames Towpath runs through Richmond. There is a very limited 4-mile network of cycle routes across Wimbledon Common. Signs indicate where you can and cannot go. There is also a leaflet explaining the route from Manor Cottage, Wimbledon Common (0208 788 7655).
Useful publications: OS Landranger Map 176. A map of Richmond Park is available from Royal Parks, Richmond Park, Richmond, Surrey TW10 5HS (0208 948 3209).
Refreshments: Cafe to the west side of the park.

40

40 Greenwich & the Thames Barrier to Erith

CATEGORY
Riverside cycle path.
DISTANCE
8 miles each way.

National Cycle Network Route 1 exits London to the east from near the Millennium Dome, following the course of the Thames as closely as possible at the start of its final leg from John o'Groats down to Dover. The character of the river changes dramatically as it broadens out across the floodplains on its way to the sea. The ride passes along a series on newly-built riverside promenades at Woolwich, Gallions Reach and Thamesmead.

STARTING POINT & PARKING
→ **The Thames Barrier,** between Greenwich and Woolwich in east London. The traffic-free section ends at Manorway on the north side of Erith (grid reference 510788).

Station: Erith or Greenwich.
TIC: Greenwich, 0208 858 6376.
Other nearby trails: Greenwich is at a crossroads of the National Cycle Network. The best nearby traffic-free section runs north from Limehouse Basin along the Regent's Canal (Grand Union Canal) and through Victoria Park to the Lee Navigation (see East of England Chapter).
Useful publications: OS Landranger Map 177. A London street map is much more useful. Sustrans *Garden of England* map (£5.99) shows this route and other traffic-free trails in Kent (eg several coastal promenades and the Canterbury to Whitstable route).

Sustrans Order Line: Call 0845 113 0065 or visit their website at www.sustrans.org.uk
Refreshments: Lots of choice for refreshments all along the way.

41 Slough Arm, Grand Union Canal, east of Slough

CATEGORY
Canal towpath.
DISTANCE
5 miles each way.

The towpath of the Grand Union Canal close to London is generally maintained to a very high standard. There are several 'arms' coming off the main canal: others are to be found at Wendover, Aylesbury and Northampton. The Slough Arm runs from Slough via Langley and Iver to the Cowley Peachey Junction (south of Uxbridge). Built in 1883, the Slough Arm was, with the exception of the Manchester Ship Canal, the last canal to be built in Britain. It goes over several aqueducts and through a long cutting. To the west of Iver the water is surprisingly clear.

STARTING POINT & PARKING
➔Cowley Peachey Junction lies 3 miles south of Uxbridge on the A408, just north of **Yiewsley** (grid reference 056800). The terminus is on the B416 Stoke Poges road to the north of Slough railway station (grid reference 979808).

Station: Yiewsley, Iver, Langley, Slough.
TIC: Windsor, 01753 743900.
Other nearby trails: The Grand Union Canal itself, Windsor Great Park.
Useful publications: OS Landranger Map 176. The *Nicholson Guide to the Waterways (South)* is packed with detail about all the canals in England and Wales to the south of Birmingham.
Refreshments: Iver, Langley and Slough.

42 The Ridgeway from Streatley Golf Club west to East Ilsley, south of Oxford.

CATEGORY
Long distance byway / bridleway.
DISTANCE
6 miles each way.

The Ridgeway is said to be the oldest 'road' in Europe, dating back over 5000 years. It runs from West Kennett, near to Avebury, to the Thames at Goring and in its entirety would make a good summer challenge for very fit cyclists on mountain bikes. East Ilsley to Warren Farm (west of Streatley) represents the final high level section of the Ridgeway to the west of the Thames. To the east of the river the trail splits rather confusingly into three strands that occasionally overlap: the Ridgeway, the Icknield Way and Swan's Way. This ride uses a chalk and flint track with a steep 300ft climb at the beginning (meaning a wonderful descent on the return trip!) but if you enjoy this you will enjoy many other sections of the Ridgeway, and if you wish to go further afield, the South Downs Way is a similar long distance chalk and stone bridleway.

NB This trail is not suitable for touring bikes nor for young children and can be very hard going in the winter when you are likely to encounter muddy sections and some very large puddles! It is best ridden on mountain bikes between mid-May and mid-October after a few dry days. There is a short section on road to reach the pubs in East Ilsley.

STARTING POINT & PARKING
➔Just north of **Streatley** on the A417 (between Reading and Didcot) and 1/4 mile beyond the A329 / A417 junction, take the no through lane (Rectory Road) to the left, leading past the golf

course. Follow this minor lane for 1 1/2 miles. At the fork by Warren Farm bear right. There is parking for about 20 cars immediately after the fork, at the end of the tarmac lane (grid reference 568813).

ON YOUR BIKES!

1. From the car parking area at the end of the lane by Warren Farm continue uphill on the track. There is a 300ft climb over a mile and you may well choose to walk all or parts of this first climb. It is the toughest part of the ride!

2. There are fine views to the left down into Streatley Warren. Keep following 'Ridgeway' signposts. After reaching the top there is a gentle 220ft descent over 2 miles then a second climb (shorter and less steep).

3. At the crossroads with a concrete track at the top of the second climb turn right following Ridgeway signs (remember this point for the return). After 1/2 mile as the concrete track

swings left into a private property continue straight ahead on track then shortly take the first track to the left signposted 'Public Bridleway' (**leaving** the Ridgeway at this point).

4. Descend gently for 1 mile. The track turns to tarmac. At the T-junction with the road by Summerdown Stables, turn right (remember this point for the return). At the one way system **dismount** and bear right towards the two pubs - the Crown & Horns or the Swan.

Station: Goring.
TIC: Wallingford, 01491 826972.
Other nearby trails: The Ridgeway can be followed west for many miles as far as Avebury. The Kennet & Avon Canal between Newbury and Reading. Waterways through Oxford.
Useful publications: OS Landranger Map 174.
Refreshments: Two pubs and a shop in East Ilsley. Lots of choice in Streatley / Goring.

43 The Ridgeway east and west from Uffington White Horse, near Wantage

CATEGORY

Long distance byway / bridleway.

DISTANCE

East from the White Horse - 7 miles each way.
West from the White Horse - 6 miles each way.

The figure of the Uffington White Horse is one of the most enigmatic in the country and is well worth visiting on a fine summer's day. The trail follows a stone and chalk track which is only suitable for mountain bikes and best ridden in the summer months after a few dry days. There are several gentle climbs and a steeper one up on to Fox Hill. If you are travelling **east** from the Uffington White Horse car park it is suggested you go as far as the A338. If you are travelling **west** from the Uffington White Horse car park it is suggested you go as far as the Shepherd's Rest pub below Fox Hill.

NB Care should be taken crossing the B4000 to the west and the B4001 to the east, both of which can get busy.

STARTING POINT & PARKING

➔ The car park for **Uffington White Horse**, just off the B4507 about 6 miles to the west of Wantage, in South Oxfordshire (grid reference 293866).

Station: Swindon.
TIC: Swindon, 01793 530328.
Other nearby trails: The Ridgeway can be followed for many miles in each direction. Sections of the Kennet & Avon Canal either side of Newbury are open to cyclists. Waterways through Oxford.
Useful publications: OS Landranger Map 174.
Refreshments: Shepherd's Rest pub at the bottom of Fox Hill, near Wanborough.

44 Oxford waterways north and south

CATEGORY

Canal towpath and riverside path.

DISTANCE

6 miles each way.

Oxford has always been a city dominated by bikes and recent developments have made cycling in the city more pleasant as the use of cars in the central area has been restricted still further. This ride explores the towpaths of two of the city's waterways: the Thames on the southern half of the ride and the Oxford Canal on the northern section. The area explored by the ride lies within the Ring Road: north and south of the Ring Road the towpaths become much rougher and narrower. There are many architectural attractions along the way including the bridge at Iffley Lock and the folly at Folly Bridge. The southern half of this ride overlaps with National Cycle Network Route 5 which continues south via a newly-built track alongside the railway to Radley and Abingdon.

NB This ride is also popular with walkers. Please ride with consideration for other users, let people know you are coming and thank them if they step aside for you. Where the path is narrow show courtesy by pulling in and letting walkers pass: you will be doing everyone a favour by creating goodwill between walkers and cyclists!

STARTING POINTS & PARKING

➔ *By bike from the centre of the city.* The canal towpath starts on Hythe Bridge Street, between the railway station and the centre of **Oxford**; the Thames towpath can be joined at Folly Bridge.
➔ *If arriving by car* it would be better to start at the northern end of the trail, near the Plough Inn (grid reference 494096) in **Wolvercote OR** the **Park & Ride car park** just off the Ring Road

44

at the south of Oxford, at the junction of the A4144 and the A423, to the east of the A34 (grid reference 519036).

ON YOUR BIKES!

1. *Starting from the south.* Exit the Park & Ride car park towards the bus stop and turn right along the shared-use pavement (away from Oxford). Go through the subway and at the first T-junction turn left. Go through a second subway then at the second T-junction turn right and follow the cycle track parallel with the Ring Road.

2. Cross a bridge over a tributary of the Thames then just before the much larger bridge over the main course of the Thames turn left downhill then left along the towpath. (Remember this point for your return).

3. Go past the lock, the Isis Tavern and past the college boathouses. At the crossroads (with the main road) by Folly Bridge go straight ahead onto a continuation of the towpath. **TAKE CARE** crossing this busy road.

4. Walk your bike through Osney Lock. Join East Street by the Waterman's Arms pub and continue in the same direction. As the street swings round to the left climb the steps to cross the small bridge over the stream.

5. Turn right along the pavement, walking your bike as far as the toucan crossing. Cross the main road onto Abbey Road opposite. At the end of the road turn left then right to cross a grey, hump-backed metal bridge. At the end of the bridge turn right.

6. Go beneath the railway bridge, cross a road then the river and at the canal towpath turn left. Follow the canal towpath for 3 miles as far as the Plough Inn in Upper Wolvercote. Retrace your steps.

Station: Oxford.
TIC: Oxford, 01865 726871.
Other nearby trails: The Ridgeway is a long distance bridleway / byway running from West Kennett to Goring on Thames. The Phoenix

Trail is a railway path between Thame and Princes Risborough.

Useful publications: OS Landranger Map 164. The *Oxford Cycling Map* shows all the traffic-free routes in Oxford plus all the quiet lanes up to 25 miles around. It is produced by CycleCity Guides, Wallbridge Mill, The Retreat, Frome BA11 5JU (01373 453533). E-mail: info@cyclecityguides.co.uk

Refreshments: Lots of choice in Oxford, most of it just off the route; Isis Tavern by the Thames, just north of the Ring Road; Plough Inn, Wolvercote.

45 The Phoenix Trail between Thame and Princes Risborough

CATEGORY

Railway path.

DISTANCE

6 miles one way, 12 miles return.

One of the most recently created railway paths in the region, the Phoenix Trail is destined to become increasingly popular as improvements are made to the links at both ends of the path and pubs start attracting cyclists off the route for lunchtime refreshments. The path has wide views of the wooded Chiltern escarpment across arable fields. Keep an eye out for the many sculptures along the way, not least the strange animals perched high up on poles about halfway along the ride.

STARTING POINTS & PARKING

→The sports ground on Horsenden Lane, **Princes Risborough** (grid reference 798027). To get here, turn off the B4444, on the southwest edge of Princes Risborough, near to the railway station, onto Picts Lane signposted 'Saunderton, Horsenden, Bledlow'. At the Give Way sign turn right over the railway bridge and immediately right again onto Horsenden Lane, a dead-end road.

The sports ground is along this lane on the right.

→Thame United FC ground at the end of Windmill Road, on the southern edge of **Thame** (grid reference 706053). You will have to park in the nearby streets.

ON YOUR BIKES!

→From Horsenden Lane, **Princes Risborough.** Follow the lane to its end, past the church. At the end of the tarmac turn left signposted 'NCN 57'. Follow this wide stone track across a field and bear right up onto the railway line.

→From **Thame.** The Phoenix Trail starts right by the football ground.

Station: Princes Risborough.

TIC: Thame, 01844 212834.

Other nearby trails: Waterways through Oxford, Wendover Woods, Ashridge Estate and the Grand Union Canal. (See East of England for these last two).

Useful publications: OS Landranger Map 165.

Refreshments: Three Horseshoes pub at Towersey, lots of choice in Thame and Princes Risborough.

46 Wendover Woods, Chilterns, southeast of Aylesbury

CATEGORY
Waymarked forestry routes.

DISTANCE
Two circuits, each of 3 miles.

There are very few Forestry Commission holdings of any size in the area immediately to the north and west of London. Wendover Woods are the one exception and are the only woodland in the area with waymarked trails aimed at recreational family cycling. There are some wonderful views and the car park at the start of the ride is very close to the highest point of the Chilterns. The woodland is mainly broadleaf so there is a fantastic display of bluebells in the late spring and a glorious riot of colour in the autumn as the trees start to lose their leaves. The only downside to this otherwise perfect combination is that with the car park / starting point at the top of the hill almost all the routes start off with a descent and finish with a climb back up to the car park. You have been warned! Wendover Woods were originally owned by the Rothschild family and were transferred to the Forestry Commission in 1939. During the Rothschild era the wood was used extensively by the family and their guests for recreational purposes - mainly shooting and horseriding. It is reported that Lord Rothschild would be driven into the woods by a team of zebras to picnic at one of his favourite spots, now known locally as 'Rothschild's Seat'.

STARTING POINT & PARKING
→From **Wendover** (southeast of Aylesbury) follow the A4011 north towards Tring. After 3 miles take the first proper road to the right towards Buckland Common and Cholesbury. The entrance to the woodland is 3/4 mile up this steep minor road on the right-hand side.

Climb on the road through the forest for about 1 mile to the car parks / information centre at the top of the hill (grid reference 889090).

ON YOUR BIKES!
1. From the Wendover Woods car park continue past the information stand on the tarmac road towards the exit. After 200 yds keep an eye out for a turning to the right by a wooden barrier marked with a green bike arrow and a 'Cyclists' sign (near the start of the orienteering course).

2. Long gentle descent with great views to the right. At the crossroads turn right (signs will tell you where you **can't** go). At a second crossroads, with a wide stone forestry road at the bottom of the hill, go straight ahead steeply uphill.

3. After 1/2 mile go straight ahead signposted 'Short Cut'. Emerge at a tarmac road. **For the short route** turn right to return to the car parks by the information stand.

4. **For the full route** turn right along the road then almost immediately bear left following the 'Fitness Track' signpost. The track is also waymarked with a green bike arrow.

5. At the first fork bear right on the upper track (there is a 'No cycling' sign to the left). At the next junction by a concrete drainage ditch turn sharply right steeply uphill. ('Halton' is

signposted to the left). Emerge by the car parks near the information stand and 'Chilterns Highest Point' signpost.

Station: Wendover.
TIC: Wendover, 01296 696759.
Other nearby trails: The Phoenix Trail between Thame and Princes Risborough. Ashridge Estate. The Ebury Way. The Grand Union Canal. (See East of England for the last three).
Useful publications: OS Landranger Map 165. The Forestry Commission produce an A4 full colour leaflet, *Cycling Wendover Woods - Recommended Cycle Routes.* This is available from: Forestry Commission, Chiltern Forest Office, Upper Icknield Way, Aston Clinton, Aylesbury, Bucks HP22 5NF (01296 625825).
Refreshments: None on route, lots of choice in Wendover.

47 Ouse Valley Trail, Milton Keynes

CATEGORY
Riverside path and railway path.
DISTANCE
8 miles each way.

For those who have not yet discovered the secret: Milton Keynes offers more miles of safe and enjoyable family cycling than any other town in the country! There is a vast network of traffic-free cycle tracks through parkland, around lakes, along canal towpaths and disused railways. It is also at a crossroads of the National Cycle Network: Route 51 passes through Milton Keynes on its way from Oxford to Cambridge, whilst Route 6 runs south from Derby down to London. The ride described below starts on the western fringes of the town, at the old bridge over the River Great Ouse between Old Stratford and Stony Stratford, running alongside the river for 4 miles on a tarmac path. You pass through a narrow tunnel through the Iron Trunk Aqueduct carrying the Grand Union Canal over the River Ouse then beneath the railway viaduct. At New Bradwell the route veers away from the river and joins the course of the dismantled railway through leafy cuttings as far as Newport Pagnell. With the aid of a *Redway Guide* (see **'Useful publications'** below), it is easily possible to plan several days out exploring the network of traffic-free trails.

STARTING POINTS & PARKING
→**Old Stratford / Stony Stratford.** From the roundabout at the junction of the A5, A508, and A422 (to the northwest of Milton Keynes), take the exit towards Old Stratford and Stony Stratford, cross the bridge over the River Ouse then take the next right signposted 'Stony Stratford Centre' and park along this road (grid reference 782410).

47

at an offset crossroads with a wide track / drive (there is a large red-brick house to your left), go straight ahead onto a continuation of the path. Go through a narrow tunnel beneath the Iron Trunk Aqueduct, carrying the Grand Union Canal.

3. Cross a bridge over a side stream and turn left to pass beneath the massive stone railway bridge. At a fork of tracks immediately after crossing the next bridge over a stream bear right away from the river.

4. At the T-junction at the end of the path turn left then at the T-junction with the road turn left then right (**TAKE CARE**) onto Newport Road. Shortly turn first right signposted 'City Centre, Blue Bridge, Bradville, V6' and soon take the first left (same sign).

5. After 200 yds turn first right (by the second of two small playgrounds). Pass beneath two large bridges then turn sharp left uphill sgnposted 'Wolverton, Stony Stratford, Blue Bridge'. At the T-junction at the top turn right signposted 'Newport Pagnell, Stantonbury, Great Linford'.

6. Follow the railway path and signs for Newport Pagnell for 2 1/2 miles*. The trail ends at Sheppards Close in Newport Pagnell.

After 1 1/2 miles, where the metal bridge crosses the Grand Union Canal you have the chance of exploring the Canal Broadwalk and the routes around Willen Lakes. You will also find refreshments north and south along the canal towpath.

Station: Milton Keynes.
TIC: Milton Keynes, 01908 558300.
Other nearby trails: There is a fantastic network of traffic-free paths throughout Milton Keynes. Try a circuit of Willen Lakes or a ride along the Grand Union Canal towpath or the Ouse Valley Trail.
Useful publications: OS Landranger Map 152. The indispensable publication for enjoying Milton Keynes by bike is the *Redway Guide*,

→ **Newport Pagnell**. From the centre of Newport Pagnell follow signs for 'Milton Keynes North' and 'Buckingham'. Turn left at the roundabout signposted 'Willen, Bedford (A422), Wellingborough (A509)' then turn right onto The Green / Broad Street (between a car dealers and an off licence). Shortly turn right onto the no through road called Sheppards Close. There is no designated car park (grid reference 855426).

ON YOUR BIKES!

1. Start from the bridge over the River Great Ouse on the road between Old Stratford and Stony Stratford (southeast of the roundabout at the junction of the A5 / A508 / A422). **TAKE CARE** crossing the road via the traffic island onto the path signposted 'Wildlife Conservation Area, Canal, New Bradwell'.

2. Go through a gate, turn left and then shortly,

48

available (free) from Milton Keynes Council. Call 01908 691 691 and ask for the Cycling Officer or alternatively request a copy by emailing: cycling@ milton-keynes.gov.uk or download a pdf image from www.mkweb.co.uk **Refreshments:** Lots of choice in Old Stratford and Newport Pagnell. Pubs just off the route where it crosses the Grand Union Canal (follow the canal either north or south).

48   Milton Keynes Redway

CATEGORY
Lakeside paths, canal towpaths, dedicated cycle network.

DISTANCE
(Just one suggested route). 3 miles around Willen Lakes plus 7 miles along the Canal Broadwalk to Linford.

It will come as a surprise to many people who are reluctant to dump their preconceived ideas that there is an excellent network of recreational cycle routes around Milton Keynes, including circuits of lakes, tree-lined canal towpaths and well-made paths across parkland. Other surprises include a Buddhist Pagoda and lots of adventure playgrounds.There are endless possibilities if you get hold of a free *Redway Guide* (see **Useful publications** below). The suggested rides below explore Willen Lakes and the Canal Broadwalk.

STARTING POINT & PARKING
→Willen Lakes on the east side of Milton Keynes, just off the M1 Jct 14 (grid reference 873405).

ON YOUR BIKES!
Willen Lakes south to Woughton on the Green
1. From the Willen Lakes car park follow the red-brick path south towards Woolstone and Kingston, keeping the water on your left. After the Watersports Centre, near to the miniature railway, ignore the first right signposted 'Milton Keynes Village, Ouzel Valley'. Bear left to stay close to the lake then shortly, at the T-junction

take the next right (the same names are on the signpost) to pass beneath road bridge.

2. Follow the River Ouzel for 2 miles, crossing three narrow cattle grids and passing a wooden bridge over the river. Soon after passing beneath a second road bridge, just before a second wooden river bridge turn sharp right passing fenced-off clumps of trees and heading towards the Canal Broadwalk.

3. Follow signs for Canal Broadwalk. Just before red-brick bridge over the canal, turn right signposted 'Woolstone, Newlands, Campbell Park'.

4. Follow the Canal Broadwalk beneath several bridges. At Bridge 81B, a wide bridge with red-brick pillars and a central span of concrete and black railings, turn right signposted 'Peace Pagoda, Willen Lake' to return to the start **OR** continue straight ahead and join the *Northern Route* at Instruction 2.

Northern Route

1. To get to the Grand Union Canal from the Willen Lakes car park follow signs for 'Newlands / Grand Union Canal / Campbell Park'. Join the canal at Bridge 81B. Turn right along the Canal Broadwalk.

2. At Bridge 79 cross to the other side and turn right. At the T-junction with Cottisford Crescent (near Marsh Drive / High Street) turn right then second left signposted 'Linford Manor'. At the almshouses turn right and follow this good path past a stone circle as far as the Black Horse pub at Bridge 76.

3. Retrace steps, cross back to the other (east) side of the canal at Bridge 78 then leave the canal at Bridge 81B, a wide bridge with red-brick pillars and a central concrete span with black railings, signposted 'Willen Lake, Peace Pagoda' to return to the start

Station: Milton Keynes.

TIC: Milton Keynes, 01908 558300.

Other nearby trails: The Grand Union Canal can be ridden from London to Daventry. The Ouse Valley Trail runs west from Milton Keynes.

Useful publications: OS Landranger Map 152. The indispensable publication for enjoying Milton Keynes by bike is the *Redway Guide*, available (free) from Milton Keynes Council. Call 01908 691 691 and ask for the Cycling Officer or alternatively request a copy by emailing: cycling@ milton-keynes. gov.uk or download a pdf image from www.mkweb.co.uk

Refreshments: Cafe at Willen Lakes Watersports Centre, pubs along the canal towpath.

48

East

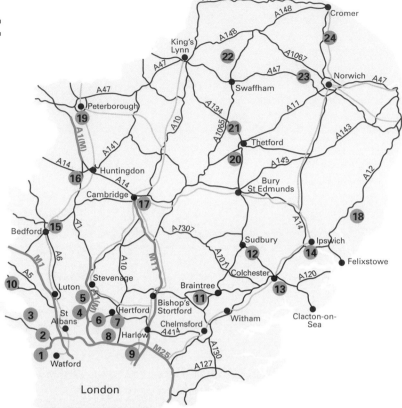

EAST TRAILS

1 Ebury Way - Rickmansworth to West Watford
2 Nicky Line - Hemel Hempstead to Harpenden
3 Ashridge Estate, northwest of Hemel Hempstead
4 Albanway from St Albans to Hatfield
5 Ayot Greenway, Wheathampstead, north of St Albans
6 Cole Green Way, west of Hertford
7 Lee Navigation from Hertford to Waltham Abbey
8 Lee Navigation - Victoria Park to Waltham Abbey
9 Epping Forest, north of London
10 Grand Union Canal - London to Norton Junction, near Daventry
11 Flitch Way, west of Braintree
12 Valley Walk, Sudbury, northwest of Colchester

13 Colchester to Wivenhoe along the riverside path
14 Alton Water, south of Ipswich
15 Priory Country Park and Willington Countryway, Bedford
16 Grafham Water, southwest of Huntingdon
17 Fulbourn Roman Road, southeast of Cambridge
18 Three Forest Cycle Trail, northeast of Ipswich
19 Peterborough Green Wheel
20 Thetford Forest, northwest of Cambridge
21 Peddars Way - Bridgham Heath to Castle Acre
22 Peddars Way from Castle Acre to Holme next the Sea
23 Marriott's Way, Norwich
24 Weavers' Way from North Walsham to Aylsham, north of Norwich

East Mountain Biking

The East of England has very few mountain biking possibilities other than those to be found in and around Thetford Forest, the Suffolk Coast forests, Epping Forest and along the Icknield Way & Peddars Way. The latter is a long distance trail that runs as a byway or bridleway for over 50 miles from Lackham, southwest of Thetford to the North Norfolk coast at Holme next the Sea. Although the maps show that there are plenty of bridleways and byways in Essex and Hertfordshire, these are predominantly very rough and muddy in winter and baked hard into bumpy corrugations in the summer.

There is no substitute for intimate local knowledge - try to explore every bridleway, byway, unclassified road, canal towpath and Forestry Commission track near to home, sift out the good from the bad and link together the best offroad sections to form your own customised route(s). The best advice is to use the months from late spring to early autumn (May to October) to do the exploration, if possible after a spell of dry weather. The same track in winter can take twice as long or even be impassable.

Note down on the map (or colour code with highlighter pen) the quality of the trail and whether it is better done in one direction or the other - it is normally better to climb on tarmac and descend offroad so that gravity can help you through any muddy bits.

Bear in mind that everyone has a different view of what constitutes a good trail: hard or technical for some is easy for others and a bit of mud for some is a quagmire for others!

Mountain Biking Information

These are possible sources:
- leaflets produced by local authorities, normally available in Tourist Information Centres
- guidebooks which can usually be found in larger, better stocked bookshops
- the staff in bike shops can often put you in contact with local riders or clubs who are sure to have done some of this research already, saving you many hours of trial and error.

East Forestry

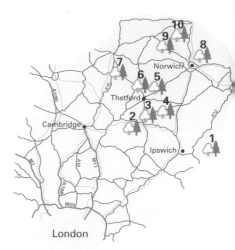

The East of England has a small densely forested centre on the sandy soils around Thetford and two reasonable sized holdings (Tunstall and Rendlesham) to the northeast of Ipswich, near the Suffolk Coast, but other than this the region is one of the least forested in the whole country.

In some forests and woods there are no waymarked routes but you are free to explore the tracks. The relevant Ordnance Survey map is mentioned. It is highly recommended that you take a map for the larger woods where it is very easy to get lost!

2 **King's Forest and Mildenhall Woods, southwest of Thetford**
OS Explorer Maps 226 & 229

4 **West Harling Heath, east of Thetford**
OS Explorer Map 230

5 **Swaffham Heath and Cockleycley Heath southeast of Swaffham**
OS Explorer Map 236

6 **Coldharbour Wood and Shaker's Wood south of Swaffham**
OS Explorer Maps 229 & 236

7 **Shouldham Warren / The Sincks,**
south of King's Lynn
OS Explorer Map 236

8 **Horsford Woods, north of Norwich**
OS Explorer Map 238

9 **Swanton Great Wood, east of Fakenham**
OS Explorer Map 251

10 **Woodlands between Holt and Sheringham**
OS Explorer Map 252

Forests and woods with waymarked trails

They are shown with a corresponding trail number and page reference.

1 **Three Forest Trail - Rendlesham, Tunstall and Dunwich, north of Ipswich**
See Route 18, page 139

3 **Thetford Forest**
See Route 20, page 141

Further Information

East Anglia Forest District
Santon Downham, Brandon, Suffolk.
IP27 0TJ
Tel: 01842 810271.

East National Cycle Network

Hull to Harwich (two maps)

369 miles.

Highlights (in the southern half of the route) include King's Lynn, the North Norfolk Coast, Walsingham Abbey, the traffic-free Marriott's Way from Reepham to Norwich, Norwich Cathedral, Framlingham Castle, Orford Castle, Snape Maltings, Constable Country, Colchester's historic town centre and the traffic-free Wivenhoe Trail.

Traffic-free sections over 3 miles:

- Wivenhoe Trail from Wivenhoe to Colchester (NCN 1)
- Marriott's Way from Reepham to Norwich (NCN 1)

Other areas for lane cycling

East Anglia has hundreds of miles of quiet lanes with gentle gradients linking small villages. As the weather tends to be much drier than on the west side of the country you have a set of excellent conditions for enjoyable cycling for day rides or longer touring. The southern part of the region is fairly densely populated but there is a lot less traffic north of an imaginary line drawn from Luton to Colchester ie **north Essex, Suffolk** and **Norfolk**. There are many attractive villages that would make good bases in Norfolk such as Castle Acre, Little Walsingham, Burnham Market, Reepham or Aylsham. Elsewhere, Thaxted in Essex or Lavenham, Framlingham and Beccles in Suffolk are all wonderful bases around which there is a delightful network of lanes to explore.

Sustrans

Listed below are the Sustrans maps that cover the National Cycle Network within the region. Some of the maps may describe routes that continue on into adjacent regions: these maps are mentioned in both chapters. The maps are not only useful for people wishing to ride the the whole route over several days; they also show all the traffic-free sections which make good day rides. The maps cost £5.99 each and are available from Sustrans.

Sustrans Order Line:
Call **0845 113 0065** or visit their website at
www.sustrans.org.uk

East Trails

1   Ebury Way, from Rickmansworth to West Watford

CATEGORY

Canal towpath and railway path.

DISTANCE

3 miles each way.

This 3-mile railway path between Rickmansworth and West Watford is surprisingly green and leafy for such a built-up area. The trail crosses the Colne, Chess and Gade rivers and if you are lucky you may even see the flash of bright blue as a kingfisher flies low over the water. The path runs parallel with then crosses the Grand Union Canal so it would be easy to vary the there-and-back ride along the railway by returning via the canal towpath. Indeed the Grand Union Canal could be followed for several miles in either direction, either south towards Uxbridge (and central London) or north towards Hemel Hempstead and Berkhamsted. As the year progresses the dominant features of the ride change from birdsong in spring to wildflowers and dragonflies in the summer then berries on blackthorn, hawthorn and bramble in the autumn, offering important food sources for the resident thrushes and blackbirds but also migrants such as redwings and fieldfares.

STARTING POINT & PARKING

➔ The most convenient car park is at **Rickmansworth Aquadrome**, although it is a little complicated to describe how to get there! Take the A404 out of Rickmansworth towards Northwood and London. At the Moor Lane roundabout where 'A4145 / Watford Road' is signposted straight on and 'London (A404)' off to the right, complete a circuit of the roundabout and head back towards Rickmansworth - the turning for the Aquadrome, Harefield Road, is on your left (grid reference 057938).

ON YOUR BIKES!

1. Exit the Aquadrome car park via the vehicle entrance then shortly before the bridge turn left onto the canal towpath. Pass beneath the main road then immediately after the Batchworth Lock Visitor Centre bear left, cross a wooden bridge to the left and follow the path.
2. With a low 'drawbridge' to the right turn left then shortly turn sharp right through metal posts / barrier and car park to join the Ebury Way.
3. Follow the dismantled railway path for 3 miles. It ends at Eastbury Road Post office on Hampermill Lane (A4125).

Station: Rickmansworth.
TIC: Hemel Hempstead, 01442 234222.
Other nearby trails: The Grand Union Canal.
Useful publications: Ordnance Survey Landranger Sheet 176. An A3 full colour leaflet of the Ebury Way is available from: The Countryside Management Service, Hertfordshire County Council, County Hall, Hertford SG13 8DN.
Refreshments: Cafe near the Batchworth Lock Visitor Centre at the start of the ride.

2   Nicky Line, from Hemel Hempstead to Harpenden

CATEGORY
Railway path.
DISTANCE
8 miles each way.

One of four short rides along railway paths in Hertfordshire, the Nicky Line runs gently downhill from Hemel Hempstead to Harpenden. The name may have come from an abbreviation of 'funicular' referring to the steep gradients along the line or from 'knickerbockers' either because the railway navvies wore such garments or because the line was considered half-size, being only single track. The Nicky Line was built in 1877 as a result of a proposal by businessmen of Hemel Hempstead to link the straw plait trade in the town with the well known hat-makers of Luton. The railway carried passengers until 1947 and also freight until 1979.

NB There are four busy roads to cross - the B487 (twice), the A5183 (near Redbourn) and the A4147 (near Eastman Way Trading Estate). **Take great care.**

STARTING POINT & PARKING
➔ From the centre of Harpenden take the A1081 Luton Road then turn left immediately after going under the railway bridge onto Park Hill. Park about 200 yds along this road (grid reference 127150). The railway path is located to your left.

Station: Harpenden.
TIC: Hemel Hempstead, 01442 234222.
Other nearby trails: The Grand Union Canal passes through Hemel Hempstead.
Useful publications: OS Landranger Map 166.
Refreshments: Lots of choice in Harpenden and Hemel Hempstead.

3

3 Ashridge Estate, northwest of Hemel Hempstead

CATEGORY
Bridleways and roads through Ashridge Estate.

DISTANCE
5-mile circuit.

Comprising over 1600 hectares of woodlands, commons, downland and farmland, the Ashridge Estate runs along the main ridge of the Chilterns from Berkhamsted to Ivinghoe Beacon. The main focal point of the Estate is the granite monument erected in 1832 in honour of the 3rd Duke of Bridgewater, father of inland navigation, who was nicknamed 'the Canal Duke'. The ride starts from this mighty monument (which you can climb!) and descends through broadleaf woodland on a series of bridleways marked with blue arrows. This is just one of many rides that could be devised in the estate. Be warned, however, that these are woodland tracks rather than specially built cycle trails so the going can become muddy in winter and after prolonged rain. Mountain bikes are recommended.

STARTING POINT & PARKING
→From the A41 / Berkhamsted follow the B4506 north for 3 1/2 miles towards Ringshall and Dunstable taking the second road to the left to the visitor centre (grid reference 970130).

ON YOUR BIKES!
1. Go past the visitor centre and straight ahead downhill on a wide track signposted with a blue arrow signposted 'Boundary Trail'. At a fork of tracks on a fast descent bear left. Follow the main track round to the left and go past a white lodge house on your left. Continue in the same direction.
2. At the road (B4506) go straight ahead **(take care)**. Gentle descent. Soon after passing a

house to the left, turn right uphill on a broad stone track (blue arrow)

3. At the next crossroads of tracks, with a red-brick barn ahead, turn right on a broad stone track. Shortly, at the next farm, bear right away from the stone track onto a grassy track (blue arrow).

4. Keep following blue arrows (ie not horseshoe signs). At the crossroads with the B4506 go straight ahead onto the lane opposite. **Take care on this short road section.** Go past 'Base Camp', round a sharp left-hand bend then shortly after a car parking area to the left turn right onto a public bridleway with an 'Icknield Way' signpost.

5. Rougher section. At the T-junction with broad gravel drive turn right then left by the white lodge house, rejoining the outward route. Climb back to the start.

Station: Tring.

TIC: Wendover, 01296 696759.

Other nearby trails: The Grand Union Canal runs close by. The Ridgeway / Icknield Way has some long bridleway sections. There are waymarked forest trails in Wendover Woods between Wendover and Tring.

Useful publications: OS Landranger Map 165. A basic map, *Ashridge Estate Cyclists' Guide* is available from: The Visitor Services Manager, Ashridge Estate, Ringshall, Berkhamsted, Hertfordshire HP4 1LX (01442 851227).

Refreshments: There is a tea kiosk open on summer weekends, next to the visitor centre. Otherwise the nearest refreshments are either in the village of Aldbury or in Little Gaddesden.

4   Albanway - from St Albans to Hatfield

CATEGORY
Railway path (waymarked as National Cycle Network 61).

DISTANCE
4 1/2 miles each way.

4

It is well worth exploring this fine wooded railway trail between these two towns, forming part of the National Cycle Network Route 61. The route runs from St Albans (Abbey Station) northeast to Old Hatfield on a fine gravel path with a deep cutting at the St Albans end. There are short sections on quiet roads at the start and finish and three other road crossings but none are particularly busy. Opened in 1865 by the Hatfield & St Albans Railway Company, the line was absorbed by the Great Northern Railway in 1883. Passenger services continued until 1951 and freight lines until the late 1960s. In 1985 the line was given a new lease of life when it was converted to a cycleway / footpath.

All that is left of Verulamium, once the most important Roman town in Britain, lies to the west of the present city of St Albans. There are the remains of a great amphitheatre and part of an underground heating system. Modern St Albans takes its name from Alban, the first

Christian martyr in Britain. The mighty abbey was founded on the hill where he was beheaded.

STARTING POINTS & PARKING

→ **St Albans** (near Abbey Railway Station). Follow the A5183 Radlett Road out of St Albans. At the traffic lights by the Abbey Theatre car park, just after a petrol station on the left but before the Abbey Railway Station, turn left on to Prospect Road. At the T-junction at the end of Prospect Road turn right and park near to the newsagents / stores. To get to the start of the trail follow the road for 300 yds, cross the railway bridge then turn immediately right and keep bearing right to go back under the bridge and join the railway path.

→ **Hatfield.** The Galleria Shopping Centre surface car park. From Jct 3 of the A1(M) follow signs for 'Galleria' then for 'A1001 Hertford'. At the roundabout by the Peugeot dealer turn right signposted 'Galleria Parking' and bear left into the surface car park. Park at the far right-hand end near to the Drive-In McDonalds at the back of the cinema complex. To get to the start of the trail exit the car park and turn right alongside

the decorative brick wall. Follow this road to its end, staying close to the wall, then climb the ramp / steps at the end of the left-hand cul-de-sac and turn right on to the tarmac path. Use the underpass, turn right, cross the bridge then turn left on to the railway path

ON YOUR BIKES!

From St Albans - see 'Starting point' above to get to start of railway path

1. Follow the railway path and cycle lane through St Albans. After almost 2 miles cross the new blue bridge over Dellfield Road.

2. Cross a road near to the Body Limits Gymnasium then continue 2 1/2 miles into Hatfield. Use the underpass to cross to the Galleria.

From Hatfield - see 'Starting point' above

1. Follow the railway path through a housing estate. After 2 1/2 miles cross a road near to the Body limits Gymnasium.

2. Shortly, cross the new blue bridge over Dellfield Road.

3. Follow for 2 miles to the end of the trail, beyond a new housing estate in St Albans

4

Station: Abbey Station, St Albans.
TIC: St Albans, 01727 864511.
Other nearby trails: The Ayot Greenway, Cole Greenway and Nicky Line all lie close by.
Useful publications: OS Landranger Map 166. *The Albanway* leaflet is available from Hertfordshire Countryside Management Service (01727 848168) or from St Albans Tourist Information Centre (01727 864511).
Refreshments: Lots of choice in St Albans.

5 Ayot Greenway, Wheathampstead

CATEGORY
Railway path.
DISTANCE
3 miles each way.

A short ride along the course of the old Luton, Dunstable & Welwyn Junction railway from Wheathampstead east to the minor road south of Welwyn with some lovely wooded sections. Many men were employed building the line but the hardest workers would have been the navvies. A day's work for two of them would be to shovel 20 tons of rock and earth into 14 horse-drawn wagons. Although the work was hard, the pay, ranging between 15 shillings and 22 shillings and sixpence per week, was better than that of farm workers so many men left the farms to work on the railway. It took two years to complete the stretch of the line between Luton and Hatfield and the first excursion over the new section ran to London. The cheapest return fare from Luton to London was two shillings and sixpence (12.5p!)

STARTING POINT & PARKING
→Free car park on East Street, **Wheathampstead** (by the Bull pub), just off the B651, about 5 miles north of St Albans (grid reference 178143).

ON YOUR BIKES!
1. From the north side of the bridge over the river (the other side from the Bull pub) take the street called Mount Road and follow the 'Bridleway to Waterend' signpost.
2. Follow along a field edge and through a bridlegate. At a T-junction with a broad stone track turn left through the subway. Ignore a left turn signposted 'Bridleway' and take the next right at a crossroads of tracks, waymarked with a bike sign.
3. The track climbs then ends at a junction with the Ayot St Peter road south of Welwyn (grid reference 221145).

Station: Welwyn North or Harpenden.
TIC: St Albans, 01727 864511.
Other nearby trails: The Nicky Line, Cole Greenway and Albanway all lie nearby.
Useful publications: OS Landranger Map 166.
Refreshments: In Wheathampstead (and Welwyn, 1 1/2 miles beyond the end of the trail on minor roads).

6 Cole Green Way, west of Hertford

CATEGORY
Railway path.
DISTANCE
4 1/2 miles each way.

The most rural of the four dismantled railways in Hertfordshire, passing through attractive woodland between the Rivers Lee and Mimram, linking Welwyn Garden City and Hertford. The trail follows the course of the old Hertford, Dunstable and Luton line. Opened in 1858 by the Hertford & Welwyn Junction Railway and carried passengers up to 1951 and converted to a walking and riding route in 1974.

STARTING POINTS & PARKING
→On the southeast edge of **Welwyn Garden City**. Follow the B195 towards Cole Green and Letty Green. At the start of the countryside at the edge of Welwyn Garden City turn right off the B195 signposted 'QE2 Hospital'. Park on Holwell Hyde Lane (grid reference 265118).

→The Cole Greenway car park near the Cowper Arms pub in **Cole Green**. Turn off the A414 following signs for 'Cole Green / Birch Green' then signs for 'Letty Green'. The car park is just beyond the Cowper Arms pub on the left (grid reference 285112).

→**Hertford** Town FC Ground. Take the A414 out of Hertford towards Hatfield. Just after the Gates Ford garage turn left on to West Street signposted 'Hertford Town FC'. About 100 yds after the end of the houses, on a left-hand bend, turn right by a high 'Cole Green Way / NCN 61' sign down a tarmac lane leading to the car park (grid reference 320120).

ON YOUR BIKES!
From Welwyn Garden City
Follow the trail for just over 4 miles. Near to the the vast, brick railway viaduct in Hertford bear right on the main track then at a T-junction of tracks turn left to pass beneath the arches into Hertford Town Football Club car park.
From Hertford
From football club car park take the track that leads towards the left-hand end of the railway arches. Going under the arches and take the first right by a white gate. Continue for 4 1/2 miles as far as the B195 at the edge of Welwyn Garden City.

Station: Hertford.
TIC: Hertford, 01992 584322.
Other nearby trails: The Ayot Greenway, Albanway and Nicky Line are all near by.
Useful publications: OS Landranger Map 166.
Refreshments: The Black Horse pub on West Street, Hertford, is just beyond the end of the railway path. Cowper Arms pub at Cole Green.

7 The Lee Navigation from Hertford to Waltham Abbey

CATEGORY

Canal towpath.

DISTANCE

Up to 13 miles each way.

Many of the best traffic-free cycling routes routes in and near London use the towpaths of the waterways that radiate from the capital - these also include the Grand Union Canal in the west of London, the Thames to the southwest and the Thames estuary east from Greenwich. The surface of the Lee Navigation towpath has recently been upgraded to a very high standard - if only all canal towpaths were as good! The whole Lee Valley (or **Lea** Valley, both spellings are used, take your pick) has become one of the best areas for recreational cycling to the north of London. The ride described here follows the Lee Navigation from its northern terminus in Hertford eastwards through the attractive town of Ware before taking a more southerly course past Cheshunt to

Waltham Abbey. This is only a suggested turnaround point: you may wish to do a much shorter ride going only as far as Ware or the pub at Dobb's Weir or perhaps you may wish to push on further right into London, joining the Thames near Limehouse Basin.

NB Care should be taken crossing the A1170 in Ware - use the cycle facility.

STARTING POINTS & PARKING

→The long stay car park near the swimming pool on Hartham Lane, **Hertford** From the centre of Hertford follow signs for the B158 (Parliament Square roundabout, The Wash, Millbridge) past the library then turn right onto Hartham Lane past Hertford Brewery to the car park (grid reference 325130).

→Highbridge car park, **Waltham Abbey**, off the A121 (grid reference 373007).

ON YOUR BIKES!

Starting from Hertford

1. From opposite the cafe near to the playing fields follow the cyclepath running parallel with the road signposted 'Ware 2 1/2'. Cross the

railway path running west from Hertford to Welwyn Garden City. Epping Forest lies to the southeast of Waltham Abbey.

Useful publications: OS Landranger Map 166. Much more useful is the very fine full colour leaflet produced by the Lee Valley Regional Park Authority, available free from: Lee Valley Park Information Centre, Abbey Gardens, Waltham Abbey, Essex EN9 1XQ (01992 702200).

Refreshments: Lots of choice in Hertford and Ware. Fish & Eels pub at Dobb's Weir. Lots of choice in Waltham Abbey. Cafe near the swimming pool in Hertford at the start of the ride.

8 The Lee Navigation from Victoria Park to Waltham Abbey

CATEGORY

Canal towpath.

DISTANCE

Up to 12 miles each way.

A superb escape from Victoria Park, Hackney via Hackney Marshes to Waltham Abbey on a recently upgraded towpath which sets a fine example against which other towpaths should measure themselves. Improvements to the River Lee started in 1424 when an Act was passed to 'scour and amend the river'. In the centuries that followed the river was gradually straightened, deepened and extended. By 1930, 130-ton barges could negotiate the Navigation to Enfield. The River Lee Country Park was established in 1967 to help meet the leisure needs of the people of London, Essex and Hertfordshire. It regenerated 10,000 acres of land and water for a wide range of sporting and leisure activities and for nature conservation. Since 1983, extensive landscaping works, habitat creation, footpath and access projects

recreation ground, then the bridge and turn left along the towpath of the Lee Navigation.

2. After 2 miles, at the bridge in Ware at the end of the towpath bear right and use the traffic islands to cross straight ahead then left to rejoin the towpath.

3. Follow this excellent cycling towpath for a further 5 miles to the Fish & Eels pub at Dobb's Weir then another 6 miles until you get to Waltham Abbey.

Station: Hertford, Waltham Abbey and several stations in between.

TIC: Hertford, 01992 584322.

Other nearby trails: The towpath alongside the Lee Navigation continues south to Limehouse Basin on the Thames. The Cole Greenway is a

have been carried out providing a valuable haven for people and wildlife. Nearly half a million trees have been planted.

NB It would also be possible to start the ride from Islington, following the Regent's Canal then the Hertford Union Canal although this can be quite busy with pedestrians.

STARTING POINTS & PARKING

→Victoria Park, **Hackney**. The southeast corner of the park at the junction of Cadogan Terrace and Jodrell Road. Follow the Hertford Union Canal to the junction with the Lee Navigation and turn left.

→Highbridge car park, **Waltham Abbey**, off the A121 (grid reference 373007).

Station: Several stations are close to the canal, enabling you to ride one way and catch the train back. Liverpool Street is the London terminal for the stations along the ride.

TIC: Hertford, 01992 584322.

Other nearby trails: Epping Forest and the Cole Greenway.

Useful publications: OS Landranger Maps 166

& 177. Much more useful is the very fine full colour leaflet produced by the Lee Valley Regional Park Authority, available free from: Lee Valley Park Information Centre, Abbey Gardens, Waltham Abbey, Essex EN9 1XQ (01992 702200).

Refreshments: Lots of choice along the way.

9   Epping Forest, north of London

CATEGORY
Forest trail.

DISTANCE
This is a suggested ride of 4 miles. There are many miles of tracks from which to make up your own routes.

Although there is no specifically waymarked bike trail in Epping Forest there is such a plethora of top grade gravel tracks that it would be possible to make up any number of routes criss-crossing this ancient woodland, owned and managed by the Corporation of London.

This ride starts from the King's Oak pub in the heart of the forest and wastes no time before diving into the wooded delights on a broad gravel track. There are some roads to cross and great care should be taken at the busier ones but in general there is good visibility at the road crossings. As long as you are prepared to wait for a clear gap in the traffic the roads should not be a deterrent to exploring Epping Forest's fine network of tracks. It is notoriously difficult to give woodland instructions so please do not get exasperated if you feel you are lost! The most important point is that you are outside cycling in beautiful woodland, you will never be that far from where you started and if you take a different route from the one described, it is not the end of the world, is it? It is best to turn up with a map (or buy one from the excellent visitor centre at High Beach). There are plenty of good quality gravel tracks, although these may become muddy in the depths of winter or after prolonged rain. There are several short hills, some of which are quite steep.

NB Great care should be taken crossing the roads, particularly the A104 which is crossed twice. Allow yourself time to gauge the speed of the traffic and wait for a clear gap in both directions.

STARTING POINT & PARKING

→ The King's Oak pub at **High Beach**, near the visitor centre in the middle of Epping Forest. This is located about 1 mile northwest of the Loughton / High Beach roundabout on the A104, the road running north from London towards the town of Epping (grid reference 411981).

ON YOUR BIKES!

1. With your back to the King's Oak pub turn right. Immediately before joining the next road turn right through a metal barrier onto a broad gravel track.

2. **Ignore** two left turns (these are the wheelchair paths). Take the next left. At the crossroads with A104 go straight ahead **WITH GREAT CARE.**

3. Bear right at the next junction, descending gently then more steeply. Climb to the next road and go straight ahead (you will pass a pond to your right).

4. On a gentle downhill take the first major wide stone track to the right. At the crossroads with the A104 **TAKE GREAT CARE** crossing straight ahead onto a continuation of the track. Continue straight ahead at the next crossroads with a minor road.

5. Take the next right then shortly turn right again. It starts flat then climbs gently. At the final road (which has a 20 mph speed limit) turn right then left. **Ignore** the turning to the right, rejoin the outward route, go past the wheelchair walk and at the road turn left to return to the King's Oak pub.

Station: Chingford, Loughton, Epping.
TIC: At the High Beach Visitor Centre, 0191 508 0028.
Other nearby trails: The Lee Navigation runs to the west of Epping Forest.
Other publications: OS Landranger Maps 167 & 177. Better still are the larger scale maps that can be purchased from the visitor centre at High Beach which show the trails in much greater detail (0191 508 0028).
Refreshments: King's Oak pub and cafe at the start. Several pubs (and odd tea waggons!) dotted around Epping Forest.

10

10 Grand Union Canal from London to Norton Junction, near Daventry

CATEGORY

Canal towpath.

DISTANCE

Anything up to 100 miles.

One of the best escapes from London (see also the Lee Navigation and the Thames Towpath), the Grand Union Canal towpath can be followed for over 100 miles to Daventry. It is **not** a route to be undertaken at speed - there are lots of walkers, anglers and barriers! The surface tends to be better closer to London, although this section is also busier with other users. There is another superb section through Milton Keynes along the Broadwalk - see page 116. The route is as follows: Ladbroke Grove, London - Uxbridge - Rickmansworth - Watford - Hemel Hempstead - Tring - Leighton Buzzard - Milton Keynes - southwest of Northampton - Norton Junction, northeast of Daventry.

NB Please read *The Waterways Code - Cycling on the towpath* at the front of the book

Start: Ladbroke Grove (near the Sainsbury's supermarket), Kensal Town, London. Beyond Uxbridge the surroundings become much greener.

Stations: All along the way.

TICs: Hemel Hempstead, 01442 234222; Milton Keynes, 01908 691691; Daventry, 01327 300277.

Other nearby trails: Thames Towpath, Milton Keynes Redway, Brampton Valley Way (Northampton to Market Harborough).

Useful publications: OS Landranger Maps 152, 165, 166 & 176. You may prefer to use the Nicholson *Ordnance Survey Guide to the Waterways. 1: South.*

Refreshments: There are refreshments all along the way.

11   Flitch Way, west of Braintree

CATEGORY

Railway path.

DISTANCE

7 miles each way.

The best of Essex's dismantled railways, the Flitch Way runs west from Braintree railway station and offers the option of a good pub at Little Dunmow, at the western end of the ride. This section of the trail continues west beyond Little Dunmow for 1 1/2 miles to the A130 south of Great Dunmow. There is another 6-mile section of the Flitch Way further west which can also be cycled although it is not as well maintained. Starting to the east of Bishop's Stortford, it runs from the minor road at Tilekiln Lane (just west of M11, Jct 8, grid reference 520213) and continues east for about 6 miles to Greencrofts, 2 miles west of Great Dunmow (grid reference 603213).

STARTING POINT & PARKING

→**Braintree** Railway Station car park (the end furthest from the station).

ON YOUR BIKES!

From Braintree

1. Follow the Flitch Way westwards from Braintree railway station car park. After 2 1/2 miles, at the far end of the old station and platform at Rayne, turn left off the railway path via a white wooden gate on to School Road then bear right. Cross the bridge over the A120 then take Mill Road, the second road to the right. After 1 mile, just before the bridge over the railway, turn right downhill by a 'Flitch Way' signpost. Descend to the railway path and turn left. **Remember** this point for the return trip.
2. After 3 1/2 miles the trail descends to the Felsted to Little Dunmow road. Turn right then sharply left, then opposite a red-brick house

bear right to rejoin the track. Immediately after passing beneath the next red-brick bridge turn right off the railway path and join a minor lane. **Remember** this point for the return. Turn left on the lane (Brook Street) then at the T-junction, turn left again for the Flitch of Bacon pub.

Station: Braintree.
TIC: Braintree, 01376 550066.
Other nearby trails: South of Bishop's Stortford, the Stort Navigation runs towards London. Epping Forest has many miles of fine tracks.
Useful publications: OS Landranger Map 167.
Refreshments: Lots of choice in Braintree, Flitch of Bacon pub in Little Dunmow.

12   Valley Walk, Sudbury, northwest of Colchester

CATEGORY

Railway path.

DISTANCE

3 miles each way.

One of few dismantled railways in Suffolk that has been converted to recreational use, this one follows the delightful River Stour which forms the boundary between Suffolk and Essex for much of its length. The trail can be linked to a picnic site by the River Stour to the southwest of Rodbridge Corner by crossing the road bridge at the end of the trail to the other bank of the river. You might also choose to head east along the network of quiet Essex / Suffolk lanes to the village pubs in Belchamp Otten, Belchamp St Paul and Pentlow.

STARTING POINT & PARKING

→The trail starts opposite the main entrance to the Leisure Pool in **Sudbury**, 15 miles northwest of Colchester. Look out for a 'Valley Walk' sign at the start of the trail. There is a large car park at the Leisure Pool.

13

Station: Sudbury (the route starts from the station).

TIC: Sudbury, 01787 881320.

Other nearby trails: The circuit of Alton Water is just south of Ipswich.

Useful publications: OS Landranger Map 155.

Refreshments: Lots of choice in Sudbury. There are pubs in the villages a few miles along quiet lanes from the end of the railway path.

13 Colchester to Wivenhoe along the riverside path

CATEGORY
Riverside path and cyclepaths through parkland.

DISTANCE
5 miles each way.

This ride links two clusters of beautiful old buildings, one in the very heart of Colchester and the other around Wivenhoe Quay, via a mixture of quiet streets, paths through parkland and (for the greater part of the ride) a traffic-free riverside path along the River Colne from the southeastern edge of Colchester past the University of Essex to Wivenhoe railway station.

It is well worth going beyond the station to explore the quay and pubs by the riverside in Wivenhoe. For those of you looking for a totally traffic-free ride it would be best to start at Wivenhoe station and turn around at the end of the cyclepath after 3 miles. However, if you are prepared to use some short sections on quiet streets you soon join another traffic-free stretch alongside the river and through parkland, arriving right in the heart of Colchester's historic city centre. As this ride is part of National Cycle Network Route 1 it is likely that the short sections on roads will be improved year on year with traffic calming and segregated cycle lanes.

STARTING POINTS & PARKING
→ The railway station car park at **Wivenhoe**, on the B1028, about 3 miles southeast of Colchester.

→ The George Hotel, **Colchester** High Street. There are several car parks in the centre of Colchester (the one by Leisure World off the A133, Cowdray Avenue, is the closest) although if arriving from outside of Colchester by car it would probably be better to start at Wivenhoe rather than battling with traffic in the centre of Colchester.

ON YOUR BIKES!

1. From the Wivenhoe railway station car park follow the trail parallel with the railway line alongside the river.

2. The railway path ends after 3 miles at Travis Perkins timber merchants. If you wish to continue into the centre of Colchester on a mixture of mainly traffic-free riverside paths with the occasional street section, cross the road at the toucan crossing and follow the cycle lane right then round to the left.

3. Follow Hawkins Road through the industrial estate (this is the busiest road of the urban section). At the T-junction at the end turn left then bear right onto the cycle lane and follow this round to the right to rejoin the riverside path.

4. Follow alongside the river and past the allotments. At the traffic lights cross the road and continue alongside the river and through parkland.

5. At the T-junction of paths by metal railings turn right to cross the bridge over the river then left along the road (Sportsway). As this road swings right turn left through parkland onto the waymarked cycle lane.

6. Exit the park, turn left uphill at the end of Middle Mill and follow this road right up to Colchester High Street.

Station: Colchester or Wivenhoe.
TIC: Colchester, 01206 282920.
Other nearby trails: The Flitch Way between Braintree and Little Dunmow.
Useful publications: OS Landranger Map 168. *Cycling in Colchester* is an A2 full colour leaflet showing all the cyclepaths in Colchester plus the whole of the Colchester to Wivenhoe route. It costs 25p and is available by sending an SAE to: Essex County Council, County Hall, Chelmsford CM1 1QH.
Refreshments: Rose & Crown pub, the Station pub, Wivenhoe; lots of choice in the centre of Colchester.

14

14 Alton Water, south of Ipswich

CATEGORY

Round-reservoir route.

DISTANCE

8-mile circuit.

This fine reservoir circuit is being improved a little more each year, making the route safer and easier with each improvement. Alton Water is also popular with watersports so on fine, breezy days you will catch sight of windsurfers racing each other across the lake with their bright sails skimming over the surface. Although this is a relatively easy and flat ride you should be warned that there is a hillier and rougher stretch on the north side of the lake between Birchwood car park and Lemons Bay. You may prefer to follow lanes for this section: maps showing the route plus the surrounding lanes are available from the cycle hire centre. There is a cafe at the visitor centre and lots of pubs just near the route so you could either follow the circuit close to the lake itself or make this part of a longer ride exploring some of the beautiful and quiet lanes on the Shotley Peninsula.

STARTING POINT & PARKING

→The **Alton Water Visitor Centre**, off the B1080 between Stutton and Holbrook, 6 miles south of Ipswich and 4 miles east of the A12 at Capel St Mary (grid reference 156354).

ON YOUR BIKES!

1. From the visitor centre keep the water to your left and follow the trail ('Alton Water Circuit') past the sailing club, over the dam wall then turn left just before the fence.

2. Certain sections on the far side of the lake are a bit rough. At the car park and road turn left over the bridge then left again through gate onto a gravel track, following the bike route signposts.

3. At the T-junction with tarmac turn right uphill for 150 yds then left onto a gravel track parallel with the road and follow this back to the start

Station: Manningtree and Ipswich.
TIC: Ipswich, 01473 258070.
Other nearby trails: The Three Forest Way lies to the east of Woodbridge.
Useful publications: OS Landranger Map 169. A leaflet is available from the cycle hire centre (01473 328873).
Refreshments: Cafe at the visitor centre; White Horse pub, Tattingstone White Horse; Wheatsheaf pub, Tattingstone; Kings Head pub, Stutton; Compasses pub, Swan Inn, Holbrook.

15 Priory Country Park and Willington Countryway, Bedford

CATEGORY

Lakeside route and railway path.

DISTANCE

1 1/2 miles around the lake and 4 miles each way along the Willington Countryway.

This ride has two parts: a short circuit of the lake in Priory Country Park plus a trip along the Willington Countryway railway path through woodland and arable land. Priory Country Park is named after the Augustinian Priory established here in the 12th century. Very little of this now remains, although the stone wall between the marina and the sailing lake formed part of the boundary. Near to Priory Country Park, at Cardington Lock, the River Ouse splits into two, the left waterway passing through the lock to the navigable part of the river. The lock was restored to full working order in the late 1970s, making it possible to cruise from Bedford to the Wash.
NB There will be a short section on road if you wish to visit the pub and/or the Dovecote in Willington.

STARTING POINT & PARKING

→Priory Country Park, Bedford signposted off the A428 Bedford /Cambridge road (grid reference 072495).

ON YOUR BIKES!

1. The railway path starts close to the car park entrance signposted 'Countryway'. Go past the water treatment works. At the T-junction with a track soon after crossing bridge over the bypass bear left. At a T-junction after the gravel pits turn right then left (bike signs).

2. At a T-junction with a narrow tarmac path with a fence ahead, turn left, follow the river, then turn right opposite the bridge. The track ends near to a lake at the Willington to Great Barford road. Retrace your steps. (On your return, to visit Willington, turn left at the end of high green wire / concrete post fence. At the road go straight ahead for the pub or turn right for 3/4 mile to see the dovecote).

Station: Bedford.
TIC: Bedford, 01234 215226.
Other nearby trails: Grafham Water lies 15 miles to the north.
Useful publications: OS Landranger Map 153.
Refreshments: Priory Marina pub at the start. The Crown pub in Willington.

16 Grafham Water, southwest of Huntingdon

CATEGORY
Round-reservoir route.

DISTANCE
8-mile circuit.

This well-signposted reservoir route on tracks and quiet roads is very popular, particularly during summer weekends. The trail uses stone and gravel paths with some gentle hills where the trail leaves the waterside. The reservoir was built in 1966 and holds 59,000 million litres of water! There is plenty of birdlife as well as attractive woodland stretches.

STARTING POINT & PARKING
→West Perry (just off the A1 between St Neots and Huntingdon). There are three main pay and display car parks - Mander Park, Plummer Park and Marlow Park. Best cycled anti-clockwise.

ON YOUR BIKES!
The route is generally well signposted. On the road section through Perry ignore left turns on Lymage Road and Chichester Way. About 400 yds after passing the Wheatsheaf pub and soon after Duberley Close on your left, turn left on to a waymarked track through Plummer Park.

Station: Huntingdon, 6 miles northeast of Grafham village.
TIC: St Neots, 01480 388788.
Other nearby trails: The country's most famous reservoir route, Rutland Water, lies 30 miles to the north. The Brampton Valley Way (Northampton to Market Harborough) lies 25 miles to the west.
Useful publications: OS Landranger Map 153. The cycle hire centre also has maps.
Refreshments: Cafes in Mander and Marlow Parks. Montagu Arms pub in Grafham and Wheatsheaf pub in West Perry.

16

17

17 Fulbourn Roman Road, southeast of Cambridge

CATEGORY
Track along the course of an old Roman Road.

DISTANCE
6 1/2 miles each way.

This ride uses a short section of the old Roman Road that used to be known as Woles or Wolves Street linking Colchester with Godmanchester. Where it crossed the Cam, a small Roman town grew up, later to become Cambridge. It offers a wonderful rollercoaster ride along a chalk track between verges of wildflowers and beneath canopies of trees, but be warned!....it should only be ridden after a dry spell in the summer months as it will be muddy in winter or after prolonged rain. Mountain bikes are recommended.

NB If you want refreshment in either Linton or Balsham you will need to spend time on public roads. (Look at Ordnance Survey Landranger Map 154 for the best minor roads to use).

STARTING POINT & PARKING
→The small car park 2 miles southwest of **Fulbourn** along the minor lane known as Shelford Road. If starting from Cambridge, take the A1307 road towards Haverhill then turn left on the outskirts of town, just after the roundabout by Addenbrooke's Hospital onto the Fulbourn Road. The car park is 1 1/2 miles along on your right (grid reference 493547).

Station: Cambridge or Great Shelford.
TIC: Cambridge, 01223 322640.
Other nearby trails: Grafham Water is 20 miles to the west. Thetford Forest lies 25 miles northeast.
Useful publications: OS Landranger Map 154.
Refreshments: In Fulbourn, Balsham or Linton (all of them are about 2 miles off the route).

18 Three Forest Cycle Trail, northeast of Ipswich

CATEGORY
Forest trails and roads.

DISTANCE
Up to 25 miles each way. The forestry sections are much shorter.

This ride links three forests near to the Suffolk Coast using a mixture of roads and forest trails. If you wish to avoid roads altogether then stick to the tracks in Tunstall and Rendlesham Forests. The full ride starts at the Forest Enterprise Offices in Rendlesham Forest then passes through Butley, Chillesford, Tunstall Forest, Snape, Aldeburgh, Aldringham and Eastbridge to finish in Dunwich. In its entirety the Three Forests Cycle Trail is more road than offroad. If you decide to concentrate on the trails in Rendlesham and Tunstall Forests it is recommended venturing out beyond the woodland as far as the Snape Maltings which are well worth visiting.

STARTING POINT & PARKING

➔Tangham House (Forest Enterprise car park),
Rendlesham Forest, east of Ipswich. Leave the
A12 at Woodbridge, northeast of Ipswich.
Follow the A1152 then the B1084 towards
Butley. After 4 miles on the B1084, take the first
road to the right (grid reference 355484).

Station: Market Wickham.
TIC: Woodbridge, 01394 382240.
Other nearby trails: Alton Water Reservoir is just
south of Ipswich.
Useful publications: OS Landranger Maps 156
& 169. A Forest Enterprise leaflet is available
from East Anglia Forest District, Santon
Downham, Brandon, Suffolk IP27 0TJ (01842
810271).
Refreshments: In Butley, Sudbourne, Snape,
Aldeburgh, Eastbridge and Dunwich.

18

19 Peterborough Green Wheel

CATEGORY
Specially-built cyclepath.
DISTANCE
10-mile circuit.

This traffic-free ride on either side of the River
Nene from Ferry Meadows Country Park to the
centre of Peterborough is part of a much larger
and more ambitious project known as the
Peterborough Green Wheel. This is a network of
cycleways, footpaths and bridleways that
provide safe, continuous routes around the city
and 'spokes' linking the Wheel to residential
areas and the city centre. The Green Wheel
celebrates over 2000 years of Peterborough's
social, cultural, economic and environmental
history through a series of sculptures and
colourful interpretation boards along the route.
Half the cost has been met by National Lottery
funding through the Millennium Commission
and the remainder raised through sponsorship
and donations. The ride described is just one
suggestion: others might include a ride along
the River Nene to the east of town or west from
Farcet towards the A15 and A1.

STARTING POINT & PARKING
➔The bridge over the River Nene by Asda in
the centre of **Peterborough** or, if coming from
outside Peterborough, better to park in Ferry
Meadows (off the A605 Oundle Road on the
west side of Peterborough) and cycle into town.

ON YOUR BIKES!
1. From the footbridge over the River Nene just
south of the centre of Peterborough (by Asda
and close to Railway World) turn right on Henry
Penn Walk alongside the river (keeping the
water to your left).
2. At the T-junction at the end of the tarmac
turn right to cross the bridge then left by the
Boat House Inn. Follow the path around the

19

parallel with railway line.

9. Stay on the tarmac path as it swings right then left to recross the railway line for a final time. Go past Railway World and take the next footbridge across the river (opposite new yellow-brick riverside houses).

Station: Peterborough.

TIC: Peterborough, 01733 452336.

Other nearby trails: There are several sections of the Peterborough Green Wheel that offer traffic-free cycling and more is being built each year. See details about the leaflet below.

Useful publications: OS Landranger Map 142. Much better is the leaflet *The Peterborough Millennium Green Wheel Cycle Map* (£1.25) available from Peterborough Environment City Trust, High Street, Fletton, Peterborough PE2 8DT (01733 760883).

Refreshments: Lots of choice for refreshments in Peterborough. Boat House Inn, near to the rowing lake. Also there is a cafe at the Ferry Meadows Country Park.

edge of the rowing lake, keeping the water to your left.

3. At the T-junction by the main road at the end of the lake turn left signposted 'Orton, Ferry Meadows'. Pass beneath the road bridge, over the river bridge, cross the railway line then turn right signposted 'Orton Meadows, Ferry Meadows, Lynch Wood'.

4. At the next T-junction turn right to cross the railway line then turn left. Cross the road with care then turn right on the tarmac path alongside the road to the visitor centre.

5. For a full circuit of the lakes follow signs for 'Bluebell Wood, Adventure Playground, Nature Reserve'.

6. **To return to Peterborough** along the south side of the River Nene, follow the tarmac path alongside the exit road from the park then turn left signposted 'Station, Orton Mere, City Centre'.

7. Keep following the tarmac path as it crosses the railway line then turn left parallel with the line signposted 'Orton Mere, City Centre'.

8. At the next junction turn left then right signposted 'Woodston City Centre' to continue

20 Thetford Forest, Thetford, northwest of Cambridge

CATEGORY

Forest trails.

DISTANCE

Brandon Park Loop - 6.5-mile circuit.
High Lodge Loop - 6.5-mile circuit

Draw a line 10 miles around Thetford and you have some of the most consistently rideable offroad tracks in all of East Anglia: the soil has a sandy base and drains well and as the land is not good enough for farming, most of it is owned by the Forestry Commission and planted with pine trees. The forestry tracks around the

Forest Centre, on the Forest Drive, off the B1107 east of Brandon (grid reference 811852).

ON YOUR BIKES!

1. From the High Lodge Visitor Centre on the Forest Drive, south of the B1107 between Brandon and Thetford follow the direction of the one way tarmac Forest Ride on a track parallel with the road. The route is well-signposted with bike symbols on yellow circles and directional arrows; follow it clockwise for 4 miles.

plantations tend to have excellent all-year round surfaces and it is possible to devise any number of loops using these tracks. However, as is the case with all forestry land, it is almost impossible to give detailed route instructions when the only landmarks are trees and more trees, so the rides described are those that the Forestry Commision has already waymarked. Route instructions are given as a back-up to avoid getting lost. Even so, it is no bad idea to carry a compass with you so that you know in which direction you are travelling. Getting lost in Thetford Forest is hardly a life-threatening experience: you are never more than 2 miles from a road, so if you do lose your way, there is no need to panic! Simply retrace your steps to where you last knew where you were or, alternatively continue in a straight line until you find a road and you should soon be able to re-orientate yourself.

NB If you link the two routes there is a crossing of the busy (and fast) B1106. Take great care with young children.

STARTING POINTS & PARKING

➔ For Brandon Park Loop, start at Mayday Farm car park, 3 miles south of Brandon along the B1106 (grid reference 795834).
➔ For High Lodge Loop, start at High Lodge

2. At a T-junction with a 2-way signpost turn left 'Mayday' if you wish to do the second loop **OR** turn right 'High Lodge' to return to the start for a short ride.
3. At the junction with the B1106 go straight ahead. **Take care** crossing this busy road.
4. Keep following the waymarked route. The second loop also runs clockwise. About 1 1/2 miles after crossing the B1106, at the fork at the forest section signposted '45' bear left.
5. After a further 2 1/2 miles at the two way signpost near to forest sections signposted '6' and '10' turn left.
6. At the T-junction by two way signpost with a radio mast to the right turn left. At the crossroads with the B1106 go straight ahead. **Take care.** After 1/2 mile rejoin the first loop, bearing left to return to the start

Station: Brandon.
TIC: Bury St Edmunds, 01284 764667
Other nearby trails: The Peddars Way is a long distance trail that runs north from Thetford to the Norfolk Coast.
Useful publications: OS Landranger Maps 143 & 144. Much better is the Forest Enterprise map, available from the Forest Centre or from Forest District, Santon Downham, Brandon, Suffolk IP27 0TJ (01842 810271).
Refreshments: At the visitor centre.

21 Peddars Way (south) from Bridgham Heath to Castle Acre

CATEGORY
Long distance trail.

DISTANCE
Up to 26 miles each way.

This ride describes the southern half of the Peddars Way. It is a linear, there-and-back ride, overall sandier, more wooded and slightly less undulating than the northern half of the trail. The starting point is not particularly auspicious - a track lying just north of a fast section of dual carriageway on the A11. If you have accommodating friends, this would be a good place to be dropped by someone who is happy to pick you up at the end of your ride. Alternatively, it would be possible to start from Castle Acre and ride south to the A11 then return to Castle Acre. The route passes through a sandy heathland of pines, silver birch and fern. There are frequent Ministry of Defence signs indicating that the area is used for training. From South Pickenham the route turns west towards the Iceni Village at Cockley Cley before skirting round Swaffham towards the valley of the River Nar. After a fast descent to the river you have a choice of leaving the Peddars Way to discover the delights of Castle Acre or of continuing northwards along the line of the long distance path as it heads towards the sea at Holme

STARTING POINT & PARKING
→ Just off the A11, about 5 miles northeast of Thetford, at grid reference 934871. Proceeding northeast from Thetford on the A1075 / A11 the route starts on a track one mile after the start of the A11 dual carriageway next to signs which read 'Danger. MOD Range' '68' and 'Peddars Way'.

ON YOUR BIKES!
From the starting point, follow 'Peddars Way'

signs along the tarmac lane northwards away from the A11. Cross the railway line. The tarmac turns to gravel then becomes a rougher track. Follow signs for 'Peddars Way' and 'Long Distance Path'.

Station: Thetford.
TIC: Fakenham, 01328 851981.
Other nearby trails: There are two waymarked trails in Thetford Forest.
Useful publications: OS Landranger Maps 132 & 144.
Refreshments: Dog & Partridge pub, Wretham; White Horse pub, Little Cressingham; Twenty Churchwardens pub, Cockley Cley; lots of choice in Swaffham; Ostrich pub, Albert Victor pub, tearooms, Castle Acre.

22 Peddars Way (North), Norfolk

CATEGORY

Long distance trail.

DISTANCE

Up to 24 miles each way.

The Peddars Way was built by the Romans in the second half of the first century AD and provides one of the finest offroad routes in all of East Anglia. The ride has been split into two sections, each of which should be manageable in a day. However, as the ride is a linear, there-and-back route, it is possible to do as much or as little as you like. The best option of all would be to have somebody drop you at the start near to Thetford and pick you up at the end when you reach the sea at Holme. The ride described here starts at the halfway point of Castle Acre, a delightful village of brick and flint which is an excellent base for both road and offroad rides. The ride is a mixture of lanes and tracks - some of the latter are likely to be hard going (ie muddy) from late autumn to late spring. There is

more tarmac at the start of the ride near to Castle Acre but the lanes carry very little traffic and are a delight in themselves, passing through broadleaf woodland. The course of the Peddars Way bridlepath and footpath run together, straight as an arrow for several miles in a generally northwesterly direction as far as Fring where the two routes diverge, rejoining in Holme next the Sea. The sea finally comes into view at the crest of the last hill before the coast, some 6 miles north of Fring. From here there is a steady downhill right out to the dunes on the coast.

STARTING POINT & PARKING

→ The Ostrich pub, Castle Acre, north of Swaffham

ON YOUR BIKES!

Route instructions south to north (Castle Acre to Holme next the Sea)
1. With your back to the Ostrich pub in Castle Acre turn right then just past the church take the first left onto South Acre Lane. Go down through ford (or use the footbridge), climb to the T-junction and turn right.
2. **Easy to miss.** After 2 miles, on a sharp left-hand bend, bear right signposted 'Unsuitable for motors' onto a broad sandy track.
3. Go through another ford (or use the bridge). At the T-junction by a grass triangle and a sign for the Stag pub turn right gently uphill. At the crossroads at the end of Low Road go straight ahead. At the T-junction bear right (no sign).
4. After 3 miles at a T-junction by a Give Way sign go straight ahead onto a broad stone track. Follow 'Peddars Way' signs.

Station: Thetford or King's Lynn.
TIC: Fakenham, 01328 851981.
Other nearby trails: There are two waymarked trails in Thetford Forest.
Useful publications: OS Landranger Maps 132 & 144.

Refreshments:
Ostrich pub, Albert Victor pub, tearooms, Castle Acre; White Horse pub, Holme next the Sea. Pubs just off the route in: Great Massingham, Harpley, Great Bircham, Docking, Sedgeford & Ringstead.

23 Marriott's Way, Norwich

CATEGORY
Railway path.

DISTANCE
Up to 24 miles each way.

Escape from the heart of Norwich into the countryside on one of the longest disused railways in the country. The route is signposted as the Wensum Valley Walk from the centre of Norwich and becomes the Marriott's Way near to Drayton. If you do not live in Norwich itself, the visitor centre at the Old Railway Station in Reepham is a good place to start. The woodlands of Mileplain Plantation are a real delight: a deep cutting planted with sweet chestnut trees, especially attractive during the changing autumn colours. The whole route is studded with a wide variety of broadleaf trees - oak, ash, hawthorn, silver birch and sycamore. The clear, gently-flowing waters of the River Wensum are crossed three times on fine old

metal bridges with wooden planking. Between Lenwade and Reepham you have the option of the full route following the Themelthorpe Loop or taking a shortcut which saves 4 miles.

STARTING POINTS & PARKING
→On the northwest side of the centre of **Norwich** at the roundabout by the River Wensum at the junction of Barn Road and St Crispins Road (grid reference 229094).
→**Drayton** - the trail crosses the A1067 between Drayton and Taverham (grid reference 176139).
→**Reepham** - the Old Railway Station is 3/4 mile north of crossroads in the centre of Reepham on the B1145 towards Aylsham, opposite the Crown pub (grid reference 102230).
→The Bure Valley Railway station in **Aylsham**, 15 miles north of Norwich along the A140 / B1354 (grid reference 195265).

ON YOUR BIKES!
Route instructions from south to north (Norwich city centre to Reepham)
1. From the Barn Road / St Crispins Road roundabout join the track alongside the river signposted 'Wensum Valley Walk'.
2. Follow signs for Hellesdon Road along a tarmac then gravel path for 5 miles, crossing one road and continuing in the same direction

(take either fork after road crossing - they join up).

3. Shortly after a triangular-shaped metal bridge over the river the railway path peters out. Descend to the left then at the T-junction with the road turn right then left onto Station Road 'No through traffic'. At the T-junction at the end of Station Road turn right then left through a gap in the wooden fence signposted 'Marriott's Way' to descend to a continuation of railway path.

4. Over the next 4 miles go straight ahead at several crossroads, following signs for 'Reepham' and 'Aylsham'.

5. At the T-junction with road turn right signposted 'Reepham 9, Aylsham 15' then after 150 yds (just past the Post Office to the right) turn left and follow the track to the left through the car park to rejoin the course of the railway.

6. Cross the river. The industrial estate begins to the left. Go straight ahead at several crossroads. Follow the Themelthorpe Loop as it swings through 180 degrees to the old railway station at Reepham

Station: Norwich Station (1 1/2 miles southeast of the start of the route) or North Walsham, which is on the Weavers' Way, enabling you to cycle one way from Norwich to North Walsham (30 miles) and catch the train back.

TIC: Norwich, 01603 66071.

Other nearby trails: In Aylsham you can link to the Weavers' Way, another dismantled railway that runs east to North Walsham. The Peddars Way lies 25 miles to the west and runs for 50 miles from near Thetford to the Norfolk Coast at Holme next the Sea.

Useful publications: OS Landranger Maps 133 & 134. Leaflet available from Department of Planning and Transportation, County Hall, Martineau Lane, Norwich NR1 2SG (01603 222230).

Refreshments: Lots of choice in Aylsham, Reepham and Norwich and just off the route in Drayton and Lenwade.

23

24

24   Weavers' Way from North Walsham to Aylsham

CATEGORY
Railway path.

DISTANCE
6 miles each way.

The Weavers' Way runs along the course of a dismantled railway from North Walsham west to Aylsham through attractive woodland and verges full of beautiful wildflowers in spring and summer. The Weavers' Way trail can easily be linked to the Marriott's Way to form one of the longest and most extensive railway path rides in the country. The trail is a stone and gravel path with a short rough section if you go beyond the end of the railway path into Aylsham. There is one major road (the A140) to cross if you go into Aylsham and a short section of the ride is on streets.

STARTING POINT & PARKING
→Small car park on Station Road, 1/2 mile to the west of the railway station, on the west side of North Walsham (grid reference 274300). North Walsham lies on the A149 about 15 miles north of Norwich.

ON YOUR BIKES!
1. From the car park on Station Road, North Walsham, follow the Weavers' Way for 4 miles. At the end of the dismantled railway track, with a house ahead, you may wish to turn around OR.....
2. *(To visit Aylsham)* ... turn right then take the first track to the left signposted 'No through road'. This section may be rough.
3. At the T-junction with the busy A140 go straight ahead **(TAKE CARE)** onto a track. At the crossroads with tarmac turn left.
4. At the T-junction at the end of Banningham Road turn right and follow into the centre of Aylsham.

Station: North Walsham.
TIC: Aylsham, 01263 733903.
Other nearby trails: The Marriott's Way starts at Aylsham and heads west to Reepham before swinging southeast to Norwich.
Useful publications: OS Landranger Map 133. Leaflet available from the Planning and Transportation Department, Norfolk County Council, County Hall, Martineau Lane, Norwich NR1 2SG (01603 222230).
Refreshments: Lots of choice in North Walsham and Aylsham.

East Midlands

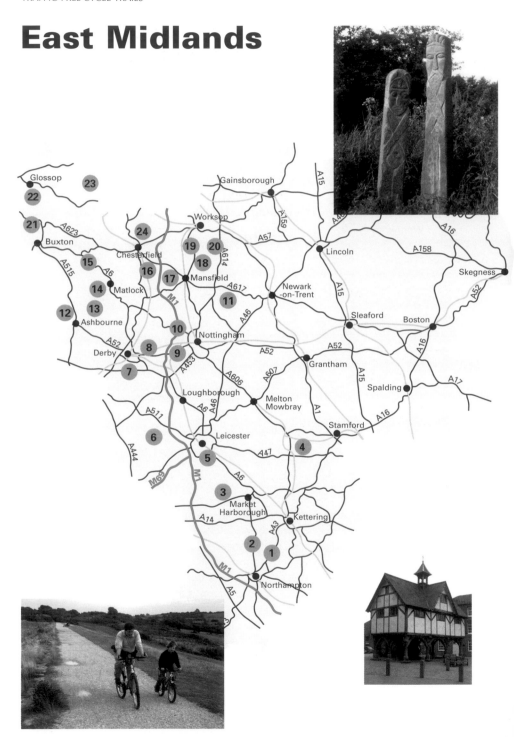

East Midlands Mountain Biking

Mountain biking in the East Midlands is fairly limited to the bridleways and byways in Derbyshire, many of which are fairly challenging as they lie within the hilly and dramatic Peak District.

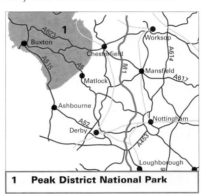

1   Peak District National Park

Most of the best tracks (and many of the more popular railway trails) are located in a 10-mile radius around Bakewell. There are several guides which cover these trails, available from good bookshops and the larger Tourist Information Centres. A few bridleway and byway sections of the Viking Way through Lincolnshire and longer sections of the Midshires Way through Leicestershire can be ridden legally.

There is no substitute for intimate local knowledge - try to explore every bridle-way, byway, unclassified road, canal towpath and Forestry Commission track near to home, sift out the good from the bad and link together the best offroad sections to form your own customised

East Midlands Forestry

The Midlands are the least forested area of Great Britain. With the exception of Sherwood Forest and the woodlands to the east of Mansfield there is very little woodland at all in the region.

In some forests and woods there are no waymarked routes but you are free to explore the tracks. The relevant Ordnance Survey map is mentioned. It is highly recommended that you take a map for the larger woods where it is very easy to get lost!

route(s). Use the months from late spring to early autumn to do the exploration, if possible after a spell of dry weather. The same track in winter can take twice as long or even be impassable.

Note down on the map (or colour code with highlighter pen) the quality of the trail and whether it is better done in one direction or the other - it is normally better to climb on tarmac and descend offroad so that gravity can help you through any muddy bits.

Bear in mind that everyone has a different view of what constitutes a good trail: hard or technical for some is easy for others and a bit of mud for some is a quagmire for others!

1   **Harry's Park Wood and Souther Wood, east of Kettering**
    OS Explorer Map 224

2   **Fineshade Wood and Wakerley Great Wood, southwest of Stamford**
    OS Explorer Map 234

3   **Twyford Wood and Morkery Wood, south of Grantham**
    OS Explorer Map 247

4   **Temple Wood and Bourne Wood, north of Peterborough**
    OS Explorer Map 248

6   **Sherwood Forest woodlands, east of Mansfield, south of Worksop**
    OS Explorer Map 270

7   **Stapleford Wood, northeast of Newark-on-Trent**
    OS Explorer Map 271

8   **Ostler's Plantation, east of Woodhall Spa, east of Lincoln**
    OS Explorer Map 273

9   **Chamber's Farm Wood, east of**

Lincoln

OS Explorer Map 273

**10   Willingham Forest and
    Willingham Woods, east of
    Market Rasen**

OS Explorer Map 282

**11   Laughton Woods, southwest of
    Scunthorpe**

OS Explorer Map 280

Forests and woods with waymarked trails

*This is shown with a corresponding trail number
and page reference.*

**5   Clipstone Forest, east of
    Mansfield**

See Route 18, page 172

Further Information

**Sherwood & Lincolnshire Forest
District**
Edwinstowe, Mansfield,
Nottinghamshire. NG21 9JL
Tel: 01623 822447

Northants Forest District
Top Lodge, Fineshade, Corby, Northants.
NN17 3BB.
Tel: 01780 444394/5

The Forestry Commission's
website is a good source of information
with details of 1600 miles of waymarked
cycling trails throughout the UK. Search
by forest name or by the nearest town
or city and the search will tell you the
grade, length and waymarking details of
the trails.

www.forestry.gov.uk/recreation

East Midlands National Cycle Network

West Midlands Cycle Route

163 miles from Oxford to Derby via Birmingham. Highlights include the ancient city of Oxford, Blenheim Palace at Woodstock, North Oxfordshire villages, Stratford-upon-Avon, the Rea Valley Route into Central Birmingham, Lichfield Cathedral and the traffic-free routes through Derby.

Traffic-free sections over 3 miles:

- Stratford upon Avon Greenway from Stratford to Long Marston (NCN 5)
- Rea Valley Route - King's Norton to Cannon Hill Park (Birmingham) (NCN 5)
- Birmingham Canal between Birmingham and Wolverhampton (NCN 5)
- Etwall to Mickleover, near Derby (NCN 5)

South Midlands Cycle Route

148 miles from Oxford to Derby via Leicester. Highlights include the ancient city of Oxford, the largely traffic-free route from Winslow through Milton Keynes to Wolverton, the Brampton Valley Way railway path between Northampton and Market Harborough, the Grand Union Canal towpath, the traffic-free route through Leicester and the railway path from Worthington into Derby.

Traffic-free sections over 3 miles:

- Route through Milton Keynes (NCN 51)
- Brampton Valley Way from Northampton to Market Harborough (NCN 6)

- Market Harborough to Foxton along the Grand Union Canal (NCN 6)
- Route through Leicester to Birstall (NCN 6)
- Cloud Trail from Derby to Worthington (NCN 6)

Derby to York Cycle Route

154 miles from Derby to York via Nottingham, Sheffield and Doncaster. Highlights include Elvaston Castle Country Park (Derby), Bestwood Country Park (Nottingham), Newstead Abbey, the traffic-free route through Sherwood Forest and Clumber Park, Rother Valley Country Park, the Old Moor Wetland Centre and the historic city of York.

Traffic-free sections over 3 miles:

- Derby to Elvaston Country Park alongside the Derwent (NCN 6)
- Blidworth to Worksop through Sherwood Forest and Clumber Park (NCN 6)
- The Elsecar Greenway from Hoyland to the Old Moor Wetland Centre (NCN 62 & 67)
- Harlington to Bentley along the Trans Pennine Trail (NCN 62)
- Riccall to York (NCN 65)

Hull to Fakenham Cycle Route (northern part of Hull to Harwich Route)

206 miles from Hull to Fakenham via Market Rasen, Lincoln, Boston, Wisbech and King's Lynn. Highlights include the Lincolnshire Wolds, Lincoln Cathedral and Castle, Boston's St Botolph Church

- Mickleover to Etwall, near Derby (NCN 68)
- Tissington Trail from Ashbourne to Sparklow (NCN 68)
- Longdendale Trail from Hadfield to the Woodhead Tunnel (NCN 68)
- Dove Valley Trail from Dunford Bridge via Penistone to Grenoside near Sheffield (NCN 62)
- Sheffield to Rotherham (NCN 6)
- Rother Valley Country Park to Staveley (NCN 67)
- Clumber Park to Blidworth (NCN 6)
- Elvaston Country Park to Derby (NCN 6)

Other areas for lane cycling

There is a huge variety of terrain within this region from the very steep and challenging lanes of the **Peak District** in the west (the best network of lanes lies to the south of Buxton) to the **fens of Lincolnshire**, one of Britain's flattest counties, in the east. If neither of these extremes appeals then the gently rolling countryside of **Leicestershire** and **Northamptonshire** with its attractive stone villages may be the solution.

(the Boston Stump) and the fine buildings of King's Lynn.

Traffic-free sections over 3 miles:
- None

Pennine Cycleway: The Peak District

178 miles of cycle route including 81 miles of the Pennine Cycleway and a circular ride linking Derby, Buxton, Holmfirth, Sheffield, Sherwood Forest and Nottingham. Highlights of the Pennine Cycleway include the Peak District National Park, Ashbourne, the Tissington Trail, Buxton and the Longdendale Trail.

Traffic-free sections over 3 miles:
(includes several extra trails in addition to those actually on Route 68, the Pennine Cycleway):

Sustrans

Listed below are the Sustrans maps that cover the National Cycle Network within the region. Some of the maps may describe routes that continue on into adjacent regions: these maps are mentioned in both chapters. The maps are not only useful for people wishing to ride the the whole route over several days; they also show all the traffic-free sections which make good day rides. The maps cost £5.99 each and are available from Sustrans.

Sustrans Order Line:
Call **0845 113 0065** or visit their website at **www.sustrans.org.uk**

East Midlands Trails

1 Brixworth Country Park / Pitsford Reservoir, north of Northampton

CATEGORY
Lakeside path.

DISTANCE
8-mile circuit of the reservoir

The cycle trail around Pitsford Water is a model of its kind, keeping you close to the water for the whole circuit, on well-maintained paths, avoiding time spent on roads, which is so often the failing of circuits around reservoirs. The lake appears to be popular with swans, anglers and windsurfers and if the wind is blowing strongly you may well witness some pretty amazing acrobatics by top class windsurfers whizzing over the surface of the lake and turning on a sixpence! Anglian Water, in conjunction with Northamptonshire County Council, has been successful in gaining a grant from the Millennium Fund to provide 'Access for All' at Pitsford Water. Brixworth Country Park is being developed to include special gardens and ponds, tracks suitable for disabled access and a link to the Brampton Valley Way. It is intended that the project will provide an opportunity for everyone to experience the wonderful countryside around Pitsford Water.

STARTING POINT & PARKING
→ The Pitsford Water Visitor Centre at Brixworth Country Park, off the A508, about 6 miles north of Northampton (grid reference 754692).

ON YOUR BIKES!
1. From the visitor centre, head downhill towards the masts of the dinghies. At the main track around the reservoir turn left, keeping the water to your right.
2. After 2 1/2 miles, at the T-junction with the road, turn right, cross the causeway across the reservoir, climb gently then turn right through

gate and bear left through the car park (ie once through the gate do **not** turn immediately right on the earth track).

3. Stay on the gravel track all the way around the reservoir. Cross a second bridge. **Ignore** the first right into the sailing club. Take the next right then turn left to return to the visitor centre.

Station: Northampton or Kettering.
TIC: Northampton, 01604 622677.
Other nearby trails: The Brampton Valley Way between Northampton (Chapel Brampton) and Market Harborough. The Market Harborough Arm of the Grand Union Canal.
Useful publications: OS Landranger Maps 141 & 152. Much more useful is the map you can get from Pitsford Water Cycle Hire (01604 881777) near the visitor centre.
Refreshments: Cafe at the visitor centre.

2 The Brampton Valley Way from Northampton to Market Harborough

CATEGORY
Railway path.
DISTANCE
Up to 14 miles each way.

The Brampton Valley Way is the longest dismantled railway path in the region, connecting Market Harborough with the outskirts of Northampton and forming part of National Cycle Network Route 6, which when complete will run all the way from London to Keswick in the Lake District. The trail includes two tunnels where you will need lights. There are some old steam locomotives and rolling stock at Chapel Brampton. The railway line was closed in 1981 and was purchased by Northamptonshire County Council in 1987. It opened for recreational use as the Brampton Valley Way in 1993. It is named after the

tributary of the River Nene - the Brampton Arm - the valley of which it follows for much of its length.

STARTING POINTS & PARKING
➔ The Bell Inn, **Market Harborough**. From the traffic lights in the centre of Market Harborough follow the A508 Northampton Road for 1/2 mile. The Bell Inn is on your left. The cycle path starts at the back of the pub (grid reference 737867).

➔ From the centre of **Northampton** follow the A5199 towards Leicester for 4 miles. Once out beyond the city limits and into the country take the first right on to Brampton Lane signposted 'Boughton, Moulton, Boughton Cold Store' then immediately turn right again into the car park (grid reference 737653).

Station: Market Harborough.
TIC: Market Harborough, 01858 821270.
Other nearby trails: Rutland Water lies 15 miles to the northeast. Brixworth Country Park (Pitsford Water) is just north of Northampton. The Grand Union Canal to the north of Market Harborough.
Useful publications: OS Landranger Maps 141 & 152.
Refreshments: Lots of pubs just off the route (use an Ordnance Survey map to get to the villages).

3 Market Harborough Arm of Grand Union Canal

CATEGORY

Canal towpath.

DISTANCE

6 miles each way.

Britain has 2000 miles of canals but only a small fraction of the towpaths are suitable for recreational cycling - the majority are too narrow, too rough, too muddy, too overgrown or a combination of all four. The Market Harborough Arm of the Grand Union Canal, part of National Cycle Network Route 6, is a splendid exception and offers a fine 12-mile there-and-back ride with good views, refreshments at a pub known as Lock 61 and a chance to visit the museum at Foxton Locks. The winding course of the canal is explained by the desire of the canal builders to hug the contours and thus avoid the need to build any locks. As the height they followed is at about 300 ft there are some fine views out into the surrounding countryside. The banks are

crowded with wildflowers and hawthorn blossom in the late spring and early summer: cow parsley, campion, vetch and willowherb add shades of white, pink and purple. It is suggested you turn around at Debdale Wharf Bridge: at this point the towpath turns to grass and the going becomes a lot rougher.

The ten locks at Foxton opened in 1814. They raise the canal by 75 feet and take an average of 45 minutes to negotiate, using 25,000 gallons of water per passage. The locks linked together the Leicestershire & Northamptonshire Union Canal and the (Old) Grand Union Canal. Following a takeover by the Grand Junction Canal, a lift was opened in 1900 to compete against the railways for traffic. It was part of a scheme to widen the route from the Derbyshire coalfields to London. The locks were refurbished for night traffic in 1909 but in 1911 the lift was mothballed to save money and the machinery was sold for scrap in 1928.

STARTING POINT & PARKING

➜From the centre of Market Harborough follow signs for 'Melton Mowbray B6047' and 'St Lukes Hospital'. After passing a garage then the Police Headquarters turn left (**before** reaching the roundabout), immediately before the Union Inn Hotel signposted 'Union Wharf South' (grid reference 727879).

ON YOUR BIKES!

1. The canal towpath starts near the Union Inn Hotel on the B6047 Melton Mowbray road. From the hotel follow signs for 'Union Wharf South'.
2. Follow the canal towpath for 6 miles, passing through Foxton. It is suggested that you go as far as Debdale Wharf. After this the towpath becomes grassy and rougher.

Station: Market Harborough.
TIC: Market Harborough, 01858 821270.

Other nearby trails: The Brampton Valley Way runs between Market Harborough and Northampton.
Useful publications: OS Landranger Map 141.
Refreshments: Lots of choice in Market Harborough. Cafe and Bridge 61 pub at (surprise, surprise!) Bridge 61.

4   Rutland Water, east of Leicester

CATEGORY
Round-reservoir route.

DISTANCE
17 miles for the circuit plus 6 miles for the Hambleton Peninsula.

Britain's favourite reservoir route offering a superb day out around the largest man-made lake in Western Europe, covering an area of 3100 acres. The ride uses a good, all-year-round track with some tarmac sections and links Egleton (near Oakham), Manton, Edith Weston, Whitwell and Upper Hambleton. The visitor centres all have something of interest: there are tropical butterflies, exotic insects and fish at the Empingham Leisure Centre, the Normanton Church and Water Museum at Normanton Leisure Centre and the Drought Garden at Barnsdale Leisure Area. There are three short sections on public roads: the section along the lane which leads from the A606 near Oakham to Hambleton Peninsula is fairly quiet, likewise the lane to Egleton. There is a busier 1 mile section east of Manton.

STARTING POINTS & PARKING
➜Pay and display car parks at Normanton, Barnsdale, Whitwell and Empingham. Rutland Water lies between Oakham (A606 / A6003) and Stamford (A1).

Station: Oakham.
TIC: Oakham, 01572 724329.
Other nearby trails: The Brampton Valley Way between Market Harborough and Northampton lies 16 miles to the southwest.
Useful publications: OS Landranger Map 141. The cycle hire outlets also have maps.
Refreshments: Pubs in Edith Weston, Empingham, Whitwell, Hambleton and Manton.

5 Leicester Great Central Way and the Canal Network

CATEGORY
Railway path, riverside path, canal towpath.

DISTANCE
3 1/2 miles each way to Watermead Park.
7 1/2 miles each way to Blaby.

By combining a dismantled railway with a towpath and a riverside path it is possible to pass right the way through Leicester from Watermead Country Park in the north to Blaby in the south on traffic-free routes or designated cycle lanes.

STARTING POINT & PARKING
→ St Margaret's Pasture car park near the Sports Centre, just off St Margaret's Way, near Abbey Park in the centre of Leicester.

ON YOUR BIKES!
North from Leicester city centre to Watermead Park.

1. At the end of the St Margaret's Pasture car park, turn left between the black railings, with the sports centre on your left.
2. Go round 1 1/2 sides of the square formed by the sports ground, then turn right over the concrete river bridge and right again signposted 'Riverside Way / Birstall'. Remember this point for your return. You will follow blue-and-white markers for the majority of the way. At the T-junction with the road cross via a pelican crossing.
3. At a T-junction just after the Museum of Technology on your left, turn right and follow the river (do not cross the steel bridge). Remember this point for your return.
4. After passing between blue metal bollards you will come to the road at a large red-brick bridge. Turn right onto the parallel footbridge with metal railings and right again at the end of

the bridge to go under the road. Remember this point for your return.
5. Follow the track close to the river, taking special care under the bridges and dismounting if you feel at all unsafe.
6. After passing beneath the major road bridge over the river you have a wide choice of tracks in Watermead Park. For this ride it is suggested you follow the river as far as the lock, cross the river and continue to the White Horse pub. Retrace your steps.

South to Blaby.

1. From St Margaret's Pasture car park return to the main road, turn left down the steps on to the towpath then turn right under the bridge.
2. Shortly after passing North Bridge (there is a lock here), fork left then soon leave the canal towpath at the next red metal bridge bearing right to cross the bridge. Shortly turn left onto

Forest Way.

3. Cross at the traffic lights at the end of Richard III Road onto the pavement on the left-hand side of the road ahead. Follow the pavement for 50 yds then use the metal ramp to climb up onto the Great Central Way.

4. Follow the track for 3 miles until the end of the tarmac then turn right by a metal gate and a wooden post signpposted 'Blue Bank Lock'.

5. Take the track to the canal towpath and follow this for 3 miles as far as Bridge 92 at Crow Mill, by the totem pole. Retrace your steps

Station: Leicester.

TIC: Leicester, 0116 299 8888.

Other nearby trails: Rutland Water is 20 miles to the east. The Brampton Valley Way (Market Harborough to Northampton) is 16 miles southeast.

Useful publications: OS Landranger Map 140. A very useful booklet for the area, *Cyclists' Leicester: Leicester Spokes Street by Street Guide to Environment City* (£2.95) is available from Leicester Spokes, PO Box 30, Leicester LE1 7GD.

Refreshments: Gazebo Cafe in the Abbey Grounds. White Horse pub, Birstall. The County Arms pub, Blaby.

6 Ashby Woulds Moira Heritage Trail, Northwest of Leicester

CATEGORY

Railway path.

DISTANCE

3 1/2 miles each way.

The signboards along this short railway path ride to the northeast of Measham offer a clear explanation not only of the area's industrial history but also of the huge efforts needed to restore nature's balance after more than 150 years of dumping mining and industrial waste without thinking through the long-term environmental consequences. As a result of these huge efforts, lakes, grassland and woodland has been created where before there were stagnant hazardous pools and a moonscape of spoils. Within a generation the area will be covered by mature trees and a visitor would never know what was previously there! In addition to the 7-mile there-and-back ride along the railway path there are three different circuits of between 1 and 2 miles in what is now called Donisthorpe Woodland.

STARTING POINT & PARKING

→ The library car park in the centre of **Measham**, just off the M42 / A42 to the northeast of Junction 11, about 9 miles southeast of Burton upon Trent (grid reference 332120).

ON YOUR BIKES!

1. From the car park by the library in the centre of Measham follow the 'Ashby Would Heritage Trail' signposts.

2. After 3/4 mile turn left to join the pavement alongside the road that passes beneath the A42, then shortly, at the next Heritage Trail signpost, turn right to rejoin the railway path.

3. Follow the blue arrows through Donisthorpe Woodland (the other coloured waymarks refer to circular rides within the park).

4. The trail ends at the Navigation Inn on the B5004 (northeast of Overseal).

Station: Burton upon Trent.

TIC: Ashby-de-la-Zouch, 01530 411767.

Other nearby trails: The Derby to Worthington Path lies 9 miles to the northeast. There are also rides in the newly created Donisthorpe Woodland Park:

Green route

Woodland Park Circular - 1.5 miles.

Purple route

Hill Street Circular - 1.1 miles.

Orange route

Moira Road Circular - 1 mile.

Useful publications: OS Landranger Map 128.

Refreshments: Lots of choice in Measham. The Navigation Inn on the B5004 at the northern end of the trail.

7   Derby to Worthington on the Cloud Trail

CATEGORY

Railway path.

DISTANCE

Up to 13 miles each way.

This route out of Derby was one of the first built by Sustrans, the Bristol-based engineering charity who were awarded £43 million in 1995 by the National Lottery to build Britain's National Cycle Network. The route has many of the best features of a Sustrans project - it starts from the very heart of the city, uses an attractive riverside path, canal towpath and a disused railway on its way from the urban centre into the heart of the countryside. Schools and colleges benefit from safe cycling routes for schoolchildren and students whilst recreational cyclists and those with young children living in Derby near the route do not have to worry about driving to the start of a cycle route as it is right there on their doorstep! As the route moves out into the countryside you will come across some beautifully painted Millennium Mileposts

and some very fine stone sculptures. This ride follows the same course as the Derby to Elvaston Castle Country Park route at the start before turning south away from the River Derwent and using a mixture of cycle tracks, a canal towpath and a dismantled railway to reach the village of Worthington which has a curious red-brick octagonal lock-up and a pub.

STARTING POINTS & PARKING

➡️ Riverside Gardens in the centre of Derby (near the bus station and the Eagle Centre Market).

➡️ If coming from outside Derby it is best to start (and park) at the south end of the trail in **Worthington**, a village about 7 miles west of Loughborough. The nearest motorway junction is M1 Jct 23. From the crossroads in Worthington by St Matthew's Church follow Breedon Lane downhill, signposted 'Cloud Trail' then shortly turn first right and follow this to the car park (grid reference 406210).

ON YOUR BIKES!

1. The ride starts in the Riverside Gardens in the centre of Derby (near the bus station and the council offices). Follow signs for the 'Riverside Path' and stay close to the river for 2 miles.
2. Go past Pride Park, the stadium for Derby County Football Club, pass beneath a low black bridge (with attached pipe!) then take the **second** of two closely spaced paths to the right.
3. Go past a lake then take the next right past the college buildings. Keep bearing left to pass beneath a bridge. After 1 mile, cross three roads in quick succession, the first and the third using toucan crossings.
4. After a further mile, near the end of the built-up area, at a crossroads with a minor lane go straight ahead signposted 'Swarkestone Lock'. ('Sinfin' is signposted to the right).
5. Pass beneath the A50, cross a bridge over the canal then turn left onto the towpath signposted 'Melbourne'.

6. After 2 miles, just before the large bridge over the river bear right and join the railway path.
7. After 4 miles the path veers right and runs parallel with the A42. Cross the bridge over the dual carriageway then bear left to rejoin the railway path.
8. After 1 1/2 miles the trail ends. If you wish to visit Worthington with its attractive church, octagonal lock-up and pub, turn left onto the minor lane then at the crossroads at the end of Breedon Lane turn left onto Church Street signposted 'Griffydam, Osgathorpe'. Follow this road through the village for 3/4 mile past the octagonal red-brick lock-up to the Malt Shovel pub.

Station: Derby.
TIC: Derby, 01332 255802.
Other nearby trails: Derby to Elvaston Castle Country Park.
Useful publications: OS Landranger Maps 128 & 129. An excellent leaflet, *Recreational Routes in and around Derby* is available from Derby City Council, Planning and Technical Services Dept, Roman House, Friar Gate, Derby DE1 1XB (01332 255021).
Refreshments: Lots of choice in Derby; Swarkestone Tearooms, at the Lock House at the start of the canal section; lots of choice in Melbourne (1 mile off the route); the Malt Shovel pub, Worthington, 3/4 mile on quiet roads beyond the end of the trail.

8   Derby to Elvaston Castle Country Park

CATEGORY

Riverside path.

DISTANCE

4 1/2 miles each way. The circuit of Elvaston Country Park adds another 2 miles.

A fine escape from the heart of Derby via a top quality track alongside the River Derwent to Elvaston Castle Country Park where there is the option of a circuit around the park. Elvaston Castle is an imposing stone and brick-built house dating from the early 19th century. It is situated in 200 acres of beautiful wood and parkland containing many rare trees planted over 150 years ago. There is an adventure playground, an ornamental garden, a topiary and a an Old English garden with herbaceous borders and a rose garden. The gardens are free and open all year round.

STARTING POINTS & PARKING:

→Riverside Gardens in the **centre of Derby** (near the bus station and the Eagle Centre Market).

→If arriving by car it would be better to start at **Elvaston Castle Country Park** (grid reference 413328). Turn off the A6005 Derby to Long Eaton road in Borrowash onto the B5010 towards Elvaston. The entrance to the park is 1 1/2 miles along on the right. (The B5010 can also be approached from the A6 Derby to Loughborough Road). From the castle head north to join the riverside path.

ON YOUR BIKES!

1. From the corner of Bass's Recreation Ground / Riverside Gardens in the centre of Derby, follow the riverside path for 4 1/2 miles. Turn off from the riverside path at the weir, signposted 'Elvaston Castle' where the pylons cross to the other side of the river.

2. At a T-junction after 1/2 mile turn left. At the T-junction at the large fir tree, turn left to visit Elvaston Castle or turn right to complete a circuit of the park.

3. (Circuit) After passing the ornate gates and statues on your left turn left on to a track. At a T-junction with a tarmac lane turn right past a walled garden then take the first track to the left to complete the loop.

Station: Derby.

TIC: Derby, 01332 255802.

Other nearby trails: The trail links with the Derby to Worthington Trail. The Nutbrook Trail runs from Long Eaton to Shipley Country Park.

Useful publications: OS Landranger Maps 128 & 129. An excellent leaflet, *Recreational Routes in and around Derby* is available from Derby City Council, Planning and Technical Services Dept, Roman House, Friar Gate, Derby DE1 1XB (01332 255021).

Refreshments: Tea rooms at Elvaston Castle.

9 Nutbrook Trail from Shipley Country Park to Long Eaton

CATEGORY
Railway path, canal towpath and specially-built cycle path.

DISTANCE
8 miles each way.

Shipley Country Park has many fine tracks within its 600 acres of landscaped parkland - should you not feel up to a 16-mile there-and-back ride to Long Eaton there are plenty of shorter options within the park itself. There are also the temptations of the American Theme Park which is situated right next door. Once you have negotiated your way up and down the hill and past the Theme Park you find yourself on a railway path that runs along the course of the old Stanton Branch Line for 5 miles down to the Erewash Canal, linking Eastwood with the River Trent at Trentlock, south of Long Eaton. You pass many fine red-brick buildings along the banks of the canal before the trail drops you somewhat abruptly in the middle of Long Eaton.

Shipley was developed in the 18th century as a country estate and coal mining area by the influential Miller-Mundy family. Following the demise of the old coal mines and opencast quarries, former railways have been transformed into leafy pathways, old reservoirs are now tranquil lakes teeming with wildlife and reclaimed spoil heaps are now large woodlands, rolling hills and wildflower meadows. The park was opened in 1976.

STARTING POINTS & PARKING
→Midland Street, **Long Eaton** (near the junction of the A6005 and the B6540, southwest of Nottingham). Parking near to the Town Hall and Asda superstore. Follow signs for 'Sandiacre Cycle Route' (grid reference 492338).

→**Shipley Country Park** (Heanor), off the A608 / A6007 to the west of Nottingham (grid reference 431452).

ON YOUR BIKES!
1. From the information board in the car park in Shipley Country Park take the gravel track signposted 'Public bridleway, Osborne Pond'. At a crossroads of tracks go straight ahead to join the railway path through the wood.
2. The track turns to tarmac. At the crossroads with lane (with Coppice House Business Centre to your right) turn right and go downhill. Continue in the same direction, staying on the tarmac path, at one point jinking left then right. Climb then descend alongside the Theme Park.
3. At the T-junction at the end of the Theme Park turn right then shortly take the first tarmac track to the left opposite a red-brick house. Follow the tarmac path for 5 miles.
4. At the canal turn right (remember this point for the return route).

5. **Easy to miss!** After 3 miles, just after passing the back of Andy Supermarket to your right, by a lock and a hump-back red-brick bridge, turn left by a 'Nutbrook Trail' signpost onto a path running parallel with towpath.

6. Follow the trail past a tall red-brick chimney as it swings left, passing through a barrier then turning right onto a tarmac path. The trail ends near Asda and the Town Hall in the centre of Long Eaton.

Station: Long Eaton.
TIC: Nottingham, 0115 915 5330.
Other nearby trails: There are more trails in Shipley Country Park.
Useful publications: OS Landranger Map 129. Leaflet available from Erewash Borough Council (0115 944 0440).
Refreshments: Long Eaton, Sandiacre, Kirk Hallam, Shipley Country Park.

10 Shipley Country Park, west of Nottingham

CATEGORY
Estate roads and tracks.
DISTANCE
This 7-mile ride is just one of many that could be devised.

A country park near to Nottingham with several miles of quiet estate roads and good quality tracks around lakes and through woodland. Buy a map from the visitor centre and explore the park at your leisure. The routes in the park can easily be linked to the Nutbrook Trail to Long Eaton. Mentioned in the Domesday Book, Shipley was developed during the 18th century as a farming and coal mining area by the influential Miller-Mundy family. Fine lodges and cottages dating from this period can still be seen around the park. Following restoration of the old coal mine sites, former railway lines have

11

become walkways and cyclepaths and reclaimed colliery spoils are now woodlands and wildflower meadows.

STARTING POINT & PARKING
→The visitor centre at the entrance to **Shipley Park**, 1 mile south of Heanor (A6007) and west of M1 Jct 26 (grid reference 431452).

ON YOUR BIKES!
1. From the car park near the visitor centre follow signs for 'Osborne's Pond' (marked with blue horseshoes). Follow the raised track through woodland, passing a pond then running

parallel with a small lane.

2. At the end of the metal railings on your right, turn right down a track by the Lakeside Business Centre. Descend then climb.

3. At the top of a steep hill turn sharp left past Nottingham Lodge signposted 'Shipley Wood'.

4. At the bottom of the hill cross the bridge over the lake and turn immediately right onto a tarmac lane. At the farm turn left onto a broad red gravel track.

5. Follow signs for Mapperley then (easily missed) take the first right signposted 'Mapperley Reservoir'.

6. Cross the tarmac lane near to the car parking area on to the track opposite, starting at a wide wooden gate (waymarked with blue horseshoes).

Station: Heanor.

TIC: Nottingham, 0115 915 5330.

Other nearby trails: The Nutbrook Trail goes south to Long Eaton. There are two trails starting from Derby, 6 miles to the southwest.

Useful publications: OS Landranger Map 129. A better map is available at the visitor centre.

Refreshments: Cafe at the visitor centre.

11   Southwell Trail, east of Mansfield

CATEGORY
Railway path.

DISTANCE
8 miles each way.

You are in Robin Hood Country here with Sherwood Forest just a few miles to the west. It would seem to stretch belief that Robin Hood had much to do with the course of the dismantled railway used in this ride but nevertheless the map shows the Robin Hood Way following the railway path between Southwell and Farnsfield. Although the ride starts from the northern edge of Southwell it is well worth exploring the centre of this grand cathedral town with its magnificent minster. The ride itself is a very pleasant outing through wooded cuttings and rich arable country glimpsed between the hedgerows. Bilsthorpe lies on the eastern edges of what was the great Nottinghamshire coal mining area, almost all of which has disappeared in the last 25 years.

The lovely cream-coloured Southwell Minster with its slender towers and spires dates from 1108. There is a magnificent stone carving called 'The Leaves of Southwell' in the Chapter House. Charles I gave himself up to the Scots Commissioners in the 17th-century Saracens Head in 1646.

STARTING POINTS &PARKING

→**Southwell**. The car park next to the Newcastle Arms pub, Southwell. From the mini-roundabout by the Saracens Head pub in the centre of Southwell, leave the A612 and follow Queen Street. At the crossroads go straight ahead onto Station Road. Immediately after the Newcastle Arms pub turn left into the car park (grid reference 707545).

→**Bilsthorpe**. The end of Forest Walk (a new housing estate), signposted 'Picnic Site' at the southern end of Bilsthorpe. Proceeding south from Bilsthorpe along the Kirklington Road, turn off the roundabout onto Forest Walk, opposite the turning to the landfill site (grid reference 650603).

Station: Fiskerton, east of Southwell.

TIC: Newark, 01636 678962.

Other nearby trails: There is a waymarked forest trail in Clipstone Forest.

Useful publications: OS Landranger Map 120.

Refreshments: The Newcastle Arms pub at the start of the trail in Southwell.

Lots of choice in Southwell itself.

12 Tissington Trail, Peak District

CATEGORY
Railway path.
DISTANCE
13 miles each way.

Together with the High Peak Trail, this is one of the most famous railway paths in the Peak District if not in the whole country. Passing through the dramatic limestone scenery of the Derbyshire Dales it climbs gently from Ashbourne up to Parsley Hay setting you up for a fantastic descent. If you ever need to persuade a non-cyclist of the joys of cycling, drop them at the top and pick them up at the bottom!

NB There is a steady drop of almost 700 ft from Parsley Hay to Ashbourne. For this reason it is worth starting at Ashbourne when you are fresh, riding uphill to Parsley Hay, leaving you with a downhill on the way back.

STARTING POINTS & PARKING:
→Mapleton Lane in **Ashbourne** (grid reference 177469).
→On the minor road east of **Thorpe** (grid reference 166503).
→On the A515 near **Alsop** (grid reference 157549).
→Car parks on the B5054 east of **Hartington** (grid reference 151611).
→There is a large pay and display car park and cycle hire centre at **Parsley Hay** (grid reference 147637).

Station: Matlock, Buxton or Uttoxeter.
TIC: Ashbourne, 01335 343666.
Other nearby trails: High Peak Trail, Carsington Water, the Monsal, Manifold and Churnett Valley Trails are all nearby.
Useful publications: OS Landranger Map 119. Peak Cycle Hire leaflet available from:

Information Group, Peak National Park Office, Aldern House, Baslow Road, Bakewell, Derbyshire DE4 1AE (01629 816200).
Refreshments: Plenty of choice in Ashbourne; soft drinks and sweets at the cycle hire / visitor centres; the Dog & Partridge pub in Thorpe and the Waterloo Inn in Biggin are just off the route; coffees and teas at Basset Wood Farm, Tissington.

13 Carsington Water, northeast of Ashbourne

CATEGORY
Round-reservoir route.

DISTANCE
8-mile circuit.

One of the country's most recently built reservoirs (1992), Carsington Water has quickly established itself as a major focus for recreational cycling, offering a circuit around the lake which is demanding enough to give young children a real sense of achievement when they complete the ride. There are two crossings of the B5035 and about 1 mile is spent on a minor road, but as the latter runs parallel with the main road, very few vehicles have any reason to use it. This lane detour to the lovely stone-built village of Hopton enables you to enjoy a stopping point at the pub about three-quarters of the way around the circuit. **NB** Take care on the two crossings of the B5035. There are several short, steep hills on the far side of the lake from the visitor centre.

STARTING POINT & PARKING
→Pay & Display car park at the **Carsington Water Visitor Centre**, 5 miles northeast of Ashbourne. Turn off the B5035 Wirksworth - Ashbourne road at the Knockerdown pub (grid reference 241517).

ON YOUR BIKES!

1. With your back to the visitor centre entrance turn left then at the corner of the building continue straight ahead on the broad gravel track.

2. Follow this obvious track with the water to your left, crossing the dam wall, following the frequent signposts.

3. The route becomes hillier! At the main road (B5035) **TAKE CARE** crossing onto the minor lane opposite. Follow the waymarks through the village of Hopton, past the Miners Arms pub.

4. At the second crossing of the B5035 **TAKE CARE** as you go straight ahead towards the car park then bear right at the fork and follow this track for 2 miles back to the start.

Station: Belper or Cromford.
TIC: Ashbourne, 01335 343666.
Other nearby trails: The High Peak Trail, Tissington Trail and Manifold Trail are close by.
Useful publications: OS Landranger Map 119. Better is the free map available from the visitor centre (01629 540696).
Refreshments: Cafe at the visitor centre. Miners Arms pub in Hopton on the far side of the lake. Pub in Carsington village.

14 High Peak Trail, west of Matlock

CATEGORY
Railway path.
DISTANCE
Up to 17 1/2 miles each way. The flattest section runs for 12 miles between Middleton Top, Parsley Hay and Sparklow.

One of the best known and most popular routes in the country, this ride offers a superb challenge in the heart of the Peak District from High Peak Junction (south of Matlock) via Middleton Top and Parsley Hay to Sparklow.

The trail runs through the limestone scenery of the White Peak and links with the Tissington Trail in the north at Parsley Hay, 10 miles southeast of Buxton. If you start at the northern end of the trail, remember it is all downhill on the outward leg, with a particularly steep section near to High Peak Junction (800 ft descent in little over 2 miles down to the A6) so you will need good brakes on the way down and strong legs on the way up.

The 33-mile Cromford & High Peak Railway was one of the earliest railways in the country, built between 1825-30. In the early days, horses were used to haul wagons along the rails.

STARTING POINTS & PARKING
→There is a large pay and display car park and cycle hire centre at **Parsley Hay**, just off the A515 about 10 miles southeast of Buxton (grid reference 147637).
→Car park at **Friden**, near the junction of the A515 and A5012 (grid reference 172607).
→**Middleton Top Visitor Centre**, southwest of Matlock on the B5035 towards Ashbourne (grid reference 276552).
→**High Peak Junction**, on the A6 south of Matlock (grid reference 315561).

Station: Matlock, Buxton or Uttoxeter.
TIC: Buxton, 01298 25106; Matlock, 01629 55082.
Other nearby trails: Tissington Trail, Carsington Water, the Monsal, Manifold and Churnett Valley Trails are all nearby.
Useful publications: OS Landranger Map 119. Peak Cycle Hire leaflet available from: Information Group, Peak National Park Office, Aldern House, Baslow Road, Bakewell, Derbyshire DE4 1AE (01629 816200).
Refreshments: Soft drinks and sweets at the cycle hire / visitor centres; Royal Oak pub at Hurdlow (north of Parsley Hay). Rising Sun pub just off the route in Middleton.

15 Monsal Trail, Bakewell, Peak District

CATEGORY
Railway path.

DISTANCE
5 miles each way.

Although the Monsal Trail runs for 9 miles from Bakewell towards Buxton, only a 4-mile section, from Bakewell northwest as far as Little Longstone, is open to cyclists. It is nevertheless well worth riding this fine trail through beautiful countryside in the southern Peak District. The ride starts with a short section on a no through road with almost no traffic. You will need to use quiet lanes to get to the pubs at Little Longstone and Great Longstone.

In 1863 the railway link between Rowsley (north of Matlock) and Manchester was completed and the Midland Railway achieved its own London to Manchester mainline route. Coal was unloaded at Bakewell Station and delivered to remote areas, while milk churns from surrounding farms were sent to London. Closure of the Peak section occurred in 1968. After 12 years of negotiation the Peak National Park finally persuaded the rail authorities to allow them to turn it into a recreational trail.

STARTING POINT & PARKING
→From the centre of **Bakewell** take the A619 towards Chesterfield. Immediately after crossing the bridge over the River Wye, turn first right onto Station Road, then right again onto Coombs Road - the car park is second on right (grid reference 224686). To get to the railway path, turn right out of the car park for 3/4 mile along this minor, no through road then turn left steeply uphill just before the railway bridge.
Station: Buxton.
TIC: Bakewell, 01629 813227.
Other nearby trails: The High Peak and Tissington Trails can both be accessed 6 miles

west of Bakewell at Parsley Hay.
Useful publications: OS Landranger Map 119. Leaflet available from: Information Group, Peak National Park Office, Aldern House, Baslow Road, Bakewell, Derbyshire DE4 1AE (01629 816200).
Refreshments: Lots of choice in Bakewell. The Crispin pub, Great Longstone and the Pack Horse Inn, Little Longstone.

16

16   Five Pits Trail, southeast of Chesterfield

CATEGORY
Railway path.
DISTANCE
6-mile circuit plus 7-mile round trip to Tibshelf Ponds ie 13 miles total.

The trail follows the course of the railway that used to serve the collieries, between Grassmoor and Tibshelf Ponds, passing through rolling countryside with fine views. There are a couple of hills which may come as a surprise to anyone expecting railway paths to be flat! One is near the start and the other near to Tibshelf.

The railways were opened in 1892 to serve the coalfield and operated initially by the Midland Railway Company's mineral line and later by the Great Central Railway Company. The railway served the five pits of Tibshelf, Pilsley,

Holmewood, Williamthorpe and Grassmoor. By 1971 the collieries had closed, causing the closure of the railway. Pilsley coal received royal patronage when Queen Mary chose to burn nothing but 'Pilsley Brights' on her drawing room fire at Buckingham Palace.

STARTING POINT & PARKING
→The Birkin Lane car park between **Temple Normanton** and **Grassmoor**, southeast of Chesterfield. Take the A617 Mansfield Road out of Chesterfield for 4 miles. Turn off south onto the B6245, then take the B6039, following signs for 'Temple Normanton' and 'Holmewood'. Turn second right. The car park is 3/4 mile along this road on your right (grid reference 413673).

ON YOUR BIKES!
1. Follow 'Five Pits Trail' signs from the car park under the bridge and continue up a steady climb. At the fork of tracks, bear left past the pond signposted 'Williamthorpe' (the right fork goes directly to Tibshelf).
2. Go past the old brick colliery. Descend to cross the bridge over the stream. At a crossroads of tracks at the top of the rise go straight ahead (Grassmoor Wheelchair Route is to the right).
3. Soon after a sweet distribution centre cross the road and continue up a ramp. Follow this road for 100 yds then cross the busy A6175, following 'Five Pits Trail' signs.
4. Cross the B6039. After a mile, turn right on the lane by Timberlane picnic site for 50 yds then turn left.
5. Follow the route through to Tibshelf, dropping down into then climbing up out of the valley formed by Westwood Brook. At the brow of the hill by the church in Tibshelf, fork left under the bridge to go under the road. The route ends at Tibshelf Ponds.
6. Retrace your steps, taking the left fork shortly after Timberland picnic site, signposted 'Grassmoor'.

Station: Alfreton, south of the route.

TIC: Chesterfield, 01246 345777.

Other nearby trails: The Pleasley Trails lie just to the east. The Staveley to Beighton Trail lies 6 miles to the north. Chesterfield Canal starts in the centre of Chesterfield. Clumber Park has several trails. Clipstone Forest. Rother Valley Country Park.

Useful publications: OS Landranger Map 120.

Refreshments: Available at The Wheatsheaf pub, Tibshelf.

17 Pleasley Trails, northwest of Mansfield

CATEGORY
Railway paths.

DISTANCE
7-mile circuit.

The Pleasley Trails are three separate railway paths lying between Pleasley, Skegby and Teversal. They are linked together to form a circular route. Deep cuttings show the exposed limestone rock of the area. The Pleasley Trails network runs along the track beds of the Great Northern Railway and the Midland Railway. The sections explored in this ride were built between 1866 and 1900. The last train ran in 1982.

STARTING POINTS & PARKING
→ The Meden Trail car park on Outgang Lane, off the A617 / B6407 roundabout in **Pleasley**. Follow the B6407 signposted 'Shirebrook' then after 200 yds turn first right to Pleasley Vale & Church. The Meden Trail car park is on the right after 3/4 mile (grid reference 510649).

→ The Teversal Trail car park in **Skegby**, on Buttery Lane, just off the B6014 Mansfield to Tibshelf Road, signposted 'Manor Estate' (grid reference 495614).

ON YOUR BIKES!
1. Go down from the car park to the stream and turn right, following the stream. Shortly after a red-brick pumping station, turn right on to the underpass beneath the road.

2. Turn right on the road by the post office and climb the hill. Take care on this section as there may be some traffic.

3. Just before the roundabout turn left onto Pit Road opposite the Pleasley Surgery. After 150 yds turn left through a wooden barrier to get to the start of the trail.

4. Follow the trail for 2 1/2 miles to the car park at Skegby. Retrace your steps for 300 yds then at the fork of tracks, bear left.

6. After 1 mile, at a crossroads of tracks, continue straight ahead uphill on to a narrower track. Descend to the road, turn right for 200 yds, go under the bridge then immediately right up the steps and right along the old railway.

7. At a T-junction by a wooden barrier and metal gate turn right for 100 yds then left to

rejoin the outward route.

Station: Alfreton, to the southwest.
TIC: Chesterfield, 01246 345777.
Other nearby trails: The Five Pits Trail lies 5 miles to the west. Clipstone Forest lies 7 miles to the east.
Useful publications: OS Landranger Map 120.
Refreshments: Carnarvon Arms, Fackley, just off the route, near Teversal.

18 Clipstone Forest, northeast of Mansfield

CATEGORY
Forest trail.
DISTANCE
6-mile circuit.

This is a well-signposted trail through this large tract of forestry land. Tracks are wide and well-maintained so this is a good ride for group cycling. There is also a much tougher mountain bike trail if you want a harder challenge. Clipstone Forest forms part of the largest single tract of woodlands in the East Midlands. Most of the forest was planted in the 1920s and 1930s. Much of the timber here has supplied local businesses particularly as pit wood for the mining industry. In some parts of the forest the heathland vegetation, once so common in Sherwood, still exists. These areas are now being kept as heathland as part of the conservation plan. There is a Robin Hood exhibition at the visitor centre.

STARTING POINT & PARKING
➔ **Sherwood Pines** car park, off the B6030, about 5 miles northeast of Mansfield (grid reference 611638).

ON YOUR BIKES!
Make your way from the car park towards the

information centre and you will come across the red markers that indicate the course of the trail. The ride is very well waymarked.

Station: Fiskerton, southeast of Southwell.
TIC: Ollerton, 01623 824545.
Other nearby trails: The Southwell Trail and Clumber Park.
Useful publications: OS Landranger Map 120. Forest Enterprise also produce a leaflet which is available at the visitor centre.
Refreshments: Cafe at the visitor centre.

19 Clumber Park to Cresswell Crags

CATEGORY
Forest tracks and bridleways.
DISTANCE
6 1/2 miles each way.

Cresswell Crags are believed to be the most northerly point in Britain where humans and animals lived during the last Ice Age and there have been many archaeological discoveries backing up the theory. It is well worth leaving yourself time to explore the area on foot once you have cycled over from Clumber Park. There are a mixture of roads, good tracks through woodland and rougher or sandier tracks, including one leading down through an atmospheric rock cutting to cross the great estates from Clumber Park through Welbeck Park to Cresswell Crags. Best to use mountain bikes. The ride is not suitable for very young children.

NB. EXTREME CARE should be taken crossing both the B6034 and the A60, particularly on the return trip. Allow yourself time to gauge the speed of the traffic before crossing.

STARTING POINT & PARKING
➔ **Clumber Park**, south of Worksop. The route

19

starts from the Cycle Hire Centre in the middle of the park. Cars are charged to enter the park.

ON YOUR BIKES!

1. From the bike hire centre turn left then follow this road to the right. Follow Clumber Lane (some estate traffic) in the same direction for 2 miles*

There are several other options to get from the bike hire centre to Truman's Lodge on forest tracks. Buy a map of the park and work out your preferred route (for example, if you follow the waymarked Red Bike Route clockwise you will get there).

2. About 300 yds after passing through Truman's Lodge bear left onto a track by a wooden barrier signposted 'Public Bridleway'. Shortly, **TAKE GREAT CARE** crossing the busy B6034 onto the bridleway opposite.

3. Continue in the same direction passing remote stone buildings. Descend through an atmospheric rock cutting. At the next house (South Lodge) turn left and go through a gate and across a field, following 'Public Bridleway'

signposts.

4. At the T-junction with tarmac turn right then shortly after passing a private road to the left take the next track left. At the next T-junction with a road turn right (remember this point for your return).

5. Go straight across at two crossroads with estate roads. **WITH GREAT CARE** cross the A60 and continue straight ahead for 3/4 mile to Cresswell Crags Visitor Centre. Retrace your steps, taking care at the two road crossings.

Station: Worksop.
TIC: Worksop, 01909 501148.
Other nearby trails: There are two waymarked trails in Clumber Park. A long traffic-free stretch of National Cycle Network 6 links Clumber Park to Blidworth, to the southeast of Mansfield. There is also a waymarked woodland circuit in Clipstone Forest. A railway path runs from Southwell to Bilsthorpe.
Useful publications: OS Landranger Map 120. This trail plus other trails near Derby, Worksop, Rother Valley Country Park, Sheffield, York and

20

parts of the Trans Pennine Trail are all shown on Sustrans *Derby to York* map (£5.99).
Sustrans Order Line: Call 0845 113 0065 or visit their website at www.sustrans.org.uk
Refreshments: Cafe at Clumber Park and at Cresswell Crags Visitor Centre

20 Clumber Park, southeast of Worksop

CATEGORY
Estate roads and paths.

DISTANCE
A variety of routes and distances are possible. This is a 5-mile circuit

Clumber Park is likely to become one of the most popular destinations for recreational family cycling in the country, ranking alongside Rutland Water and the Peak District railway trails. This is due to the superb infrastructure of bike hire with all sorts of bikes and trailers available, the excellent mix of quiet estate roads, broad gravel tracks through woodlands, waymarked circuits and beautiful settings with the famous old stone bridge and chapel. There is an excellent visitor centre and cafe and plenty of places to choose for a picnic or barbecue in the thousands of acres of parkland. It is also on the Sustrans National Route 6 which runs north from Derby to York and if you arrive by bike there is no entry fee to pay to get into the park!

This ride is a 5-mile circuit around the lake using gravel tracks and short sections on road. For a small charge it is a very good idea to buy the large colour map of Clumber Park showing all the tracks. There is a car park charge.

NB There is some light traffic on the estate roads. The park is busier in high season.

STARTING POINT & PARKING

➔Clumber Park lies southeast of Worksop (east of M1 Jct 30). There are five entrances to the park - off the A57 from the north, off the B6034 to the west and off the A614 to the east. The main car park is near the chapel, restaurant and shops.

ON YOUR BIKES!

1. From the main car park near to the chapel, go back towards the road. As the road swings right, and a road turns off to the left, turn left on to a parallel track (near to a large oak tree). Ignore the first left towards the buildings. After 200 yds, turn left onto a cobbled path leading towards the water's edge. At the lake turn right.
2. Stay on the main track bearing left past a small red-brick outbuilding. At the T-junction with the road turn left over the bridge then immediately left again. Follow the main track close to the water.
3. Cross the dam / weir and follow the track alongside the lake as it swings to the left.
4. Join tarmac, cross the bridge over the lake then take the first track to the left. After 150 yds, at a junction of tracks, turn right.
5. The track turns to tarmac. At the cricket ground turn left and follow this tarmac lane past the barrier back to the car park at the start.

Station: Worksop.

TIC: Worksop, 01909 501148.

Other nearby trails: Another route, a 13-mile circuit with red waymarks also explores Clumber Park. There is a waymarked trail in Clipstone Forest, 6 miles to the south. National Cycle Network Route 6 from Clumber to Blidworth is largely traffic-free.

Useful publications: OS Landranger Map 120. Much better is the map produced by the park which can be purchased from The Clocktower Shop, Clumber Park, Worksop, Notts S80 3BE (01909 474468). Also from the cycle hire centre (01909 476592).

Refreshments: Clumber Restaurant, in the park.

21 Sett Valley Trail, Hayfield, southeast of Manchester

CATEGORY

Railway path.

DISTANCE

3 miles each way.

A short section of railway path on the western edge of the Peak District with fine views east towards Kinder Scout. It is worth visiting the New Mills Heritage Centre and the Torrs Riverside Park in New Mills.

NB You will need to go on road if you wish to visit New Mills.

STARTING POINT & PARKING

➔Sett Valley Visitor Centre in **Hayfield**. Turn off the A624 Glossop to Chapel-en-le-Frith road on to the A6015 to New Mills then first right on to Station Road (grid reference 035869).

ON YOUR BIKES!

Follow the trail towards New Mills. The trail ends at St Georges Road where a sign indicates that there is no cycling beyond this point. If you wish to go further you will either need to dismount and push your bikes through Riverside Park to The Torrs waterfalls (this will involve some steps) or go by road into New Mills: turn right on St Georges Road, right again at the T-junction at the bottom, cross the river then turn left into New Mills.

Station: New Mills.

TIC: Glossop, 01457 855920.

Other nearby trails: The Middlewood Way lies west of New Mills The Longdendale Trail.

Useful publications: OS Landranger Map 110. A leaflet is available from Hayfield Information Centre (01663 746222).

Refreshments: Hot drinks at the visitor centre. Lots of choice in New Mills (this will involve a short road section).

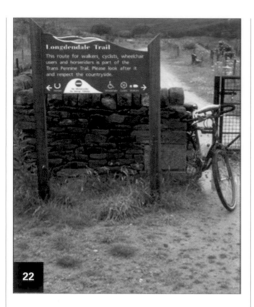

22 Longdendale Trail, east of Manchester

CATEGORY
Railway path.
DISTANCE
6 1/2 miles each way.

The route runs along the side of Longdendale following the course of the old railway from Hadfield to the Woodhead Tunnel (A628) past a string of reservoirs lying at the bottom of the valley. The scenery is spectacular, if a little spoiled by the line of pylons that runs parallel with the trail.

The railway through Longdendale provided the first railway link between Manchester and Sheffield. The first passenger train ran in 1845. The Woodhead Tunnel was one of the great achievements of the early years of the railway age. After 136 years of operation the line was finally closed in 1981. The five reservoirs of Bottoms, Valehouse, Rhodeswood, Torside and Woodhead were completed in 1877 and formed the largest artificial expanse of water in the world at the time.

NB There is a 330 ft climb from Padfield to the Woodhead Tunnel.

STARTING POINT & PARKING
→Trail car park in **Hadfield** (grid reference 024962). Turn off the A57 Manchester to Glossop road just south of Hollingworth at the roundabout by the Spread Eagle pub and Woolley Bridge pub onto Woolley Bridge Road. At the next roundabout by The Lamp pub turn right onto Station Road towards then through the centre of Hadfield. Just before the railway bridge over the road there is a car park to the left at the start of the trail.

Station: Padfield.
TIC: Glossop, 01457 855920.
Other nearby trails: The route is part of the Trans Pennine Trail that crosses the country: the next traffic-free section to the east, the Upper Don Trail runs from Dunford Bridge towards Penistone (see page 246). The Sett Valley Trail runs between New Mills and Hayfield (south of Glossop on the A624). There is a trail around the edge of the Upper Derwent Valley Reservoir.
Useful publications: OS Landranger Map 110. The three maps covering the whole of the Trans Pennine Trail are available from from Sustrans.
Sustrans Order Line: Call 0845 113 0065 or visit their website at www.sustrans.org.uk
Refreshments: Only in Hadfield.

23 Upper Derwent Valley Reservoirs, between Manchester and Sheffield

CATEGORY
Round-reservoir(s) route.
Distance
Anything from 5 miles - the circuit of the northern part of Ladybower - to 16 miles which

is the circuit of all three reservoirs.

A magnificent ride amid the beauty of woodland, lakes and moorland alongside the reservoirs in the Upper Derwent Valley. Various routes are possible from the Ladybower Reservoir and Fairholmes Visitor Centre - circuits of one, two or three of the reservoirs. The easiest ride is the there-and back ride along the west side of Derwent and Howden Reservoirs, starting from the visitor centre. The rides use a mixture of tarmac, fine stone tracks and slightly rougher tracks on the east side of Howden Reservoir. There are several small climbs.

NB The road up from the A57 to the visitor centre carries a reasonable amount of traffic at the height of the season, but the cars are probably carrying other cyclists to get to the start!

STARTING POINT & PARKING
→ Turn off the A57 Sheffield to Glossop road on the west side of the viaduct over **Ladybower Reservoir**. The visitor centre lies 2 1/2 miles up this road (grid reference 173894).

ON YOUR BIKES!
(A full circuit of all three lakes, starting with an anti-clockwise ride around the upper two lakes. Only appropriate for mountain bikes. An easier ride uses the road on the west side of Derwent Reservoir)
1. From the visitor centre, cross to the other side of the reservoir via the bridge, signposted 'Road closed except for access to premises'. Follow the tarmac past, then away from the dam, climbing for 300 yds. After a short stone wall, turn sharp left onto a broad track.
2. Follow this broad stone track for 4 1/2 miles, passing a second dam and a second lake until you see a stone bridge down to your left, signposted 'Hope Woodlands via Packhorse Bridge'. Cross the bridge.
3. Follow the road back alongside the reservoirs.

You will descend to cross each 'arm' of the reservoir and climb again after each crossing.
4. At the visitor centre, you may wish to do a second loop, around Ladybower Reservoir, in which case continue along the road down to the A57, turn left onto the viaduct (use the pavement) then 50 yds past the end of the bridge turn sharp left onto a tarmac track signposted 'Public Bridleway'
5. Follow this back to the start, following the road beneath the dam.

Station: Hope Station is south of Ladybower Reservoir.
TIC: Glossop, 01457 855920.
Other nearby trails: The Longdendale Trail is just north of Glossop.
Useful publications: OS Landranger Map 110.
Refreshments: Hot drinks, cakes and sweets available at the visitor centre.

24 Chesterfield Canal

CATEGORY
Canal towpath.
DISTANCE
5 miles each way.

At the Tapton Lock Visitor Centre about 1 mile north of the start of the ride in Chesterfield you will come across a sign which indicates that following the canal south will lead to Chesterfield whereas following it north will lead to Istanbul! The explanation is that the Chesterfield Canal towpath is part of the Southern Link of the Trans Pennine Trail and the Trans Pennine Trail itself is part of the much larger European Long Distance Footpath system which extends right down as far as Turkey!

A bold and imaginative product of the early years of the Industrial Revolution, the prime purpose of the Chesterfield Canal was to take Derbyshire's coal to new markets. The original surveys were done by the famous canal engineer, James Brindley, although he did not live to see its opening in 1777. For its time it was a magnificent piece of engineering with the country's longest tunnel (at the time) at Norwood and one of the earliest examples of a large staircase of locks at Thorpe Salvin. The route of the Chesterfield Canal follows the River Rother valley out of the town and Tapton Lock is the first of five carrying the canal down to Staveley. The lock fell into disuse and was restored in the late 1980s. Each lock gate weighs approximately one ton and was manufactured from solid oak at the Rochdale Canal Workshops.

STARTING POINT & PARKING

➔ The car park in the centre of **Chesterfield** near the Chesterfield Hotel and Chesterfield College (just west of the railway station). To get to the start of the canal, follow Brimington Road

24

(B6543 / A619) towards Tapton / Brimington / Staveley, turn first left onto Holbeck Close then after 100 yds, shortly after the Chesterfield Canal information board, bear right onto a narrow path (grid reference 388716).

ON YOUR BIKES!

Once you have found the start in Chesterfield no instructions are needed as it is hard to lose a canal! The route ends where the canal ends, at the barrier on the western edge of Staveley (grid reference 430746). There are plans to improve the route north to connect up with the dismantled railway path that leads on to Killamarsh, Beighton and the Rother Valley Country Park.

Station: Chesterfield.
TIC: Chesterfield, 01246 345777.
Other nearby trails: The Trans Pennine Trail continues north via the Staveley to Beighton railway path to the Rother Valley Country Park.
Useful publications: OS Landranger Maps 119 & 120. Various leaflets about the canal can be obtained from the Tapton Lock Visitor Centre.
Refreshments: Lots of choice in Chesterfield. Limited refreshments at the visitor centre at Tapton Lock.

25   Staveley to Beighton, southeast of Sheffield

CATEGORY
Railway path and lakeside circuit
DISTANCE
3-mile circuit of the lakes plus 6 miles each way from Beighton to Staveley.

With its craft centre, exhibitions, cafe, plentiful wildfowl plus a variety of rides and walks Rother Valley Country park is an ideal place to spend the day. A 3-mile circuit of the two lakes may be all the cycling that you want to do but if you are interested in a longer challenge then there is a dismantled railway on the western side of the lakes that runs 6 miles south from Beighton to Staveley through a mixture of wooded cuttings and open stretches with views out into the surrounding countryside. The ride forms part of both the Trans Pennine Trail (the southern link from Chesterfield through Sheffield to Barnsley) and also National Cycle Network Route 6 which runs north from Derby via Nottingham, Worksop, Sheffield and Doncaster to York. The two routes join at the southern end of the lake, so don't be confused if you see a mixture of 'Route 6' 'Route 67' and 'Trans Pennine Trail' signs.

Set in 750 acres of countryside, Rother Valley Country Park offers an enormous range of leisure and recreational activities on both land and water. At the centre of the park stands a historic complex of buildings based around Bedgreave Mill, now the visitor centre. Bedgreave New Mill was built near the site of earlier mills and dates from the late 1700s. Next to the visitor centre is a cafe and craft centre.

STARTING POINT & PARKING

Rother Valley Country Park, accessed from the A618 to the southeast of Sheffield, between Killamarsh and Aston, southwest of M1 Jct 31. Or Staveley, on the A619 between Chesterfield and Worksop

ON YOUR BIKES!

1. From the Rother Valley Country Park Visitor Centre make your way to the lakeside and turn right. Pass between the two lakes and continue alongside the water.
2. You could either continue the circuit of the lake for a 3-mile ride OR for a link to the Trans Pennine Trail, when you reach a point opposite the Sailing Club (on the other side of the water) and with a double metal gate and a wooden bridlegate across the path, turn right under the railway bridge then turn left onto the old railway path following signs for Killamarsh and Staveley.
3. Follow this trail for 5 miles, at one point passing through a small car park and following the Trans Pennine Trail up to the left.
4. The easy trail ends at a point where a bridge with steps crosses a railway (just north of Staveley). It is suggested you turn around at this point* and return to the visitor centre, completing the circuit of the lake.
* If you continue south along the Trans Pennine Trail, a short rough section will take you to the Chesterfield Canal.

Station: Woodhouse Mill, east of Sheffield.
TIC: Sheffield. 0114 221 1900.
Other nearby trails: Clumber Park is just south of Worksop. Chesterfield Canal.
Useful publications: OS Landranger Map 120. Sustrans *Derby to York* map (£5.99) shows this and many other traffic-free sections of the National Cycle Network in the Sheffield area.
Sustrans Order Line: Call 0845 113 0065 or visit their website at www.sustrans.org.uk
Refreshments: Cafe at the visitor centre. Pubs in Staveley, Renishaw, Killamarsh.

West Midlands

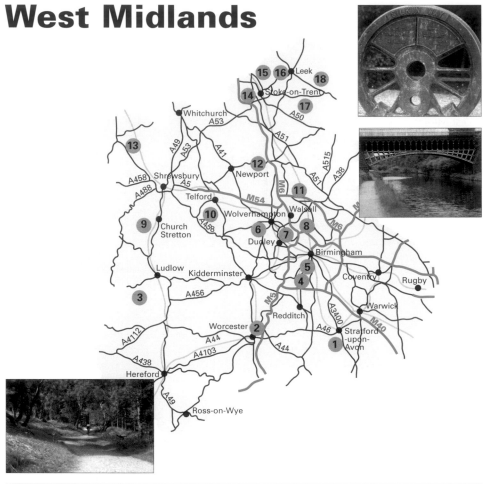

WEST MIDLANDS TRAILS

1	Stratford Greenway, southwest of Stratford upon Avon	10	Silkin Way, south of Telford
2	Worcester - the River Severn, the canal and the racecourse	11	Cannock Chase, north of Birmingham (3 routes)
3	Shropshire Woodlands (7 routes)	12	Stafford to Newport Greenway, south of Stoke
4	Birmingham & Worcester Canal	13	Nescliffe Hill Country Park, north of Shrewsbury
5	Rea Valley Cycle Route, Birmingham	14	Salt Way, northwest of Stoke
6	Kingswinford Railway Walk, southwest of Wolverhampton	15	Biddulph Valley Trail from Congleton to Biddulph
7	Birmingham & Black Country Canal Cycleway	16	Rudyard Lake, near Leek
8	Sutton Park, north of Birmingham	17	Churnet Valley Trail, west of Ashbourne
9	Long Mynd Ridge, Church Stretton	18	Manifold Trail, northwest of Ashbourne

West Midlands Mountain Biking

The best mountain biking in the West Midlands is in Cannock Chase (see Route 11, page 197) and the Shropshire hills. Church Stretton would be a good base to explore three areas: the tracks on the Long Mynd; the area west towards the border with Wales; and the tracks on Wenlock Edge and Brown Clee Hill to the east.

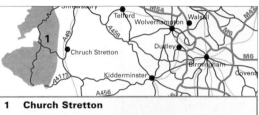

1   Church Stretton

The area to the south and west of Bishop's Castle also offers a good number of bridleways and byways. Most of the best riding near to Ludlow uses the forestry holdings to the southwest mentioned in 'Shropshire Woodlands' (Route 3, page 185).

There is no substitute for intimate local knowledge - try to explore every bridleway, byway, unclassified road, canal towpath and Forestry Commission track near to home, sift out the good from the bad and link together the best offroad sections to form your own customised route(s). The best advice is to use the months from late spring to early autumn (May to October) to do the exploration, if possible after a spell of dry weather. The same track in winter can take twice as long or even be impassable.

Note down on the map (or colour code with highlighter pen) the quality of the trail and whether it is better done in one

Mountain Biking Information

These are possible sources:

- leaflets produced by local authorities, normally available in Tourist Information Centres
- guidebooks which can usually be found in larger, better stocked bookshops
- the staff in bike shops can often put you in contact with local riders or clubs who are sure to have done some of this research already, saving you many hours of trial and error.

direction or the other - it is normally better to climb on tarmac and descend offroad so that gravity can help you through any muddy bits.

Bear in mind that everyone has a different view of what constitutes a good trail: hard or technical for some is easy for others and a bit of mud for some is a quagmire for others!

West Midlands Forestry

With the exception of Cannock Chase and the woodlands of Shropshire, the West Midlands have few forestry holdings of any size. By good fortune, almost all of these larger holdings have some form of waymarked trails in them. The main entry under 'Shropshire Woodlands' (Route 3, page 185) brings together all the forest trails in the county.

In some forests and woods there are no waymarked routes but you are free to explore the tracks. The relevant OS map is mentioned. It is highly recommended that you take a map for the larger woods where it is very easy to get lost!

1   Haugh Wood, east of Hereford
OS Explorer Map 189

3   Wyre Forest, west of Kidderminster
OS Explorer Map 218

5   Bishop's Wood, east of Market Drayton
OS Explorer Map 243

6   Swynnerton Old Park, southwest of Stoke
OS Explorer Map 258

Further Information

West Midlands Forest District,
Lady Hill, Birches Valley, Rugeley, Staffs.
WS15 2UQ
Tel: 01889 586593

Forests and woods with waymarked trails

They are shown with a corresponding trail number and page reference.

2   Shropshire Woodlands
See Route 3, page 185
● Eastridge Wood, Snailbeach, southwest of Shrewsbury
● Bury Ditches, south of Bishop's Castle, west of Craven Arms
● Hopton Titterhill, northeast of Knighton
● Mortimer Woods, southwest of Ludlow
● Wapley Hill, southeast of Knighton
● Shobdon Hill Wood, south of Wigmore, northwest of Leominster
● Mere Hill Wood, south of Wigmore, northwest of Leominster

4   Cannock Chase, north of Birmingham
See Route 11, page 197

The Forestry Commission's website is a good source of information with details of 1600 miles of waymarked cycling trails throughout the UK. Search by forest name or by the nearest town or city and the search will tell you the grade, length and waymarking details of the trails.

www.forestry.gov.uk/recreation

West Midlands
National Cycle Network

West Midlands Cycle Route

163 miles from Oxford to Derby via Birmingham. Highlights include the ancient city of Oxford, Blenheim Palace at Woodstock, North Oxfordshire villages, Stratford-upon-Avon, the Rea Valley Route into Central Birmingham, Lichfield Cathedral and the traffic-free routes through Derby.

Traffic-free sections over 3 miles:

* Stratford upon Avon Greenway from Stratford to Long Marston (NCN 5)
* Rea Valley Route - King's Norton to Cannon Hill Park (Birmingham) (NCN 5)
* Birmingham Canal between Birmingham and Wolverhampton (NCN 5)
* Etwall to Mickleover near Derby (NCN 5)

Sustrans

Listed below are the Sustrans maps that cover the National Cycle Network within the region. Some of the maps may describe routes that continue on into adjacent regions: these maps are mentioned in both chapters. The maps are not only useful for people wishing to ride the the whole route over several days; they also show all the traffic-free sections which make good day rides. The maps cost £5.99 each and are available from Sustrans.

Sustrans Order Line:
Call **0845 113 0065** or visit their website at
www.sustrans.org.uk

Other areas for lane cycling

There is a major contrast within this region: the eastern half is flatter with almost all the big conurbations - Stoke, Wolverhampton, Birmingham and Coventry - and most of the people, whereas the western half, with the exceptions of Telford and Shrewbury, is almost exclusively rural with all the hills. It is in **Herefordshire** and **Shropshire**, in the western half that you will find the best network of quiet lanes and myriad attractive towns and villages that are good bases from which to explore the area: try Ludlow, Church Stretton, Tenbury Wells, Bishop's Castle, Hay on Wye or Upton on Severn. The other areas worth exploring are in the **far north of Staffordshire**, up into the Peak District National Park and the **south of Warwickshire** where it borders with the northern Cotswolds.

West Midlands

1 Stratford Greenway, southwest of Stratford upon Avon

CATEGORY
Railway path.

DISTANCE
5 miles each way.

Finding the start of the trail will be your hardest task when you choose to explore this railway path running southwest from Shakespeare's Stratford and crossing the River Avon on a fine metal bridge. It forms part of the West Midlands Cycle Route from Oxford to Birmingham (National Cycle Network Route 5).

NB There is a short section on road if you wish to visit the pub at Long Marston.

STARTING POINT & PARKING
→It is very hard to give detailed instructions to get to the car park at the start! If you follow signs for the race course and the B439 to Bidford-on-Avon you will pick up signs for the Stratford Greenway (grid reference 196541).

ON YOUR BIKES!
The trail ends after 5 miles at the industrial estate in Long Marston, but you will need to leave before the end if you wish to go to the pub in Long Marston: on your outward journey from Stratford, cross the road at Milcote car park, then at the second row of white-painted, upright railway sleepers by a line of telegraph poles, turn right by Railway Cottage. At the T-junction at the end of Wyre Lane, turn right for 200 yds for the Masons Arms pub.

2

Station: Stratford.

TIC: Stratford, 01789 293127.

Other nearby trails: The Stratford Greenway is part of Sustrans National Cycle Network Route 5 from Oxford to Birmingham. It uses short traffic-free sections along the Stratford upon Avon Canal towpath to the north of Stratford and also in the Arrow Valley Park through Redditch.

Useful publications: OS Landranger Map 151.

Refreshments: Masons Arms pub, Long Marston (just off the route).

2   Worcester - the River Severn, the canal and the racecourse

CATEGORY

Riverside path, canal towpath, round race course track.

DISTANCE

A total of 6 miles.

Three short rides starting from the western side of the bridge over the River Severn in Worcester, exploring the banks of the mighty Severn, Worcester Race Course and a section of the Worcester & Birmingham Canal. Do not try to do a circuit of the race course when there is a race meeting going on!

STARTING POINT & PARKING

➔ The car park on the west side of the river bridge heading away from Worcester town centre. Follow signs for 'A44 Leominster' over the bridge then immediately turn left (grid reference 847547).

ON YOUR BIKES!

Race course.

Cross to the north side of the bridge via the traffic lights, follow the river then cross a pedestrian bridge to do a circuit around the

outside of the race course. Return to the car park.

River Severn.

Stay on the south side of the main road and follow the River Severn south for 1 mile, keeping the water to your left.

Link to the canal.

Stay on the south side of the main road but turn right over the bridge, walking your bike along the pavement then turn right again and follow the riverside path (with the water to your right) as far as the Diglis Basin. Cross the lock and turn left to link with the Worcester & Birmingham Canal Towpath. If you wish, follow the canal towpath past the Commandery for 2 1/2 miles as far as Lock 7, Bridge 15, near to Perdiswell Leisure Centre, changing sides at Bridges 5 and 13. After this the path deteriorates.

Station: Worcester.

TIC: Worcester, 01905 726311.

Other nearby trails: Stratford Greenway, Stratford upon Avon or trails in Birmingham.

Useful publications: OS Landranger Map 150.

Refreshments: Lots of choice in Worcester.

3   Shropshire Woodlands (7 routes)

CATEGORY

Woodland trails.

DISTANCE

Various distances.

There are several short waymarked woodland trails in the beautiful unspoilt Welsh Border country, also known as the Marches. It is best to get hold of the leaflets mentioned in 'Useful publications' and use these in conjunction with the appropriate Ordnance Survey Landranger map.

Snailbeach / Eastridge Woods, southwest of Shrewsbury

Ordnance Survey Landranger Map 126 / grid reference 373023.

A 4-mile circuit of Eastridge Woods with several climbs, starting from the village of Snailbeach, just off the A488 about 12 miles southwest of Shrewsbury. Short sections of quiet lanes are used near to Snailbeach to access the woodlands. The forest trails lie to the north and east of the village.

Bury Ditches, south of Bishop's Castle

Ordnance Survey Landranger Map 137 / grid reference 33483.

A hilly woodland circuit around an Iron Age Fort 5 miles to the south of Bishop's Castle which itself lies about 20 miles south of Shrewsbury on the A488. Follow the B4385 southeast out of Bishop's Castle towards Lydbury North. After 2 miles turn right onto the minor road to Lower Down and Bury Ditches.

Hopton Titterhill, northeast of Knighton

Ordnance Survey Landranger Map 137 / grid reference 348778.

Hopton Mountain Bike Trail offers the freedom to explore some 860 acres of woodland. Select your route by visiting the numbered marker posts located at the track and path junctions. To get the most out of the woodland, it is essential to obtain the leaflet produced by the Forestry Commission, Marches Forest District, Whitcliffe, Ludlow, Shropshire SY8 2HD (01584 874542). The car park is about 12 miles west of Ludlow and 1 mile west of the hamlet of Hopton Castle, near the junction of the B4367 and B4385.

Mortimer Woods, southwest of Ludlow

Ordnance Survey Landranger Map 137 / grid reference - see below.

Woodland trail running from near Overton towards High Vinnalls car park and picnic area. Start from the car park on the B4361 about 4

miles south of Ludlow, just beyond Overton (grid reference 500720) or from High Vinnalls car park on the minor road between Ludlow and Wigmore (grid reference 474732).

Wapley Hill, east of Presteigne

Ordnance Survey Landranger Map 137 / grid reference 360622.
3-mile circuit to the base of Wapley Hill Fort. This lies just off the B4632 about 4 miles east of Presteigne.

Shobdon Hill Wood, south of Wigmore

Ordnance Survey Landranger Map 137 / grid reference - see below.
4-mile linear route from Uphampton to Covenhope (grid reference 397634 or 40/643). Located west of Mortimer Cross, at the junction of the A4110 and the B4632.

Mere Hill Wood, south of Wigmore

Ordnance Survey Landranger Map 137 / grid reference - see below.
3-mile linear route from Covenhope to the summit of Mere Hill and down to Aymestrey (grid reference 407643 or 425624). Located

north of Mortimer Cross - at the junction of the A4110 and the B4632.

TICs: Shrewsbury, 01743 350761; Ludlow, 01584 875053.
Useful publications: OS Landranger Maps 126 & 137. A pack of five laminated leaflets called *Cycling for Pleasure in the Marches* (£9.50) shows several of the forestry routes in Shropshire. There is also a free leaflet called *Countryside and Woodland Cycle Trails.* Both publications are available from Shropshire Books, 7 London Road, Shrewsbury SY2 6NW (01743 255043).

4   Birmingham & Worcester Canal

CATEGORY
Canal towpath.
DISTANCE
6 miles each way, 12 miles return.

A section of the canal is used as part of National Cycle Network Route 5 from Reading

to Birmingham. The surface is excellent but as this is also a popular walking route please show consideration to other users. The ride starts from Gas Street Basin in the centre of Birmingham and ends abruptly at King's Norton Tunnel, one of the longest in the country.

STARTING POINTS & PARKING

→ **Gas Street Basin** located in the centre of Birmingham.

→ The towpath ends at **King's Norton Tunnel** (also known as Wast Hill Tunnel) which is located near the junction of Shannon Road and Primrose Hill in the Hawkesley / Walker's Heath area (grid reference 048780).

ON YOUR BIKES!

From the Gas Street Basin in the centre of Birmingham, follow signs for the Worcester & Birmingham Canal for 6 miles as far as King's Norton tunnel.

Station: Birmingham / King's Norton.
TIC: Birmingham, 0121 643 2514.
Other nearby trails: The Birmingham & Black Country Canal Cycleway. Rea Valley route. Sutton Park.
Useful publications: OS Landranger Map 139.
Refreshments: Lots of choice in the centre of Birmingham.

5   Rea Valley Cycle Route, Birmingham

CATEGORY
Riverside path through parkland.
DISTANCE
4 miles each way.

Forming part of the National Cycle Network through Birmingham, the Rea Valley Route follows the River Rea (at times more like a stream) through the delights of Cannon Hill Park where there are always fantastic displays of flowers, shrubs and rare ornamental trees. Beyond Cannon Hill Park the ride follows a tarmac path alongside the river through Stirchley and onto a short section of the Worcester & Birmingham Canal. It ends at King's Norton Park where there is a playground for children. To the north of Cannon Hill Park the NCN Route uses traffic-calmed streets and specially-built contraflow lanes to take you right into Centenary Square.

The River Rea is 15 miles long and rises southwest of Birmingham in Waseley Country Park, flowing northeast across the city to join the River Tame near to Spaghetti Junction. Although a small river, it has been called the 'Mother of Birmingham' as it has played a vital role in the development of the city, particularly in the Digbeth area where there was a small settlement hundreds of years ago. Over twenty mills once flourished along the Rea Valley, many of them built for corn grinding but during the Industrial Revolution they provided water power for Birmingham's industries.

STARTING POINTS & PARKING
→ **Cannon Hill Park**, central Birmingham. The car park lies off the A441 (Pershore Road), just to the south of Edgbaston Cricket Ground (grid reference 067841).
→ **King's Norton Park**, on Westhill Road, just

south of the junction of the A441 Pershore Road with the A4040 Watford Road and the B4121 Middleton Road (grid reference 050792).

ON YOUR BIKES!

1. From the lodge at the north end of Cannon Hill Park follow the cycle track through the park. Continue in the same direction with the river close by to your right.

2. The tarmac path swings right to cross the river via a brick and metal bridge. Shortly, the track joins Kitchener Road. Turn first left onto Cecil Road then at the T-junction turn left then right onto a continuation of the riverside path.

3. Follow the Rea Valley Route and signs for 'Stirchley, King's Norton'. At the next busy road (Cartland Road) go straight ahead via a toucan crossing onto a continuation of the riverside path.

4. At the T-junction with the trading estate road turn right to cross bridge then immediately left. At the crossroads with Fordhouse Lane use the toucan crossing to go straight ahead signposted 'Kings Norton, Northfield'.

5. At the end of the cyclepath by a tall wooden signpost turn left on the quiet estate road (Dacer Close) then shortly first left. Follow 'Rea Valley Route' signs to join the Worcester & Birmingham Canal towpath. Turn left along the towpath.

6. At the second bridge over the canal you will need to cross to the towpath on the other side. **Easy to miss.** Immediately after passing a red-brick bridge with a '72' plaque on it, turn right by a large red-brick house away from the towpath signposted 'Rea Valley Route. King's Norton'. Cross the playing fields then cross Pershore Road. The ride ends at the west edge of King's Norton Park at the junction of Wychall Lane and Westhill Road.

Station: Birmingham.
TIC: Birmingham, 0121 643 2514.
Other nearby trails: The Birmingham & Worcester Canal. The Birmingham & Black Country Canal. Sutton Park. The Kingswinford Railway Path.
Useful publications: OS Landranger Map 139.
Refreshments: Cafe in Cannon Hill Park.

5

6   Kingswinford Railway Walk, southwest of Wolverhampton

CATEGORY
Railway path.

DISTANCE
10 miles each way.

Despite its proximity to the conurbation of Wolverhampton, this ride along the disused railway of the Kingswinford line has a very fine, wooded, countryside feel to it. The trail is well-maintained with the exception of the extreme southern end near Pensnett which is somewhat neglected. Otherwise it is apparent that real pride is taken in keeping the trail in top condition. Along its whole length the trail runs parallel with the Staffordshire & Worcestershire Canal. Indeed you have the option of extending your ride northwards by following the canal towpath for a few miles before turning around.

Wombourne is about halfway along the trail so you can go north or south from this point.

STARTING POINT & PARKING
→ **Wombourne**. Turn off the A449 Wolverhampton to Kidderminster road at the roundabout near Wombourne where the A463 joins the A449 signposted 'Kingswinford Railway Walk'. Follow signs for **Trysull** on to Billy Buns Lane then just before a brown and cream coloured railway bridge turn right onto a track signposted 'Kingswinford Railway Walk' (grid reference 940870).

ON YOUR BIKES!
North from Wombourne
1. From the car park turn right onto the cycle track. Continue for 3 miles to Castlecroft and a further 3 miles to Aldersley Stadium.
2. At Aldersley you can either retrace your steps or continue further north on the Staffordshire & Worcestershire Canal towpath. To get to the

7 Birmingham & Black Country Canal Cycleway

CATEGORY

Canal towpath.

DISTANCE

Up to 14 miles each way.

Although it is often stated that Birmingham has more miles of canals than Venice, (there are over 130 miles of canals in Birmingham and the Black Country) this does not translate, unfortunately, into a fine network of broad, smooth, gravel towpaths that would immeasurably improve the life of every cyclist in Birmingham. With the exception of the Main Line Canal between Birmingham and Wolverhampton, cycling is undertaken on a *de facto* rather than *de jure* basis. The hub of the canal network in Birmingham lies around Digbeth Basin and Gas Street Basin. To the northwest the canal from Birmingham to Wolverhampton, known simply as the Birmingham Canal or the Main Line, is variable in quality and rarely pretty - this is a trip past the sinews of a muscular, industrial city with metal foundries and hot metal smells. As the Birmingham Canal in its entirety forms part of the National Cycle Network it may be assumed that over the next few years it will all be improved up the excellent standard to be enjoyed near to the centre of the city.

By 1769 the engineer James Brindley had completed the first of Birmingham's canals from Wednesbury to Newhall, then to a wharf beyond Gas Street Basin, where the Holiday Inn now stands. By 1772 the Old Main Line extended to Wolverhampton. The canal created rapid growth in industry - coal and building supplies were brought in and manufactured goods carried out. In the next half century the canal system spread rapidly and expanding trade brought great congestion. In the 1820s

canal, descend on the right-hand road and keep bearing right to pass beneath the railway bridge. At the road turn left then left again to pass for a second time beneath the railway bridge. Join the canal at Tunstall Water Bridge (no. 63) and turn left. The towpath quality is good for about 3 miles, as far as the A449.

South from Wombourne

The railway path can be followed south for 3 1/2 miles as far as a set of wooden steps by a car crusher's yard. Beyond here the trail gets rougher. It ends at Fens Pool Nature Reserve.

Station: Wolverhampton.

TIC: Wolverhampton, 01902 312051.

Other nearby trails: The Birmingham & Black Country Canal Towpath runs from the centre of Birmingham to the centre of Wolverhampton.

Useful publications: OS Landranger Map 139.

Refreshments: Excellent tea shop at Wombourne Station. Pubs just off the route.

Thomas Telford constructed a straight canal, the New Main Line, running parallel at a lower level to the Old Main Line. Despite advances in canal planning the Galton Valley cutting was still dug out by men using picks, shovels and wheelbarrows.

NB Please read *The Waterways Code - Cycling on the towpath* at the back of the book

STARTING POINTS & PARKING

→The **National Indoor Arena** in the centre of Birmingham. If arriving by car the towpath can be joined at any point along the route from central Birmingham via Smethwick, Tipton, Coseley and Broad Street Basin to Wolverhampton. Parking in the side streets.

ON YOUR BIKES!

From the centre of Birmingham to Wolverhampton

With your back to the National Indoor Arena turn right, with the water to your left. There are occasionally paths on both sides of the canal. Keep an eye out for the signs indicating where you change sides. The path can be followed for up to 14 miles to Wolverhampton. You may wish to turn around when the surface deteriorates.

Stations: Wolverhampton, Tipton, Birmingham New Street.
TIC: Birmingham, 0121 643 2514.
Other nearby trails: The Kingswinford Railway Walk runs south from Wolverhampton through Wombourne to Pensnett.
Useful publications: OS Landranger Map 139. The *Birmingham Cycling Map* is produced by CycleCity Guides, Wallbridge Mill, The Retreat, Frome BA11 5JU (01373 453533). E-mail: info@cyclecityguides.co.uk
Refreshments: All along the way.

8   Sutton Park, north of Birmingham

CATEGORY
Country park trails.
DISTANCE
A 3-mile circuit is described but there are several miles of tracks and bridleways through Sutton Park. Use the map available from the visitor centre to plan your routes around the park.

Sutton Park is on the edge of a large city, not unlike Richmond Park in London, where you often have to remind yourself that you are less than a couple of miles from a huge conurbation where millions of people are living and working. Sutton Park offers a sense of wide open spaces, with grassland and woodland and a plethora of tracks to explore. The park has considerably improved since through traffic was banned. There is no specifically waymarked cycle trail - this is just one of many that you could easily devise yourself. The best way of exploring the park is by buying the map from the visitor centre and giving yourself plenty of time to explore - the map will tell you the areas where cycling is **not** allowed.

STARTING POINT & PARKING
→Sutton Park Visitor Centre, off the A5127 on the west side of Sutton Coldfield, north of Birmingham (grid reference 115958).

ON YOUR BIKES!
1. From the visitor centre climb up to the four-way junction of roads ('Keepers Pool Only' is signposted straight ahead). Do **not** go towards Keepers Pool but turn left on the road with a single gate barrier.
2. At a major junction of tracks go straight ahead. At a tarmac crossroads just beyond a barrier turn right, passing a car parking area on your left. Go through the next barrier.
3. At the Jamboree Stone turn left onto a broad,

red gravel track.

4. Fast descent. Cross the stream. **Easy to miss.** About 200 yds **before** the main road (you will hear the traffic and glimpse it through the trees) turn left onto a less well-defined path. There is a signpost down to your left 'Ground nesting birds - please keep dogs on lead'.

5. Continue straight ahead on the main track through the woodland. Go through the car park and turn left onto the road. Go past Longmoor Pool.

6. At a tarmac crossroads go straight ahead through a wooden barrier to rejoin the outward route back to the visitor centre.

Station: Sutton Coldfield.
TIC: Birmingham, 0121 693 6300
Other nearby trails: The Birmingham & Black Country Canal Cycleway links the city centres of Birmingham and Wolverhampton. The Kingswinford Railway Walk runs from Pensnett (west of Dudley) to Aldersley Stadium, north of Wolverhampton. There are several waymarked trails in Cannock Chase.
Useful publications: OS Landranger Map 139.

Leaflet available from the visitor centre, Sutton Park, Sutton Coldfield, West Midlands B74 2YT (0121 355 6370). *The Birmingham Cycling Map*, a comprehensive cyclists' map of Birmingham is produced by CycleCity Guides, Wallbridge Mill, The Retreat, Frome BA11 5JU (01373 453533). E-mail: info@cyclecityguides.co.uk
Refreshments: At the visitor centre.

9 Long Mynd Ridge Ride, Church Stretton

CATEGORY
Moorland ridge path.

DISTANCE
5 each way.

This is not a recognised cycle trail in the same way as a railway path or a waymarked forestry route, it is merely a suggested route along a bridleway on top of a spectacular range of hills with the most magnificent views on a clear day. As such it is not worth doing in poor visibility as the whole point of the ride is the views! It is one of the few rides in the country where you should beware of gliders that are taking off or landing - the route passes a gliding club set high on the Long Mynd. It is suggested that you turn around a couple of miles beyond the gliding club where the gradient of the bridleway suddenly steepens but if you are feeling very brave and fit there is nothing to stop you devising a circular ride on a mixture of quiet lanes and bridleways, dropping steeply down into the valley of the River Onny then climbing back up to the starting point at Shooting Box.

NB This is a tough ride and should only be attempted on mountain bikes. It is not suitable for very young children and involves a long gentle climb of almost 400 ft back to the starting point. That said, it is an exhilarating ride with fantastic views on a clear day.

STARTING POINT & PARKING

→ The Long Mynd is just off the A49 above **Church Stretton**. From the centre of Church Stretton follow signs for 'Burway / Long Mynd'. Follow this very steep and narrow road to the top of the hill. At the fork at the top bear right signposted 'Youth Hostel'. Just before the start of the descent there is a small, grassy car park to the right by a wooden post with 'Shooting Box' on it (grid reference 421954).

ON YOUR BIKES!

1. From the Shooting Box car park cross the road onto the climbing track opposite, signposted 'Polebank'. Continue climbing, going straight ahead at a crossroads of tracks to reach the summit and the toposcope showing all the surrounding hills.
2. Descend to the road, bear right and continue descending. Climb then descend again. At the

9

Midland Gliding Club bear left on the road and pass to the left of the club building.

3. At the major fork of tracks with a 'No Right of Way' sign to the left, bear right on the lower, grassy track signposted 'Plowden'.

4. It is suggested that you continue for a further 2 miles until the land starts dropping away steeply. Retrace your steps, taking care on the lane section.

Station: Church Stretton.
TIC: Church Stretton, 01694 723133.
Other nearby trails: There are woodland trails at Bury Ditches (south of Bishop's Castle) and Hopton Titterhill (northeast of Knighton) plus several more in the woodlands to the southwest of Ludlow. See under 'Shropshire Woodlands' (page 185).
Useful publications: OS Landranger Map 137.
Refreshments: None on the route. The nearest is in Church Stretton.

10   Silkin Way, Telford

CATEGORY
Railway path.
DISTANCE
5 miles each way.

This ride explores the area where the Industrial Revolution started: the iron bridge over the River Severn in the village of Ironbridge was a major step on the route which saw Great Britain rise to industrial pre-eminence throughout the world in the late 18th century and most of the 19th century. The iron wheel used as the motif for the Silkin Way is an indication of the area's industrial past. The route, starting in the heart of the New Town of Telford, uses a dismantled railway for much of its course, passing through deep rock cuttings and thickly wooded stretches. The Severn is reached at Coalport where there is a pub on the other side of the lovely bridge over the river.

At Coalbrookdale in 1709, Abraham Darby started to experiment with methods of smelting iron ore using coke instead of charcoal. A maker of iron-bellied pots and household pans, Darby's clever innovations were later used to create monsters! Two of these iron monsters, David and Sampson, now feature in the Open Air Museum at Blists Mill. They are two mighty furnace engines that together gave sterling service for just over a century, pumping air into the Prioslee furnace, like a giant pair of bellows.

STARTING POINTS & PARKING
→Town Park car park in the centre of **Telford**, which lies about 1 mile southeast of M54 Jct 5 (grid reference 700082).
→The China Museum, **Coalport**, on the road alongside the River Severn, parallel with the A442 the south of Telford, south of M54 Jct 4 (grid reference 698024).

ON YOUR BIKES!
The route is signposted with an iron wheel logo
1. From the Town Park car park in the centre of Telford go into the park through the green metal gates, continue straight ahead along a road with humps and a white painted cycle lane (pass to the right of the public conveniences).

2. Exit the park, ignore two car parks to the left and take the next left downhill by a black metal barrier and a wooden 'Silkin Way' signpost. Descend to cross the bridge and turn sharp right. Continue in the same direction along the railway path, **taking good care to remember this point** for the return trip.

3. Pass beneath four bridges, cross Chapel Lane onto a continuation of the railway path. Cross a second minor lane. Shortly, pass beneath the road bridge and turn right (there is a wooden 'Silkin Way' signpost). This soon runs on the pavement alongside the main road, passing the turn to Blists Hill Victorian Town.

4. Go beneath two narrow metal bridges and follow the pavement as it bears left away from

the road.

5. At the T-junction by the Brewery Inn go straight ahead onto a continuation of the path then bear right to arrive at the end of the path, Coalport Bridge and the Woodbridge Inn.

Station: Telford or Wellington.

TIC: Telford, 01952 238008.

Other nearby trails: There are three waymarked forest trails in Cannock Chase to the north of Cannock.

Useful publications: OS Landranger Map 127. A good booklet is produced by Wrekin Council, Leisure Dept, PO Box 213, Civic Offices, Telford TF3 4LD (01952 202419).

Refreshments: Lots of choice in Telford. Woodbridge Inn at Coalport.

11 Cannock Chase, north of Birmingham (3 routes)

CATEGORY

Forest trail.

DISTANCE

The Sherbrook Valley Route is 9 miles long.

Cannock Chase is the largest Forestry Commission holding in the West Midlands. In character it is far from the dense blocks of conifers that cloak hillsides in Wales and Scotland – there are many open, sandy spaces, a pleasant mixture of broadleaf and coniferous trees and more important from the cyclist's point of view, a large network of bridleways, many of which are well-drained broad, stone-based tracks where it is possible to cycle all year round. The ride is largely a descent in the first half down the course of Sherbrook Valley and largely a climb in the second half up Abraham's Valley. Cannock Chase is the remnant of a vast royal hunting forest (chase). At 17,000 acres it is the smallest mainland Area of Outstanding Natural Beauty in Britain. Much of Cannock Chase is recognised by English Nature

as a Site of Special Scientific Interest.

STARTING POINT & PARKING

→ At the **Cannock Chase Visitor Centre**, 4 miles southwest of Rugeley (grid reference 005154). Turn off the A460 onto the B5013 towards Cannock then first right onto the minor road (Brindley Heath Road). The visitor centre is located about 1 mile along this road, on the right.

ON YOUR BIKES!

1. Exit the visitor centre car park back towards the road. Turn right, following the green and white bike signs, passing the overflow car park to your right. At the T-junction by the tall pines turn left.

2. At the T-junction at the end of Marquis Drive turn right (take care). Just before the crossroads and the Give Way sign cross the road onto the cyclepath and continue straight ahead at the next road onto a woodland track.

3. Keep following the green bike signs. You will need to turn right then left at two T-junctions. At the road continue straight ahead.

4. At the T-junction at the bottom of the descent turn left. At the bottom of the dip, just before the path starts climbing again turn right to continue downhill.

5. Continue in the same direction, basically downhill although there is one short climb on a sweeping bend. At the crossroads at the bottom of a long descent, by a 'Stepping Stones' signpost turn right.

6. At the T-junction (with a car park away to your left) turn right uphill. Steep then steady climb.

7. Go past a low red-brick building (Army Cadet Force). At the crossroads with the road go straight ahead onto a narrow track (take care crossing the road). At the T-junction with the wide forest track turn right then right again. After a few hundred yards turn left to rejoin the outward route.

8. Cross the road then bear left onto the next

11

road for 100 yds. Take the first road to the left
(Marquis Drive) then first right to return to the
visitor centre.

Station: Rugeley.

TIC: Stafford, 01785 240204

Other nearby trails: There are two other
waymarked routes in Cannock Chase - the
Pepperslade Route (4 1/2 miles) and the Lady
Hill Route (4 miles). The Stafford to Newport
Greenway is a dismantled railway running west
from Stafford.

Useful publications: OS Landranger Maps 127
& 128. A leaflet can be purchased from the
visitor centre or from the County Countryside
Officer, Shire Hall, Market Street, Stafford ST16
2LQ (01785 277264).

Refreshments: None on the route. There is a
pub in Little Haywood, just to the north of the
lowest point of the ride (at the bottom of
Sherbrook Valley, near Instruction 6). Otherwise
you will need to go into Cannock or Rugeley.

12 Stafford to Newport Greenway

CATEGORY

Railway path.

DISTANCE

3 1/2 miles each way.

A short ride on a dismantled railway to the west
of Stafford, best seen in late spring / early
summer when the wildflowers are at their most
colourful. There are plans to continue the
section open to cyclists beyond the present
finish towards Newport.

The line was built in 1849 by the Shropshire
Union Railway and ran from Stafford to
Newport and Wellington and beyond, being an
important link between the Midlands and
Wales. The line was used for 115 years until
1964 when the last steam engine plied its way
along the line carrying a wreath to mourn its
passing.

STARTING POINTS & PARKING

→ **Stafford**. Take the A518 towards Telford. Turn off this road at the new housing estate at Castlefields. Follow Martin Drive from the first roundabout by Castlefields then go straight ahead at the second roundabout on to the narrow lane signposted 'No Through Road'. There is a car park along to the left (grid reference 908234).

→ There is also a car park at the western end of the trail, north of **Haughton** (grid reference 862213).

ON YOUR BIKES!

From Stafford. Exit the car park, turn left along the narrow lane then at the end of the factories on the right turn right to join the railway path. Follow for 3 1/2 miles as far as a small car park, where the trail ends.

Station: Stafford.
TIC: Stafford, 01785 240204
Other nearby trails: The Silkin Way runs south of Telford. There are plenty of forest tracks in Cannock Chase to the southeast of Stafford.
Useful publications: OS Landranger Map 127.
Refreshments: The Red Lion pub, Derrington.

13 Nescliffe Hill Country Park, north of Shrewsbury

CATEGORY

Cycle track through country park.

DISTANCE

5-mile circuit.

In 1990 Shropshire County Council purchased the area which encompasses the country park with its prominent ridge of sandstone hills. The 160-acre park includes impressive woodland walks, an Iron Age hill fort, an ancient green lane, panoramic views and Humphrey Kynaston's Cave - Shropshire's own Robin Hood!

STARTING POINT & PARKING

➜ Nescliffe Hill Country Park is located just off the A5 about 10 miles northwest of Shrewsbury (grid reference 385199).

Station: Shrewsbury.
TIC: Shrewsbury, 01743 350761.
Other nearby trails: There is a waymarked woodland trail in Eastridge Woods near to Snailbeach, south of Shrewsbury (see page 185). The Silkin Way runs south from Telford.
Useful publications: OS Landranger Map 126. A leaflet called *Nescliffe Hill Country Park* is available from Countryside Service, Shropshire County Council, Column House, Shrewsbury SY2 6NW (01743 255043).
Refreshments: Pub in Nescliffe.

14 Salt Way, northwest of Stoke

CATEGORY
Railway path.
DISTANCE
3 miles each way.

A short, well-maintained stretch of dismantled railway from Hassall Green southeast to Alsager, northwest of Stoke, through attractive woodland and a good family pub at the end of the ride.

The railway was built by the North Staffordshire Railway Company in 1858 with the primary function of carrying minerals to and from Stoke-on-Trent. The Trent & Mersey Canal proved vital in the construction of the line as many of the bulky materials were transported by narrowboat. The line began as goods only, expanded to take passengers then reverted to goods only between 1930 and 1970 when it finally closed. The old course of the railway is rich in species of flowers, birds and butterflies.
NB. If you decide to go to the pubs at either end

of the trail there are short road sections.

STARTING POINT & PARKING

➜ Turn off the A533 about 2 1/2 miles south of Sandbach (M6, Jct 17) opposite the New Inn pub onto New Inn Lane, signposted 'Hassall Green, Wheelock'. Go under the motorway and take the first right into the car park (grid reference 775583).

ON YOUR BIKES!
Follow the trail eastwards away from the car park. At the second road (the B5078) turn right, walking your bikes along the pavement, to go to another excellent watering hole called the Wilbraham Arms pub.

Station: Alsager.
TIC: Stoke, 01782 284600.
Other nearby trails: The Biddulph Valley Trail is 5 miles east of Alsager. Rudyard Lake is 9 miles to the east.
Useful publications: OS Landranger Map 118.
Refreshments: The Lockside Cafe and Romping Donkey pub in Hassall Green are both about 1/2 mile from the start. The Wilbraham Arms pub is located at the eastern end of the trail, about 200 yds along the B5078 towards Alsager.

15 Biddulph Valley Trail, Congleton

CATEGORY
Railway path.
DISTANCE
5 miles each way.

The raised track bed of the old Biddulph Valley Line provides fine views towards the Peak District. The ride passes through woodland and beneath a magnificent viaduct near Congleton on its way south to Biddulph.
The Biddulph Valley Line was opened in 1859.

14

As Congleton's main arterial link with the Potteries it provided the town's economic lifeblood with the movement of freight of every description from straw to war weapons. It lasted 109 years and the final train ran in 1968. In 1980 Congleton Borough Council bought the line from British Rail and the line was put into service once again to provide recreation for local people and a refuge for wildlife.

STARTING POINTS & PARKING

→ **Congleton**. The track / lane to the right of the Brunswick Wharf Depot opposite Brook Street Garage and petrol station, 1/2 mile out of Congleton on the A54 Buxton Road (grid reference 865634).

→ **Biddulph**. Leave the A527 Congleton to Stoke road at the traffic lights at the southern end of Biddulph, turning on to Newpool Road, signposted 'Mow Cop / Brown Lees'. The trail starts beneath the railway bridge after 200 yds (grid reference 878568).

Station: Congleton.
TIC: Congleton, 01260 271095.
Other nearby trails: The Rudyard Lake Trail lies 4 miles to the east.
Useful publications: OS Landranger Map 118.
Refreshments: In Congleton or Biddulph.

16   Rudyard Lake, near Leek

CATEGORY
Railway path.
DISTANCE
4 1/2 miles each way.

A delightful ride alongside Rudyard Lake with colourful yachts and dinghies set against a background of steep wooded slopes. The ride goes from Rushton Spencer (off the A523 south of Macclesfield) along the east side of Rudyard Lake to the western edge of Leek.
The young Kiplings spent their courting days

here and named their first son, Rudyard, after the area. Rudyard Lake is a feeder reservoir for the Caldon Canal and was a very popular Victorian resort.

STARTING POINTS & PARKING

→Car park near the Knot Inn at **Rushton Spencer**, just off the A523, about 8 miles south of Macclesfield (grid reference 936625).

→The **southern end of Rudyard Lake** - turn off the A523 Leek to Macclesfield road, about 2 miles northwest of Leek onto the B5331, signposted 'Rudyard Lake'. Just after going under a railway bridge turn left into the car park (grid reference 956578).

→**Leek**. Turn off the A523 Macclesfield Road on to the road next to the Dyers Arms pub. The tarmac lane becomes a track. Join the railway path at the bridge (grid reference 973567).

ON YOUR BIKES!

North from the lake car park
Follow the broad track alongside the eastern side of the lake. At the end of the lake, shortly after going under a bridge you will come to a wide parking area. After 150 yds turn right at a 'Staffordshire Way' signpost to rejoin the course of the railway. (This section can get muddy). Follow for a further 1 1/2 miles, passing the Knot Inn pub in Rushton Spencer.
South from the lake car park
The trail runs for 1 1/2 miles to the outskirts of Leek, ending near a large field

Station: Congleton.
TIC: Congleton, 01260 271095.
Other nearby trails: The Biddulph Valley Trail lies 5 miles to the west. The Manifold Way starts at Waterhouses, on the A523, about 8 miles southeast of Leek.
Useful publications: OS Landranger Map 118.
Refreshments: Knot Inn pub in Rushton Spencer.

17

17 Churnet Valley Trail, west of Ashbourne

CATEGORY
Railway path.
DISTANCE
4 miles each way.

The Churnet Valley Trail is a railway path through woodland at the southwest edge of the Peak District, running from Oakamoor, east of Stoke on Trent to Denstone. Keep an eye out for the dramatic Gothic-style castle in Alton village to the south of the trail, built by Pugin, the 19th-century architect famous for his work on the House of Commons. You will probably be aware of music drifting over from Alton Towers Theme Park which lies in parkland to the north of the valley.

STARTING POINTS & PARKING
→The car park in **Oakamoor** is just off the B5417 at the bottom of the hill just to the west

of the bridge over the River Churnet, by the Cricketers Arms pub. Go past a second pub (the Admiral Jervis) to the end of the second car park and fork left to get to the start of the trail (grid reference 054444).

→The Village Hall car park, on the B5032 in **Denstone**, 5 miles north of Uttoxeter. From the car park, go past the petrol station and turn left just before the telephone box on to the Churnet Railway Trail (grid reference 099410).

Station: Uttoxeter.
TIC: Ashbourne, 01335 343666.
Other nearby trails: The Tissington Trail starts in Ashbourne, 8 miles to the northwest of Denstone. The Manifold Trail starts at Waterhouses, 6 miles northeast of Oakamoor.
Useful publications: OS Landranger Map 119 or 128.
Refreshments: The Tavern, Denstone. The Admiral Jervis pub and Cricketers Arms, Oakamoor.

18   Manifold Trail, northwest of Ashbourne

CATEGORY
Railway path.
DISTANCE
8 miles each way.

Along with the High Peak and Tissington Trails the Manifold Trail is one of the most popular trails in the Peak District. The scenic railway path follows the course of two rivers, the Manifold and the Hamps from Waterhouses (west of Ashbourne) via Wettonmill to Hulme End. The River Manifold appears and disappears: during the drier months it takes an underground course, leaving just the dry, stony river bed and tree-lined banks. High above the wooded hillsides are accessible caves. The Manifold Trail dips in the middle, at the junction of the Rivers Hamps and Manifold, so

there is a gentle climb from this point (Weags Bridge) north to Hulme End or south to Waterhouses.

The Leek & Manifold Valley Light Railway was opened in 1904, closed in 1934 and was converted to recreational use in 1937. It was a narrow-gauge railway designed by E.R. Calthrop who had tested and proved his ideas on the Barsi Light Railway in India.

NB There is one busy road (the A523) to cross at Waterhouses. The trail uses a short section of quiet lane for about 1 1/2 miles.

STARTING POINTS & PARKING
→**Hulme End**, 12 miles southwest of Bakewell. Turn off the B5054 just to the west of the Manifold Valley pub (grid reference 103594).
→**Waterhouses**, 9 miles northwest of Ashbourne. Turn off the A523 Ashbourne to Leek road at Ye Olde Crown Hotel in Waterhouses, signposted 'Cauldon Lowe, Cheadle, Manifold Track'. Go under the bridge and immediately left into the car park (grid reference 085501). To get to the start of the trail go to the far end of the car park and follow the waymarks.

Station: Uttoxeter, 10 miles to the south.
TIC: Ashbourne, 01335 343666.
Other nearby trails: The Tissington Trail lies 4 miles to the east of Hulme End along the B5054. The Churnet Valley Trail from Oakamoor to Denstone lies 6 miles south of Waterhouses.
Useful publications: OS Landranger Map 119. Leaflet available from: Information Group, Peak National Park Office, Aldern House, Baslow Road, Bakewell, Derbyshire DE4 1AE (01629 816200).
Refreshments: The Manifold Valley at Hulme End. Various tea shops and refreshment vans along the way. Ye Olde Crown at Waterhouses.

North-West

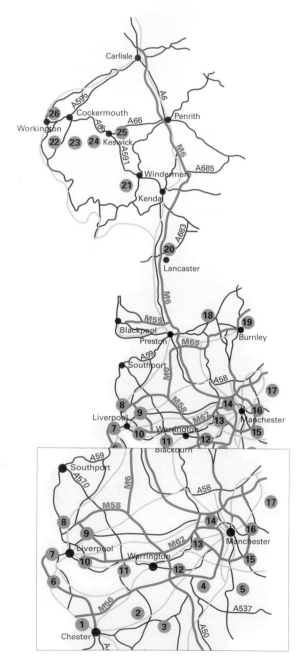

North-West Mountain Biking

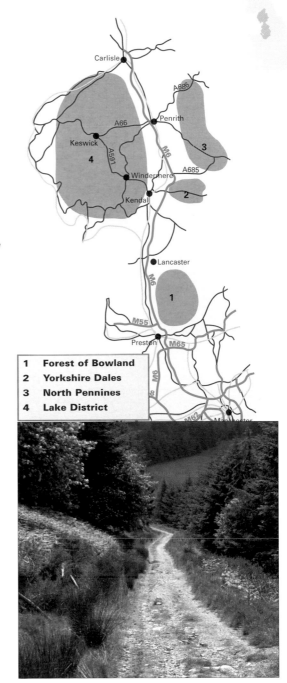

With the exception of the odd track in the Forest of Bowland in Lancashire, for example Salter Fell or the track alongside the River Dunsop north from Dunsop Bridge, the only real mountain biking in the North-West region is to be found in Cumbria. There are books and leaflets too numerous to mention describing rides in this beautiful area, which can be obtained in good bookshops or in the local Tourist Information Centres.

Within Cumbria, the best rides are those which do not overlap with very popular walking trails in the heart of the Central Fells ie it is better to go to the fringes of the National Park: north of Keswick around the back of Skiddaw; south of Penrith on Askham Fell; between the valleys of Longsleddale and Trout Beck northeast of Windermere; or between the Duddon Valley and Coniston Water in the southwest corner of the National Park.

There are also some 'expedition' style crossings of the Pennines on bridleways to the northeast of Appleby-in-Westmorland, and strange though it may seem, part of the Yorkshire Dales National Park is located in Cumbria. There are many tracks around Sedbergh in the Howgills that offer tough but exhilarating mountain biking.

1	Forest of Bowland
2	Yorkshire Dales
3	North Pennines
4	Lake District

North-West Forestry

The North-West divides into two as far as forestry is concerned: the southern half is one of the least forested areas of the country, with only two forestry holdings, at Delamere, to the east of Chester, and Gisburn to the north of Burnley; by contrast Cumbria and the Lake District is considerably more forested with visitor centres and waymarked trails at Grizedale and Whinlatter and several more holdings where cycling is possible. Although parts of Kielder Forest lie within the North-West, all the routes there are covered in the North-East chapter.

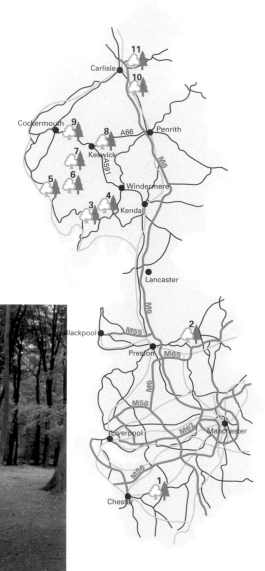

In some forests and woods there are no waymarked routes but you are free to explore the tracks. The relevant Ordnance Survey map is mentioned. It is highly recommended that you take a map for the larger woods where it is very easy to get lost!

3   **Broughton Moor and Hardknott Forest, west of Coniston Water**
    OS Outdoor Leisure Map 6

5   **Miterdale and Blengdale Forest, east of Sellafield, West Cumbria**
    OS Outdoor Leisure Map 6

6   **Ennerdale Forest, east of Ennerdale Water, Lake District**
    OS Outdoor Leisure Map 6

8   **Dodd Wood, north of Keswick, Lake District**
    OS Outdoor Leisure Map 4

9   **Setmurthy Common, east of Cockermouth, Lake District**
    OS Outdoor Leisure Map 4

10 **High Stand Plantation, southeast of Carlisle**
    OS Outdoor Leisure Map 5

11 **Kershope Forest, northeast of Carlisle**
    OS Explorer Map 315

Forests and woods with waymarked trails

They are shown with a corresponding trail number and page reference.

1   **Delamere, east of Chester**
    See Route 2, page 211

2   **Gisburn, north of Burnley**
    See Route 18, page 228

4   **Grizedale, west of Windermere**
    See Route 21, page 230

7   **Whinlatter Forest, west of Keswick**
    See Route 24, page 233

The Forestry Commission's

website is a good source of information with details of 1600 miles of waymarked cycling trails throughout the UK. Search by forest name or by the nearest town or city and the search will tell you the grade, length and waymarking details of the trails.

www.forestry.gov.uk/recreation

Further Information

North West England Forest District
Grizedale, Hawkshead, Ambleside, Cumbria. LA22 0QJ.
Tel: 01229 860373

North-West National Cycle Network

C2C / Sea to Sea Cycle Route

140 miles from Whitehaven or Workington on the West Cumbrian coast over the Pennines to Sunderland or Tynemouth on the North Sea coast. Highlights include: the route through the Lake District, the delightful wooded, riverside railway path to the east of Keswick, the crossing of the Pennines with a highpoint of 2000ft between Nenthead and Allenheads and the long, gentle, almost entirely traffic-free descent for the final 35 miles.

Traffic-free sections over 3 miles:

- Whitehaven to Rowrah (NCN 71)
- Keswick to Threlkeld (NCN 71)
- The Waskerley Way from Rookhope to Consett (NCN 7)
- Consett to Sunderland railway path (NCN 7)

Sustrans

Listed below are the Sustrans maps that cover the National Cycle Network within the region. Some of the maps may describe routes that continue on into adjacent regions: these maps are mentioned in both chapters. The maps are not only useful for people wishing to ride the the whole route over several days; they also show all the traffic-free sections which make good day rides. The maps cost £5.99 each and are available from Sustrans.

Sustrans Order Line:
Call **0845 113 0065** or visit their website at
www.sustrans.org.uk

- The Derwent Valley Walk from Consett to Newcastle (NCN 14)
- Newcastle to Tynemouth along Hadrian's Way (NCN 72)

Trans Pennine Trail (west): Irish Sea to the Pennines

215 miles from Southport to Hull via Liverpool, Manchester, Barnsley, Doncaster and Selby. Highlights in this section include the sculpture at the start point on the Irish Sea in Southport; the deep stone cuttings along the Liverpool Loop Line; wide views of the Mersey from Pickering's Pasture; Sale and Chorlton Water Parks in south Manchester; and the Longdendale Trail climbing from Hadfield to the Woodhead Tunnel alongside the string of reservoirs in the valley below.

Traffic-free sections over 3 miles:

- Cheshire Lines Path from Ainsdale near Southport to Maghull in north Liverpool (NCN 62)
- Liverpool Loop Line from Aintree to Halewood (NCN 62)
- St Helen's Canal from Spike Island to Sankey Bridges (NCN 62)
- Thelwall to Altrincham along the railway path (NCN 62)

- River Mersey through south Manchester (NCN 62)
- The Longdendale Trail from Hadfield to the Woodhead Tunnel (NCN 62 and 63)

Pennine Cycleway: The Peak District

178 miles of cycle route including 81 miles of the Pennine Cycleway and a circular ride linking Derby, Buxton, Holmfirth, Sheffield, Sherwood Forest and Nottingham. Highlights of the Pennine Cycleway include the Peak District National Park, Ashbourne, the Tissington Trail, Buxton and the Longdendale Trail.

Traffic-free sections over 3 miles:

(includes several extra trails in addition to those actually on Route 68, the Pennine Cycleway):

- Mickleover to Etwall, near Derby (NCN 68)
- Tissington Trail from Ashbourne to Sparklow (NCN 68)
- Longdendale Trail from Hadfield to the Woodhead Tunnel (NCN 68)
- Dove Valley Trail from Dunford Bridge via Penistone to Grenoside, Sheffield (NCN 62)
- Sheffield to Rotherham (NCN 6)
- Rother Valley Country Park to Staveley (NCN 67)
- Clumber Park to Blidworth (NCN 6)
- Elvaston Country Park to Derby (NCN 6)

Pennine Cycleway: South Pennines & the Dales

124 miles from Holmfirth in the South Pennines through the Yorkshire Dales to Appleby-in-Westmorland in the Eden Valley. Highlights include the beautiful and challenging lanes through the South Pennines between Holmfirth and Burnley; the canal towpath between Burnley and Colne; the Yorkshire Dales, particularly the lanes through Kingsdale and Dentdale; the handsome town of Appleby-in-Westmorland.

Traffic-free sections over 3 miles:

- Burnley to Barnoldswick along the Leeds & Liverpool Canal (NCN 68)

Other areas for lane cycling

There is a good and lane network with plenty of easy cycling in the **far southwest of Cheshire** bordering on Wales to the west and Shropshire to the south. Tarporley, Bunbury and Beeston are attractive villages in the area. Moving north from here there is a great swathe of the region dominated by the vast cities and suburbs of Liverpool and Manchester, densely populated as far north as a line from Blackpool to Burnley; traffic is generally heavy. Beyond here there is an attractive web of lanes around the fringes of the **Forest of Bowland** with the fine settlements at Chipping, Dunsop Bridge and Slaidburn. It is north of here, however, that there is the most fantastic of cycling opportunities, from the **Lune Valley** north to the **Eden Valley**; in the western reaches of the **Yorkshire Dales National Park**; and of course the **Lake District** and **Cumbria**. The best lane cycling here lies outside of the Central Fells, where all the roads tend to be busy. For easier Cumbrian cycling try the area south and west of Carlisle along the **Solway Firth** with fine views of both Scottish and English.

North-West Trails

1 Chester (Mickle Trafford) to Queensferry (Connah's Quay)

CATEGORY
Railway path.

DISTANCE
10 miles each way.

Chester is a most attractive town full of half-timbered buildings. This newly-built trail forms part of National Cycle Network Route 5 which runs along the north coast of Wales from Holyhead on Anglesey to join the Trans Pennine Trail east of Liverpool. The ride starts from Mickle Trafford, on the northeast side of Chester and goes west to Hawarden Bridge Station, on the north side of Connah's Quay. The trail runs through north Chester, parallel with Kingsway and Brook Lane, passing Chester College then through Blacon. The Mickle Trafford to Dee Marsh railway line once carried steel to and from the steelworks on the banks of the Dee at Hawarden Bridge.

STARTING POINTS & PARKING
→ **Hawarden Bridge Station** on the north side of the River Dee to the north of Connah's Quay, west of Chester (grid reference 312696).

→ Saughall Road, **Blacon**, just south of its junction with Blacon Avenue (grid reference 373681).

→ **Brook Lane**, north of Chester centre east of the A5116 Liverpool Road (grid reference 409675).

Station: Chester.
TIC: Chester, 01244 402111.
Other nearby trails: Delamere Forest Park.

Useful publications: OS Landranger Map 117. An excellent leaflet *The Millennium Cycle Route in Cheshire* is available from the Countryside Management Service, Cheshire County Council (0151 327 5145).
Refreshments: Lots of choice in Chester.

2 Delamere Forest, east of Chester (2 routes)

CATEGORY
Forestry trails.
DISTANCE
Hunger Hill Trail – 4 miles; White Moor Trail – 7 miles.

There are very few Forestry Commission holdings of any size in the southern half of the North-West region - you would need to go to Cumbria (or Wales) for that - but whilst Delamere Forest Park is not particularly large it does have two waymarked cycle routes which are ideal for family cycling - broad gravel tracks with a few gentle hills but nothing to really worry about. Starting from the visitor centre the ride crosses and recrosses the railway line, passing through mixed broadleaf and conifer woodland, with a fine display of wildflowers in the spring and early summer. Delamere Forest was once the royal hunting preserve of the Earls of Chester - the visitor centre has displays of Delamere's history. The forest is noted for kestrels, sparrowhawks, foxes and badgers.

NB A minor road needs to be crossed twice. The traffic can be travelling quite fast on this road so take care.

STARTING POINT & PARKING
→ Forestry Commission Visitor Centre, Linmere, Delamere, just off the B5152, about 6 miles south of M56, Jct 12 (grid reference 548704).

ON YOUR BIKES!
From the car park by the Delamere Forest Visitor Centre return towards the public road and take the first left over a bridge with a 'No entry' (for cars) signpost. You will come to an obvious crossroads of tracks where you have a choice:
Hunger Hill Trail
4 miles, blue arrows, to the right
White Moor Trail
7 miles, white arrows, to the left.

Station: Delamere.
TIC: Chester, 01244 402111.
Other nearby trails: The Whitegate Way starts 3 miles to the east.
Useful publications: OS Landranger Map 117. *Delamere Forest Guide Map* can be purchased from Forest Enterprise, Linmere, Delamere, Cheshire (01606 882167).
Refreshments: At the visitor centre. There is a cafe at the old station just by the main road.

3 Whitegate Way, east of Chester

CATEGORY

Railway path.

DISTANCE

3 miles each way east from the car park; 4 miles each way west to Cuddington.

There aren't many cycle trails in the country that end at a salt mine, as the Whitegate Trail does just to the north of Winsford. The railway path is predominantly wooded through the cuttings with views across to arable farmland and pasture on the more open sections. As with so many of these railway paths the Whitegate Way is at its best either in late spring / early summer when the young leaves are a fresh green and the verges and woodland are full of bright wildflowers, or in late autumn when the leaves are changing colour and the path is carpeted with all shades of yellow and red. Some sections of this route are not that well drained so in winter and after rain you may well encounter several muddy sections. The Whitegate Line was opened in 1870 to transport salt from the mines and works along the west bank of the River Weaver. The line closed in 1966. The old railway is now managed for maximum benefit of wildlife as well as providing an attractive environment for people to enjoy. Trees are coppiced in a traditional form of woodland management whereby the trees are cut down to ground level every 6-8 years. This encourages tremendous re-growth and provides useful timber for poles and logs.

STARTING POINT & PARKING

➜ The car park for the Whitegate Way is at **Marton Green**, to the north of the A54 between Kelsall and Winsford (about 10 miles west of M6 Jct 18). Turn onto Clay Lane, **opposite** a lane signposted 'Budworth'. After 1 mile, just before a railway bridge, bear right downhill signposted 'Whitegate Way' for the car park (grid reference 615680).

ON YOUR BIKES!

The route follows the course of the old railway so it is impossible to get lost! From the car park you can:

Head east (turn right) for 3 miles until you reach the T-junction with the road by the salt mines.
OR
Head west (turn left) for 4 miles until you come to a huge railway bridge over the trail by Ravenscough in Cuddington.

Station: Cuddington.
TIC: Nantwich, 01270 610983.
Other nearby trails: Delamere Forest Trails.
Useful publications: OS Landranger Maps 117 & 118. Leaflet available from The Rangers' Office, Linmere Picnic Site, Station Road, Delamere, Northwich, Cheshire CW8 2JQ (01606 889941).
Refreshments: None on route. Pub in Cuddington

4   Tatton Park, northwest of Knutsford

CATEGORY

Estate roads.

DISTANCE

There are 8 miles of quiet estate roads within Tatton Park. There are also two suggested rides, using some tracks, known as the Old Hall Circuit and the Tatton Tour.

There is a charge to enter this country estate by car so there is very little traffic on the estate roads within the park. As a result it is a fine place to cycle, exploring the attractive parkland which has been a refuge for deer for hundreds of years. You can buy a family ticket for combined admission to all the attractions. The Old Hall displays 500 years of history; Home Farm explains how the wealth of Tatton Hall was derived from agriculture and at the stables

the vital role of the horse on a country estate is brought to life; the Mansion juxtaposes majestic staterooms and the life of the servant 'below stairs'.

NB There is traffic on the estate roads but it is travelling slowly and signs tell motorists to be aware of cyclists. There is more traffic during summer weekends, so plan accordingly.

STARTING POINT & PARKING

→ Follow signs off the A556 which runs between Junction 7/8 of the M56 and Junction 19 of the M6 between Altrincham and Knutsford. There is a charge to enter the park.

Station: Knutsford.
TIC: Knutsford, 01565 632611.
Other nearby trails: The Middlewood Way from Marple to Macclesfield lies 8 miles to the east.
Useful publications: OS Landranger Maps 109 & 118. The park also produces a map, available from the visitor centre.
Refreshments: Restaurants and refreshments near the mansion.

5 Middlewood Way, south of Manchester

CATEGORY
Railway path.

DISTANCE
10 miles each way.

A fine long stretch of dismantled railway, much of it in woodland, running south from Marple, southeast Manchester via Higher Poynton and Bollington to Macclesfield, on the edge of the Peak District. During the Industrial Revolution, many local industries flourished in this area, especially silk, coal, cotton and stone. Rail and canal links with Stockport were built so that products could be moved more easily. The Macclesfield, Bollington & Marple Railway was opened in 1869 and was in use until 1970. In the early 1980s work was carried out to reopen the routes for recreational use and the Middlewood Way was opened in 1985.

STARTING POINTS & PARKING
→ Tesco supermarket just off the roundabout at the start of the A523 dual carriageway to the north of **Macclesfield** (grid reference 919741).
→ Adlington Road car park by the viaduct in **Bollington**, 3 miles northeast of Macclesfield, by the Dog & Partridge pub, signposted 'Middlewood Way' (grid reference 931782) or at the Cycle Hire Centre on Grimshaw Lane, Bollington.
→ Poynton Coppice and Higher Poynton, east of **Poynton** and the A523 (grid reference 945834).
→ **Marple.** Turn off the A626 Stockport to Glossop road in Marple, opposite the Rose Hill Post Office (close to the Railway pub) onto Railway Road, signposted 'Middlewood Way / Station car park'. Look for a sign for the start of the Middlewood Way in the far left-hand corner of the car park (grid reference 949888).

Stations: Marple, Middlewood and Macclesfield.
TIC: Macclesfield, 01625 504114.
Other nearby trails: The Sett Valley Trail runs between New Mills and Hayfield, to the southeast of Marple. Rudyard Lake lies 10 miles south of Macclesfield. The Biddulph Valley Line starts from Congleton, 10 miles southwest of Macclesfield.
Useful publications: OS Landranger Maps 109 & 118. *Pathways from the Past* leaflet available from Cheshire Countryside Rangers, Adlington Road, Bollington, Cheshire (01625 573998) or Leisure Services (01625 504504). A comprehensive cyclists' map of Manchester is produced by CycleCity Guides which shows all the city's recreational routes and best commuter routes. Available by sending £4.95 payable to CycleCity Guides, Wallbridge Mill, The Retreat, Frome BA11 5JU (01373 453533). E-mail: info@cyclecityguides.co.uk
Refreshments: Lots of choice in Marple, Bollington and Macclesfield.

6 Wirral Country Park (Hooton to West Kirby), on the Wirral Peninsula

CATEGORY
Railway path.

DISTANCE
Up to 12 miles each way. The southern section is of a much higher quality so you may wish to shorten the ride considerably.

Improvements are happening at a rapid pace on this 12-mile railway path along the west side of the Wirral. At present large parts are divided into two sections, one for walkers and the other for horseriders and cyclists. This can become very confusing as the paths occasionally change sides and vary considerably in quality. Always show courtesy to other path users and if by any chance you find yourself on the walkers' side, slow right down and keep smiling! The improvement has

6

started at the southern end of the path, from Hooton Station, and so far reaches as far as Neston. The improvements have created a far better surface on the path as it runs through broadleaf woodland, banks of wildflowers and, as you proceed north, you will enjoy views of the Dee Estuary to the west. On the outskirts of Neston you will pass through an amazing rock cutting where you feel as though Indiana Jones might suddenly swing across the path on a hanging creeper! Pick marks can still be seen in the sandstone which was gouged out by hand.

Wirral Country Park is based on the former 12-mile Hooton to West Kirby Branch Line Railway. It opened in 1866 and ran for 90 years carrying freight and passengers and for a further 6 years carrying just freight. The dismantled railway became Britain's first country park in the late 1960s. The most important remaining feature of railway days is the station at Hadlow Way, Willaston which still looks as it might have done in the 1950s.

STARTING POINTS & PARKING

→ **Hooton Railway Station** car park (Park & Ride car park), to the northwest of Ellesmere Port and just west of the M53 Jct 5. Follow the A41 towards Chester then turn first right onto the B5133 to get to the station (grid reference 350782).

→ The visitor centre, at the end of the minor road through **Thurstaston**, off the A540 between Heswall and West Kirby (grid reference 237836).

ON YOUR BIKES!

1. Exit Hooton Station car park, cross the railway line via the road bridge then turn immediately left to descend to the Wirral Way, at first running parallel with the railway line on a fairly narrow track.

2. The track widens and the surface improves after the first bridge. (Much of the Wirral Way

6

will be brought up to this standard over the next few years, as time and money allows). The Wirral Way briefly joins a lane then bears right onto a continuation of the trail, at first parallel with the lane.

3. Pass through an amazing rock cutting. At the crossroads with the road (Bushell Road to the right, Mellock Lane to the left, Station Road ahead) continue straight on, signposted 'Wirral Way'. Continue in the same direction. At the mini-roundabout at the end of Station Road turn left then on a sharp left-hand bend turn right. (It is better to cross the road before the bend). Climb to rejoin the course of the railway path.

4. At the junction with the next road (Neston Cricket Club is to your left) turn right then second left signposted 'Wirral Way'.

5. Views of the Dee Estuary open up to the left. About 3 miles after Neston Cricket Club, at the T-junction with a road, turn right along Riverbank Road / Davenport Road, quiet residential roads with new houses. After 1/2

mile bear right to rejoin the railway path.

6. After 2 miles go past Thurstaston Visitor Centre.

7. The Wirral Way ends after a further 3 miles at the busy A540 in West Kirby.

Station: Hooton or West Kirby.

TIC: Birkenhead, 0151 647 6780.

Other nearby trails: North Wirral Coastal Park runs from Hoylake to the Seacombe Ferry Terminal. The Liverpool Loop Line runs from Halewood to Aintree. There are waymarked trails in Delamere Forest. The Whitegate Way runs from Cuddington to Winsford.

Useful publications: OS Landranger Maps 108 & 117.

Refreshments: Coach & Horses pub, Neston. Lots of choice just off the route in Heswall. Refreshments at Thurstaston Visitor Centre. Lots of choice in West Kirby.

7   North Wirral Coastal Park, Liverpool

CATEGORY
Coastal promenade.
DISTANCE
8 miles each way.

A time will come when there will be an unbroken, top quality cyclepath around the edge of the Wirral, from the Seacombe Ferry Terminal round to Hoylake, Heswall and Neston. Until that time enjoy the first stretch that is open and ready, from the ferry terminal through New Brighton to Meols on the eastern edge of Hoylake. It is an open breezy ride that starts with wonderful views across the Mersey with the famous ferry plying its trade between Seacombe and the Royal Liver Buildings. Further north on the other side of the Mersey is the Port of Liverpool with hundreds of cranes loading and unloading containers. After passing through the Victorian resort of New Brighton the path runs alongside a golf course with big open

7

skies and the vast expanse of Liverpool Bay to the north. The trail known as the North Wirral Coastal Park ends at Meols but if you want to extend the ride it is possible to link up with the Wirral Way in West Kirby by using roads through Hoylake for about 3 miles.

New Brighton was established in the 1830s by James Atherton who hoped that it would come to outrank the resort of Brighton on the south coast. In Victorian times there was a tower even higher than the one at Blackpool. North Wirral Coastal Park is well known for its wildlife, especially wading birds which visit during their migration - oystercatcher, dunlin, redshank and turnstone for example. Leasowe Lighthouse was built in 1763 as one of several beacons used to guide ships safely into the Mersey estuary.

STARTING POINTS & PARKING

→ The **Seacombe Ferry Terminal** on the west side of the Mersey, Liverpool (grid reference 326908). No cars are allowed along the promenade between the ferry terminal and New Brighton. There is parking in the side streets or at New Brighton.

→ Dove Point on Meols Parade, the coastal road on the eastern edge of **Hoylake**, by a sign which says 'No unauthorised vehicles' (grid reference 235907).

ON YOUR BIKES!

1. From the Seacombe Ferry Terminal follow the broad (traffic-free) road north with the River Mersey to your right.
2. The route goes through New Brighton, turning west and running along the cycleway on the pavement then continues in the same direction with the golf course to your left.
3. Follow this traffic-free route for 5 miles. It stops at Dove Point near Meols Parade, on the eastern edge of Hoylake.

Station: New Brighton.

TIC: Liverpool, 0151 708 8854.
Other nearby trails: The Wirral Way. The
Otterspool Promenade on the other side of
the Mersey.
Useful publications: OS Landranger Map 108.
Much more useful is the excellent *Liverpool
Cycle Map* (£3.00) showing traffic-free routes,
recommended routes, waymarked routes and
the National Cycle Network in the Liverpool
area. Available from: Merseyside Cycling
Campaign, 11 Beaconsfield Street, Liverpool L8
2UU (0151 727 4584).
E-mail: neil@cyclingsolutions.co.uk
Refreshments: Lots of choice in New Brighton.

8 Cheshire Lines Path, north of Liverpool

CATEGORY
Railway path.
DISTANCE
7 miles each way.

The trail runs from the outskirts of Liverpool to
the coast south of Southport, following the old
Cheshire Lines railway across the West
Lancashire Moss. This is the first railway path
section of the Trans Pennine Trail, followed to

the east by the Liverpool Loop Line. Moss is an
old Lancashire word meaning marsh, and like
much of this part of the West Lancashire Plain,
this was former marshland drained in the 19th
century to produce richly fertile farmland. The
pine woods near the railway line are one of the
last sanctuaries of the red squirrel.

STARTING POINTS & PARKING
→ Maghull, off the A59 to the north of the
M57, Jct 7. The railway path starts from the
B5422 (Sefton Lane) to the west of Maghull, just
west of the Sefton Drive turning (grid reference
364017).
→ Moor Lane, a minor road off the A565 to the
southeast of Ainsdale, between Formby and
Southport (grid reference 325102).

Station: Maghull or Ainsdale.
TIC: Southport, 01704 533333.
Other nearby trails: Liverpool Loop Line.
Useful publications: OS Landranger Map 108.
Another useful publication is the excellent
Liverpool Cycle Map (£3) showing traffic-free,
recommended and waymarked routes and the
National Cycle Network. Available from:
Merseyside Cycling Campaign, 11 Beaconsfield
Street, Liverpool L8 2UU (0151 727 4584).
E-mail: neil@cyclingsolutions.co.uk
Refreshments: Lots of choice in Maghull
and Ainsdale.

9 Liverpool Loop Line (Halewood & Aintree)

CATEGORY
Railway path.
DISTANCE
10 miles each way.

The railway path runs along wooded
embankments and between sandstone cuttings
around the eastern edge of Liverpool, from

Halewood (southwest of M62 Jct 6) through Knotty Ash and Walton to the A59 just south of Aintree Station. There are extensive views as far as the Pennine foothills. Opened in 1879, the Liverpool Loop Line was planned to provide a direct route to the Lancashire coast from Chehire and Warrington, bypassing central Liverpool. The line was used for 90 years and has since been converted to recreational use, forming part of the Trans Pennine Trail which crosses the country from Southport to Hull. Halewood Triangle was once a busy railway junction. However, now the trains have gone the area has been developed into an attractive country park with recreational facilities and is served by a visitor centre.

STARTING POINTS & PARKING
→ **Halewood Triangle Country Park**, southwest of M62 Jct 6 (grid reference 439862). The railway line runs along the northeast edge of the park.
→ **Walton Hall Park**, north Liverpool, west of M57 Jct 4/5 (grid reference 375952). The trail runs just to the east of the park.
→ The trail (signposted as the Trans Pennine Trail) can be picked up from **Aintree railway station** (grid reference 366979).

Station: Halewood.
TIC: Liverpool, 0151 708 8854.
Other nearby trails: The Cheshire Lines Path starts 5 miles north of Walton (the northern end of the Liverpool Loop Line).
Useful publications: OS Landranger Map 108. Much more useful is the excellent *Liverpool Cycle Map* (£3) showing traffic-free routes, recommended routes, waymarked routes and the National Cycle Network in the Liverpool area. Available from: Merseyside Cycling Campaign, 11 Beaconsfield Street, Liverpool L8 2UU (0151 727 4584). E-mail: neil@cyclingsolutions.co.uk
Refreshments: Halewood Visitor Centre. In West Derby (Mill Lane) and Rice Lane.

10

10 Liverpool - the Otterspool Promenade

CATEGORY
Promenade alongside the Mersey.

DISTANCE
5 miles each way.

The regeneration of Albert Dock has been the driving force behind the improvement along the whole length of the River Mersey from Cressington and Otterspool to the Royal Liver Buildings. A broad, top grade promenade now sweeps alongside the river for 5 miles with wide open views across the water to the Wirral. The path is popular with walkers, joggers and cyclists but is wide enough to accommodate all three without trouble. Albert Dock houses the Beatles Museum amongst others and offers a model of what can be done in terms of inner city regeneration. If you want to enjoy the quintessential Liverpool experience why not take the ferry across the Mersey? Opened in

1846 as England's gateway to the New World, Albert Dock is the largest group of Grade 1 listed buildings in Great Britain. It fell into disuse but has now been revamped into a quayside complex featuring watersports and a museums. Alongside Animation World, The Beatles Story, the Tate Galley and the Maritime Museum are a number of speciality shops and restaurants.

STARTING POINTS & PARKING
→ The **Liver Buildings**, in the centre of Liverpool.
→ The south end of the Otterspool Promenade. Turn off the A561 just west of Cressington Station down Riversdale Road, following signs for 'Liverpool Cricket Ground'. There is a car park at the end. Descend to the riverside promenade and turn right (grid reference 385852).

ON YOUR BIKES!
It is hard to lose something as large as the River

11

Mersey! Stay close to the water and you won't go far wrong. There are one or two short diversions away from the promenade but you soon return to the water's edge. From the Royal Liver Buildings you could easily catch a ferry to Seacombe on the other side and continue north along the traffic-free promenade that runs to New Brighton and around the coastline of the Wirral to Hoylake.

Station: Liverpool.
TIC: Liverpool, 0151 708 8854.
Other nearby trails: On the other side of the Mersey there is a cyclepath from the Seacombe Ferry Terminal to New Brighton and on to the North Wirral Coastal Park. Also the Liverpool Loop Line (Halewood), the Cheshire Lines Path (Maghull - Ainsdale) and Saint Helen's Canal (Widnes).
Useful publications: OS Landranger Map 108. Much more useful is the excellent *Liverpool Cycle Map* (£3) showing traffic-free routes, recommended routes, waymarked routes and the National Cycle Network. Available from: Merseyside Cycling Campaign, 11 Beaconsfield Street, Liverpool L8 2UU. (0151 727 4584). E-mail: neil@cyclingsolutions.co.uk
Refreshments: Lots of choice for refreshments in Albert Dock.

11   Saint Helen's Canal, Widnes (east of Liverpool)

CATEGORY
Canal towpath.
DISTANCE
5 1/2 miles each way.

Several rides in this book use sections of the Trans Pennine Trail, the path that crosses the country from Southport on the West Coast to Hull and the North Sea Coast, officially opened at the end of 2000. This ride along St Helen's Canal is surprisingly green, quiet and secluded for a setting so much in the heart of the industrial area between Liverpool and Manchester. Do not be surprised to see herons and even kingfishers along this stretch of water. The pub at Fiddler's Ferry offers a welcome refreshment stop and is a good turnaround point for an 8-mile ride. If you want to extend the ride you can easily follow the Trans Pennine Trail signposts through Warrington on a mixture of tracks and quiet streets to join the railway path from Warrington to Altrincham. Spike Island and the surrounding area was the birthplace of the British chemical industry and the Catalyst Museum explains the industry's history with photgraphs, slide shows and working machines. Since 1975 the area has been transformed into a green space and haven for wildlife.

STARTING POINT & PARKING

→ The Catalyst Museum car park in **Widnes**, just north of the Runcorn - Widnes Bridge (grid reference 513842). Follow the brown and white signs from the A562 / A533 / A557. (East of Liverpool).

ON YOUR BIKES!

1. From the corner of the Catalyst Museum car park by the path leading to the museum entrance, bear left towards the locks. Cross the narrow bridge and turn left alongside the canal.
2. After 4 miles you will go past the Ferry Tavern pub.
3. The towpath ends after a further 1 1/2 miles. It is possible to continue eastwards on the Trans Pennine Trail by following signposts through Warrington on quiet roads and sections alongside the River Mersey and the Manchester Ship Canal to join the next long traffic-free section which runs along a railway path from Warrington through Lymm to the outskirts of Altrincham.

Station: Warrington.
TIC: Warrington, 01925 442180.

Other nearby trails: This route is part of the Trans Pennine Trail. To the east the next traffic-free section is the railway path from Warrington to Altrincham. There are three more traffic-free routes just to the west: the Liverpool Otterspool Promenade, the Cheshire Lines Path and the Liverpool Loop Line.
Useful publications: OS Landranger Map 108. Much more useful is the excellent *Liverpool Cycle Map* (£3) showing traffic-free routes, recommended routes, waymarked routes and the National Cycle Network in the Liverpool area. Available from: Merseyside Cycling Campaign, 11 Beaconsfield Street, Liverpool L8 2UU (0151 727 4584). E-mail: neil@cyclingsolutions.co.uk
Refreshments: Excellent pub called Ferry Tavern at Fiddler's Ferry.

12 Warrington to Altrincham (between Manchester and Liverpool)

CATEGORY
Railway path.
DISTANCE
7 1/2 miles each way.

There is a signboard at the western end of this trail, at the bottom of the approach ramp on the outskirts of Warrington, that places this short ride within a much wider context: not only is Warrington to Altrincham part of the Trans Pennine Trail stretching from coast to coast but the Trans Pennine Trail itself is part of the European Long Distance Footpath system which links such far-flung destinations as Geneva, Istanbul, St Petersburg and Riga! Finding the car park and the start of the ride on the west side of Altrincham can be hard work! Once on the trail it is impossible to get lost and the top grade surface enables you to bowl along through open countryside and woodland with verges full of

12

wildflowers in the late spring and early summer. This is a good ride for conversation - no hills, a wide track and good visibility so you can put the world to rights while keeping yourself fit! It would be easy to extend this ride westwards by following the Trans Pennine Trail signs through Warrington to join St Helen's Canal to Widnes.

STARTING POINTS & PARKING

→ **Altrincham** (grid reference 751889). From the M6 or the M56 follow the A556 north towards Altrincham. Go past the left turn to Dunham Massey (B5160) then after 1/2 mile, on a sharp right-hand bend, take the **second** of two closely-spaced left turns onto Highgate Road. This becomes Gorsey Lane. At the T-junction (mini-roundabout) turn left onto Oldfield Road (which becomes Seamons Road). Cross the bridge over the canal (traffic lights) then 150 yds after passing the Bay Malton pub turn left into the car park. **Beware the height barrier!**

→ **Bradshaw Lane**, on the southeast edge of

Warrington, just north of the junction of the A50 and the A56, close to the Latchford Locks on the Manchester Ship Canal (grid reference 638871).

ON YOUR BIKES!

The route is well signposted and easy to follow. If you are travelling from east to west the M6 is about 6 miles along the trail (three-quarters of the total distance from Altrincham to Warrington).

Station: Warrington or Altrincham.
TIC: Altrincham, 0161 912 5931.
Other nearby trails: This is part of the Trans Pennine Trail. To the west is Saint Helen's Canal, to the east the next traffic free section is the Mersey River through South Manchester.
Useful publications: OS Landranger Map 109.
Refreshments: Bay Malton pub, west of Altrincham, Star pub at Lymm, Railway Inn, Dunham Woodhouses.

13 Mersey River through South Manchester

CATEGORY
Riverside path.

DISTANCE
West from the visitor centre - 1 mile each way; east from the visitor centre - 2 1/2 miles each way.

Forming part of the Trans Pennine Trail, this route alongside the River Mersey through Sale Water Park not only offers an existing ride alongside the river and around Chorlton Water but promises much more in the future when the quality of the riverside path is improved to the east. In the meantime enjoy the open green spaces alongside the River Mersey with its profusion of wildflowers and birdlife.

Occupying the site of the old Barlow Hall Farm, 170-acre Chorlton Water Park is now one of the most popular sites in the Mersey Valley. Like Sale Water Park a mile downstream, the lake at Chorlton was excavated in the early 1970s to provide gravel for the M60 motorway. Since then the area has been developed to cater for all kinds of recreational activities in a country-side setting. During winter months the lake is visited by large numbers of ducks including Pochard, Tufted Duck and Goldeneye.

STARTING POINTS & PARKING
→ The visitor centre at **Sale Water Park** (Trafford Watersports Centre) off the M60 Jct 8 (grid reference 804989).

→ The church in **East Didsbury**, just off the A5145 to the west of the A34 and to the north of M63 Jct 3 (grid reference 847904).

ON YOUR BIKES!
With your back to the entrance to the visitor centre go straight ahead on the narrow path running parallel with the road. Continue in the same direction to join the River Mersey by a sluice control building (remember this point for your return). At this point you have a choice:

West
Turn left on the track alongside the river. Follow this for 1 mile as far as the railway line and the next bridge over the river. From this point you can return on the higher or lower track. There is also a track on the other side of the river but it is rougher. Return to the sluice control building.

East
Turn right along the river then cross the bridge over the river (by Jacksons Boat pub) and turn right. After 1 mile, opposite a metal bridge with anti-climbing barbs go through the barrier and turn left down to Chorlton Water Park. Complete a circuit of the lake, return to this point on the River Mersey then go back to the visitor centre.

Station: Sale or East Didsbury.
TIC: Manchester, 0161 234 3157.
Other nearby trails: The Middlewood Way runs from Marple (east of Stockport) to Macclesfield. The Trans Pennine Trail continues west from Altrincham to Warrington.
Useful publications: OS Landranger Map 109. A comprehensive cyclists' map of Manchester is

produced by CycleCity Guides which shows all the city's recreational routes and best commuter routes. Available from CycleCity Guides, Wallbridge Mill, The Retreat, Frome BA11 5JU (01373 453533).
E-mail: info@cyclecityguides.co.uk
Refreshments: Cafe adjacent to the visitor centre. Jackson's Boat Inn at Jackson's Bridge

14 Salford Looplines, West Manchester

CATEGORY
Railway path.
DISTANCE
5 miles each way.

The old railway line skirts Worsley Wood and offers the opportunity to visit the famous Worsley Canal Basin on the Bridgewater Canal. There are two separate trails, the lower arm is called the Tyldesley Loopline to Ellenbrook and the upper arm is referred to as the Roe Green Loopline to Little Hulton. The Looplines have become a valuable wildlife corridor, encouraging the free movement of plants and animals into the heart of the urban area. The old railways were some of the earliest to be converted to cyclepaths in the North-West region.

STARTING POINT & PARKING
→**Monton Green** (east of M60, Jct 12). Car park in Duke's Drive Recreation Ground / Broadoak Park just off Parrin Lane to the west of its junction with Monton Green, near Monton church (grid reference 764995).

Station: Patricroft or Walkden
TIC: Manchester, 0161 234 3157.
Other nearby trails: Ashton Canal, Mersey River, Warrington to Altrincham.
Useful publications: OS Landranger Map 109. Better is the *Greater Manchester Cycling Map* produced by CycleCity Guides, Wallbridge Mill, The Retreat, Frome BA11 5JU (01373 453533). E-mail: info@cyclecityguides.co.uk
Refreshments: Pubs, cafes at Monton Green and Worsley Canal Basin.

14

15 Reddish Vale Cycle Trail, southeast Manchester

CATEGORY
Railway path and tracks in country park.

DISTANCE
3-mile circuit.

Pass through rich flower meadows, experience the sights and sounds of nature under the woodland canopy and follow the course of the River Tame south from the Reddish Vale Visitor Centre as it gently meanders its way through the valley. There is a suggested waymarked loop (white on green circular waymarks with 'Reddish Vale Cycle Trail' written on them) at the southern end of the trail, crossing the River Tame on the two bridges in the park

STARTING POINT & PARKING
→ Reddish Vale Visitor Centre, at the junction of Reddish Vale Road and Mill Lane, in **Reddish**, southeast of Manchester city centre and north of M60 Jct 27. Reddish Vale Road lies to the east of Reddish Road (B6167) very close to Reddish South railway station (grid reference 904934).

Station: Brinnington or Reddish South.
TIC: Manchester, 0161 234 3157.
Other nearby trails: The Middlewood Way runs south from Marple, the Mersey River through South Manchester goes through Sale Water Park. A railway path runs from Warrington to Altrincham.
Useful publications: OS Landranger Map 109. A leaflet, *Reddish Vale Cycle Trail* is available from: Stockport Metropolitan Borough Council, Community Services Division (0161 474 4434) or from the Reddish Vale Visitor Centre (0161 477 5637).
Refreshments: Cafe near the visitor centre.

16 Ashton Canal, from Manchester to Ashton-under-Lyne

CATEGORY

Canal towpath.

DISTANCE

7 miles each way.

This ride starts in the heart of Manchester and runs east towards the Pennine foothills. The ride starts from Jutland Street/Ducie Street in Central Manchester and runs east through Bradford, Openshaw, Fairfield and Guide Bridge to Portland Basin/Portland Street in Ashton-under-Lyne. There is a gentle climb alongside locks. The Ashton Canal was opened in 1797, linking four other canals: Bridgewater, Rochdale, Huddersfield and Peak Forest. By the 1830s it was carrying over half a million tonnes of coal and limestone. The growth of railways and then roads took away much of its business and it was closed in 1958. It was reopened in 1974 and now forms part of the popular Cheshire Ring.

STARTING POINTS & PARKING

→ Portland Basin, **Ashton-under-Lyne** (near Asda Superstore, grid reference 935985).

→ Ducie Street Basin, near Piccadilly Station in **Central Manchester** (grid reference 848982).

Stations: Manchester Piccadilly, Guide Bridge and Ashton-under-Lyne.

TIC: Manchester, 0161 234 3157.

Other nearby trails: The Middlewood Way runs south from Marple to Macclesfield. Mersey River through South Manchester (Sale Water Park).

Useful publications: OS Landranger Map 109. Better by far is either an A-Z street atlas or the *Greater Manchester Cycling Map* produced by Cycle City Guides, Wallbridge Mill, The Retreat, Frome BA11 5JU (01373 453533). E-mail: info@cyclecityguides.co.uk

Refreshments: Lots in Ashton and Manchester.

17 Tame Valley Trail, northeast of Manchester

CATEGORY

Railway path.

DISTANCE

3 miles each way.

Follow the River Tame, a tributary of the River Mersey, from Brownhill Visitor Centre in Uppermill via Greenfield to Mossley down the steep-sided river valley along the course of an old railway line, the Micklehurst Loop Line, that used to serve the mills. There is plenty of architectural interest against a background of moorland scenery. The former cotton mill village of Uppermill is now a popular tourist centre with the Saddleworth Museum of local history located in an old woollen mill and speciality shops along the main street.

NB Take care crossing the A670 from Brownhills Visitor Centre, the A669 at Greenfield and the A635 near The Roaches.

STARTING POINT & PARKING

→ Brownhill Visitor Centre, Uppermill (grid reference 996064), on the A670, about 5 miles east of Oldham, Manchester.

ON YOUR BIKES!

From the visitor centre, cross the A670 **with care** onto Brownhill Road and climb for about 1/4 mile to the brow of the hill. The trail starts on the right, going through a narrow gate.

Stations: Greenfield and Mossley, each 1/2 mile from the Tame Valley Trail.

TIC: Oldham, 0161 627 1024.

Other nearby trails: The route is likely to be extended down the Tame Valley via Stalybridge to the Ashton Canal. The Middlewood Way starts south of Marple. The Longdendale Trail runs east from Hadfield.

Useful publications: OS Landranger Map 109. Leaflet available from Tame Valley Countryside Warden Service (0161 342 3306).

Refreshments: Lots of pubs and cafes in Uppermill and Delph. Pubs in Greenfield and Mossley.

18   Gisburn Forest, north of Clitheroe

CATEGORY

Waymarked forest trails.

DISTANCE

Three routes of 6 - 10 miles.

There are three waymarked trails in this small forestry holding north of Clitheroe. This is the only Forestry Commission holding worth mentioning between Manchester and the Lake District; indeed, Gisburn Forest and Delamere Forest near to Chester are the only holdings south of Cumbria in the North-West region.

STARTING POINT & PARKING

→ Cocklet Hill, on the minor road which crosses the B6478 Slaidburn to Long Preston road 4 miles northeast of **Slaidburn**, and 10 miles north of Clitheroe (grid reference 745551).

Station: Long Preston.
TIC: Clitheroe, 01200 425566.
Other nearby trails: The River Lune Cycleways start in Lancaster
Useful publications: OS Landranger Map 103.
Refreshments: None on the route.

19   Pendle Cycleways from Colne to Brierfield

CATEGORY

Canal towpath.

DISTANCE

5 miles each way.

Three canals were built to cross the Pennines between Liverpool and Hull: the Huddersfield Narrow Canal and the Rochdale Canal took more direct lines whereas the Leeds & Liverpool, used in this route between Burnley and Colne, made the most of the gap created by the tributaries of the River Aire and River Calder, reaching its highest point just north of Colne. Think about those poor navvies 200 years ago as you cycle along the towpath!

STARTING POINTS & PARKING

→ Greenfield Road (near the railway station), **Colne**, at the northern end of the M65 to the north of Burnley (grid reference 880397). Follow Greenfield Road across a crossroads with Whitewalls Drive to Barrowford Locks and bear left along the towpath.

→ The Finsley Gate crossing of the canal in the centre of **Burnley**, just south of the TIC and bus station.

Stations: Colne, Nelson, Brierfield & Burnley.
TIC: Burnley, 01282 455485.
Other nearby trails: There are waymarked woodland trails in Gisburn Forest, 10 miles north of Clitheroe.
Useful publications: OS Landranger Map 103. *The Pendle Cycleways* is available from the Highways & Transport Services, Booth Street, Nelson, Lancashire BB9 7PX (01282 617731).
Refreshments: In Colne, Nelson, Brierfield & Burnley.

20 Lune Cycleways, Lancaster

CATEGORY
Railway and riverside paths.
DISTANCE
Lancaster to Glasson Dock - 4 1/2 miles each way; Lancaster to Caton (Bull Beck) - 5 miles each way; Lancaster to Morecambe - 3 miles each way.

The Lune Cycleways are three traffic-free rides linked by a 1-mile section of quiet roads in Lancaster. The most popular recreational trail runs from Lancaster to Caton (and Bull Beck), following the River Lune to just beyond the wide bend in the river known as the Crook o' Lune; a second recreational trail runs south to the marina and the old docks at Glasson with wide views over the estuary; there is also an urban spur of three miles from Lancaster into Morecambe. The path to the north follows the course of the old Lancaster to Wennington railway, opened in 1850 and passing beneath the remarkable Lune Aqueduct carrying the Lancaster Canal. To the south the trail runs along the old Lancaster to Glasson Dock Railway which ran for 60 years from 1887 to 1947.

STARTING POINTS & PARKING
→ **Lancaster** city centre, on the southern side of the new Millennium Bridge.

→ **Glasson Dock** car park at the southern end of the bike path (grid reference 445561).

→ **Crook o' Lune** picnic site, signposted off the A683 about 4 miles northeast of Lancaster (grid reference 522646).

ON YOUR BIKES!

The Morecambe to Lancaster path is connected to the Lancaster to Caton path via the splendid new Millennium bridge.

To connect the Caton trail to the Glasson trail, from the end of the Caton path in the centre of Lancaster, turn right under the railway bridge, left at the first T-junction and left again almost immediately at the T-junction with the river, onto New Quay Road. The traffic-free path starts near the industrial estate, at first a bit rough, it soon improves.

Station: Lancaster.
TIC: Lancaster, 01524 32878.
Other nearby trails: Gisburn Forest, north of Clitheroe.
Useful publications: OS Landranger Maps 97 & 102. Lealeft available from: County Publicity Department, Lancashire County Council, County Hall, Preston, Lancashire PR1 8XJ (01772 263399).
Refreshments: Lots of choice in Lancaster. Pubs and cafe in Glasson Dock. Ship Inn, The Cottage tearoom in Caton.

21 Grizedale Forest, southwest of Ambleside, Lake District (5 routes)

CATEGORY
Forest trails
DISTANCE
2 - 14 miles

Grizedale is the main forestry area in the Lake District with several waymarked trails. Pick up a leaflet describing all the trails from the visitor centre and explore the woodland with all its amazing sculptures.

STARTING POINTS & PARKING

➔ The Grizedale Visitor Centre is located on a minor road 4 miles southwest of Hawkshead (10 miles south of Ambleside) (grid reference 335944).

DISTANCE	GRADE / WAYMARK

Goosey Foot Tarn

2 miles	Easy-Moderate	Red

Start: Moor Top car park, on the road towards Hawkshead (grid reference 343964)
Recommended ride direction: anti-clockwise

Grizedale Tarn

6 miles	Moderate / Black

Start: Bogle Crag car park, on the road towards Satterthwaite (grid reference 338933)
Recommended ride direction: clockwise

Moor Top

7 miles	Moderate / Purple

Start: Grizedale Visitor Centre

Hawkshead Moor

10.5 miles	Demanding / Green

22

Start: Grizedale Visitor Centre; Moor Top car park, on the Hawkshead road; or High Cross car park, on the B5285 west of Hawkshead (grid reference 332987).
Recommended ride direction: clockwise

Silurian Way

14 miles	Demanding / Orange

Start: Grizedale Visitor Centre
Recommended ride direction: clockwise

NB The minor road between Hawshead and Satterthwaite is used for about 1 mile on the Moor Top route and for 3 miles on the Silurian Way route.

Station: Windermere.
TIC: Hawkshead, 01539 436525.
Other nearby trails: Whinlatter Forest, west of Keswick, also has waymarked forest trails.
Useful publications: OS Landranger Map 97. Leaflet available from Forest Enterprise, South Lakes Forest District, Grizedale, Hawkshead, Ambleside LA22 0QJ (01229 860010).
Refreshments: At the visitor centre. Pub in Satterthwaite.

22 Whitehaven to Rowrah, West Cumbria

CATEGORY
Railway path.
DISTANCE
9 miles each way.

This is the first section of Sustrans C2C Route (National Cycle Network Routes 7 & 71), a long distance trail which crosses the Pennines and reaches the East Coast at Sunderland (or Tynemouth). The trail climbs slowly away from the industrial Cumbrian Coast at Whitehaven via Moor Row, Cleator Moor and Rowrah towards the western fells of the Lake District. If you are feeling fit you can easily link this ride to

the trail alongside Ennerdale Water, taking you right into the heart of the fells.

The Whitehaven to Rowrah line was built in the 1850s and passes through an area dotted with old mines and quarries which formed the basis of West Cumbria's rapid growth through the second half of the 19th century. By 1900 the population of Cleator Moor had grown to 10,000. The villages and towns remain but the mines and quarries which created them have largely gone, leaving only old mine buildings and spoil heaps.

STARTING POINT & PARKING
The trail starts from **Whitehaven Harbour** by heading south along Preston Street (the B5345 towards St Bees), signposted as the 'C2C'. If in doubt, the trail runs close to the present railway line for the first couple of miles, crossing and recrossing three times as the trail heads south. There are several car parks in Whitehaven and also at Rowrah (grid reference 055185).

Station: Corkickle, south of Whitehaven.
TIC: Whitehaven, 01946 852939.
Other nearby trails: Ennerdale Water. Whinlatter Forest.
Useful publications: OS Landranger Map 89. Leaflet available from West Cumbria Groundwork Trust, Crowgarth House, 48 High Street, Cleator Moor, Cumbria CA25 5AA (01946 695678).
Refreshments: Lots of choice in Whitehaven. Pubs in Cleator Moor and Rowrah.

23 Ennerdale Water on the west side of the Lake District

CATEGORY
Woodland trail.
DISTANCE
6 miles each way.

Although this is not a waymarked forestry trail as such, it nevertheless offers an attractive ride through forestry on wide stone forest roads with

23

views over Ennerdale Water and unlike most non-waymarked forest routes, it is very hard to get lost. You can either go for a there-and-back ride or form a circuit by crossing the River Liza just below the youth hostel and following the river on the south side as far as the eastern end of Ennerdale Water, where you recross to rejoin the outward trail.

NB There is a 500ft climb from the start to the highpoint near to Black Sail Hut Youth Hostel.

STARTING POINT & PARKING
➔ The car park at the end of the minor road leading east from **Ennerdale Bridge**, 10 miles east of Whitehaven (grid reference 110152).

Station: Whitehaven.
TIC: Whitehaven, 01946 852939.
Other nearby trails: Whitehaven to Rowrah. Workington Railpaths.
Useful publications: OS Landranger Map 89.
Refreshments: None on the route. The nearest is at Ennerdale Bridge.

24 Whinlatter Forest Park, west of Keswick (2 routes)

CATEGORY
Forest trail.
DISTANCE
5 and 7 miles.

There are two waymarked routes on steep woodland trails through this spectacularly set Forestry Commission holding west of Keswick. The short loop is waymarked with orange bike signs, the longer route with purple bike signs. If you are looking for easier forest trails, try Grizedale Forest, south of Hawkshead. Open daily, the visitor centre uses films, computers and a unique working model to depict the life of a working forest. Information about activities in the forest and the work of the Education Service can be obtained from the visitor centre staff who will be happy to help you plan your day in the forest.

NB The B5292 must be crossed on both loops.

24

Remember also that the forest roads are used by walkers and forestry vehicles and take special care when negotiating bends and blind summits.

STARTING POINT & PARKING

→ **Whinlatter Forest Visitor Centre** on the B5292 between Keswick and Cockermouth (grid reference 208245).

Station: Workington.
TIC: Keswick, 01768 772645.
Other nearby trails: Keswick Railway Path, Whitehaven Railway Path, Ennerdale Water.
Useful publications: OS Landranger Map 89. A leaflet (£1.25) can be purchased from Whinlatter Forest Park, Braithwaite, Keswick CA12 5TW (01768 778469).
Refreshments: At the visitor centre.

25 Keswick Railway Path, Lake District.

CATEGORY
Railway path.
DISTANCE
4 miles each way.

This short, delightful trail starting from the Old Railway Station, Keswick (near the Leisure Pool) crosses and recrosses the scenic River Greta on its way towards Threlkeld. Here you have several options to vary your return route to Keswick by following quiet, attractive lanes, for example via Castlerigg Stone Circle. As this is the Lake District you should be aware that these lane options will involve several steep hills. If you are searching for tougher offroad challenges there are spectacular tracks to the north of Skiddaw or along the Old Coach Road over Matterdale Common, east of Keswick. The latter is an option on the C2C ('Coast to Coast'), Sustrans' most popular long distance route on the National Cycle Network.

25

STARTING POINT & PARKING

→ At the old railway station in **Keswick**, near the Leisure Pool. Keswick is in the northern half of the Lake District, west of M6, Jct 40 (grid reference 270237).

Station: Nowhere nearby. Penrith or Workington are both 16 miles away.
TIC: Keswick, 01768 775043.
Other nearby trails: Keswick lies on the course of the C2C Route. There are waymarked trails in nearby Whinlatter Forest.
Useful publications: OS Landranger Map 90.
Refreshments: Lots of choice in Keswick. Pubs in Threlkeld.

26 Workington Rail Paths, West Cumbria

CATEGORY
Railway path.
DISTANCE
6 miles each way.

The west coast of Cumbria was home to a great deal of heavy industry based around the high grade deposits of iron ore. The industry has now gone and the tramways and old railways have been converted to recreational use. This ride goes from High Harrington, in the southern outskirts of Workington, north through Workington then east to Camerton. From the bridge over the River Derwent in Workington there is a 250ft climb north to Camerton and a 200ft climb south to High Harrington.

STARTING POINTS & PARKING

→ The centre of **Workington** (near the bus station / Tourist Information Centre).
→ **High Harrington**, on the A597 to the south of Workington (grid reference 999255).
→ **Seaton / Camerton**, to the northeast of Workington (grid reference 037313). Follow National Cycle Network Route 71 signs.

Station: Workington.
TIC: Whitehaven, 01946 852939.
Other nearby trails: There is a railway path from Whitehaven to Rowrah, a trail alongside Ennerdale Water and waymarked forestry routes in Whinlatter Forest.
Useful publications: OS Landranger Map 89.
West Cumbria Cycle Network is available from: Groundwork West Cumbria, 48 High Street, Cleator Moor, West Cumbria (01946 813677).
Refreshments: Lots of choice in Workington. Pubs in High Harrington, Seaton and Camerton.

Yorkshire

YORKSHIRE TRAILS

1	Rother Valley Country Park south of Sheffield
2	Wharncliffe Woods, northwest of Sheffield
3	Sheffield to Rotherham via the Five Weirs Walk
4	Upper Don Trail from Penistone to Wharncliffe Woods or Dunford Bridge
5	Dove Valley Trail, southwest of Barnsley
6	Barnsley to the Old Moor Wetland Centre along the Trans Pennine Trail
7	Doncaster to Harlington along the Trans Pennine Trail
8	Aire & Calder Navigation Towpath, southeast from Leeds
9	Leeds & Liverpool Canal along the Aire Valley, west of Leeds
10	Harland Way, southeast of Harrogate
11	York to Overton
12	York to Riccall
13	Hudson Way from Beverley to Market Weighton, northwest of Hull
14	Hull to Hornsea Trail
15	Hull to South Holderness Trail
16	Cleveland Way from Sutton Bank, North York Moors
17	Boltby Forest, east of Northallerton
18	Rudland Rigg, north of Kirkbymoorside
19	Dalby Forest, northeast of Pickering (4 routes)
20	Scarborough to Whitby Railway Path

Yorkshire Mountain Biking

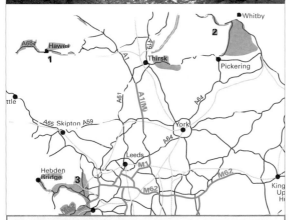

1   **Yorkshire Dales**
2   **North York Moors**
3   **Central Pennines**

Mountain Biking Information

These are possible sources:

- leaflets produced by local authorities, normally available in Tourist Information Centres
- guidebooks which can usually be found in larger, better stocked bookshops
- the staff in bike shops can often put you in contact with local riders or clubs who are sure to have done some of this research already, saving you many hours of trial and error.

The region offers the aficionado some of the finest mountain biking in England with a plethora of excellent well-drained tracks in the Yorkshire Dales and the North York Moors.

There are scores of possibilities in the Yorkshire Dales right from the far north in upper Swaledale and Arkengarthdale down through the centrally located Wensleydale (Bainbridge or Aysgarth would be good bases) to the southern tracks around Settle, Horton in Ribblesdale, Malham and Grassington. Outside the National Park boundary, the hill country west from Ripon towards Nidderdale and around Pateley Bridge also offers a vast range of possibilities.

The North York Moors, although less well provided than the Yorkshire Dales with bridleways and byways, have as compensation great swathes of forestry, a drier climate and sandier soils which tend to drain better. There are some fine ridge rides such as Rudland Rigg to the north of Kirkbymoorside and the Cleveland Way to the north of Sutton Bank Visitor Centre. Even the there-and-back ride along the Scarborough to Whitby railway path is more of a mountain bike challenge than a Sunday afternoon pootle.

Further south, well away from the two National Parks, Hebden Bridge and Todmorden are good bases for exploring the Central Pennines to the northwest of Huddersfield.

Yorkshire Forestry

With the exception of Wharncliffe Woods to the northwest of Sheffield, all of Yorkshire's Forestry Commission holdings are located to the northeast of the county, in or near the North York Moors National Park, with several large holdings to the north of Pickering.

In some forests and woods there are no waymarked routes but you are free to explore the tracks. The relevant Ordnance Survey map is mentioned. It is highly recommended that you take a map for the larger woods where it is very easy to get lost!

2   **Yearsley Moor, northeast of Easingwold**
    OS Explorer Map 299

3   **Scawton and Wass Moor woodlands, along the A170 east of Thirsk**
    OS Outdoor Leisure Map 26

4   **Over Silton Moor, east of Northallerton**
    OS Outdoor Leisure Map 26

5   **Arncliffe Wood, northeast of Northallerton**
    OS Outdoor Leisure Map 26

7   **Langdale, Broxa, Wykeham, Sneaton High Moor and Harwood**

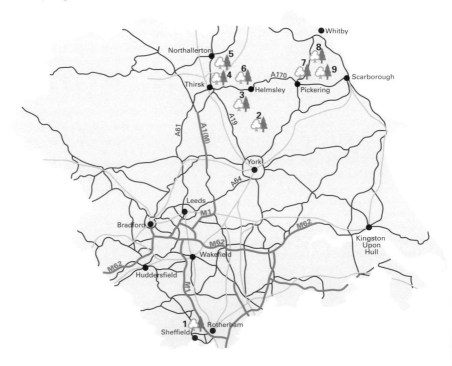

Dale, northeast of Pickering

OS Outdoor Leisure Map 27

8   **Cropton Forest, north of Pickering**

OS Outdoor Leisure Map 27

Forests and woods with waymarked trails

They are shown with a corresponding trail number and page reference.

The Forestry Commission's website is a good source of information with details of 1600 miles of waymarked cycling trails throughout the UK. Search by forest name or by the nearest town or city and the search will tell you the grade, length and waymarking details of the trails.

www.forestry.gov.uk/recreation

Further Information

North York Moors Forest District

Outgang Road, Pickering, North Yorks. YO18 7EL

Tel: 01751 472771

Yorkshire National Cycle Network

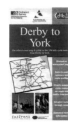

Derby to York Cycle Route

154 miles from Derby to York via Nottingham, Sheffield and Doncaster. Highlights include Elvaston Castle Country Park (Derby), Bestwood Country Park (Nottingham), Newstead Abbey, the traffic-free route through Sherwood Forest and Clumber Park, Rother Valley Country Park, the Old Moor Wetland Centre and the historic city of York.

Traffic-free sections over 3 miles:

- Derby to Elvaston Country Park alongside the Derwent (NCN 6)
- Blidworth to Worksop through Sherwood Forest and Clumber Park (NCN 6)
- The Elsecar Greenway from Hoyland to the Old Moor Wetland Centre (NCN 62 & 67)
- Harlington to Bentley along the Trans

Sustrans

Listed below are the Sustrans maps that cover the National Cycle Network within the region. Some of the maps may describe routes that continue on into adjacent regions: these maps are mentioned in both chapters. The maps are not only useful for people wishing to ride the the whole route over several days they also show all the traffic-free sections which make good day rides. The maps cost £5.99 each and are available from Sustrans.

Sustrans Order Line:
Call **0845 113 0065** or visit their website at
www.sustrans.org.uk

Pennine Trail (NCN 62)
- Riccall to York (NCN 65)

White Rose Cycle Route

123 miles from Hull to Middlesbrough via York. Highlights include Beverley Minster, the Yorkshire Wolds, the historic city of York and the North York Moors. Traffic-free sections over 3 miles:

- The Hudson Way from Beverley to Market Weighton (NCN 66)
- Riccall to York (NCN 65)
- York to Overton (NCN 65)

Trans Pennine Trail (central): Derbyshire & Yorkshire

215 miles from Southport to Hull via Liverpool, Manchester, Barnsley, Doncaster and Selby. Highlights in this section include the Chesterfield Canal, Rother Valley Country Park, Wharncliffe Woods, the Earth Centre and the Aire & Calder Navigation into Leeds.

Traffic-free sections over 3 miles:
- Chesterfield Canal north of Chesterfield (NCN 67)
- Staveley to Beighton Railway Path (NCN 67)
- Sheffield to Rotherham along the River Don (NCN 6)
- Grenoside to Penistone along the Upper Don Trail (NCN 67)
- Silkstone Common to Bolton upon Dearne along the Dove Valley Trail (NCN 62)
- Harlington to Sprotborough along the River Dearne and Don (NCN 62)

- Royston to Walton along the Barnsley Canal north of Barnsley (NCN 67)
- The Aire & Calder Navigation from Woodlesford into Leeds (NCN 67)

Trans Pennine Trail (east): Yorkshire to the North Sea

215 miles from Southport to Hull via Liverpool, Manchester, Barnsley, Doncaster and Selby. Highlights in this section include Cusworth Country Park (Doncaster), lanes across the Vale of York, the historic town of Selby, York, views over the River Humber, the North Sea at Hornsea.

Traffic-free sections over 3 miles:
- Sprotborough to Bentley (NCN 62)
- Riccall to York (NCN 65)
- The Hornsea Rail Trail from Hull to Hornsea (NCN 65)

Pennine Cycleway: South Pennines & the Dales

124 miles from Holmfirth in the South Pennines through the Yorkshire Dales to Appleby-in-Westmorland in the Eden Valley. Highlights include the beautiful and challenging lanes through the South Pennines between Holmfirth and Burnley; the canal towpath between Burnley and Colne; the Yorkshire Dales, particularly the lanes through Kingsdale and Dentdale; the handsome town of Appleby-in-Westmorland.

Traffic-free sections over 3 miles:
- Burnley to Barnoldswick along the Leeds & Liverpool Canal (NCN 68)

Other areas for lane cycling

Much of the southern half of Yorkshire is dominated by the huge conurbations of Sheffield / Rotherham and Leeds / Bradford with several other large towns such as Huddersfield, Wakefield, Barnsley and Doncaster: lots of traffic and few roads free of it. In the northern half there is an amazing choice; from the steep challenges of the **Yorkshire Dales** and the **North York Moors** to the easier rolling countryside of the **Yorkshire Wolds** and the almost flat **Vale of York** and **Holderness**.

Yorkshire Trails

1

1   Rother Valley Country Park, south to Staveley

CATEGORY

Reservoir circuit within a country park and a railway path.

DISTANCE

3-mile circuit of the lake. A further 6 miles each way from Beighton to Staveley.

With its craft centre, exhibitions, cafe, plentiful wildfowl plus a variety of rides and walks, Rother Valley Country Park is an ideal place to spend the day. At the centre of the park stands a historic complex of buildings based around Bedgreave Mill, now the visitor centre. A 3-mile circuit of the two lakes may be all the cycling you want to

do but if you are interested in a longer challenge there is a dismantled railway on the western side of the lakes that runs 6 miles south from Beighton to Staveley through a mixture of wooded cuttings and open stretches with countryside views. The ride forms part of both the Trans Pennine Trail (the southern link from Chesterfield through Sheffield to Barnsley) and also National Cycle Network Route 6 which runs north from Derby via Nottingham, Worksop, Sheffield and Doncaster to York. The two routes join at the southern end of the lake, so don't be confused if you see a mixture of 'Route 6', 'Route 67' and 'Trans Pennine Trail' signs.

STARTING POINT & PARKING

→Rother Valley Country Park Visitor Centre, 6

miles southeast of Sheffield (grid reference 455825). Closest motorway: M1, Jct 31.

ON YOUR BIKES!

The route may be signposted as the Trans Pennine Trail, Route 6 or Route 67.

1. From the Rother Valley Country Park Visitor Centre make your way to the lakeside and turn right (ie keep the water to your left). Pass between the two lakes and continue alongside the water.

2. You could either continue the circuit of the lake for a 3-mile ride **OR** for a link to the Trans Pennine Trail, when you reach a point opposite the Sailing Club (on the other side of the water) and with a double metal gate and a wooden bridlegate across the path, turn right under the railway bridge then turn left onto the old railway path following signs for Killamarsh and Staveley.

3. Follow this trail for 5 miles, at one point passing through a small car park and following the Trans Pennine Trail up to the left.

4. The easy trail ends at a point where a bridge with steps crosses a railway (just north of Staveley). It is suggested you turn around at this point* and return to the visitor centre, completing the circuit of the lake.

If you continue south along the Trans Pennine Trail, a short rough section will take you to the Chesterfield Canal.

Station: Kiveton Bridge Station.
TIC: Sheffield, 0114 221 1900.
Other nearby trails: At the southern end of the Staveley to Beighton railway path you can easily link to the Chesterfield Canal.
Useful publications: OS Landranger Map 120. The *Trans Pennine Trail (Central)* map (£4.95) available frrom Sustrans shows this trail and several other traffic-free routes in the area.
Sustrans Order Line: Call 0845 113 0065 or visit their website at www.sustrans.org.uk
Refreshments: Cafe at the visitor centre.

2 Wharncliffe Woods, northwest of Sheffield

CATEGORY
Waymarked forestry route.

DISTANCE
3-mile circuit (or longer options on woodland tracks if you take a map with you).

There are few large Forestry Commission woodlands in the area and even fewer with waymarked trails so Wharncliffe Wood, lying just north of Sheffield, is something of an exception. There are two trails waymarked, one described as difficult using narrow, twisting tracks, the other uses the broad forestry roads but also involves a long climb back to the start, as is inevitable with any ride that starts on top of a hill! If you are looking for a longer ride it would be quite feasible to drop down the hillside towards the bottom of the valley of the River Don on forestry tracks and head north along the railway path that leads to Penistone and Dunford Bridge, all offroad and traffic-free. Further afield, to the west of Sheffield there are some superb traffic-free trails in the Upper Derwent Valley.

The Wharncliffe and Grenoside area has been extensively used by man since the Iron Age, first as a base for hunting groups then later as a source of querns or hand mills for grinding grain. This gave rise to the original name 'Querncliff'. In the medieval period parts of the chase were enclosed as a deer park and in more recent times much mining and quarrying has taken place for coal, ganister and fire clay in Wharncliffe and building stone in Grenoside.

STARTING POINT & PARKING

→There is a car park in the woods at the top of the hill off the minor road that leads north from **Grenoside** to **Wortley**, about 5 miles northwest of Sheffield (grid reference 325950).

ON YOUR BIKES!

1. From the car park go through the metal barrier and continue downhill following black and green bike route waymarks. Ignore a left turn, take the next turning to the right.
2. Ignore the next left turning, continue on to a T-junction (grid reference 307947) turn left* and carry on downhill.
*or for a longer route turn right here to explore the lower part of the forest. You will need Ordnance Survey Landranger Map 110 to help find your way.
3. Ignore another left turn. At a major crossroads of tracks go straight ahead then shortly follow the main track round to the left.
4. Long climb. At the T-junction turn right onto the steepest climb of the day to return to the start.

Station: Sheffield.
TIC: Sheffield, 0114 221 1900.
Other nearby trails: Traffic-free sections of the Trans Pennine Trail run from Worsbrough Mill Country Park (on the A61 south of Barnsley) to Silkstone Common in the west (Dove Valley Trail) and to Bolton upon Dearne in the east (Barnsley to Old Moor Wetlands Centre). The Five Weirs Walk links the centre of Sheffield via the River Don to the centre of Rotherham. There are trails in Rother Valley Country Park to the southeast of Sheffield.
Useful publications: OS Landranger Map 110.
Refreshments: There are refreshments available at Grenoside.

3 Sheffield to Rotherham via the Five Weirs Walk

CATEGORY
Riverside path.
DISTANCE
7 miles each way.

With just one short diversion away from the water to the north of Sheffield centre, the trail follows the course of the River Don and the Sheffield & Keadby Canal between the centres of the Sheffield and Rotherham for almost 7 miles. The route follows National Cycle Network Route 6, which also forms a spur off the main east-west Trans Pennine Trail from Hull to Southport, so you may see a mixture of signs. Route 6 runs all the way from London to Keswick in the Lake District.

STARTING POINT & PARKING

→**Sheffield**. The riverside path starts on Leveson Road, off Attercliffe Road (A6178) to the northeast of the city centre where the railway bridge crosses the road and the river.
→**Rotherham**. The trail starts south from Rotherham Central railway station, running alonside Don Street to join the riverside path.
→If coming from outside Sheffield or Rotherham the best place to park is at the **Meadowhall Shopping Centre**, off the M1 jct 34.

Stations: Sheffield or Rotherham.
TICs: Sheffield, 0114 221 1900; Rotherham, 01709 823611.
Other nearby trails: There are trails in Wharncliffe Woods to the northwest of Shefffield; Rother Valley Country Park and the Staveley to Beighton Railway Path lie to the southeast.
Useful publications:
OS Landranger Map 111. More useful is the *Sheffield Cycling Map* showing recommended cycle routes in the centre of the city, available

from Pedal Pushers (0114 258 1605).
Rotherham Cycling Map produced by CycleCity Guides, Wallbridge Mill, The Retreat, Frome BA11 5JU (01373 453533). E-mail: info@cyclecityguides.co.uk.
Sustrans *Derby to York* map (£5.99) and *Trans Pennine Trail (Central)* map (£4.95).
Sustrans Order Line: Call 0845 113 0065 or visit their website at www.sustrans.org.uk
Refreshments: Lots of choice all along the way.

4 The Upper Don Trail from Penistone east to Wharncliffe Woods or west to Dunford Bridge

CATEGORY
Railway path and woodland trail.

DISTANCE
Penistone to Dunford Bridge - 6 miles each way; Penistone to Wharncliffe Crags - 6 miles each way.

The Trans Pennine Trail crosses the Pennines between Longdendale and Dunford Bridge, passing above the Woodhead Tunnels which used to carry the railway line. So from Dunford Bridge (at 985 ft) down to the end of the ride at the River Don south of Thurgoland (at 490 ft) there is a drop of 500 ft over almost 12 miles. Take into account the likelihood of the wind blowing from the west and you soon see that it is normally a lot quicker heading east downhill with the wind behind you than heading west uphill into the wind! Penistone is an attractive stone-built town with plenty of choices of refreshment. Heading west from here the views are of dry-stone walls and sheep-grazed moorland in the Upper Don Valley. There is a welcome pub at Dunford Bridge, the turnaround point. To the east of Penistone the trail is increasingly wooded as it drops height. The ride could easily be linked either to the Dove Valley Trail, by following the Trans Pennine Trail signs from Oxspring to Silkstone Common or Wharncliffe Woods, by joining the forestry track just south of the A616.

STARTING POINTS & PARKING
➔**Penistone** lies 7 miles west of Barnsley on the A628 (west of M1 Jct 37). Follow signs for the free car park in Penistone, just south of the main part of the village, near to the fire station (grid reference 245034)
➔An alternative start is from the forest road off

the minor road between **Oughtibridge** and **Grenoside** on the northwest outskirts of Sheffield (grid reference 315934).

→ There is a car park in **Dunford Bridge** at one end of the trail (grid reference 159024). Dunford Bridge is about 10 miles south of Huddersfield.

ON YOUR BIKES!

The route is well signposted as the Trans Pennine Trail or the Upper Don Trail.
From the car park in Penistone follow the gravel track across the open land ahead and join the railway path. Either: turn left (**west**) for Dunford Bridge (6 miles, gentle 300 ft climb) or turn right (**east**) for Wharncliffe Woods (6 miles, gentle 200 ft descent)

Station: Penistone.
TICs: Sheffield, 0114 221 1900; Holmfirth. 01484 222444.
Other nearby trails: Waymarked trails in Wharncliffe Woods. Dove Valley Trail and the Trans Pennine Trail from Barnsley to the Old Moor Wetlands Centre.

Useful publications: OS Landranger Map 110. Available from Sustrans, the *Trans Pennine Trail (Central)* and *Trans Pennine Trail (West)* maps (£4.95 each) show this trail and several other traffic-free routes in the area.
Sustrans Order Line: Call 0845 113 0065 or visit their website at www.sustrans.org.uk
Refreshments: Pub at Dunford Bridge. Lots in Penistone. Pub just off the route in Oxspring.

5 Dove Valley Trail, southwest of Barnsley

CATEGORY
Railway path.
DISTANCE
Up to 10 miles each way.

Whilst passing through the picturesque rolling countryside to the south of Barnsley it is gratifying to see the enormous efforts that have been made to transform the ugly spoil heaps and wastelands of the coal mining industry into green and wooded areas. There is a real case of nature being actively encouraged to heal over scars and one wonders whether any present inhabitant would recognise the place in 50 years time when the trees have had a chance to mature and the hard edges of the massive

earth moving exercises have been softened by the growth of grass and wildflowers. The Worsbrough Bank Railway was opened in 1880 to allow large amounts of Lancashire-bound coal traffic to bypass the serious bottleneck of Barnsley. The Bank included 2 1/2 miles of 1 in 40 gradient, one of the steepest gradients in the country and a severe obstacle to heavily-laden westbound coal trains. In 1952 the line was electrified, one of the first such schemes in Britain. The 142-minute journey from Wath to Dunford Bridge was whittled down to 66 minutes! The track was closed in 1981.

NB You will probably prefer to use the pavement for 200 yds from the car park at Worsbrough Mill to the point where the Trans Pennine Trail crosses the A61. Heading east, care should be taken crossing the B6100 in Worsbrough, close to the start of the ride. You should also be aware that there is a gentle 270ft descent from Silkstone Common east to the Old Moor Wetland Centre.

STARTING POINT & PARKING

→The Pay & Display car park at **Worsbrough Mill Country Park**, 3 miles north of Jct 36 of the M1, along the A61 towards Barnsley (grid reference 352034).

ON YOUR BIKES!

Exit Worsbrough Country Park car park and turn left along the main A61 (push your bike along the pavement for 200 yds) to the point where the Trans Pennine Trail crosses the road. From here you can go 4 miles west to Silkstone Common or 6 miles east to Wombwell and the Old Moor Wetland Centre. The route is signposted as 'Trans Pennine Trail' or 'Dove Valley Trail'.

Route west to Silkstone Common. Turn left off the A61 onto the old railway path and climb gently for 4 miles, crossing the M1. The railway path ends at the southern edge of Silkstone Common (just before the old tunnel). Here you have a choice of turning round and making your way straight back to Worsbrough, going into Silkstone Common for refreshments or following the Trans Pennine Trail further west on a mixture of rougher tracks and minor roads to join the next railway section from Oxspring to Penistone and Dunford Bridge.

Route east to the Old Moor Wetland Centre. Cross the A61 **with care** onto the railway path leading east signposted 'Public Bridleway'. After 1 1/2 miles pass beneath a railway viaduct then keep bearing right to cross two bridges over the A633. A track from Barnsley joins from the left (remember this point for your return). Go past a Go Kart circuit, Wombwell FC ground and a Thomas the Tank Engine model. Cross into the Old Moor Wetland Centre and complete a circuit of the lake. Return back to Worsbrough Country Park.

Station: Silkstone or Wombwell.
TIC: Barnsley, 01226 206757.

Other nearby trails: The Dove Valley Trail is part of the Trans Pennine Trail which runs from Southport to Hull. To the west the trail goes on to Penistone, to the east to Doncaster, with spurs south towards Wharncliffe Woods and northwest into Barnsley.

Useful publications: OS Landranger Maps 110 & 111. The *Trans Pennine Trail (Central)* map (£4.95), available from Sustrans, shows several other traffic-free routes in the area.

Sustrans Order Line: Call 0845 113 0065 or visit their website at www.sustrans.org.uk

Refreshments: In Silkstone, Worsbrough and Wombwell.

6 Barnsley to the Old Moor Wetland Centre along the Trans Pennine Trail

CATEGORY
Railway path.
DISTANCE
7 miles each way.

Barnsley has been the headquarters for the development of the Trans Pennine Trail over the last decade. This route is a spur linking Barnsley with the main trail (which passes to the south of the town) taking you east towards Bolton upon Dearne and to the wonderfully landscaped Old Moor Wetland Nature Reserve which has covered over old industrial scars. It could easily be extended in almost any direction: north from Stairfoot towards Wakefield and Leeds, west from Wombwell along the Dove Valley Trail towards Penistone, east from the Wetland Reserve towards Sprotborough or south from the Reserve along the Elsecar Greenway towards Sheffield. A copy of the *Trans Pennine Trail Map (Central)* is highly recommended

STARTING POINTS & PARKING
→**Barnsley.** The trail starts just to the east of the Alhambra Centre. Go through the subways towards the A635 Doncaster Road and take the first minor road to the left over the railway - the trail starts on your right after 200 yds (grid reference 352060). Go past Wombwell FC ground and a Thomas the Tank Engine model. Cross into the Old Moor Wetland Centre, complete a circuit of the lake and return back to Barnsley.

→**The Old Moor Wetland Centre,** west of Bolton upon Dearne, near the junction of the A633 and the A6195 (grid reference 423022). **Station:** Barnsley.
TIC: Barnsley, 01226 206757.
Other nearby trails: The next traffic-free section of the Trans Pennine Trail to the east runs from

Harlington to Doncaster. To the west the Dove Trail and Upper Don Trail lie close by.

Useful publications: OS Landranger Map 111. Available from Sustrans, the *Trans Pennine Trail (Central)* map (£4.95) shows all the traffic-free routes in the area.

Sustrans Order Line: Call 0845 113 0065 or visit their website at www.sustrans.org.uk

Refreshments: Lots of choice in Barnsley.

7 Doncaster to Harlington along the Trans Pennine Trail

CATEGORY
Railway path, riverside path and newly-built cyclepath.

DISTANCE
9 miles each way.

The Earth Centre is a visionary exhibition centre created amid the wasteland left over from decades of mining. It has acted as a catalyst to regenerate the whole of the surrounding area, greening the spoil heaps and showing how the future can take greater account of renewable sources of energy and make better use of recycling the world's dwindling resources. The ride starts on the outskirts of Doncaster and follows the course of a dismantled railway to the first viaduct over the river. There is a lovely stretch along the wooded banks of the River Don through the attractions of Sprotbrough and up a steep climb to the second viaduct. The trail leads right past the Earth Centre and along the valley of the River Dearne to Harlington. The River Don was once a major route for transporting goods across the country. Water traffic still uses the River Don near to Sprotbrough. The valley has a richly interwoven industrial and ecological heritage. Sprotbrough Flash, an expanse of open water, was created by subsidence from coalmining at Cadeby and Denaby Main. Sir Walter Scott worked on his novel *Ivanhoe* whilst staying at the Boat Inn in Sprotbrough.

7

STARTING POINT & PARKING

The car parks by the shopping centre near B&Q, on the A638 northwest of **Doncaster** (grid reference 559044).

ON YOUR BIKES!

1. From the car park by B&Q, return to the main road, turn left (away from Doncaster) down to the cyclepath and turn left again signposted 'Sprotbrough, Cusworth Cycle Route'. Follow this railway path for 2 1/2 miles.
2. Just **before** the huge viaduct over the river descend steeply via the steps to the right. Follow alongside the river for 3 miles, passing beneath the A1 road bridge, alongside the locks and the Boat Inn at Sprotbrough.
3. Continue along the broad stone track climbing steeply to join the right-hand end of the tall viaduct ahead. Continue on the track past the Earth Centre.
4. At the road cross straight ahead then turn right over the wooden bridge and join a railway path. Follow this for 1 1/2 miles. Opposite a footbridge over the river turn right onto a track.
5. This turns to tarmac. At the T-junction (at the end of Mill Lane) turn left as far as the Harlington Inn.

Station: Doncaster
TIC: Doncaster, 01302 734309.
Other nearby trails: The route is part of the Trans Pennine Trail which continues west to Barnsley or along the Dove Trail and Upper Don Trail.
Useful publications: OS Landranger Map 111. Available from Sustrans, the *Trans Pennine Trail (Central)* and *Trans Pennine Trail (East)* maps (each £4.95) show this trail and several other traffic-free routes in the area.
Sustrans Order Line: Call 0845 113 0065 or visit their website at www.sustrans.org.uk
Refreshments: Lots of choice in Doncaster. Boat Inn, Sprotborough. Harlington Inn, Harlington.

8 Aire & Calder Navigation Towpath, southeast from Leeds

CATEGORY

Canal towpath.

DISTANCE

6 miles each way.

An attractive section along this important commercial waterway, starting from the Royal Armouries Museum on Clarence Road in the centre of Leeds and running past Thwaite's Mill Industrial Museum southeast to Woodlesford Metro Train Station. The ride forms the northernmost part of the spur of the Trans Pennine Trail that comes off the main East - West route at Stairfoot near Barnsley going north to Leeds via the west Wakefield.

NB Please read *The Waterways Code - Cycling on the towpath* at the front of the book

STARTING POINTS & PARKING

→Royal Armouries Museum on the southeast edge of the **centre of Leeds** located on Clarence Road, just off the A61 Wakefield Road (grid reference 306331).
→**Woodlesford** railway station, just off the A642 to the southeast of Leeds (grid reference 368291).

Station: Leeds or Woodlestord.
TIC: Leeds, 0113 242 5242
Other nearby trails: The Leeds & Liverpool Canal runs northwest from Leeds city centre. The Trans Pennine Trail spur continues south towards Barnsley, on a mixture of traffic-free paths and quiet roads / streets.
Useful publications: OS Landranger Map 104. Better is the *Leeds Cycling Map* produced by CycleCity Guides, Wallbridge Mill, The Retreat, Frome BA11 5JU (01373 453533). E-mail: info@cyclecityguides.co.uk
Refreshments: At either end of the ride.

9 Leeds & Liverpool Canal along the Aire Valley, west of Leeds

CATEGORY
Canal towpath.
DISTANCE
Up to 13 miles each way.

Running west from Granary Wharf in the centre of Leeds to Horsforth and Shipley this rides uses the towpath of the oldest surviving Trans-Pennine waterway, exploring this green corridor west along Airedale. The Leeds & Liverpool Canal was opened between Bingley and Shipley in 1777 and barges were soon carrying coal, chemicals, limestone and wool between Lancashire and Yorkshire. Nowadays leisure craft and anglers are the main users of this picturesque canal. The canal corridor, however has managed to retain its rich industrial heritage.

STARTING POINTS & PARKING
→Granary Wharf in the **centre of Leeds**, just west of the railway station.
→**Shipley** railway station, west of Leeds (grid reference 150374).

Stations: Leeds or Shipley.
TIC: Leeds, 0113 242 5242.
Other nearby trails: The Aire & Calder Navigation runs southeast from Leeds city centre.
Useful publications: OS Landranger Map 104. Leaflet available from British Waterways, Pottery Road, Wigan WN3 5AA. Better is the *Leeds Cycling Map* produced by CycleCity Guides, Wallbridge Mill, The Retreat, Frome BA11 5JU (01373 453533). E-mail: info@cyclecityguides.co.uk
Refreshments: Lots of choce in Shipley and Leeds. Pubs just off the route at Apperley Bridge, Rodley and Newlay.

10 Harland Way, southeast of Harrogate

CATEGORY
Railway path.
DISTANCE
3.5 miles each way (plus 1 mile to reach Spofforth Castle).

Follow this railway path from Wetherby through gentle countryside to the village of Spofforth with its medieval castle. Wetherby is an ancient market town overlooking the River Wharfe with a handsome stone bridge downstream from the ancient weir which once powered the town's corn mill. The town was an important staging post on the Great North Road to Scotland; one

of the staging inns, The Angel, was known as 'Halfway House' because it was midway between London and Edinburgh. Spofforth Castle (or its ruins) date from the 14th century; it was really a large fortified house rather than a castle.

NB There is one busy road to cross (A661) to visit Spofforth village and its castle.

STARTING POINT & PARKING

→Old station car park, Linton Road, **Wetherby**. Follow the A661 from the centre of Wetherby towards Harrogate. Bear left at first junction to Linton (grid reference 397484).
Station: Harrogate.
TIC: Wetherby, 01937 582706.
Other nearby trails: York to Overton and York to Riccall.
Useful publications: OS Landranger Map 104.
Refreshments: Lots of choice in Wetherby. The Railway Inn in Spofforth.

11   York to Overton

DISTANCE
4 miles each way.
CATEGORY
Riverside path.

Forming part of the White Rose Cycle Route from Hull to Middlesbrough (National Cycle Network Route 65), this short ride starts near the heart of the beautiful walled city of York and runs parallel with the broad, slow-moving River Ouse. The ride crosses the grazed Rawcliffe Meadows - a managed 25 acres of wildflowers and birdlife. You will pass several curious sculptures - seats looking like horse-drawn carriages and farm implements, a weather vane with a bicycle and dog and a metalwork globe with depictions of York Cathedral and the walled city. If you choose to go on to the National Trust property and tearoom at

Beningbrough Hall you will need to use quiet lanes for a further 5 miles.

STARTING POINTS & PARKING
→The River Ouse end of Marygate in the **centre of York** (on the other side of the river from the railway station).
→If you are coming from outside York it would be better to start from **Rawcliffe Bar Park & Ride** car park near the junction of the A19 with the Ring Road to the north of the city (grid reference 575548).

Station: York.
TIC: York, 01904 620577.
Other nearby trails: York to Riccall. There is another railway path in the centre of York (the Foss Island Railpath) which runs eastwards for 3 miles from the Wigginton Road (B1363) near to the hospitals to Osbaldwick.
Useful publications: OS Landranger Map 105. York City Council produces an excellent cycle map for the city which can be purchased from: The Cycling Officer, City of York Council, Environment and Development Services, 9 St Leonard's Place, York YO1 2ET (01904 613161).
Refreshments: Lots of choice in York. You may wish to carry on along National Cycle Network Route 65 for a further 5 miles on quiet lanes to the teashop in the National Trust property at Beningbrough Hall (open spring to autumn).

12   York to Riccall Cycle Path

CATEGORY
Railway path.
DISTANCE
10 miles each way.

The trail links the cycle-friendly city of York with the village of Riccall in the Vale of York running across a flat, arable landscape. It starts alongside the River Ouse in the heart of the city,

65, is a spur off the main Trans Pennine Trail from Southport to Hull and also forms part of the White Rose Cycle Route from Hull to Middlesbrough via York.

STARTING POINTS & PARKING

Ouse Bridge (railway station side) in the centre of York at the junction of Skeldergate and Micklegate.
If arriving by car the route can be picked up from the **Tadcaster Road Park & Ride** or in Ricall village.

ON YOUR BIKES!

Follow Skeldergate southwards signposted 'Bishopthorpe, Selby' then bear first left onto Terry Avenue to stay close to the river and pass beneath Skeldergate Bridge. This becomes a no through road. Follow the red tarmac path as it swings away from the river. Cross the road, cross the race course and follow signs for Riccall and Selby.

Station: York.
TIC: York, 01904 620577.
Other nearby trails: The York to Overton Route. There is another railway path in the centre of York (the Foss Island Railpath) which goes past the racecourse, through the village of Bishopthorpe then over the swing bridge at Naburn, built to permit large vessels to go up the river as far as York. The ride uses the fomer East Coast main line which was threatened with subsidence by the development of the huge Selby coalfield in the 1970s. A new stretch of main line was paid for by the National Coal Board and opened in 1983. The old route was then converted to recreational use by Sustrans, one of their earliest projects. The path, waymarked as National Cycle Network Route runs eastwards for 3 miles from the Wigginton Road (B1363) near to the hospitals to Osbaldwick.

Useful publications: OS Landranger Map 105. York City Council produces an excellent cycle map for the city which can be purchased from: The Cycling Officer, City of York Council, Environment and Development Services, 9 St Leonard's Place, York YO1 2ET (01904 613161).

Refreshments: Lots of choice in York. Pubs in Bishopthorpe and Riccall.

13   Hudson Way from Beverley to Market Weighton, northwest of Hull

CATEGORY

Railway path.

DISTANCE

11 miles each way.

Explore the rolling hills of the southern Yorkshire Wolds on this railway path linking the towns of Beverley and Market Weighton. The handsome town of Beverley was the county town of the old East Riding of Yorkshire and is famous for its magnificent Minster and historic town walls. Market Weighton developed as a result of its strategic location on trade routes between the Wolds and the Vale of York. The Hudson Way is part of the old railway line that linked York to Hull from 1865 until 1965 when it was shut under the famous Beeching Axe.

NB There is one busy road to cross - the B1248 north of Cherry Burton. Take care at this point.

STARTING POINTS & PARKING

→**Beverley**. Car park just off the A1035 Beverley bypass to the north of the town (grid reference 028416)

→**Market Weighton**. Old station site, north of Station Road, off St Helen's Square behind the parish church (grid reference 070420).

Station: Beverley.

TIC: Beverley, 01482 867430.

Other nearby trails: At its western end it links to the Market Weighton to Bubwith Trail. Two nearby trails start from Hull - one to Hornsea and the other to South Holderness.

Useful publications: OS Landranger Maps 106 & 107.

Refreshments: Lots of choice in Beverley and Market Weighton. Cafe in Kiplingcotes Station. Pubs just off the route in Goodmanham and Etton.

14   Hull to Hornsea Trail

CATEGORY

Railway path.

DISTANCE

13 miles each way.

The trail follows the line of the old railway across the central part of Holderness from the centre of Hull via New Ellerby to the East Coast resort of Hornsea. A Hull timber merchant by the name of Joseph Wade was the driving force behind the building of the railway that he hoped would develop Hornsea into a fashionable resort. The line opened in 1864 and ran for 101 years before being closed down in 1965. Hornsea Mere is the largest freshwater lake in Yorkshire, rich in birdlife.

NB You have to cross the A165 south of Skirlaugh. There are also roads to negotiate in Hull and Hornsea.

STARTING POINTS & PARKING

→Dansom Lane, off Clarence Street / Holderness Road (A165), just east of **Hull city centre**, and the bridge over the River Hull (grid reference 108300).

→**Skirlaugh picnic site**, on the A165 about 2 miles to the south of the village (grid reference 153375).

→The police station in **Hornsea** (grid reference 206475).

Station: Hull.

TIC: Hull, 01482 223559.

Other nearby trails: The Hull to Holderness Trail also starts from Hull.

Useful publications: OS Landranger Map 107. Hull Cycle Map available from Department of Environmental Services, Essex House, Manor Street, Hull HU1 1YD (01482 593346).

Refreshments: Hull and Hornsea. The Railway Inn near the old station in Ellerby.

15 Hull to South Holderness

CATEGORY
Railway path.
DISTANCE
Up to 13 miles each way.

Starting close to the centre of Hull, the railway
path runs to the north of the Humber Estuary
through Hedon and Keyningham almost to the
village of Patrington with its magnificent church
known as 'The Queen of Holderness'. Although
mainly on a good gravel and grass track, there
are rough sections at the eastern end. The Hull
& Holderness Railway was built to serve the
new coastal resort of Withernsea and opened in
1853. It was soon bringing thousands of people
to the seaside, not only from Hull but from as

far away as Nottingham and Newcastle. It was
closed in 1965. Now lying a couple of miles
inland, Hedon was an important port on the
Humber in medieval times, exporting wool and
cloth. It has many fine buildings including a
magnificent church .

NB Patrington is 1 mile beyond the end of the
railway path along the A1033 (take care).

STARTING POINTS & PARKING
➔Southcoates Lane, **Hull**, north of Alexandra
Dock and HM Prison, just off the A1033 Hedon
/ Withernsea Road (grid reference 125297).
➔**Hedon**, on the B1240 Sproatley road on the
northern edge of the village (grid reference
190291).
➔The path ends at the A1033, about 1 mile to
the west of **Patrington** (grid reference 300234).

Station: Hull.
TIC: Hull, 01482 223559.
Other nearby trails: The Hull to Hornsea Trail
also starts in the centre of Hull.
Useful publications: OS Landranger Map 107.
Hull Cycle Map available from: Department of
Environmental Services, Essex House, Manor
Street, Hull HU1 1YD (01482 593346).
Refreshments: Hull, Hedon, Patrington.

16 Cleveland Way from Sutton Bank, North York Moors

CATEGORY
Wide stone track across moorland.
DISTANCE
10 miles each way.

There are two very similar trails in the North
York Moors that use broad ridge tracks with
wonderful views over the surrounding hills -
Cleveland Way and Rudland Rigg. They are

16

rougher and tougher than railway trails but if you have mountain bikes and are reasonably fit they are real 'roof of the world' experiences. This section of the Cleveland Way has a convenient starting point at the Sutton Bank Visitor Centre, on the A170 between Thirsk and Pickering. The ride is mainly on a broad stone track with several steady climbs. There will be some mud in winter and after prolonged rain. There is a rough bridleway alternative with fabulous views that runs parallel to the lane heading north from the visitor centre that starts about 1 mile north of the centre (turn off the road at Dialstone Farm). The suggested turnaround point is the car park where the Cleveland Way meets the minor lane that climbs up from Osmotherley (grid reference 479959).

NB For the 3 1/2 miles closest to the visitor centre you have the choice of a quiet lane or a narrow bridleway.

STARTING POINT & PARKING

→The visitor centre at the top of **Sutton Bank**, on the A170 between Thirsk and Helmsley (grid reference 515830).

Station: Thirsk.
TIC: Sutton Bank, 01845 597246.
Other nearby trails: Rudland Rigg is a similar stone track across the North York Moors starting from north of Kirkbymoorside.
Useful publications: OS Landranger Map 100.
Refreshments: At the visitor centre, or try Chequers Cafe, a mile beyond the northern end of the track, along a quiet lane.

18

17 Boltby Forest, North York Moors, east of Northallerton

CATEGORY
Waymarked forest routes.

DISTANCE
4 - 12 miles.

There are three waymarked woodland routes in the most westerly of the forestry holdings in the North York Moors National Park. Located on the western scarp of the North York Moors, it offers wonderful views over the northern Vale of York. The descriptions provided by Forest Enterprise are as follows:

GREEN ROUTE
Beginners / Family, 4 miles
Follows forest roads with shallow climbs and descents.

RED ROUTE
Challenging / Strenuous, 7 miles
A wide range of climbs and descents and some technical singletrack on a combination of grass tracks and forest roads. Very wet during winter months.

BLACK ROUTE
Very difficult / Highly technical, 12 miles
Demanding climbs, forest tracks and technical singletrack on grass and woodland trails. Very wet during winter months. Experienced, good bike handling skills and a high level of fitness required.

STARTING POINT & PARKING

→The roadside car park at the top of Sneck Yate Bank (grid reference 510877), about 4 miles along the minor road towards Hawnby that goes north from Sutton Bank Visitor Centre, off the A170 Thirsk to Helmsley road.

Station: Thirsk, Northallerton
TIC: Pickering, 01751 473791.

Other nearby trails: The Cleveland Way (a fine ridge ride) near to Boltby Forest. Rudland Rigg is another good ridge ride to the north of Kirkbymoorside. There are more forestry trails in Dalby Forest.

Useful publications: OS Landranger Map 100. A leaflet can be purchased from Forest Enterprise, North York Moors, Outgang Road, Pickering, North Yorkshire YO18 7EL (01751 472771). E-mail: n.york.moors.fdo@forestry.gov.uk

Refreshments: None on the routes. The nearest are at Sutton Bank Visitor Centre or Thirsk.

18 Rudland Rigg, North York Moors

CATEGORY
Wide, stone-based moorland track.

DISTANCE
Up to 10 miles each way.

A book could be written about the finest ridge rides in the country where you have the benefit of enjoying fantastic views all around without the grind of climbing all the way to the top of the hill. In that respect, Rudland Rigg would be an ideal candidate for inclusion. It is a route best undertaken on mountain bikes on summer's day with good visibility. The ridge track starts 6 miles north of Kirkbymoorside, a town on the A170 on the southern edge of the North York Moors, and runs northeast across the moors. Although this is essentially a ridge ride, there are nevertheless three hills to climb: the first is the longest and steepest (450ft over 2 miles). It is suggested you turn around at the third summit, not long after crossing the old railway line, at the top of Greenhow Moor, above the forest below. After this the path drops steeply for almost 900 ft to join the lane to Ingleby Greenhow.

STARTING POINT & PARKING
➔There is no specific car park but room for several vehicles at the start of the track (grid reference 659927), to the north of Kirkbymoorside and Gillamoor in the North York Moors.

19 Dalby Forest, northeast of Pickering, North York Moors (4 routes)

CATEGORY
Waymarked forest routes.

DISTANCE
6 - 8 miles.

The North Riding Forest Park is made up of 27,000 hectares of woodland, including Dalby, Langdale and Sneaton Forests. There are four waymarked trails ranging from easy family routes through to tough, technical challenges. The descriptions provided by Forest Enterprise are as follows:

GREEN ROUTE
Beginners / Family, 6 miles
A short ride mainly on the high plateau around Adderstone. Mixed terrain of forest roads and grass tracks, with a few short climbs and descents.

Start: Adderstone Field car park (grid reference 883897), south of Staindale Lake, about 5 miles along the toll road from the Low Dalby Visitor Centre, reached by heading north from Thornton-le-Dale, near Pickering.

BLUE ROUTE
Easy / Moderate, 8 miles
A longer but simple route on mixed terrain of forest roads and grass track, with some climbs and descents, steep in places.

Station: Battersby Junction.
TIC: Pickering, 01751 473791.
Other nearby trails: There is another similar moorland ridge track that follows the Cleveland Way northwards from the Sutton Bank Visitor Centre.
Useful publications: OS Landranger Map 94.
Refreshments: None on route. The nearest is in Gillamoor.

Start: Low Dalby Visitor Centre, reached by heading north from Thornton-le-Dale, near Pickering.

RED ROUTE
Challenging / Technical
A long route on variable terrain of forest roads and grass singletrack trails. Some steep climbs and descents, needing good technical ability.

Experienced, good bike handling skills and a high level of fitness required.

Start: Low Dalby Visitor Centre, reached by heading north from Thornton-le-Dale, near Pickering.

BLACK ROUTE
Very difficult / Highly technical, 6 miles
A short but challenging route, on variable terrain of mainly grass singletrack trails and some forest roads. Some very steep climbs and purpose-built descents, needing a high level of technical ability. Experienced, good bike handling skills and a high level of fitness required.

Start: Adderstone Field car park (grid reference 883897), south of Staindale Lake, about 5 miles along the toll road from the Low Dalby Visitor Centre, reached by heading north from Thornton-le-Dale, near Pickering.

Station: Scarborough.
TIC: Pickering, 01751 473791.
Other nearby trails: The Scarborough to Whitby Railway Path lies 12 miles to the east. Guisborough Forest is 25 miles to the northwest. There are also trails in Boltby Forest.
Useful publications: OS Landranger Maps 94 & 101. A map can be purchased from the visitor centre or from the Forest Enterprise office in Pickering, 01751 472771.
email: n.york.moors.fdo@forestry.gov.uk
Refreshments: Low Dalby Visitor Centre. Jingleby Farm tea rooms, at the northern end of the Red and Green routes.

20 Scarborough to Whitby Railway Path, North York Moors

CATEGORY
Railway path.
DISTANCE

Up to 18 miles each way.

The trail lies within the North York Moors National Park and follows a spectacular route along the North Yorkshire Heritage Coast from Scarborough via Scalby, Cloughton, Ravenscar, Robin Hood's Bay and High Hawsker to Whitby. For a railway path this is a tough route with two long climbs on a mixture of good and rough stone tracks. Mountain bikes are recommended. The first climb goes from Scarborough to Ravenscar (625 ft) and the second north from Robin Hood's Bay towards Whitby (250 ft).

NB There are two busy roads to cross (the A165 north of Scalby and the A171 near High Hawsker, south of Whitby) and several short sections on quiet roads through Robin Hood's Bay, Ravenscar and Scalby.

STARTING POINTS & PARKING
→Safeway car park in **Scarborough**, on Manor Road, northwest of the town centre, near the cemetery (grid reference 030887).
→The trail can also be picked up in Scalby, Cloughton, Ravenscar and Robin Hood's Bay.
→From the roundabout in the centre of **Whitby** by the Town Council Offices follow Chubb Hill Road up past the Museum and Art Gallery and turn right onto Southend Gardens. The trail starts here (grid reference 894106).

Station: Scarborough or Whitby.
TICs: Scarborough, 01723 373333; Whitby, 01947 602674.
Other nearby trails: Waymarked forest trails in Dalby Forest, west of Scarborough.
Useful publications: OS Landranger Maps 94 & 101. A leaflet is also produced by Scarborough District Council, 01723 373333.
Refreshments: Lots of choice in Scarborough, Robin Hood's Bay and Whitby. Cafe in Ravenscar.

North-East

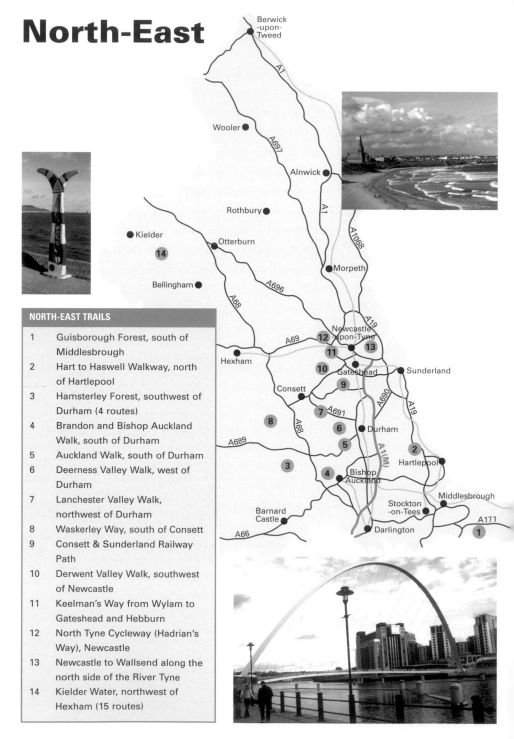

NORTH-EAST TRAILS

1   Guisborough Forest, south of Middlesbrough
2   Hart to Haswell Walkway, north of Hartlepool
3   Hamsterley Forest, southwest of Durham (4 routes)
4   Brandon and Bishop Auckland Walk, south of Durham
5   Auckland Walk, south of Durham
6   Deerness Valley Walk, west of Durham
7   Lanchester Valley Walk, northwest of Durham
8   Waskerley Way, south of Consett
9   Consett & Sunderland Railway Path
10 Derwent Valley Walk, southwest of Newcastle
11 Keelman's Way from Wylam to Gateshead and Hebburn
12 North Tyne Cycleway (Hadrian's Way), Newcastle
13 Newcastle to Wallsend along the north side of the River Tyne
14 Kielder Water, northwest of Hexham (15 routes)

North-East Mountain Biking

There are mountain biking possibilities on bridleways and byways in the region from the North Pennines in County Durham right up to the border with Scotland including several trails in the heart of the Cheviot Hills.

Alwinton would be a good base for the Cheviots, Kielder for the many trails in Kielder Forest and Allendale for the tracks in the North Pennines. An interesting feature of the Ordnance Survey map covering the Cheviots is how all the bridleways are shown right up to the border with Scotland then they stop: Scotland has a different Rights of Way system and maps do not tell you where you have a right to ride. One can only hope that the Access legislation will clarify the situation.

There is no substitute for intimate local knowledge - try to explore every bridleway, byway, unclassified road, canal towpath and Forestry Commission track near to home, sift out the good from the bad and link together the best offroad sections to form your own customised route(s). The best advice is to use the months from late spring to early autumn (May to October) to do the exploration, if possible after a spell of dry weather. The same track in winter can take twice as long or even be impassable.

Note down on the map (or colour code

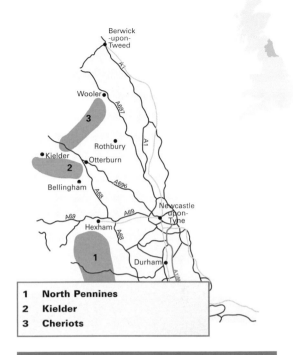

1 North Pennines
2 Kielder
3 Cheriots

Mountain Biking Information

These are possible sources:

- leaflets produced by local authorities, normally available in Tourist Information Centres
- guidebooks which can usually be found in larger, better stocked bookshops
- the staff in bike shops can often put you in contact with local riders or clubs who are sure to have done some of this research already, saving you many hours of trial and error.

with highlighter pen) the quality of the trail and whether it is better done in one direction or the other - it is normally better to climb on tarmac and descend offroad so that gravity can help you through any muddy bits.

Bear in mind that everyone has a different view of what constitutes a good trail: hard or technical for some is easy for others and a bit of mud for some is a quagmire for others!

North-East Forestry

The North-East has one massive forest holding at Kielder, including Wark and Redesdale and several smaller ones lying in an arc to the south, west and north of the main centres of population around Teeside and Tyneside.

To the south of Middlesbrough lies Guisborough Forest, to the southwest of Durham is Hamsterley Forest and well to the northwest of Newcastle, up into the heart of Northumberland there are holdings around Rothbury and into the Cheviot Hills.

In some forests and woods there are no waymarked routes but you are free to explore the tracks. The relevant Ordnance Survey map is mentioned. It is highly recommended that you take a map for the larger woods where it is very easy to get lost!

3   Chopwell Wood, southwest of Newcastle
OS Explorer Map 307

4   Slaley Forest, south of Hexham
OS Outdoor Leisure Map 43

6   Harwood Forest, southwest of Rothbury
OS Outdoor Leisure Map 42

7   Cragside Country Park, east of Rothbury
OS Outdoor Leisure Map 42

8   Harbottle Wood, south of Alwinton, in the Cheviot Hills
OS Outdoor Leisure Map 16

9   Thrunton Wood, north of Rothbury
OS Explorer Map 322

10   Kidland Forest, north of Alwinton, in the Cheviot Hills
OS Outdoor Leisure Map 16

Forests and woods with waymarked trails

They are shown with a corresponding trail number and page reference.

1   **Guisborough, south of Middlesbrough**
    See Route 1, page 268

2   **Hamsterley Forest, southwest of Durham**
    See Route 3, page 270

5   **Kielder Forest**
    See Route 14, page 281

The Forestry Commission's website is a good source of information with details of 1600 miles of waymarked cycling trails throughout the UK. Search by forest name or by the nearest town or city and the search will tell you the grade, length and waymarking details of the trails.

www.forestry.gov.uk/recreation

Further Information

Kielder Forest District
Eals Burn, Bellingham, Hexham, Northumberland
NE48 2AJ
Tel: 01434 220242

North-East National Cycle Network

Three Rivers Cycle Route

135 miles from Newcastle to Sunderland and Middlesbrough. Highlights include Newcastle's bridges, Tynemouth, North Tyne Cycleway, Derwent Valley Trail, Consett to Sunderland railway path, National Glass Centre, Stadium of Light, Lanchester Valley Walk, Durham and Castle Eden Walkway Country Park.

Traffic-free sections over 3 miles:

- Hart to Haswell Railway Path (NCN 14).
- North Tyne Cycleway (NCN 72).
- Derwent Valley Trail (NCN 14).
- Consett to Sunderland Railway Path (NCN 7).
- Lanchester Valley Walk (NCN 14).

Pennine Cycle Way (North)

150 miles from Appleby-in-Westmorland

Sustrans

Listed below are the Sustrans maps that cover the National Cycle Network within the region. Some of the maps may describe routes that continue on into adjacent regions: these maps are mentioned in both chapters. The maps are not only useful for people wishing to ride the the whole route over several days; they also show all the traffic-free sections which make good day rides. The maps cost £5.99 each and are available from Sustrans.

Sustrans Order Line:

Call **0845 113 0065** or visit their website at **www.sustrans.org.uk**

---

or Penrith to Berwick-upon-Tweed. Highlights include the Eden Valley, the crossing of the Pennines, Hadrian's Wall, views of the Cheviots, Northumberland National Park, the Union Suspension Bridge and the town walls of Berwick.

Traffic-free sections over 3 miles:

- Lambley Viaduct to Haltwhistle (NCN 68).

Coast & Castles Cycle Route

200 miles from Newcastle to Edinburgh via Berwick-upon-Tweed, Kelso and Innerleithen. Highlights include North Tyne Cycleway to Tynemouth, the Northumbrian Coast, Warkworth Castle, Bamburgh Castle, Berwick's town walls, views of the River Tweed, Kelso town square, Floors Castle, Melrose Abbey, the Moorfoot Hills and Edinburgh.

Traffic-free sections over 3 miles:

- North Tyne Cycleway to Tynemouth (NCN 72).
- The Innocent Railway, Edinburgh (NCN 1).

Other areas for lane cycling

In the southern half of the area the best lane cycling is in the **far southwest of County Durham** around Barnard Castle and Upper Teesdale or west of Corbridge in the **Tyne Valley**. Further north, once beyond Morpeth and Ashington, it is hard to go wrong: **Northumberland** is one of the least densely populated counties in England and there is a fine

Pennine
Cycleway
North

sustrans

network of quiet lanes through big, open country. There are five busy A roads to avoid: the A1, A697, A1068 and A68 and A696, but such is the network of lanes in the area that it is easy to devise routes that avoid not only these but almost all the B roads as well, leaving you with glorious cycling on some of the quietest lanes in the whole of England.

North-East Trails

1 Guisborough Forest, south of Middlesbrough

CATEGORY

Railway path and forest trails.

DISTANCE

Railway path - 3 miles each way. Forest routes - 5 or 12 miles.

A Forestry Commission holding which stretches up the steep escarpment of the North York Moors south of the market town of Guisborough, once the ancient capital of Cleveland. This route combines a railway path trail with a tougher challenge in the hills. The railway path is flat with a good surface. The forest trails are steeper and rougher and mountain bikes are recommended.

Blue route (Easy / Moderate, 5 miles) - follows forest roads and grass tracks with small climbs and descents.

Black route (Very Difficult / Highly Technical, 12 miles) - demanding climbs and technical singletrack descents on a combination of forest roads and grass tracks.

STARTING POINT & PARKING

→Pinchinthorpe Forest Visitor Centre, to the west of Guisborough, just south of the junction of the A173 with the A171 (grid reference 585154).

ON YOUR BIKES!

From Pinchinthorpe Visitor Centre go west along the railway for 2 miles (to its junction with the existing railway) or east along the railway path and up into Guisborough Woods.

Station: Nunthorpe, 1 mile west of the western end of the railway path.

TIC: Guisborough, 01287 633801.

Other nearby trails: Dalby Forest lies 20 miles southeast. Scarborough to Whitby railway path. Rudland Rigg is a trail over the North York Moors.

Useful publications: OS Landranger Maps 93 & 94. A map can be purchased from the Guisborough Forest Visitor Centre, Pinchinthorpe Station, Pinchinthorpe, Guisborough, Cleveland TS14 8H (01287 631132) or from the Forest Enterprise office in Pickering (01751 472771). E-mail: n.york.moors.fdo@forestry.gov.uk

Refreshments: None on the ride. Lots of choice in Guisborough.

2 Hart to Haswell Walkway, north of Hartlepool

CATEGORY
Railway path.

DISTANCE
9 miles each way.

Running from Hart Station (on the A1086 north of Hartlepool) through Hesleden and past Shotton Colliery to Haswell, this railway path offers good views of the coast and Cleveland Hills A good gravel path from Hart to Castle Eden and then grassier and rougher - mountain bikes are recommended. There are many ongoing developments of traffic-free paths in this part of the world with links underway for Haswell north to Seaham and Ryhope and south from Wingate along the Castle Eden Walkway towards Stockton. Shotton Colliery was once famous for having the biggest pit heap in the UK, described by J.B. Priestley as a 'depressing smoking volcano'. The colliery was first opened in 1840 and by 1913 employed over 1800 men producing 400,000 tons of coal. The colliery closed in 1972.

NB There are three road crossings, including the busy A181 north of Wingate.

STARTING POINT & PARKING
→ **Hart Station**, just off the A1086 between Hartlepool and Blackhall Colliery (grid reference 479365). Or Hesleden, Castle Eden Inn, Shotton Colliery (old station) and Haswell.

Station: Hartlepool, 4 miles southeast of Hart Station.

TIC: Hartlepool, 01429 869706.

Other nearby trails: The Brandon & Bishop Auckland Walk, the Auckland Way, the Deerness Valley Walk, and the Lanchester Valley Walk all lie less than 10 miles to the west. The Consett & Sunderland Cycleway lies 10 miles to the north.

Useful publications: OS Landranger Maps 88 & 93. This and many other traffic-free trails between Teeside and Tyneside are shown on the Sustrans *Three Rivers Cycle Route* map (£5.99).

Sustrans Order Line: Call 0845 113 0065 or visit their website at www.sustrans.org.uk

Refreshments: Pubs along the way in each village.

3

3 Hamsterley Forest, southwest of Durham (4 routes)

CATEGORY
Waymarked forest routes.

DISTANCE
3 - 10 miles.

Set in Upper Weardale, where the North Pennines meet the West Durham Moors, Hamsterley Forest covers an area of 2000 hectares with of woodlands. Both the red squirrel and the roe deer are native to the forest and there is a huge variety of birdlife. There are four waymarked trails in this popular destination. Mountain bikes are recommended and there are several hills.

NB The routes follow the Forest Drive for a part of their length, expect light traffic.

Windy Bank Trail (Beginners / Family, green waymarks, 3 miles, 10% singletrack, recommended direction: clockwise) - forest roads, mostly good surfaces and gentle gradients. Suitable for most ages and levels of fitness. *Start: Hamsterley Forest Visitor Centre.*

Spurlswood Valley Ride (Easy / Moderate, blue waymarks, 9 miles, 20% singletrack, recommended direction: clockwise) - mostly forest road, varied terrain with moderate gradients, suitable for experienced cyclists of average fitness. *Start: Hamsterley Forest Visitor Centre*

Neighbour Moor Tour (Challenging / Strenuous, red waymarks, 10 miles, 35% singletrack, recommended direction: clockwise) - variable surface and terrain, with prolonged ascents and descents. Suitable for experienced cyclists with a good level of fitness. *Start: Grove car park (grid reference 067299).*

Bedburn Bash (Very Difficult / Technical, black waymarks, 7 miles, 50% singletrack, recommended direction: anti-clockwise). This is a narrow singletrack route with varied surfaces and steep terrain. A high level of skill and fitness is required, with offroad riding experience.
Start: Hamsterley Forest Visitor Centre.

STARTING POINT & PARKING

→Hamsterley Forest Visitor Centre, 1 mile from Hamsterley village, 15 miles southwest of Durham (grid reference 092313). A toll is payable on the road from Bedburn to the visitor centre.
Station: Bishop Auckland, 9 miles to the east.
TIC: Bishop Auckland, 01388 604922.
Other nearby trails: The Auckland Walk and the Brandon and Bishop Auckland Trail start from Bishop Auckland.
Useful publications: OS Landranger Map 92. A Forest Enterprise leaflet is available at the visitor centre (01388 488312) or from Kielder Forest District Office (01434 220242).
Refreshments: Refreshment kiosk at the visitor centre. Pub in Hamsterley village.

4 Brandon and Bishop Auckland Walk, south of Durham

CATEGORY
Railway path.
DISTANCE
9 1/2 miles each way.

There are wonderful views over the Wear Valley on this attractive route which was originally built to carry coal and coke for the industry in Wearside and Tyneside. It runs from the northern end of the vast Newton Cap Viaduct, just north of Bishop Auckland via Willington and Brandon to the Broompark picnic area on the B6302, just west of Durham and uses a gravel path, stony in places with a few gentle hills. About 3 miles north of Newton Cap there is a brief urban section through Willington. After another 3 miles you will see Brancepeth Castle, essentially a 13th-century castle built to replace a Saxon stronghold, much restored in the 19th century.

NB Take care crossing the A690 near Willington.

3

STARTING POINTS & PARKING

→ **Newton Cap Viaduct** car park, just off the A689 Crook Road, on the north side of Bishop Auckland (grid reference 204306).

→ **Broompark** car park west of Durham. From the A167 take the A690 towards Crook then first right on the B6302. The car park is about 3/4 mile along this road, towards Ushaw Moor (grid reference 251415).

Station: Bishop Auckland or Durham (2 miles north of the end of the route).

TIC: Durham, 0191 384 3720.

Other nearby trails: The Auckland Way starts to the east of Bishop Auckland. There are links from Broompark picnic site to the Deerness Valley Walk and the Lanchester Valley Walk.

Useful publications: OS Landranger Maps 88, 92 & 93. A fine set of laminated route cards covering seven railway paths in County Durham can be purchased from: The Countryside Group, Environment & Technical Services Dept., Durham County Council, County Hall, Durham DH1 5UQ (0191 383 4144).

Refreshments: Lots of choice in Bishop Auckland. Pubs in Hunwick, Willington and Brancepeth.

5 Auckland Walk, south of Durham

CATEGORY

Railway path.

DISTANCE

4 miles each way.

An attractive tree-lined route with gentle gradients from Spennymoor to the outskirts of Bishop Auckland offering fine views over the Wear Valley towards the hills of the North Pennines. Although it is a stone-based path, it is rough in places so mountain bikes are recommended. The trail passes through countryside which was once part of the Bishop's Park as evidenced by the names of the farms along the route such as 'Old Park Farm' and 'Bishop's Close'. Further on you go past Auckland Park which was the Bishop's deer park, serving his palace with meat, game and fish. Binchester was originally a substantial Roman Fort on Dere Street which was built to bring supplies to the Roman armies in the north. The line was built in two stages. In 1841 the section between Byers Green and Spennymoor was opened as part of the Clarence Railway

Company serving Port Clarence on Teeside. This was used to carry coal from around Byers Green and Willington. In 1885 NER opened the route between Byers Green and Bishop Auckland and the whole line was then used by passengers. The line was closed in 1939.

NB If you choose to go from the south end of the trail into Bishop Auckland you will need to use the busy A689 for about 1 mile.

STARTING POINT & PARKING
→Whitworth Road car park, near Whitworth Hall, **Spennymoor**, south of Durham (grid reference 245337).
Station: Bishop Auckland.
TIC: Bishop Auckland, 01388 604922.
Other nearby trails: The Brandon to Bishop Auckland Walk starts from the north of Bishop Auckland.
Useful publications: OS Landranger Map 93. A fine set of laminated route cards covering seven railway paths in County Durham can be purchased from The Countryside Group, Environment & Technical Services Dept., Durham County Council, County Hall, Durham DH1 5UQ (0191 383 4144).
Refreshments: Lots of choice in Bishop Auckland.

6 Deerness Valley Walk, west of Durham

CATEGORY
Railway path.
DISTANCE
8 miles each way.

The landscape of this area was shaped by the coalmining industry in the 19th century, although little sign of heavy industry is left nowadays as the area has greened over. The trail runs west from Durham through Esh Winning and Waterhouses to the B6299 at Stanley Crook, crossing and re-crossing the River Deerness along a tree-lined route that reaches the edge of the Durham Dales. There is a steep climb at the Stanley Crook end of the ride. The ride uses an old railway line that was opened in 1858 and carried coal out of the valley for nearly a hundred years. The branch closed in 1951 but continued to be used one day a year for the Durham Miners' Gala.

NB If you choose to go into Durham or Crook from either end of the trail you will need to use busy roads.

STARTING POINT & PARKING
→**Broompark** picnic site, west of Durham (grid reference 251415). From the A617 take the A690 towards Crook then turn first right on the B6302. The car park is about 3/4 mile along this road, towards Ushaw Moor.

Station: Durham Station is 2 miles from Broompark car park.
TIC: Durham, 0191 384 3720.
Other nearby trails: The Lanchester Valley Walk and the Brandon to Bishop Auckland Walk also start from Broompark car park.
Useful publications: OS Landranger Maps 88 & 92. A fine set of laminated route cards covering 7 railway paths in County Durham can be purchased from: The Countryside Group,

Environment & Technical Services Dept.,
Durham County Council, County Hall, Durham
DH1 5UQ (0191 383 4144).
Refreshments: Pubs and cafe in Esh Winning
and Crook. Pub at Hamilton Row (west of
Waterhouses).

7   Lanchester Valley Walk, northwest of Durham

CATEGORY
Railway path.
DISTANCE
12 miles each way.

The trail climbs between Durham (Broompark
car park) and Consett, following the River
Browney to Lanchester then Backgill Burn to
Hownsgill Viaduct, across predominantly arable
land. Opened in 1862, the railway was built to
carry iron ore to Consett Steelworks and coal
from Langley Park and finally closed in 1965.
Located about 3 miles from the start, Langley

Park has been used by film-makers to portray
typical pit village life. To the left of the railway
path there is a purpose-built handball wall.
Handball was a popular game within the mining
community. Lanchester lies on Dere Street, the
Roman supply route from York to Scotland and
for centuries it has been a busy market town.
The history of Consett steelmaking began in
1837 when large deposits of coal and iron ore
were found. They helped to transform a small
village into an industrial town almost overnight.
The last furnaces closed in the 1980s and now
little remains of the industrial infrastructure.

STARTING POINTS & PARKING
→**Broompark** picnic site, west of Durham (grid
reference 250415). From the A617 take the
A690 towards Crook then first right on the
B6302. The car park is signposted to the left.
→Also at Langley Park, Malton, Lanchester and
Hownsgill Viaduct (grid reference 099494).

Station: Durham Railway Station is 2 miles from
Broompark car park.

TIC: Durham, 0191 384 3720.

Other nearby trails: There are links from Broompark car park to the Deerness Valley Walk and the Brandon to Bishop Auckland Walk. From Consett you can join the Waskerley Way, the Consett to Sunderland Railway Path and the Derwent Walk.

Useful publications: OS Landranger Map 88. A fine set of laminated route cards covering 7 railway paths in County Durham can be purchased from: The Countryside Group, Environment & Technical Services Dept., Durham County Council, County Hall, Durham DH1 5UQ (0191 383 4144).

Refreshments: Lots of choice in Lanchester and Consett. Pub in Langley Park.

8 Waskerley Way, south of Consett, County Durham

CATEGORY
Railway path.

DISTANCE
9 1/2 miles each way.

A dramatic route which climbs 900ft from Hownsgill Viaduct, south of Consett via Rowley and Waskerley to the B6278 at Weatherhill Summit (north of Stanhope) in the heart of the Durham Dales with fine views across the moors and reservoirs. Mountain bikes are recommended for the stony and grassy path. There is a steep descent to Stanhope if you choose to go down here for refreshments. The Waskerley Way mainly follows the western part of the former Stanhope & Tyne railway which was built in 1834 to carry limestone, lead and iron from Weardale and coal from Medomsley to the River Tyne. An old smelt waggon stands as a reminder of the nearby Consett Steel Works which closed in 1980. The mighty Hownsgill Viaduct is made of two and a half million bricks and stands 150 ft high.

NB: Sections of the relatively busy B6278 are used to access Stanhope.

STARTING POINTS & PARKING
→ **Hownsgill Viaduct** car park, signposted off the A692 between Consett and Castleside (grid reference 099494).

→ Also at **Rowley Station**, **Waskerley** picnic site and **Meeting Slacks**.

Station: Prudhoe (to the north), Chester-le-Street or Durham (to the east), all 10-12 miles from the start, although much of this is on railway paths.

TIC: Durham, 0191 384 3720.

Other nearby trails: The trail joins three other cycle routes at Hownsgill Viaduct - the Consett to Sunderland Railway Path, the Derwent Valley Walk and the Lanchester Valley Walk.

Useful publications: OS Landranger Maps 87 & 88 (and 92 if you are going into Stanhope). A fine set of laminated route cards covering seven railway paths in County Durham can be purchased from: The Countryside Group, Environment & Technical Services Dept., Durham County Council, County Hall, Durham DH1 5UQ (0191 383 4144).

Refreshments: In Consett and Stanhope.

9 Consett and Sunderland Railway Path

CATEGORY
Railway path.

DISTANCE
Up to 22 miles each way.

The trail runs along one of Britain's oldest railways, the Stanhope & Tyne, built in 1834. The line was mainly used to carry raw materials to the Consett Steelworks and steel from Consett to the shipyards of Sunderland. When the track was lifted in 1985, Sustrans converted the path to recreational use and have since decorated

the trail with many sculptures made from scrap metal and stone. There are also the famous earthwork sculptures by Andy Goldsworthy known as The Lampton Worm and The Maze. The trail runs right past the Beamish North of England Open Air Museum with artefacts recovered from all over Northern England illustrating the industrial and social background of the region. The ride forms part of the C2C, the National Cycle Network Route that runs from the Cumbrian Coast to the North Sea. This may be waymarked as 'C2C' or 'Route 7'.

The course of the trail is as follows: Hownsgill car park off the A692 to the south of Consett via Leadgate, Annfield Plain, Stanley, Chester-le-Street and Washington to Sunderland. There is a drop of over 800 ft from Consett to Sunderland, almost all of this occurs between Annfield Plain and Washington, so plan accordingly.

NB There are short road sections near Washington and in Sunderland.

STARTING POINTS & PARKING
→**Hownsgill** car park, off the A692, south of Consett. (grid reference 099494).
→Also at Consett, Annfield Plain, Stanley, Beamish, Chester-le-Street and James Steel Park, Washington and Sunderland.

Station: Chester-le-Street, Sunderland.
TIC: Sunderland, 0191 553 2000.
Other nearby trails: At Hownsgill Viaduct the trail links to the Waskerley Way, the Lanchester Valley Walk and the Derwent Valley Walk.
Useful publications: OS Landranger Map 88.
Sustrans *Three Rivers Cycle Route* map (£5.99), showing this and many other traffic-free trails in the area between Middlesbrough and Newcastle.
Sustrans Order Line: Call 0845 113 0065 or visit their website at www.sustrans.org.uk
Refreshments: Lots of choice along the way.

10

10 Derwent Valley Walk, southwest of Newcastle

CATEGORY

Railway path.

DISTANCE

11 miles each way.

Running along the course of the old Derwent Valley Railway, the trail follows the River Derwent, a tributary of the Tyne, passing through meadows and broadleaf woodland as it climbs gradually southwest from Swalwell Visitor Centre (Blaydon) via Winlaton Mill, Rowlands Gill, Hamsterley and Ebchester to Lydgetts Junction near Consett where there are links to several other trails. About halfway along the ride at Pontburn and Fogoesburn viaducts you may catch glimpses of red squirrel in the surrounding treetops. Dere Street, the old Roman road from York to Scotland, crossed the River Derwent at Ebchester and was guarded by

a fort (Vindomara). Shotley Bridge was once a hive of industry. In 1687 swordmakers from Solingen in Germany settled here. The swiftly flowing river provided power for the mills, local iron was available and there was plenty of timber to make charcoal for iron smelting. The Cutlers' Hall and the Crown & Crossed Swords pub are all that remain as evidence of a once-thriving industry.

NB Four busy roads are crossed and there is a short section (1/4 mile) on road at Rowlands Gill.

STARTING POINTS & PARKING

→ **Swalwell Visitor Centre**, beside Blaydon Rugby Club, signposted off the A694 and the B6317 between Blaydon and Dunston, west of Newcastle-upon-Tyne (grid reference 197620).
→ Also at Rowlands Gill, Pontburn Wood, Ebchester, Shotley Bridge and Lydgetts Junction.

Station: Newcastle upon Tyne.

TIC: Newcastle upon Tyne, 0191 261 0610.

Other nearby trails: From the Lydgetts Junction (Consett) end of the trail there are links to the Lanchester Valley Walk, the Waskerley Way and the Consett to Sunderland Path. The last two of these form part of Sustrans C2C Route. From the Swalwell end the trail links to the Keelman's Way.

Useful publications: OS Landranger Map 88. A fine set of laminated route cards covering 7 railway paths in County Durham can be purchased from: The Countryside Group, Environment & Technical Services Dept., Durham County Council, County Hall, Durham DH1 5UQ (0191 383 4144).

Refreshments: Pubs in Rowlands Gill, Ebchester and Shotley Bridge.

11 Keelman's Way from Wylam to Gateshead and Hebburn (South Tyne Cycleway)

CATEGORY
Riverside path, railway path, specially-built cyclepath, some urban road sections.

DISTANCE
Up to 14 miles each way,.

The trail runs along the south side of the Tyne from Wylam (just over the border in Northumberland) via Blaydon and Dunston to Gateshead and the Riverside Park in Hebburn. The route is well-signposted throughout as Keelman's Way, the South Tyne Cycleway or National Cycle Network Route 14. There are several short road sections, most notably between Newburn Bridge and the bridge carrying the A1 over the Tyne and then also beneath the Tyne Bridge in Gateshead but these are subject to constant improvement. As there is a traffic-free route along the north side of the river you could easily cross over then back

again. If you want a shorter, completely traffic-free route, cross Newburn Bridge (4 miles east of Wylam) and return to Wylam via Hadrian's Way (National Cycle Network Route 72).

STARTING POINTS & PARKING
→**Wylam** railway station, about 10 miles west of Newcastle city centre between the A69 and the A695 (grid reference 120644).

→**Hebburn** Riverside Park, along the south side of the Tyne, east of Gateshead (grid reference 301647).

Station: Wylam, Blaydon, Hebburn.

TIC: Newcastle, 0191 261 0610.

Other nearby trails: The route links to the North Tyne Cycle Way (Hadrian's Way) and the Derwent Valley Walk.

Useful publications: OS Landranger Map 88. A Keelman's Way leaflet is available from the Planning Dept, Gateshead MBC, Civic Centre, Regent St, Gateshead NE8 1HH, 0191 433 3000.

Refreshments: All along the way.

12 North Tyne Cycleway (Hadrian's Way), Newcastle

CATEGORY
Railway path.

DISTANCE
9 miles each way.

There are trails both sides of the Tyne east from Wylam. The North Tyne Cycleway runs from the countryside setting of Wylam (just inside Northumberland) to the Quayside in the heart of Newcastle and could be followed further east along Hadrian's Way, National Cycle Network Route 72 to Wallsend, North Shields and Tynemouth. One could catch a train from Newcastle to Wylam and cycle back into town with the prevailing westerly wind on your back. The path runs through Tyne Riverside Country

Park and along a recently built stretch through Newburn Riverside, through Scotswood on a railway path up above the river then drops down to the Tyne finishing under the magnificent bridges in the heart of the city. There are several cyclepaths in the area so look out for signs for 'Hadrian's Way' 'National Cycle Network Route 72' and 'City Centre'. It is not sufficient to say 'Follow the river' as the trail is occasionally set back from the water or up above the Tyne on the railway path through Scotswood.

STARTING POINTS & PARKING
→Wylam, Newburn Leisure Centre or Newcastle Quayside (the Swing Bridge).

Station: Wylam, Newcastle.
TIC: Newcastle, 0191 261 0610.
Other nearby trails: South of the Tyne, the Keelman's Way runs from Wylam to Hebburn Riverside Park (west of Jarrow). You can continue along the north side of the Tyne from Newcastle city centre to Wallsend and Tynemouth on Hadrian's Way. The Derwent Valley Walk runs from near the Metro Centre southwest to Consett.
Useful publications: OS Landranger Map 88. Better is the *Tyneside Cycling Map* produced by CycleCity Guides, Wallbridge Mill, The Retreat, Frome BA11 5JU (01373 453533).
E-mail: info@cyclecityguides.co.uk
Refreshments: All along the way.

13 Newcastle upon Tyne to Wallsend along the north side of the River Tyne

CATEGORY
Railway path and specially-built cycle path.
DISTANCE
5 miles each way.

From Newcastle city centre, east to Segedunum Roman Fort, Baths and Museum in Wallsend (the eastern end of Hadrian's Wall) alongside the Tyne then up above the river along the course of an old railway, passing the mighty cranes of the shipyards of Swan Hunter below. This route forms part of the famous C2C cycle route that starts in West Cumbria and finishes at Tynemouth. If you want to sample the final section of this trail, follow signs for NCN Route 72 and 1 past Royal Quays and North Shields to the castle at the mouth of the river.

NB There is a whole network of traffic-free paths in North Tyneside worth mentioning briefly.

From Royal Quays North Sea Ferry Terminal near North Shields northwest to Backworth then west through Burradon and Wide Open to Dinnington (this is the start of the Reivers Cycle Route, waymarked as 'Cycle Route 10')

Along the Coxlode Waggonway starting from close to the DSS buildings in Longbenton, east to the Rising Sun Country Park.

STARTING POINT & PARKING
→Quayside by Tyne Bridge in the centre of Newcastle. Keep the river to your right and follow signs for 'C2C' 'NCN 72' and 'Tynemouth'. The trail takes you right to Segedunum Roman Fort, off Buddle Street in Wallsend.

Station: Newcastle upon Tyne.
TIC: Newcastle, 0191 261 0610

Other nearby trails: The North Tyne Cycleway and Keelman's Way run west from the city centre on both sides of the Tyne. The Derwent Valley Walk runs from near the Metro Centre southwest to Consett.

Useful publications: OS Landranger Map 88. Better is the *Tyneside Cycling Map* produced by CycleCity Guides, Wallbridge Mill, The Retreat, Frome BA11 5JU (01373 453533). E-mail: info@cyclecityguides.co.uk

Refreshments: Lots of choice along the way.

14 Kielder Water, Northumberland (15 routes)

CATEGORY
Waymarked forestry trails.

DISTANCE
Most of the routes are 5-10 miles. The two longest are 17 miles.

Kielder Water is the second largest man-made lake in Western Europe and Kielder Forest is the largest man-made forest in Britain covering over 600 square kilometres. There are 15 waymarked routes, two of which are waymarked blue and the rest are waymarked red with the number of the route in the centre of the red arrow. The trails use minor roads, forestry roads and tracks. The leaflet indicates the percentage of tarmac / forest road / track and the amount of climbing in each route. The two longest routes (including the reservoir circuit) use sections of the access road to Kielder Castle Visitor Centre.

STARTING POINTS & PARKING
→ Kielder Castle Visitor Centre, on the minor road west from Bellingham (40 miles northwest of Newcastle-upon-Tyne) or from Leaplish Waterside Park or Tower Knowe Visitor Centre located along the west side of the reservoir.

Station: Hexham, 20 miles to the southeast.
TIC: Bellingham, 01434 220616.
Other nearby trails: There are 15 waymarked cycle routes in the forest.
Useful publications: OS Landranger Map 80. A leaflet (£2) showing routes in the Kielder Forest area is available from Forest Enterprise, Kielder Forest District, Ealsburn, Bellingham, Hexham, Northumberland NE48 2AJ (01434 220242).
Refreshments: Cafe at Kielder Castle. Pub in Kielder village

	MILES	GRADE	HT GAIN
Bull Crag	6	Moderate	Very low
Cranecleugh	5	Easy	Low
Cross Crags	6	Easy	Low
Humble Loop	10	Moderate	Medium
Swinburne Selection (3 routes: a, b, c)	6 – 10	Mod./Demanding	Medium
Kielder Water Circuit	16	Moderate	Low
Border Railway Route	7	Easy	Very low
Scaup	8	Easy	Low
Castle Hill	7.5	Easy	Low
Sidwood	17	Demanding	High
Kershope	7	Easy	Low
Cross Border Trail (A)			
via Scotch Knowe - linear route	13	Moderate	High
Cross Border Trail (B)			
via Bloodybush - linear route	17	Demanding	High
Archercleugh		Trail Quest Cyclo Orienteering	
Leaplish Crags	Offroad	Extreme mountain biking	

Wales

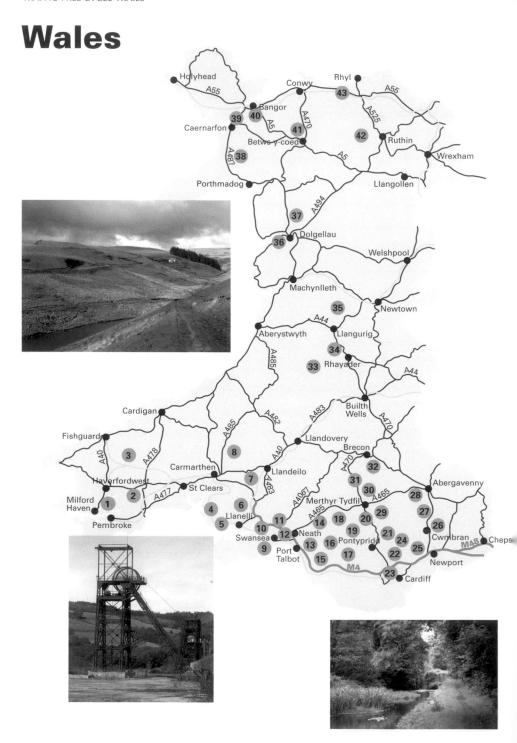

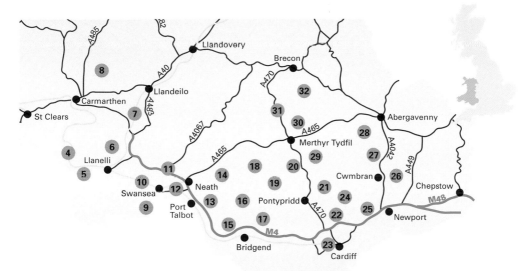

WALES TRAILS

1 Brunel Trail, north of Pembroke	24 Sirhowy Country Park, northwest of Newport
2 Canaston Woods, east of Haverfordwest	25 Newport Canal to Crosskeys
3 Llys-y-Frân Reservoir, northeast of Haverfordwest	26 Newport Canal to Pontypool
	27 Pontypool to Blaenavon
4 Pembrey Country Park, west of Llanelli	28 Llanfoist to Govilon, southwest of Abergavenny
5 Millennium Coastal Park from Llanelli to Kidwelly, west of Swansea	29 Cwm Darran Country Park, southeast of Merthyr Tydfil (4 routes)
6 Llanelli to Tumble - Swiss Valley Trail	
7 Llyn Llech Owain Country Park, southwest of Llandeilo	30 Taff Trail from Merthyr Tydfil towards Pontsticill Reservoir
8 Brechfa Forest, northeast of Carmarthen	31 Garwnant Forest, north of Merthyr Tydfil (2 routes)
9 Swansea Bikepath along the seafront	32 Taff Trail from Talybont Reservoir to Taf Fechan
10 Swansea & the Clyne Valley	
11 Swansea Canal, northeast of Swansea	33 Claerwen Reservoir, west of Rhayader
12 Neath Canal, east of Swansea	34 Elan Valley Trail, west of Rhayader
13 Port Talbot from Bryn to Goytre	35 Hafren Forest, west of Llanidloes
14 Neath Canal from Neath to Glyn Neath	36 Mawddach Trail from Dolgellau to Barmouth
15 Tondu to Pyle, northwest of Bridgend	37 Coed y Brenin Forest, north of Dolgellau (5 routes)
16 Afan Argoed Countryside Centre, northeast of Port Talbot	
17 Ogmore Valley, north of Bridgend	38 Lôn Eifion from Caernarfon to Bryncir,
18 Neath to Pontypridd High Level Route	39 Lôn Las Menai from Caernarfon to Y Felinheli
19 Rhondda Community Routes, Treorchy	
20 Taff Trail from Abercynon to Merthyr Tydfil	40 Lôn Las Ogwen from Bangor to Tregarth
21 Hengoed Viaduct to Trelewis, northwest of Newport	41 Gwydyr Forest, Betws y Coed
	42 Llyn Brenig Reservoir, southwest of Denbigh
22 Taff Trail from Castell Coch to Glyntaff	43 Colwyn Bay & Rhos-on-Sea to Prestatyn
23 Taff Trail from Cardiff to Tongwynlais	

Wales Mountain Biking

Wales has some of Britain's finest mountain biking: the purpose-built singletrack Forestry Commission trails are at the cutting edge of the sport; Powys is among the best counties in the UK for top quality byways and bridleways; there are excellent trails in the Brecon Beacons and many large Forestry Commission holdings throughout the country. However, the trails are not spread evenly through Wales: with the exception of Brechfa Forest there is little mountain biking in West Wales; there are no bridleways on Anglesey and very few on the Lleyn Peninsula. By contrast there 's good riding on the Clwyd Hills and Snowdonia has developed a successful voluntary agreement that allows mountain bikers to the top of Snowdon outside busy times.

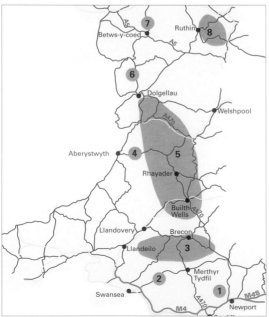

1. Cwmcarn

The Twrch Mountain Bike Trail has testing climbs, swooping descents and demanding technical sections in 9.6 miles (15.5 km) of almost pure singletrack. The trails can be ridden all year and vary from open and flowing hard pack to tight, technical and rooty. In places the trail hugs the sides of some very steep wooded slopes whilst in others it sweeps along open ground with dramatic views of the Bristol Channel.

2. Afan Argoed

Twisty, rooty, rocky and in places wildly exposed, the singletrack in the Afan Valley is an enthusiast's dream. The trails have been carved out of the steep forested slopes and the valley has been transformed into singletrack heaven. The **Penhydd Trail** explores the south side of the valley with lung-bursting climbs and amazing singletrack descents. The **Wall Trail** tackles the much steeper north side of the valley via superb flowing single-track with amazing views of the valley.

3. The Brecon Beacons

The best trails lie south of Brecon and in the Black Mountains: there is a long ride south of Brecon through a pass at almost 2000ft (600mts) to the reservoirs above Merthyr Tydfil, some short, tough rides around the hub of Talybont and many great trails in the Black Mountains.

4. Nant yr Arian

The **Summit Mountain Bike Trail** (10 miles) offers superb views and awesome riding on flowing twisty single track. The **Syfydrin Trail** (22 miles) takes in the entire Summit Trail and leads you out onto the high open hills with stunning views. The **Pendam Trail** (6 miles) combines sections of the 'Summit' and 'Syfydrin' trails for a taste of the fantastic riding and scenery available. Although the shortest route at Nant yr Arian, it includes lots of technically challenging singletrack and some hard climbs.

5. Powys

This vast, spectacular, sparsely-populated county has the densest concentration of bridleways and byways in all Wales. There is superb mountain biking around the Llyn Brianne Reservoir west of Llanwrtyd Wells and from Rhayader in the Elan Valley. The border country around Radnor Forest offers myriad trails and in the north there are testing challenges in the Berwyn Hills.

6. Coed y Brenin

From beautiful river valleys to wild hilltops, with forest road climbs giving way to brilliant purpose-built singletrack descents, Coed y Brenin has something to offer mountain bikers of all abilities. For more details see page 320.

7. Betws y Coed

The Marin Mountain Bike Trail (16 miles / 25kms) is a BIG RIDE! Big climbs, big descents, brilliant singletrack and awesome scenery. Most of the climbs are on forest roads giving you time to take in views of Snowdonia. The singletrack varies from very tight, technical and rocky to wonderfully open and flowing, from dark forest to exposed ridgelines.

8. Clwyd Hills

This compact range of hills in northeast Wales has a series of loops that can be ridden singly or linked together for a full day out. The views out into the Vale of Clwyd are stupendous. It is one of those areas to keep exploring until you have perfected your favourite routes.

www.mbwales.com

Wales Forestry

Wales has a far higher proportion of forested land than England. Ten miles either side of an imaginary north-south line from Conwy to Cardiff contains more forestry than all of Southern England, East Anglia and the Midlands put together. In addition, Wales has been at the forefront of developing purpose-built singletrack mountain bike trails through various of its holdings in the region (listed below). Even in the more densely populated area of South Wales and the Valleys there are large holdings, many of which have waymarked routes.

Forests and woods with waymarked trails

They are shown with a corresponding trail number and page reference.

1 Canaston, west of Narberth
See Route 2, page 291

3 Brechfa, northeast of Carmarthen
See Route 8, page 296

4 Afan Argoed, east of Neath *
See Route 16, page 303

5 Rhondda Community Routes, west of the Rhondda
See Route 19, page 305

6 Cwmcarn, northwest of Newport *
See page 284

7 Garwnant, north of Merthyr Tydfil
See Route 31, page 315

8 Nant Yr Arian, east of Aberystwyth *
See page 285

9 Hafren, west of Llanidloes
See Route 35, page 318

10 Coed y Brenin, north of Dolgellau *
See Route 37, page 320

13 Gwydyr, near Betws y Coed *
See Route 41, page 324

* There are purpose-built singletrack mountain bike trails in these woodlands
www.mbwales.com

Further Information

Coed y Mynydd Forest District
(Mid & Northwest Wales)
Government Buildings, Arran Road, Dolgellau,
Gwynedd. LL40 1LW
Tel: 01341 422289

Coed y Gororau Forest District
(Mid & Northeast Wales)
Powells Place, Powells Lane, Welshpool,
Powys. SY21 7JY
Tel: 01938 557400

Llanymddyfri Forest District *(Mid & West Wales)*
Llanfair Road, Llandovery, Carmarthenshire. SA20 0AL
Tel: 01550 720394

Coed y Cymoedd Forest District *(South Wales)*
Resolven, Neath. SA11 4DR
Tel: 01639 710221

This second list features forests / woods in popular tourist areas such as Snowdonia or Anglesey in which you are free to explore the tracks but where there are no waymarked routes; it is highly recommended that you take the relevant Ordnance Survey 1:25,000 scale map with you for the larger woods where it is very easy to get lost!

2   Pembrey Forest, west of Llanelli
Part of country park
OS Explorer Map 164

11   Beddgelert, north of Porthmadog
Snowdonia National Park
OS Outdoor Leisure Map 17

12   Moel Famau, on top of the popular Clwyd Hills, east of Ruthin
OS Explorer Map 265

14   Newborough, southwest Anglesey
Good, flat, family cycling
OS Explorer Map 262

There are also many other forestry holdings throughout Wales, far too many to mention them all here; these are represented on the map with a Forestry Commission logo. In order to find out more exact locations, look at the most recent edition of the relevant Ordnance Survey map: any of the forest areas shaded green which also have a thin purple border around the edge of the forest are owned by the Forestry Commission and you are allowed to ride there (forestry works permitting).

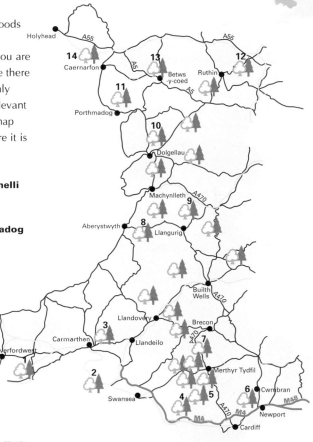

> **The Forestry Commission's** website is a good source of information with details of 1600 miles of waymarked cycling trails throughout the UK. Search by forest name or by the nearest town or city and the search will tell you the grade, length and waymarking details of the trails.
>
> **www.forestry.gov.uk/recreation**

Wales National Cycle Network

Lôn Las Cymru: North and South (two maps)

250 miles from Holyhead to Cardiff via Caernarfon, Dolgellau, Machynlleth, Builth Wells, Brecon and Merthyr Tydfil. Highlights include the lanes across Anglesey, Caernarfon Castle, the traffic-free paths near Caernarfon, Harlech Castle, Coed y Brenin Forest, the Mawddach Trail (Dolgellau), the Centre for Alternative Technology, the Upper Wye Valley, the Brecon Beacons, the Taff Trail and Chepstow Castle.

Traffic-free sections over 3 miles:

- Lôn Las Menai from Y Felinheli to Caernarfon (NCN 8)
- Lôn Eifion from Caernarfon to Bryncir (NCN 8)
- Mawddach Trail from Barmouth to Dolgellau (NCN 8)
- Taff Trail south of Talybont on Usk to Cardiff (NCN 8)

Sustrans

Listed below are the Sustrans maps that cover the National Cycle Network within the region. Some of the maps may describe routes that continue on into adjacent regions: these maps are mentioned in both chapters. The maps are not only useful for people wishing to ride the the whole route over several days; they also show all the traffic-free sections which make good day rides. The maps cost £5.99 each and are available from Sustrans.

Sustrans Order Line:
Call **0845 113 0065** or visit their website at
www.sustrans.org.uk

Celtic Trail: West and East (two maps)

140 miles from Fishguard to Chepstow with several route alternatives. Highlights include the Pembrokeshire Coast, St David's, the Brunel Cycle Trail (Pembroke), Tenby, the Llanelli Millennium Coastal Path, the Swansea Seafront Promenade, the Neath to Pontypridd High Level Route, Margam Country Park, the traffic-free route from Trelewis to Newport along railway paths and canal towpaths, Chepstow Castle.

Traffic-free sections over 3 miles:

- Brunel Cycle Trail from Neyland to Johnston (NCN 4)
- Llanelli Millennium Coastal Path (NCN 4)
- Clyne Valley Country Park from Swansea to Gowerton (NCN 4)
- Swansea Seafront Promenade (NCN 4)
- Neath to Pontypridd High Level Route (NCN 47)
- Pyle to Tondu railway path (NCN 4)
- Trelewis to Newport via Sirhowy and Crosskeys (NCN 47)

Other areas for lane cycling

With the exception of a dozen busy A roads and the densely populated, built-up triangle of South Wales between Llanelli, Abergavenny and Newport, the problem you will find in devising cycle rides in Wales is not avoiding the traffic but avoiding the hills! The island of **Anglesey** is the only large area in all of Wales where you will find a fine network of easy cycling. Elsewhere it is a case of the odd easy road along a valley but more frequently a mix of steep climbs, fine views and thrilling descents. Some of the attractive towns in **Mid Wales** such as Dolgellau, Machynlleth, Llanidloes, Rhayader, Presteigne, Hay on Wye, Brecon or Llandovery make excellent bases for a weekend or longer.

Wales Trails

1 The Brunel Trail from Neyland to Johnston, north of Pembroke

CATEGORY

Railway path.

DISTANCE

5 miles each way.

A gentle climb from Neyland Marina, north of Pembroke, through Westfield Pill Nature Reserve alongside the Daugleddau estuary up to Johnston where there is a chance of refreshment. The trail uses the bed of the Great Western Railway line, built between 1852-6 under the direction of Isambard Kingdom

Brunel, the most famous of all Victorian engineers. Neyland developed after the opening of the line as the terminus of the Great Western Railway, initially attracting passenger ships, although this trade ceased at the end of the 19th century. The village remained a busy fishing port until the middle of the 20th century.

STARTING POINT & PARKING

Car park at the end of **Neyland Marina**, just off the B4325 to the north of Pembroke Dock (grid reference 968057).

Station: Johnston.
TIC: Pembroke, 01646 622388.
Other nearby trails: Llys-y-frân Reservoir to the

northeast of Haverfordwest. Trails in Canaston Woods near to Narberth.

Useful publications: Ordnance Survey Landranger Map 158. An A3 leaflet, *Brunel Cycle Route* which describes a 14-mile route using part of the railway path costs 20p is available from local Tourist Information Centres.

Refreshments: Available at Neyland Marina and Johnston.

2 Canaston Woods, east of Haverfordwest

CATEGORY
Waymarked woodland trails

DISTANCE
3 miles of surfaced tracks plus bridleways

There is one 'lollipop'-shaped, waymarked route in this 420-acre Forestry Commission ancient woodland holding, using good, stone-based tracks appropriate for families, with a chance to explore further by using unsurfaced bridleways (which can be muddy in wet weather). The route starts from near Blackpool Mill, which has a tearoom, and runs east to the far edge of Canaston Wood, crossing the busy A4075 about halfway along. Originally part of the Slebech Estate, the woods are all that is left of a much larger forest of oak, ash and hazel. Smaller trees were used for firewood whereas the larger oaks were used for building and shipbuilding. Large amounts of wood were also converted into charcoal and used to fuel the iron foundry that existed near Blackpool Mill.

NB The busy A4075 has to be crossed after about 1 mile.

STARTING POINT & PARKING
➔ The car park near **Blackpool Mill**, located on the minor road leading southwest towards Minwear off the A4075, near the junction of the

A4075 with the A40 at Canaston Bridge, between Haverfordwest and Narberth (grid reference 060145).

Station: Narberth.
TIC: Haverfordwest, 01437 763110.
Other nearby trails: Brunel Trail (Neyland to Johnston Railway Path), Llys-y-frân Reservoir.
Useful publications: OS Landranger Map 158. A leaflet, *Canaston Cycle Trails* is available from South Pembrokeshire Partnership for Action with Rural Communities (SPARC) (01834 860965).
Refreshments: Tearoom at Blackpool Mill (summer only). Lots of choice in Narberth. If you are happy to use quiet lanes you could cycle to the Stanley Arms pub at Landshipping, about 5 miles southwest of Blackpool Mill.

3 Llys-y-frân Reservoir, northeast of Haverfordwest

CATEGORY
Round-reservoir ride.

DISTANCE
8-mile circuit.

An excellent route around one of the few reservoirs in West Wales. There are also a couple of short steep climbs where you may prefer to get off your bike and walk. Although the surface of the trail is largely stone and gravel, there are occasional awkward muddy stretches, so mountain bikes are recommended. There are also several short hills with some steep sections.

STARTING POINT & PARKING
➔ At the visitor centre at the southern end of the lake (grid reference 040244). The reservoir is well-signposted from the A40 between Haverfordwest and Narberth.

Station: Clarbeston Road.
TIC: Haverfordwest, 01437 763110.
Other nearby trails: Brunel Trail (Neyland to Johnston Railway Path, north of Pembroke).
Useful publications: OS Landranger Map 158.
Refreshments: At the visitor centre.

4 Pembrey Country Park, west of Llanelli

CATEGORY
Broad stone track around a country park.

DISTANCE
4-mile circuit.

Set halfway along the long traffic-free section of the Celtic Trail that runs from Kidwelly to Llanelli, Pembrey Country Park offers a waymarked circuit running just inside the perimeter of the grounds that takes you through the stands of pines and among the sand dunes. The park was once the site of a Royal Ordnance factory producing munitions for Allied Forces during the Second World War. Llanelli Borough Council bought the site in 1977 and initiated a vast programme of land reclamation. Among other attractions at Pembrey Country Park are a dry ski slope, a toboggan run, a nine hole Pitch and Putt course, an adventure playground, nature trails and an orienteering course together with a visitor centre and cafe. The nearby sandy beach of Cefn Sidan is 8 miles long and has won the Blue Flag Award many times.

STARTING POINT & PARKING
→ At the **Pembrey Country Park** Visitor Centre, signposted off the A484 between Llanelli and Kidwelly (grid reference 413007).

Station: Burry Port.
TIC: Llanelli, 01554 772020.
Other nearby trails: The Celtic Trail passes

through Pembrey Park. The section from Kidwelly to the Wildfowl & Wetlands Centre southwest of Llanelli is one of the finest traffic-free sections of the whole route. A railway path climbs gently from Llanelli to Tumble (the Swiss Valley Trail).

Useful publications: OS Landranger Map 159. Leaflet available from the visitor centre.

Refreshments: Cafe at the visitor centre.

5 Llanelli Millennium Coastal Park (Llanelli to Kidwelly), west of Swansea

CATEGORY
Coastal promenade.

DISTANCE
Up to 18 miles each way.

Massive earth-moving equipment was deployed over more than two years to create the magnificent coastal park where once there was post industrial dereliction. The great earth works include two award-winning earth bridges over the mainline railway. This section is already one of the most popular sections of the Celtic Trail (National Cycle Network Route 4) stretching from Pembrokeshire to Chepstow. Enjoy the wonderful views across to the Gower Peninsula. This would be a good ride to use in conjunction with the train, catching the train from Llanelli to Kidwelly into the prevailing westerly wind and cycling back to the start. Two ideas for shorter rides would be from Kidwelly to the Pembrey Forest Visitor Centre or from the Wildfowl & Wetlands Centre to Pembrey Forest.

NB You will need to use the B4308 for about 1 mile if you start in Kidwelly.

STARTING POINTS & PARKING
→ The centre of **Kidwelly**, on the A484 west of Llanelli.

→ **Pembrey Country Park**, off the A484 between Kidwelly and Llanelli (grid reference 413007).

→ At the Wildfowl & Wetlands Centre, off the A484 to the southeast of **Llanelli** (grid reference 531985).

ON YOUR BIKES!

You are following the Celtic Trail and NCN 4 signs

1. From the church in the centre of Kidwelly follow the B4308 south towards the main road (A484) and Burry Port.

2. Climb then descend. Immediately **before** the roundabout, cross the B4308 onto the pavement / cyclepath and follow this round to the right, parallel with the main Llanelli road (A484) for 1/2 mile.

3. Where the pavement ends, opposite a road turning on the left to Pinged, turn right to pass under a low railway bridge and join a path along the raised embankment with the estuary to your right.

4. At the end of the track turn left down steps, cross the small bridge over the drainage ditch, turn right onto the concrete track and then bear right towards the forest, following 'Route 4' signs.

5. The well-waymarked ride goes past Pembrey Country Park, past dunes along the coast, around Burry Port Docks, alongside the railway line and around the southern edge of Llanelli to the Wildfowl & Wetlands Centre.

Station: Llanelli or Kidwelly.

TIC: Llanelli, 01554 772020.

Other nearby trails: There is a circuit in Pembrey Forest. A railway path runs north from Llanelli to Tumble (the Swiss Valley Trail).

Useful publications: OS Landranger Map 159. Sustrans *Celtic Trail - West* map (£5.99) shows all the traffic-free trails around Llanelli plus the course of the Celtic Trail in West Wales (Fishguard to Swansea).

Sustrans Order Line: Call 0845 113 0065 or visit their website at www.sustrans.org.uk

Refreshments: Cafe at the Wildfowl & Wetlands Centre. Cafe at Pembrey Country Park. Lots of choice in Kidwelly.

6

6 Llanelli to Tumble (the Swiss Valley Trail)

CATEGORY

Railway path.

DISTANCE

11 miles each way.

Llanellli has become something of a focus for traffic-free trails in the development of the National Cycle Network in South Wales: it lies at a halfway point in the magnificent Millennium Coastal Park with trails running west towards Kidwelly and east towards Swansea while this route climbs up from Sandy Water Park into the rolling hills above the town. Near its northern end a signposted road route leads away from the railway path on quiet lanes to the National Botanic Garden of Wales at Middleton Hall. There is a gentle 550 ft climb from Llanelli to beyond Cynheidre so you are faced with a fantastic gravity-aided return back to the start.

STARTING POINTS & PARKING

→Sandy Water Park, **Llanelli**. This lies just off the A484 Burry Port / Kidwelly Road on the west side of Llanelli (grid reference 497005).

→**Tumble**, just off the A476 Llandeilo road, about 10 miles north of Llanelli (grid reference 537115).

Station: Llanelli.
TIC: Llanelli, 01554 772020.
Other nearby trails: The Llanelli Millennium Coastal Park has a cyclepath running west to Kidwelly and east towards Swansea.
Useful publications: OS Landranger Map 159. Sustrans *Celtic Trail - West* map (£5.99) shows all the traffic-free trails around Llanelli plus the course of the Celtic Trail in West Wales (Fishguard to Swansea).
Sustrans Order Line: Call 0845 113 0065 or visit their website at www.sustrans.org.uk
Refreshments: Lots of choice in Llanelli. Waun Wyllt Country Inn in Horeb

7   Llyn Llech Owain Country Park, southwest of Llandeilo

CATEGORY
Cycle path in country park.
DISTANCE
3-mile circuit.

This small country park southwest of Llandeilo makes the most of the woodland and lakes within its boundaries, offering a circuit that takes you in and among the park's natural attractions. The visitor centre stands beside the lake enjoying splendid views of Llyn Llech Owain and the surrounding area. It also houses an exhibition describing the history and natural history of the country park as well as information on how the site is being managed.

During the bird nesting season (approximately April to August) live TV pictures from nest sites are transmitted to the visitor centre.

STARTING POINT & PARKING

→The Country Park is located 6 miles southwest of Llandeilo and just to the north of the junction of the A476 and the A48 at Cross Hands (grid reference 566151).

Station: Llandeilo.
TIC: Llandeilo, 01588 824226.
Other nearby trails: There are several routes in Brechfa Forest to the northwest of Llandeilo.
Useful publications: OS Landranger Map 159.
Refreshments: At the visitor centre.

8 Brechfa Forest, northeast of Carmarthen (4 routes)

CATEGORY
Waymarked forest trails
DISTANCE
6 - 12 miles

Lying almost 20 miles to the northeast of Carmarthen, Brechfa Forest is one of the few areas in West Wales where there are traffic-free or mountain bike routes. Four waymarked trails cater for all abilities. The descriptions provided by Forest Enterprise are as follows:

White route (Fun route, 7.5 miles) - an easy route along the Aborgorlech Valley, mostly along forest roads but with some hills and muddy sections to liven things up!
Start: Aborgorlech car park on the B4310, about 17 miles northeast of Carmarthen (grid reference 587337).

Yellow route (Fun route, 10 miles) - take a tour around this spectacular section of Brechfa Forest, which climbs gently onto a plateau giving wide panoramic views over Mid Wales. This is a newly-developed family route along forest roads with a short downhill section on a wide track.
Start: Brechfa picnic area, on the minor to Llanllwni, off the B4310 to the north of Brechfa (grid reference 523319).

Green route (Sport route, 5.6 miles) - a circular route over moderate terrain for reasonably fit riders who are willing to have a go! The route follows forest roads and narrow tracks through a quiet part of Brechfa Forest and crosses a couple of streams at fords.
Start: Byrgwm car park, 3 miles southwest of Abergorlech (grid reference 546316).

Red Route (Expert route, 8.7 miles) - ride through the verdant woodlands, along forest roads and narrow singletrack. This route involves steep climbs and awesome descents and crosses the Abergorlech at a ford. Scary!
Start: Aborgorlech car park on the B4310, about 17 miles northeast of Carmarthen (grid reference 587337).

Station: Llandeilo, 10 miles southeast of Abergorlech.
TIC: Carmarthen, 01267 231557.
Other nearby trails: Three trails in Swansea. The Afan Argoed Countryside Centre lies northeast of Port Talbot.
Useful publications: OS Landranger Map 146. A good leaflet is available from: The Forest District Manager, Forest Enterprise, Llanymyddfri Forest District, Llanfair Road, Llandovery, Dyfed SA20 0AL (01550 720394).
Refreshments: The Black Lion, at Abergorlech.

9

9 Swansea Bikepath (along the seafront)

CATEGORY
Railway path / seafront promenade.

DISTANCE
5 miles each way.

The wide curving sweep of Swansea Bay is the perfect setting for a bike path and by good fortune (and visionary planning) such a path exists running from the award-winning Maritime Quarter in the centre of the city round to Mumbles along the route of the former Mumbles railway which carried the first passenger train in the world. The route has wonderful views across Swansea Bay to Mumbles Head, which marks the start of the Gower Peninsula. There are cafes, restaurants and pubs in Mumbles in a picturesque setting which includes the 12th-century Oystermouth Castle guarding the landward approach to Gower. The ride forms part of National Cycle Network Route 4, the Celtic Trail, which continues along the traffic-free Clyne Valley Country Park towards Gowerton and Llanelli.

STARTING POINT & PARKING
→ The Maritime Quarter in the centre of Swansea. Parking is also available opposite the University and in Mumbles.

Station: Swansea.
TIC: Swansea, 01792 468321.
Other nearby trails: There is a cyclepath up the Clyne Valley. A section of the Swansea Canal towpath can be ridden from Clydach to Ynysmeudwy.
Useful publications: OS Landranger Map 159. *Swansea Bay Cycling* leaflet is available from Swansea Tourist Information Centre (01792 468321).
Refreshments: In the Maritime Quarter or in Mumbles.

10 Swansea and the Clyne Valley

CATEGORY
Railway path.
DISTANCE
5 miles each way.

A spur leads off the main Swansea seafront cyclepath from Blackpill to follow a route alongside the Clyne River through Clyne Valley Country Park, providing a delightful wooded trail that runs northwest to Gowerton. The nearby Clyne Gardens are famous for colourful azaleas and rhododendrons. The trail follows the line of the old LMS Railway which used to link Swansea to the Midlands via Mid Wales. The Clyne Valley bikepath forms part of the Celtic Trail, National Cycle Network Route 4, that runs from Pembrokeshire to Chepstow. There is a steady 300ft climb from the coast to the highpoint between Dunvant and Gowerton. Heading west from here the Celtic Trail uses minor lanes, then crosses the Loughor Bridge before joining the next splendid traffic-free section past the Wildfowl & Wetlands Centre to link with the Llanelli Millennium Coastal Park.

STARTING POINT & PARKING
→It is best to use the seafront bike path to access the start of the Clyne Valley Spur at Blackpill. There is parking in Mumbles or opposite the University on the main road around Swansea Bay (A4067).

Station: Swansea or Gowerton.
TIC: Swansea, 01792 468321
Other nearby trails: The Swansea Bikepath runs along the seafront from the Maritime Quarter to Mumbles. The Swansea Canal towpath can be ridden between Clydach and Ynysmeudwy.
Useful publications: OS Landranger Map 159. A leaflet, *Swansea Bay Cycling* is available from Swansea Tourist Information Centre (01792 468321).
Refreshments: Available in Dunvant and Gowerton.

11 Swansea Canal, northeast of Swansea

CATEGORY
Canal towpath.
DISTANCE
6 miles each way.

In their heyday the Neath and Swansea Canals brought thousands of tons of coal down from the pits in the Swansea Valley and the Vale of Neath. Both were superceded by the railways and now plans have been drawn up to restore both waterways. This ride uses the canal towpath from Clydach, north of Swansea, through Pontardawe to Ynysmeudwy. The towpath is of mixed quality: there are some good gravel stretches and some rougher, narrower sections.

STARTING POINTS & PARKING
→ **Clydach**, on the B4603 to the north of M4 Jct 45. The canal starts at the junction of the B6403 and B4291 (grid reference 695014).
→**Ynysmeudwy**, at the roundabout by the junction of the A4067 with the B4603 (grid reference 741058).

Station: Swansea or Neath.
TIC: Swansea, 01792 468321.
Other nearby trails: There are two good cyclepaths in Swansea. The Neath Canal runs along the next valley to the east. There are several waymarked trails starting at the Afan Argoed Country Park (northeast of Port Talbot).
Useful publications: OS Landranger Maps 160 & 170.
Refreshments: Available in Clydach and Pontardawe.

12 Neath Canal, east of Swansea

CATEGORY

Canal towpath.

DISTANCE

5 miles each way.

This ride from Tonna southwest to Briton Ferry (near Neath) uses a recently improved section of the canal towpath which used to link the coalfields of the Neath Valley with the port at Briton Ferry, where you are still likely to see some big ships moored. The ride forms part of the northern braid of the Celtic Trail between Swansea and Pontypridd, signposted as National Cycle Network Route 47. This links in Neath to the High Level Route, a strenuous challenge for mountain bikes. In their heyday in the mid 1800s, the Neath and Tennant Canals were extremely prosperous, with up to 200,000 tons of coal alone being moved annually on the Neath Canal. However, their prosperity was short-lived and soon affected by the coming of the railway in 1851. By 1880 almost all coal traffic was being carried by rail.

STARTING POINT & PARKING

→The car park for **Tonna Canal Basin**, just off the A465 to the northeast of Neath. Follow signs for the B4434 to Tonna, Clyne and Melincourt, cross the River Neath and turn left immediately after the Railway Tavern into the car parking area (grid reference 774993). To get to the trail, cross the road and follow the canal towpath southwest towards Briton Ferry. Turn around where the canal ends.

Station: Neath.

TIC: Swansea, 01792 468321.

Other nearby trails: There is another section of the canal towpath which can be followed from Resolven northeast to Glyn Neath. The Neath to Pontypridd High Level Route is a tough challenge along forest roads between the two towns.

Useful publications: OS Landranger Map 170.

Refreshments: Lots of choice in Neath. Railway Tavern in Tonna.

12

13

13 Port Talbot: Bryn to Goytre (Wildbrook Estate)

CATEGORY
Railway path.
DISTANCE
3 miles each way.

A 3-mile section of the Cwm Dyffryn railway path through woodland that could not contrast more dramatically with the heavy industry of Port Talbot less than a couple of miles away. There is good access from Bryn south into the adjoining Margam Forest or north into the woodlands above Afan Argoed with its plethora of trails. There is a steady descent of almost 400 ft from Bryn to Wildbrook Estate in Goytre where the trail ends. The trail follows a stream called Ffrwd Wyllt, a name to test the language skills of all non-Welsh speakers!

STARTING POINT & PARKING
➔Park on the roads near to the Royal Oak pub in **Bryn**, on the B4282 east of Port Talbot (grid reference 818920).

Station: Port Talbot.
TIC: Swansea, 01792 468321.
Other nearby trails: There are several routes starting in Afan Argoed Country Park. Two sections of the Neath Canal are rideable - from Briton Ferry to Tonna and from Resolven to Glyn Neath.
Useful publications: OS Landranger Map 170.
Refreshments: Royal Oak pub, Bryn.

14 Neath Canal, between Neath and Glyn Neath

CATEGORY
Canal towpath.
DISTANCE
3 1/2 miles each way.

There are plans for the whole length of the Neath Canal from Briton Ferry to Glyn Neath to be restored to its former glory. This section from Blaengwrach to Resolven, alongside the new stretch of the A465 shows what it could look be like in the future. It would improve the ambience if they could build a soundproof screen between the towpath and the dual carriageway! The canal was built to transport the raw materials and manufactured goods of the valley's early industries and mines more efficiently than the pack horse and waggon routes. Cargoes included timber, coal, lime, finished iron and copper and even gunpowder and cannon balls during the Napoleonic wars. Not all traffic was industrial. Large landowners often had pleasure boats on the canals and the favourite Sunday School outing was a trip from Neath to the beach at Jersey Marine, often completed to the accompaniment of the local brass band.

STARTING POINT & PARKING

➜The car park at the **Resolven Basin** just off the A465 to the north of Resolven (grid reference 826030). The route ends on the B4242 to the west of Glyn Neath (grid reference 866059).

Station: Neath.

TIC: Swansea, 01792 468321.

Other nearby trails: Another section of the canal can be explored southwest from Tonna to Briton Ferry. There are several waymarked trails in Afan Argoed Country Park on the A4107 to the north of Port Talbot.

Useful publications: OS Landranger Maps 160 & 170.

Refreshments: Pubs in Resolven, Tonna. Pubs and cafes in Neath.

14

15 Tondu to Pyle, northwest of Bridgend

CATEGORY

Railway path and specially-built cyclepath.

DISTANCE

7 miles each way.

This section of the Celtic Trail from Tondu Environment Centre (north of Bridgend) west to the Frogpond Wood Nature Reserve in Pyle uses some unusual wooden decking winding its way through the Parc Slip Nature Park to keep you up above the soft ground beneath. The nature park has recorded 28 butterfly species, rare wading birds pass through during the migrating seasons and several scarce damselfly and dragonfly species breed here. There are Scheduled Ancient Monuments at either end of the trail: Cebn Cribwr Ironworks near to Pyle and Tondu Ironworks near to Tondu. The trail could easily be linked at its eastern end to the Ogmore Valley route taking you right up to Nant Y Moel.

STARTING POINT & PARKING

➜**Parc Slip Nature Park Visitor Centre** (grid reference 881841), just off the B4281 between Aberkenfig and Pyle (about 2 miles west of M4 Jct 36). From the starting point the trail runs for about 1 mile to the east and 6 miles to the west.

Station: Bridgend.

TIC: Bridgend, 01656 654906.

Other nearby trails: The route is part of the Celtic Trail (Fishguard to Chepstow). The Ogmore Valley Community Route runs up the Ogmore Valley to Nant-y-Moel. There are several routes in Afan Argoed Country Park.

Useful publications: Ordnance Survey Landranger Map 170. An excellent full colour leaflet *Guide to the Tondu to Pyle Community Route* is available from: Groundwork Bridgend, The Environment Centre, Maesteg Road, Tondu,

16

Bridgend CF32 9BT (01656 722315). Sustrans *Celtic Trail - East* map (£5.99) covers this and and many other traffic-free trails nearby.
Sustrans Order Line: Call 0845 113 0065 or visit their website at www.sustrans.org.uk
Refreshments: In Tondu or Kenfig Hill.

16 Afan Argoed Country path, northeast of Port Talbot

CATEGORY
Railway path, forestry trails.
DISTANCE
8 miles each way plus optional 6-mile round trip from Cymer to Glyncorrwg.

The Afan Argoed Countryside Centre is an excellent base for many rides in the Afan Valley. There are railway paths and waymarked forestry tracks on both sides of the valley heading southwest to Pontrhydyfen and northeast to Blaengwynfi. Spurs lead off to Efail Fach from Pontrhydyfen and to Glyncorrwg from Cymer. There are also two tough, technical mountain bike trails know as the Penhydd Trail and the Wall Trail. New mountain bike trails will soon be opening from Glyncorrwg. The Countryside Centre has a hands-on exhibition demonstrating the landscape and history of the Afan Valley. The South Wales Miners' Museum portrays the social history of the valleys mining communities.

Mountain bike trails
The Penhydd Trail (orange waymarks, 13.7 miles, 1800ft of climbing). This is a varied trail combining forest road climbs with tight, technical, switchback trails through mixed woodland and open flowing singletrack through open ground with great views. Not suitable for novices.

→**The Wall Trail** (red waymarks, 14.3 miles, 1500ft of climbing). This trail essentially

traverses the north side of the Afan Valley on singletrack, which varies from fast, open and flowing to tight, technical and rooty.

STARTING POINT & PARKING
→Afan Argoed Countryside Centre, on the A4107 northeast of Port Talbot near M4 Jct 40 (grid reference 821951).

Station: Maesteg or Port Talbot.
TIC: Swansea, 01792 468321.
Other nearby trails: Neath Canal northeast of Resolven. Ogmore Valley railway path from Blackmill to Nant y Moel.
Useful publications: OS Landranger Map 170. The Forestry Commission produce a fine map which can be purchased from the countryside centre (01639 850564). Another leaflet, *Afan - Mountain Biking in the Forest* has details of the two mountain bike rides.
Refreshments: At the countryside centre. Pubs in Efail Fach, Pontrhydyfen, Cymer and Blaengwynfi.

17 Ogmore Valley, north of Bridgend

CATEGORY
Railway path.
DISTANCE
7 miles each way.

This ride up the Ogmore Vale from Brynmenyn (north of Bridgend) through Blackmill to Nant y Moel is a splendid example of what can be done with the old railway lines that used to bring coal down from the Welsh valleys to the coast now that the region finds itself in a post-coal mining era. There is a steady climb from south to north setting you up for a much easier return leg back to the start. The southern end of the ride forms part of the Celtic Trail which runs from Pembrokeshire to Chepstow.

17

STARTING POINT & PARKING

➔The garage / pub / post office and stores in **Blackmill**, at the junction of the A4093 and A4061, about 4 miles north of the M4, Jct 36. Park just beyond the Fox & Hounds pub and garage (grid reference 933867). The path starts on the other side of the river. It runs 2 miles south to Brynmenyn or 5 miles north to Nant y Moel.

Station: Aberkenfig (north of Bridgend).
TIC: Bridgend, 01656 654906.
Other nearby trails: The Celtic Trail runs from Pembrokeshire to Chepstow - the next traffic-free section to the west runs from Tondu to Pyle. There are waymarked trails in Afan Argoed Country Park northeast of Port Talbot. The Rhondda Community Forest Routes start in Cwmparc, to the west of Treorchy (in the

Rhondda Valley).
Useful publications: OS Landranger Map 170. Sustrans *Celtic Trail - East* map (£5.99) shows all the traffic-free sections along the National Cycle Network between Swansea and Newport.
Sustrans Order Line: Call 0845 113 0065 or visit their website at www.sustrans.org.uk
Refreshments: In Blackmill, Ogmore Vale and Nant y Moel.

18 Neath to Pontypridd High Level Route

CATEGORY
Forestry roads and quiet lanes.
DISTANCE
Up to 22 miles each way.

The High Level Route is one of the toughest rides in the book, climbing to almost 2000 ft. The route, which is part of the Celtic Trail, crosses the vast swathes of forestry that lie between Neath and Pontypridd with fantastic views north over the Black Mountain and down into the Vale of Neath. As both Neath and Pontypridd have stations, the train could be used to complete one leg by public transport, enabling you to make the most of the prevailing westerly wind. Another option would be to take the train from either Newport or Cardiff to Neath: once you have cycled from Neath to Pontypridd you have the option of following the largely traffic-free Taff Trail down to Cardiff or the Celtic Trail down to Newport

STARTING POINTS & PARKING
➔You may choose to use the train to make this a each way trip in which case the ride starts from Neath railway station. Otherwise, to avoid all the urban bits.....
➔The car park at Mosshouse Wood on the minor lane to the northeast of **Neath** (grid reference 773982). The minor lane is called

Fairylands Road, off the B4434 towards Tonna.
➔ The car park by the Brynffynon Inn in
Llanwonno to the northwest of Pontypridd (grid
reference 031956).

Station: Neath or Pontypridd.
TICs: Swansea, 01792 468321; Pontypridd.
01443 409512
Other nearby trails: The Taff Trail in Pontypridd.
The Ogmore Vale Community Route. Routes in
Afan Argoed Country Park. Neath Canal routes.
Useful publications: OS Landranger Map 170. A
fine leaflet, *The High Level Route* is available
from Sustrans.
Sustrans Order Line: Call 0845 113 0065 or
visit their website at www.sustrans.org.uk
Refreshments: Lots of choice in Neath
and Pontypridd. The Brynffynon Inn at
Llanwonno.

19   Rhondda Community Routes, Treorchy

CATEGORY

Forest trail.

DISTANCE:

12 miles each way.

South Wales is not all old mining valleys: it has
hundreds of square miles of forestry and in
some cases there are waymarked forest trails,
such as these up above the Rhondda Valley,
once the greatest coal-producing area in the
world. There are three possible starting points
for the ride which is basically a high level
(1500-2000 ft) linear north-south route, with a
spur off it down into the valley at Treorchy. Two
possible starts are from the car parks at the
highpoints on the main roads (A4061 & A4107)

19

leading out of the Rhondda Valley and the other, at Cwmparc west of Treorchy, starts from the valley floor and involves a lot more climbing. In addition to the very steep climb up from Treorchy there is a steady climb at the northern end of the route to the highpoint at Mynydd Beili-glas (almost 2000 ft!). If you have started from Cwmparc and want to make the ride into a circuit you could come back down the A4061.

STARTING POINTS & PARKING

The route is waymarked with red markers 'Rhondda Community Route'.

➔ Cwmparc, west of **Treorchy**, off the A4061 Treorchy to Bridgend road (grid reference 947962). This will involve you in a very steep climb at the start.

➔ The car park at the top of the pass on the A4061 north of **Treherbert** (grid reference 922025).

➔ The car park on the A4107 Port Talbot Road between **Treorchy and Blaengwynfi** (grid reference 918957).

Station: Treorchy.

TIC: Pont Nedd Fechan, 01639 721795.

Other nearby trails: There is a railway path in Ogmore Vale. There are several waymarked trails from Afan Argoed Country Park, northeast of Port Talbot. The route overlaps with the High Level Route on the Celtic Trail. The Taff Trail goes through Pontypridd.

Useful publications: OS Landranger Map 170. Leaflet available from Rhondda Borough Council (01443 680669).

Refreshments: In Treorchy.

20 The Taff Trail from Abercynon to Merthyr Tydfil

CATEGORY

Railway path and quiet dead-end roads.

DISTANCE

8 miles each way.

This section of the Taff Trail climbs 270ft from the Navigation Inn in Abercynon north through Quakers Yard and Aberfan to the Rhydycar

Leisure Centre in Merthyr Tydfil. In the northern half of the ride the path is largely up above the valley giving wide views of the rows of terraced houses so typical of the South Wales valleys. North of Quakers Yard the trail follows the route of the Pen-y-darren Tramroad, the scene in 1804 of the first ever steam locomotive railway journey, powered by Richard Trevithick's Engine. Part of the tramroad is a scheduled ancient monument and has not been surfaced. The original trackbed and stone sleepers remain and care should be taken when riding this section. The memorial gardens in Aberfan commemorate the terrible disaster in 1966 when the tips slipped, crushing many houses and the village school, tragically killing over 100 children.

STARTING POINTS & PARKING

→ The Navigation Inn, **Abercynon**, near the junction of the B4275 and the A470 (grid reference 085949).

→ Rhydycar Leisure Centre, **Merthyr Tydfil**, just south of the railway station (grid reference 050055).

Station: Merthyr Tydfil, Abercynon North and several stations in between.
TIC: Merthyr Tydfil, 01685 379884.
Other nearby trails: The Taff Trail runs north to Brecon and south to Cardiff. A railway path runs through Sirhowy Valley Country Park. There are two canal towpaths starting from near Newport - one to Crosskeys and the other to Pontypool. The High Level Route from Pontypridd to Neath climbs to 2000 ft as it crosses large blocks of forestry between the two towns.
Useful publications: OS Landranger Maps 160 & 170. Or Sustrans *Lôn Las Cymru (South)* map (£5.99), available from Sustrans.
Sustrans Order Line: Call 0845 113 0065 or visit their website at www.sustrans.org.uk
Refreshments: Lots of choice in Merthyr Tydfil. Several pubs along the way.

21 Hengoed Viaduct to Trelewis, northwest of Newport

CATEGORY
Railway path and newly-built cyclepath.

DISTANCE
6 miles each way.

A quick glance at a map of South Wales shows how the development of the mining valleys channelled the coal down railway lines to the docks at Cardiff and Newport. Most of these lines have now gone but many have been converted to recreational use. This trail is a bit of a hybrid: for much of its length it runs parallel to an existing railway line on a specially built cyclepath. The ride, starting a few miles north of Caerphilly, forms part of the Celtic Trail or National Cycle Network Route 47, and climbs gently from Hengoed Viaduct through Nelson and Trelewis to Taff Bargoed.

STARTING POINT & PARKING

→ **Hengoed Viaduct**, near the junction of the A472 and the B4252 in Ystrad Mynach, which lies 12 miles along the A469 to the north of Cardiff (grid reference 156949).

Station: Hengoed.
TIC: Caerphilly, 029 2088 0011.
Other nearby trails: The southern part of the route is part of the Celtic Trail. The Taff Trail is easily accessed from Trelewis. The Sirhowy Valley Country Park lies to the east.
Useful publications: OS Landranger Map 171. This and many other traffic-free trails in the area are shown on the Sustrans *Celtic Trail - East* map (£5.99) available from Sustrans.
Sustrans Order Line: Call 0845 113 0065 or visit their website at www.sustrans.org.uk
Refreshments: Trelewis.

22 The Taff Trail from Castell Coch to Glyntaff

CATEGORY
Woodland path and railway path.

DISTANCE
6 miles each way.

This section of the Taff Trail goes north from the fairytale castle of Castell Coch (Tongwynlais), through woodlands and along a railway path, finishing at the cemetery at Glyntaff. You are warned that there is a very steep hill at the start where you will need to push your bike through the magnificent beech woods. Castell Coch was designed in the 1870s by the architect William Burges for his patron the third Marquess of Bute and occupies the site of a genuine medieval stronghold.

22

STARTING POINT & PARKING
→Castell Coch car park, just north of M4 jct 32 (follow signs). The trail starts almost opposite the castle with a steep push up through beechwoods (grid reference 130826).

Station: Cardiff.
TIC: Cardiff, 0292 022 7281
Other nearby trails: The Taff Trail continues north towards Brecon. A railway path runs through Sirhowy Country Park. There are two canal towpaths starting from near Newport - one to Crosskeys and the other to Pontypool.
Useful publications: OS Landranger Map 171 or Sustrans *Lôn Las Cymru (South)* map (£5.99).
Sustrans Order Line: Call 0845 113 0065 or visit their website at www.sustrans.org.uk
Refreshments: Cafe inside Castell Coch (you will need to pay to get in). Pubs in Tongwynlais.

23 The Taff Trail from Cardiff to Tongwynlais

CATEGORY
Riverside path, specially-built cyclepath and minor roads.

DISTANCE
6 miles each way.

The 53-mile Taff Trail runs north from Cardiff to Brecon, largely traffic-free, along a mixture of riverside paths, railway paths and forestry roads. It climbs gently to Merthyr Tydfil then more steeply before dropping down into Talybont in the Usk Valley and turning west to Brecon. Five of the best traffic-free sections are described in the book. The most southerly part, described here, from Cardiff Central railway station past the Millennium Stadium north to Tongwynlais, passing through parkland alongside the River Taff on an attractive broad gravel track. The trail is signposted variously as 'The Taff Trail', 'Lôn Las Cymru' and 'National Cycle Network Route 8'.

23

All three run together to Brecon. It is suggested you turn around in Tongwynlais at the end of the traffic-free section but you may prefer to follow roads through the village and climb steeply to visit fairytale Castell Coch. A good 30 mile ride involves catching a train from Cardiff to Merthyr Tydfil and cycling back downhill to Cardiff.

STARTING POINT & PARKING

→ From **Cardiff Central** railway station head towards the Millennium Stadium, following Taff Trail, Lôn Las Cymru or National Cycle Network Route 8 signs.

Station: Cardiff.

TIC: Cardiff, 0292 022 7281

Other nearby trails: The Taff Trail continues north to Brecon. The next traffic-free section starts north of Castell Coch.

Useful publications: OS Landranger Map 171 or Sustrans *Lôn Las Cymru (South)* map (£5.99).

Sustrans Order Line: Call 0845 113 0065 or visit their website at www.sustrans.org.uk

Refreshments: Lots of choice in Cardiff. Pubs in Tongwynlais.

24 Sirhowy Valley Country Park, northwest of Newport

CATEGORY
Railway path.
DISTANCE
5 miles each way.

The valleys of South Wales are synonymous with coal mining. Now that the pits have all closed, more and more of the old railways that used to transport coal down to the docks are being converted to recreational use. Sirhowy Valley Country Park not only has a section of railway path but also two waymarked mountain bike trails in the steep woodlands above the valley. General information about the park is available from the Full Moon Visitor Centre where there is also a small display about the industrial and natural history of the valley. The trail through the park to Wyllie is part of the Celtic Trail and can easily be linked to the route from Hengoed Viaduct to Trelewis (or from the Cross Keys end to the canal towpath down to Newport).

STARTING POINT & PARKING

➜At the car park just off the roundabout at the junction of the A467 and A4048 to the west of Crosskeys, northwest of M4 Jct 28 (grid reference 214914).

Station: Hengoed (Ystrad Mynach).
TIC: Newport, 01633 842962.
Other nearby trails: The Newport to Crosskeys Canal lies 1 mile to the east. To the northwest the Celtic Trail crosses the Hengoed Viaduct on its way to Trelewis along the newly built cyclepath.
Useful publications: OS Landranger Map 171. A leaflet, *Map & Guide to Sirhowy Valley Country Park* is available from the visitor centre.
Refreshments: Pub in Wyllie.

25 Newport Canal (Fourteen Locks) to Crosskeys

CATEGORY
Canal towpath.
DISTANCE
5 miles each way.

One of two canals that run north from Newport. For such a built-up area the canal represents a fine green corridor with an excellent wide, gravel towpath and views of hills rising to over 1000 ft at its northern end. The ride between Newport and Crosskeys forms part of the Celtic Trail that crosses Wales from Fishguard in Pembrokeshire to Chepstow.

STARTING POINT & PARKING
The picnic site / visitor centre by the **Fourteen Locks** just off the B4591 to the northwest of M4 Jct 27, west of Newport (grid reference 281887).

Station: Newport.
TIC: Newport, 01633 842962.
Other nearby trails: The Newport to Pontypool Canal shares the same start. The Celtic Trail continues westwards from Crosskeys via a railway path in the Sirhowy Valley Country Park. The Taff Trail runs north from Cardiff.
Useful publications: OS Landranger Map 171.
Refreshments: In Newport, Risca and Crosskeys, just off the canal.

26 Newport Canal (Fourteen Locks) to Pontypool

CATEGORY
Canal towpath.
DISTANCE
9 miles each way.

This is the second of two canals running north from Newport. Although longer than the ride from the Fourteen Locks to Crosskeys, there are sections where the canal has been built over, particularly through Cwmbran. However, as the route forms part of the National Cycle Network, it is superbly signed and if you are feeling fit you could link this to the Pontypool to Blaenavon trail to create a long and enjoyable day out. Wherever the canal has been built over (particularly in the Cwmbran area) the excellent National Cycle Network waymarking will keep you on track. Follow the '46' signposts.

STARTING POINT & PARKING
→ The picnic site / visitor centre by the **Fourteen Locks**, just off the B4591 to the northwest of M4 Jct 27, west of Newport (grid reference 281887).

ON YOUR BIKES!
Go downhill along the towpath past the locks and parallel with the M4. After 1 1/2 miles alongside the motorway, **leave** this towpath (which continues towards Newport), turn left beneath the M4 and follow the other branch of the towpath north.

Station: Newport, Cwmbran and Pontypool.
TIC: Newport, 01633 842962.
Other nearby trails: The Newport to Cross Keys Canal shares the same start. There is a railway path through the Sirhowy Valley Country Park, to the west of Cross Keys. The Pontypool to Blaenavon railway path is also part of National Cycle Network Route 46.
Useful publications: OS Landranger Map 171.
Refreshments: In Newport, Cwmbran and Pontypool, just off the route.

27 Pontypool to Blaenavon

CATEGORY
Railway path and specially-built cyclepath.
DISTANCE
9 miles each way.

This part of Sustrans grand vision in South Wales, will create a route from Newport through Cwmbran, Pontypool and Blaenavon and then via the Clydach Valley to

Abergavenny, here linking with Lôn Las Cymru (National Cycle Network Route 8) that runs between Cardiff and Holyhead. Work is ongoing at the northern end from Blaenavon to Brynmawr, Clydach and Abergavenny. The path climbs steadily as it heads north from Pontypool to Blaenavon, meaning the trip down to Pontypool is a lot easier. Blaenavon played a significant part in the Industrial Revolution in the 19th century: the town became the home of mine owners, managers and workers of the ironworks and Big Pit Colliery when first established. Many of the schools, shops and chapels built in those early days are still standing today: the town contains 17 listed buildings, including Blaenavon Ironworks, one of the best preserved examples of 18th-century ironworks in Western Europe. At Big Pit Mining Museum you can experience going underground in a real colliery.

STARTING POINTS & PARKING

→Hanbury Road, **Pontypool**. This lies just east of the roundabout at the junction of the A472 and A4043 at the southern end of Pontypool (grid reference 283007).

→Big Pit Mining Museum, **Blaenavon** (grid reference 238087).

Station: Pontypool.
TIC: Blaenavon, 01495 792615.
Other nearby trails: The Newport to Pontypool Canal links with this trail. The Newport to Crosskeys Canal is in the next valley to the west.
Useful publications: OS Landranger Maps 161 & 171.
Refreshments: Pubs and cafes near the route.

27

28 Llanfoist to Govilon railway path, southwest of Abergavenny

CATEGORY
Railway path.
DISTANCE
3 miles each way.

A short, scenic section of railway path that climbs from Llanfoist to Govilon near to Abergavenny, a town which is known as the gateway to the dramatic beauty of Mid Wales. As an alternative to a there-and-back route you could use the network of quiet, steep and almost traffic-free lanes to return to the start. In the long term this will form part of a largely traffic-free route from Abergavenny via Clydach and Blaenavon down to Newport.

NB There is a short section on road from the post office in Llanfoist to the start of the route.

STARTING POINT & PARKING
→In a road called The Cutting, by the post office in Llanfoist, just off the A465 to the southwest of Abergavenny (grid reference 286134).

ON YOUR BIKES!
At the crossroads by the Llanfoist Inn turn right then shortly after the car saleroom and a street called The Cedars on the right take the next narrow tarmac track to the right (signposted as a no through road). Immediately turn left onto the old railway path.

Station: Abergavenny.
TIC: Abergavenny. 01873 857588.
Other nearby trails: The Taff Trail runs through Talybont on Usk, 15 miles to the west. There is a railway path from Pontypool to Blaenavon.
Useful publications: OS Landranger Map 161.
Refreshments: In Llanfoist.

28

29 Cwm Darran Country Park, southeast of Merthyr Tydfil (4 routes)

CATEGORY
Railway path and forest trails
DISTANCE
Railway path - 4 miles each way. Mountain bike rides - 1.7 to 5.5 miles.

Cwm Darran Country Park is tucked away in the Darran Valley, 6 miles southeast of Merthyr Tydfil. Displays in the visitor centre show the history of the park's development from mining valley to award-winning country park. There is a dismantled railway path that descends gently over 4 miles down to Bargoed in the Rhymney Valley and three other waymarked mountain bike routes in the park which are tougher and steeper.

Mountain bike routes:

Moderate Route	1.7 miles
Green waymarks	

Intermediate Route	3.0 miles
Orange waymarks	

Challenging Route	5.5 miles
Red waymarks	

STARTING POINT & PARKING

→Cwm Darran Country Park, on the minor road between the A469 to the north of Bargoed and the A465 to the east of Merthyr Tydfil (grid reference 119030).

Station: Bargoed.

TIC: Merthyr Tydfil, 01685 379884.

Other nearby trails: The Taff Trail runs from Cardiff to Brecon via Pontypridd and Merthyr Tydfil. There is a dismantled railway in Sirhowy Valley Country Park to the west of Risca and Cross Keys. The Rhondda Community Routes are waymarked forestry trails in the woodland to the west of Treorchy.

Useful publications: OS Landranger Map 171. A leaflet is produced by Caerphilly County Borough Council showing the mountain bike trails in Parc Cwm Darran (01443 864312).

Refreshments: At the visitor centre. Pub in Deri and several pubs in Bargoed.

30 The Taff Trail from Merthyr Tydfil towards Pontsticill Reservoir

CATEGORY

Railway path and purpose-built cyclepath.

DISTANCE

5 miles each way.

North of Merthyr Tydfil the Taff Trail finally leaves behind the densely populated industrial area and heads for the hills, passing through woodlands and over tall viaducts to the first of the reservoirs in the Brecon Beacons at Pontsticill. There is a climb of 350 ft from the Rhydycar Leisure Centre to the end of the railway path. Built in 1824 for the Crawshay family, the local ironmasters, Cyfartha Castle in Merthyr Tydfil is now a museum and art gallery, open to the public, set in 160 acres of rolling parkland.

NB There are several short sections of road through Merthyr Tydfil before joining the railway path off the Swansea Road (A4102) to the south of Cefn Coed Viaduct.

STARTING POINT & PARKING

→Rhydycar Leisure Centre, Merthyr Tydfil, just south of Merthyr Tydfil railway station. Follow the Taff Trail signs carefully through Merthyr Tydfil. It largely follows the river, crossing it several times.

Station: Merthyr Tydfil.
TIC: Merthyr Tydfil, 01685 379884.
Other nearby trails: The Taff Trail continues north to Brecon. There is a long and challenging traffic-free section from Talybont to Taf Fechan Forest. There are waymarked forestry routes in Garwnant Forest.
Useful publications: OS Landranger Map 160. Or Sustrans Lôn Las Cymru (South) map (£5.99).
Sustrans Order Line: Call 0845 113 0065 or visit their website at www.sustrans.org.uk
Refreshments: Lots of choice in Merthyr Tydfil.

31 Garwnant Forest, north of Merthyr Tydfil (2 routes)

CATEGORY
Forest trail.
DISTANCE
5 or 11 miles.

Garwnant Forest lies just north of the old industrial town of Merthyr Tydfil, but here you are in a completely different world of woodland, lakes and reservoirs on the southern edge of the Brecon Beacons National Park. There are two waymarked loops in the forest, starting from the visitor centre. The trails climb several hills, some of them steep and a short section of a minor road is used in both routes. The shorter route climbs away from the visitor centre on forest roads heading west then south to drop down to the Llwyn-on Dam before

returning to the visitor centre on the road alongside the reservoir. The second, tougher loop carries on south to explore the adjacent Penmoelallt Forest.

STARTING POINT & PARKING

→Garwnant Visitor Centre, just off the A470, about 6 miles north of Merthyr Tydfil (grid reference 005132).

Station: Merthyr Tydfil.
TIC: Merthyr Tydfil, 01685 379884.
Other nearby trails: The Taff Trail runs from Cardiff to Brecon and passes through Merthyr Tydfil.
Useful publications: OS Landranger Map 160. A leaflet can be purchased from the visitor centre (01685 723060).
Refreshments: At the visitor centre.

32 The Taff Trail from Talybont Reservoir to Taf Fechan

CATEGORY
Railway path.

DISTANCE
5 1/2 miles each way.

This is one of the toughest railway paths in the country with one long, steady climb of almost 900 ft southwest from the Talybont Reservoir dam to Torpantau / Taf Fechan Forest. At 1440 feet this is the highest point on the Taff Trail with breathtaking views. From here the Taff Trail takes a downhill course almost all the way to Cardiff. If you are not aiming to do the whole of the Taff Trail and you are turning around at the top, you are rewarded with a wonderful descent. Please note, it is not worth trying to turn this into a circular ride using the road the complete the loop as the gradients are very steep on the narrow, twisting lane and will give you a fraction of the pleasure to be gained from the railway path descent.

STARTING POINT & PARKING
➔At the picnic site on the road south from Talybont-on-Usk towards Pontsticill (grid reference 106208). Talybont lies on the B4558, about 6 miles southeast of Brecon. The trail runs along the east side of Talybont Reservoir and is joined by crossing the dam at its northern end.

Station: Merthyr Tydfil.
TIC: Brecon, 01874 622485.
Other nearby trails: The Taff Trail continues south to Merthyr Tydfil and Cardiff. A short (2.5 mile) section of the Monmouthshire & Brecon Canal east from the Canal Basin in Brecon is designated as a cyclepath.
Useful publications: OS Landranger Maps 160 & 161 or Sustrans *Lôn Las Cymru (South)* map (£5.99).
Sustrans Order Line: Call 0845 113 0065 or visit their website at www.sustrans.org.uk
Refreshments: Lots of choice in Talybont on Usk.

33 Claerwen Reservoir, west of Rhayader

CATEGORY
Broad stone track alongside reservoir.

DISTANCE
6 miles each way.

The reservoirs in the Elan Valley were built at the turn of the century to collect water for the ever-expanding population of Birmingham. There are two main traffic-free rides in the area, this one and the (easier) Elan Valley Trail. Both are there-and-back routes but if you are fit and have a good map you can easily work out much tougher, circular mountain bike challenges. This ride can either start from the Elan Valley Visitor Centre or from the dam at the eastern end of the reservoir and goes west for 6 miles along the north shoreline of the Claerwen Reservoir. This is a fairly exposed and remote route at over 1000ft with several steady climbs and descents on a broad but at times rough stony surface, so it is best undertaken on mountain bikes by reasonably fit riders. It is suggested you turn around at the end of the reservoir, but you could could continue west to the pub at Ffair Rhos. The wind is normally westerley which helps on your return.

STARTING POINT & PARKING

➔There is car parking space at the dam at the **eastern end of Claerwen Reservoir**, 10 miles to the southwest of Rhayader. Alternatively you may wish to start from the Elan Valley Visitor Centre. The minor, dead-end road between the visitor centre and Claerwen carries very little traffic.

Station: Llandrindod Wells.
TIC: Rhayader, 01597 810591.
Other nearby trails: The Elan Valley Trail, north from the visitor centre.
Useful publications: OS Landranger Map 147.
Refreshments: Cafe at the visitor centre (seasonal). Lots of choice in Rhayader.

34

34 Elan Valley Trail, west of Rhayader

CATEGORY
Railway path.
DISTANCE
8 miles each way.

This spectacular trail climbs past three reservoirs in the heart of beautiful Mid Wales following the line of the old Birmingham Corporation Railway, which was built at the start of the 20th century to help construct the reservoirs to supply the growing needs of Birmingham. The ride climbs 165ft from the Elan Valley Visitor Centre past Caban Coch and Garreg Ddu Reservoirs with their fine dams and an ornamental water tower, to the end of Pen y Garreg Reservoir leaving you with a very fine descent back to the start. When the reservoirs are full you will be rewarded with the sight of millions of gallons of water cascading over the dam walls.

STARTING POINT & PARKING

→ The **Elan Valley Visitor Centre** at the end of the B4518, about 3 miles to the southwest of Rhayader in Mid Wales (gid reference 928647).

Railway: Llandrindod Wells.
TIC: Rhayader, 01597 810591.
Other nearby trails: There is also a route along the north shore of Claerwen Reservoir.
Useful publications: OS Landranger Map 147. A leaflet, *Elan Valley Trail* is available for a small charge from the Rhayader Tourist Information Centre or from the Elan Valley Visitor Centre (01597 810880).
Refreshments: Cafe at the visitor centre (from mid-March to the end of October). Lots of choice in Rhayader.

34

35 Hafren Forest, west of Llanidloes

CATEGORY
Waymarked forestry route.
DISTANCE
6-mile circuit (black waymarks).

Much of Mid Wales is blanketed with forests but there are relatively few waymarked routes. Without waymarking it is very easy to get lost! So make the most of this trail near to the attractive town of Llanidloes in beautiful Mid Wales. The minor road at the start is also part of Lôn Las Cymru, or National Cycle Network Route 8, that runs for 250 miles from Holyhead to Cardiff. The forest trails cross the infant River Severn, the longest river in Britain, on its circuitous course towards the Bristol Channel.

STARTING POINT & PARKING
→ The picnic site 6 miles due **west of Llanidloes** on the minor road that goes through Glan-y-nant and Old Hall (grid reference 858869).

Station: Caersws.
TIC: Llanidloes, 01686 412065.
Other nearby trails: The Elan Valley Trail and Claerwen Reservoir to the west of Rhayader.
Useful publications: OS Landranger Map 136.
Refreshments: None on route, the nearest is in Llanidloes.

36 Mawddach Trail from Dolgellau to Barmouth

CATEGORY
Railway path.
DISTANCE
9 miles each way.

Forming part of Lôn Las Cymru (National Cycle Network Route 8) which runs from Holyhead to

36

Cardiff, the Mawddach Trail is one of the most scenic railway paths in the country, running along the spectacular and atmospheric Mawddach Estuary. More beautiful than the Camel Trail in Cornwall with a fraction of the visitors! The trail starts right from the heart of the handsome grey stone town of Dolgellau, from the corner of the main car park by the bridge over the river. The George III Hotel at Penmaenpool is superbly located and very popular with cyclists for coffees, lunches and teas. At the western end of the trail you have to cross the wonderful old wooden railway bridge to get to Barmouth.

NB There is a short section on road in Barmouth, which has a tricky right turn if you are eastbound (ie travelling from Barmouth towards Dolgellau).

STARTING POINTS & PARKING
→The main car park in **Dolgellau** by the bridge over the river (grid reference 728179).

→Car park at **Penmaenpool**, on the A493 to the west of Dolgellau (grid reference 695185)
→Car park on the south side of Barmouth Bridge at **Morfa Mawddach Station** (grid reference 628142)
→The harbour in **Barmouth** (grid reference 613157).

Station: Barmouth.
TIC: Dolgellau, 01341 422888.
Other nearby trails: Forest trails in Coed y Brenin north of Dolgellau. Railway path south from Caernarfon to Bryncir.
Useful publications: OS Landranger Map 124. A free leaflet showing the four railway paths in Gwynedd is available from: Planning & Economic Development Department, Gwynedd Council, Caernarfon, Gwynedd LL55 1SH (01286 672255).
Refreshments: Lots of choice in Dolgellau. George III at Penmaenpool (also does coffees and teas). Lots of choice in Barmouth.

37

37 Coed y Brenin Forest, north of Dolgellau (5 routes)

CATEGORY

Forest trails

DISTANCE

7 - 22 miles

A large Forestry Commission holding in North Wales which has adopted a very positive attitude to recreational cycling with five waymarked trails. Only the Fun Route is suitable for novices or children (over 10 years old). The Sport Route and the three Expert Routes contain singletrack and technical sections and are **not** for novices! This is a hilly area! The descriptions provided by Forest Enterprise are as follows:

Fun Route (yellow waymarks, 6.8 miles, 650ft of climbing) - a route which is suitable for novices

but not for children under 10 years old, There are two short cuts for the weary, which will reduce the time taken.

Sports Route (orange waymarks, 9.3 miles, 560ft of climbing) - a combination of some of the best bits of the trails including some brilliant singletrack sections such as 'Flightpath' and 'R74'

Red Bull Trail (blue posts with 'Red Bull' logo, 7 miles, 1080ft of climbing) - a wide variety of tracks and trails, from wide, fast forest roads, rocky, rough and tumble tracks to technical singletrack. Includes delights such as 'Al's Loop' 'The Rocky Horror Show' and 'The Root of All Evil'.

mbr Trail (blue posts with 'mbr' logo, 13.7 miles, 985ft of climbing) - this trail explores some of the quieter parts of the forest with some tough climbs and lots of technical singletrack. In particular look out for 'Pink Heifer' and 'The

Pinderosas', both long flowing gradual descents.

Karrimor Trail (blue posts with 'karrimor' logo, 23.6 miles, 3645ft of climbing) - one of the best mountain bike experiences in Europe. A huge variety of terrain from forest roads to some of the finest singletrack, huge climbs and long sweeping descents make this trail only suitable for experienced mountain bikers.

STARTING POINT & PARKING
→**Coed y Brenin Visitor Centre**, off the A470, about 9 miles north of Dolgellau (grid reference 716276).

Station: Barmouth.
TIC: Dolgellau, 01341 422888.
Other nearby trails: The Mawddach Trail between Barmouth and Dolgellau lies 9 miles south of the visitor centre.
Useful publications: OS Landranger Map 124. A Forest Enterprise leaflet is available from Coed y Brenin Visitor Centre.
Refreshments: At the visitor centre.

38 Caernarfon to Bryncir (Lôn Eifion)

CATEGORY
Railway path
DISTANCE
Up to 12 miles each way.

A good long stretch of dismantled railway starting near the atmospheric castle in Caernarfon and climbing south alongside the Welsh Highland Railway past Llanwnda and Penygroes to Bryncir with wonderful views west out to Caernarfon Bay and east to the foothills of Snowdonia. The highpoint is reached after almost 500ft of climbing, just below the radio mast, about 2 miles south of Penygroes. The path forms part of Sustrans National Cycle

Network Route 8, known as Lôn Las Cymru which links Holyhead to Cardiff. You may wish to break your journey with a visit to the Inigo Jones Slateworks at Groeslon, about 4 miles south of Caernarfon, to see craftsmen cut, shape and polish raw slate slabs into practical products such as steps, kitchen worktops and a multitude of craft items. There is also a cafe attached.

STARTING POINT & PARKING
→Car park by Caernarfon Castle in the centre of Caernarfon (grid reference 479627).

ON YOUR BIKES!
Follow the road from the castle past the Harbour Offices and after 300 yds bear left beneath the sculptured arch onto the railway path, following signs for 'Lôn Eifion' and 'National Cycle Network 8'.

Station: Bangor.

TIC: Caernarfon, 01286 672232.

Other nearby trails: Lôn Las Menai (Caernarfon to Y Felinheli) starts from the north of Caernarfon.

Useful publications: OS Landranger Maps 115 & 124. A free leaflet showing the four railway paths in Gwynedd is available from: Planning & Economic Development Department, Gwynedd Council, Caernarfon, Gwynedd LL55 1SH (01286 672255).

Refreshments: Lots of choice in Caernarfon. Several pubs along the route. Cafe at the Inigo Jones Slateworks at Groeslon

39 Caernarfon to Y Felinheli (Lôn Las Menai)

CATEGORY

Railway path.

DISTANCE

4 miles each way.

This 4-mile section of dismantled railway links Caernarfon with the old slate harbour of Port

Dinorwig (Y Felinheli). There are views of the Menai Strait and across the water to the island of Anglesey. Caernarfon is dominated by the towers and battlements of the mighty castle, built for Edward I in the 13th century to command the entrance to the Menai Strait. Its unique polygonal towers, intimidating battlements and colour-banded walls were designed to echo Constantinople, the imperial power of Rome and the dream castle 'the fairest that man ever saw' of Welsh myth and legend. In 1969 the castle gained worldwide fame as the setting for the investiture of Prince Charles as Prince of Wales.

STARTING POINTS & PARKING

→ The Victoria Dock, Caernarfon (grid reference 479632). From here, follow signs for 'Lôn Las Menai' and 'National Cycle Network Route 8'.

→ In Y Felinheli, park by the Gardffon Inn, down by the waterside (grid reference 525677).

Station: Bangor.

TIC: Caernarfon, 01286 672232.

Other nearby trails: There are two other nearby railway paths - from Caernarfon to Bryncir (Lôn

Las Eifion) and from Bangor to Tregarth (Lôn Las Ogwen). The two Caernarfon routes form part of Sustrans National Cycle Network Route 8 (Lôn Las Cymru) from Holyhead to Cardiff.

Useful publications: OS Landranger Map 115. A free leaflet showing the four railway paths in Gwynedd is available from: Planning & Economic Development Department, Gwynedd Council, Caernarfon, Gwynedd LL55 1SH (01286 672255).

Refreshments: Lots of choice in Caernarfon, cafe and Garddfon Inn in Y Felinheli.

40 Bangor to Tregarth (Lôn Las Ogwen)

CATEGORY
Railway path.
DISTANCE
4 1/2 miles each way.

One of three dismantled railways in this part of the world (the other two start in Caernarfon) with fine views of the spectacular mountains of Snowdonia. The path climbs steadily from the coast at Porth Penryn (Bangor) south through Maesgeirchen and Glasinfryn to Tregarth, following the valley of the River Cegin. The disused narrow gauge railway on which the path is built was constructed by the Penrhyn Estate to transport slate from the quarries at Bethesda for export at Porth Penrhyn. There are well-advanced plans to continue this route southwards through Bethesda right into the heart of Snowdonia (Llyn Ogwen and Capel Curig).

STARTING POINTS & PARKING
➜**Abercegin** (Bangor), just off the A5122 (grid reference 592725)
➜The western edge of **Tregarth**, 4 miles to the south on the B4409 (grid reference 600680).
Station: Bangor.
TIC: Bangor, 01248 352786.

Other nearby trails: There are two trails runing north and south from Caernarfon. The Mawddach Trail links Barmouth to Dolgellau. Waymarked forest trails in Coed y Brenin.

Useful publications: OS Landranger Map 115. A free leaflet showing the four railway paths in Gwynedd is available from: Planning & Economic Development Department, Gwynedd Council, Caernarfon, Gwynedd LL55 1SH (01286 672255).

Refreshments: Lots of choice in Bangor. Pub in Tregarth.

41 Gwydyr Forestry Commission, Betws y Coed

CATEGORY
Forest trails.

DISTANCE
8 and 11 miles.

The most well known and popular trail in Gwydyr Forest is a tough and technical waymarked mountain bike ride called the Marin Trail, 15.5 miles long with almost 1500ft of climbing and plenty of challenging singletrack. This is only for experienced riders. There is also an easier trail to the south of Betwys y Coed using wider forest roads although this does involve using the A5 briefly to exit the village, so it is not appropriate for young children.

STARTING POINT & PARKING
→Betws y Coed, near the junction of the A470 and A5 on the western edge of Snowdonia. There are long stay car parks in the village. Best to arrive early during busy periods.

→For the southern trail you must follow the A5 towards Bangor for 1/2 mile. The route starts soon after the Oakfield Inn. The route is best ridden anti-clockwise for the clearest waymarking.

→The starting point for the Marin Trail is about 3 miles north of Betws y Coed, on a minor road off the B5106 that starts opposite the link road to Llanrwst (grid reference 790610).

Station: Betws y Coed.
TIC: Betws y Coed, 01690 710665.
Other nearby trails: Two railway paths start in Caernarfon. There are more waymarked forestry routes in Coed y Brenin Forest, 25 miles to the south.
Useful publications: OS Landranger Map 115. More useful is the Forestry Commission map of Gwydyr Forest which can be bought at the Y Stablau Information Centre.
Refreshments: Lots of choice in Betws y Coed.

41

42 Llyn Brenig Reservoir, southwest of Denbigh

CATEGORY

Round reservoir ride.

DISTANCE

10-mile circuit.

Set in the Denbigh Moors, Llyn Brenig is one of the few reservoirs in North Wales with an attractive, largely traffic-free circuit of the water. The trail uses a mixture of forestry roads and minor roads. The circuit of the reservoir starts from the visitor centre. There are several gentle hills and two sections on road, including almost 2 miles on the busier B4501 to the north of the reservoir so take extra care on this stretch. The eastern half of the ride is completely traffic-free so if you wish just to do this bit (about a 7-mile round trip from the visitor centre to the car park by the archaeological trail), turn left out of the visitor centre, keeping the water on your left and doing the circuit anti-clockwise.

STARTING POINT & PARKING

→At the visitor centre on the B4501, about 6 miles north of Cerrigydrudion and 10 miles **southwest of Denbigh** (grid reference 967547).

Station: Betws y Coed.
TIC: Ruthin, 01824 703992.
Other nearby trails: The seafront promenade from Prestatyn to Rhos-on-Sea.
Useful publications: OS Landranger Map 116.
Refreshments: At the visitor centre.

43 Colwyn Bay (Rhos-on-Sea) to Prestatyn

CATEGORY

Seafront promenade.

DISTANCE

Up to 16 miles each way.

43

A superb breezy open ride along the seafront between Rhos-on-Sea (Colwyn Bay) in the west and Prestatyn in the east with fine views of wooded hills rising steeply away from the coast. It is worth checking the wind on this ride: try to cycle into the wind (it is normally from the west) at the start of the ride when you are fresh and have it behind you on the return half of the ride, or alternatively catch a train one way into the wind. The ride is part of National Cycle Network 5 which runs from Holyhead on the island of Anglesey to Chester (and beyond here, all the way across England to Reading).

STARTING POINT & PARKING

→The Tourist Information Centres at either Rhos-on-Sea or Prestatyn.

Station: Colwyn Bay or Prestatyn.
TICs: Rhos-on-Sea, 01492 548778; Prestatyn, 01745 889092.
Other nearby trails: There are two railway paths starting from Caernarfon and one from Bangor.
Useful publications: OS Landranger Map 116.
Refreshments: Lots of choice along the way.

Scotland

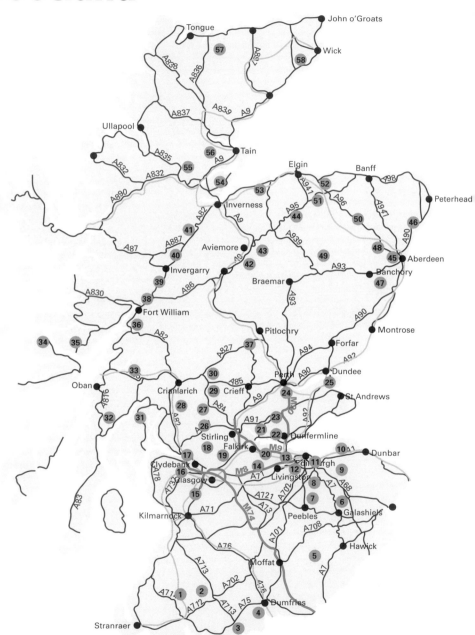

SCOTLAND TRAILS

Scotland Mountain Biking

Mountain biking in Scotland is on a very different basis from England and Wales: there is no Rights of Way network marked clearly on Ordnance Survey maps so at first glance it is impossible to know where you can and can't ride legally.

Compensation lies in the fact that there are vast swathes of Forestry Commission land where you can be sure that you DO have a right to ride and there is a growing network of purpose-built singletrack trails in the Seven Stanes mountain bike centres in Southern Scotland and also around Fort William. Mention should be made of the following guides:

101 Mountain Bike Routes in Scotland Harry Henniker (Mainstream Publishing). £14.99. ISBN 1-85158-936-8

The series of guides covering the Scottish Glens by Peter Koch-Osborne, published by Cicerone Press and all priced at £5.99:

Mountain Bike Guide: Cairngorm Glens
Mountain Bike Guide: Atholl Glens
Mountain Bike Guide: Glens of Rannoch
Mountain Bike Guide: Glens of Trossach
Mountain Bike Guide: Angus Glens
Mountain Bike Guide: Argyll
Mountain Bike Guide: Great Glen
Mountain Bike Guide: Knoydart and Morv

Scotland Forestry

Scotland is by far the most forested region of the United Kingdom. Forestry holdings stretch from the southwest in Dumfries and Galloway right up to Wick, only a few miles from John o'Groats. There is an exciting new development in Southern Scotland called the Seven Stanes Project which will create seven centres of mountain biking excellence with a variety of purpose-built single track trails.

Forestry with waymarked trails

There are several Forestry Commission leaflets describing dozens of waymarked trails in Scotland. You will need to call the nearest Tourist Information Centre or Forest District Office to obtain the leaflet. The barebone details of the trails are included within this guide but the leaflets are essential for the maps they contain:

Cycling in the Forest - Galloway Forest Park (p. 335)
7 Stanes Mabie (p. 338)
7 Stanes Dalbeattie (p. 339)
A Guide to the Walks and Cycle Trails in Craik Forest (p. 340)
Glentress Forest Trailquest - Orienteering on a Bicycle (p. 342)
Cycling in the Scottish Borders booklet (for the other Glentress Routes) (p. 342)
Kingdom of Fife Millennium Cycleways Forest Routes (p. 354)
A Guide to Queen Elizabeth Forest Park (p. 358)

Cycling in the Forest
- Argyll Forest Park (p. 362)
Cycling in the Forest
- West of Scotland (p. 363)
Loch Awe Up Close (p. 364)
Leanachan Forest Trailquest -
Orienteering on a Bicycle (p. 367)
Cycling in the Forest
- The Great Glen (p. 368)
Cycling & Skiing in the Forest -
Strathspey (p. 370)
Cycling in the Forest
- North East Scotland (p. 374)
A Guide to Forest Walks and Trails in Culbin Forest (p. 378)
Cycling in the Forest
- Northern Highlands (p. 378)

Other forestry holdings

There are many other forestry holdings throughout Scotland where it would be possible to devise your own routes on the forestry roads. There are far too many to list here: as a short cut, open out the relevant Ordnance Survey 1:50,000 Landranger Map and any of the forest areas shaded green which also have a thin purple border around the edge of the forest are owned by the Forestry Commission and you are allowed to ride there (forestry works permitting).

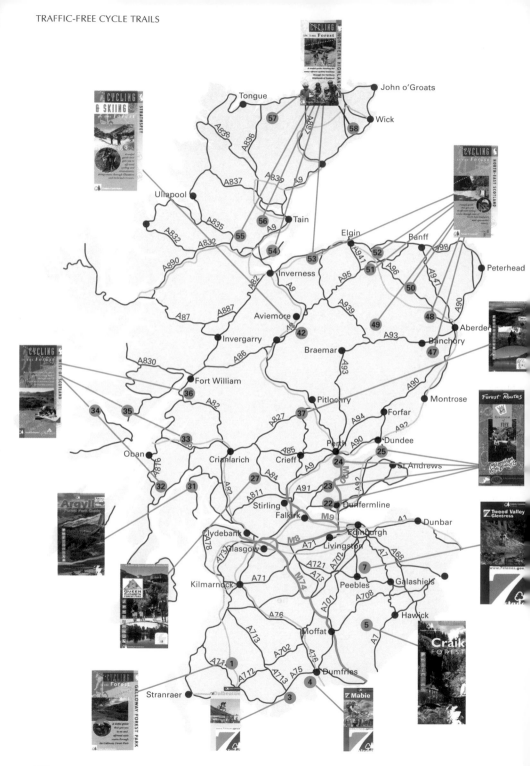

Tongue

John o'Groats

57

Wick

58

Ullapool

A838

A836

A89

A837

A835

A832

56

Tain

55

A9

54

Elgin

Banff

53

A941

52

Peterhead

A96

51

A798

A832

A890

50

A95

A941

48

A90

Inverness

Aberdeen

A87

A887

A9

A939

49

A93

Banchory

Invergarry

42

47

A830

A86

Braemar

A93

Fort William

36

A82

Pitlochry

Montrose

34

35

A827

37

A94

Forfar

33

A85

Crieff

A9

A90

Dundee

A92

Oban

Crianlarich

Perth

25

St Andrews

32

31

27

A84

A91

24

23

A82

A811

Stirling

22

Dunfermline

Clydebank

Falkirk

M9

Glasgow

M8

A71

Edinburgh

Dunbar

Livingston

A1

A68

A721

7

Kilmarnock

A71

A73

Peebles

Galashiels

A76

A101

A708

Hawick

5

Moffat

A7

1

A711

A702

A76

A713

Stranraer

A712

A713

A75

Dumfries

4

3

Further Information

North Scotland Region

Buchan Forest District
Ordiquill, Portsoy Road, Huntly,
Aberdeenshire AB54 4SJ
Tel: 01466 794161

Dornoch Forest District
Hilton of Embo, Dornoch,
Sutherland IV25 3PW
Tel: 01862 810359

Fort Augustus Forest District
Strathoich, Fort Augustus,
Inverness-shire PH32 4BT
Tel: 01320 366322

Inverness Forest District
Tower Road, Smithton, Inverness IV1 2NL
Tel: 01463 791575

Kincardine Forest District
Kirkton of Durris, Banchory,
Kincardineshire AB31 3BP
Tel: 01330 844537

Lochaber Forest District
Torlundy, Fort William,
Inverness-shire PH33 6SW
Tel: 01397 702184

Lorne Forest District
Millpark Road, Oban, Argyll PA34 4NH
Tel: 01631 566155

Moray Forest District
Balnacoul, Focahabers,
Morayshire IV3 7LL
Tel: 01343 820223

Tay Forest District
Inverpark, Dunkeld, Perthshire PH8 0JR
Tel: 01350 727284

West Argyll Forest District
Whitegates, Lochgilphead, Argyll
PA31 8RS
Tel: 01546 602518

South Scotland Region

Cowal and Trossachs Forest District
Aberfoyle, Stirling FK8 3UX
Tel: 01877 382383

Ae Forest District
Ae Village, Parkgate, Dumfries DG1 1QB
Tel: 01387 860247

Scottish Borders Forest District
Weavers Court, Forest Mill,
Selkirk TD7 5NY
Tel: 01750 721120

Scottish Lowlands Forest District
New Lanark Mills, Level 6, Mill 3,
New Lanark ML11 9DB
Tel: 01555 660 190

Galloway Forest District
Creebridge, Newton Stewart DG8 6AJ
Tel: 01671 402420.

The Forestry Commission's website
This is a good source of information
with details of 1600 miles of waymarked
cycling trails throughout the UK. Search
by forest name or by the nearest town
or city and the search will tell you the
grade, length and waymarking details
of the trails.

www.forestry.gov.uk/recreation

Scotland National Cycle Network

The Lochs & Glens Cycle Route (two maps: North and South)

428 miles from Inverness to Carlisle via Aviemore, Pitlochry, Callander, Glasgow, Ayr, Gatehouse of Fleet and Dumfries. Highlights include Aviemore and views of the Cairngorms, the pass of Drumochter, Pitlochry, the route alongside Loch Tay, Glen Ogle, the traffic-free route through the Trossachs, Loch Lomond, traffic-free routes through Glasgow, the Ayrshire Coast, Galloway Forest Park, the Solway Firth.

Traffic-free sections over 3 miles:

- Killin to Kingshouse through Glen Ogle (NCN 7)
- Strathyre to Callander past Loch Lubnaig (NCN 7)
- Loch Venachar (Callander) to Aberfoyle (NCN 7)
- Loch Lomond to Glasgow Cycleway (NCN 7)
- Johnstone to Kilbirnie (NCN 7)
- Glentrool village to Gatehouse Station via Clatteringshaws Loch (NCN 7)

Coast & Castles Cycle Route

200 miles from Newcastle to Edinburgh via Berwick-upon-Tweed, Kelso and Innerleithen. Highlights include North Tyne Cycleway to Tynemouth, the Northumbrian Coast, Warkworth Castle, Bamburgh Castle, Berwick's town walls, views of the River Tweed, Kelso town square, Floors Castle, Melrose Abbey, the Moorfoot Hills and Edinburgh.

Traffic-free sections over 3 miles:

- North Tyne Cycleway to Tynemouth (NCN 72)
- The Innocent Railway, Edinburgh (NCN 1)

Edinburgh to Aberdeen Cycle Route

170 miles from Edinburgh to Aberdeen via Dunfermline, Dundee and Montrose. Highlights include the ancient city of Edinburgh, Falkland Palace, Tenstmuir Forest, Broughty Castle (Dundee), the coast of Angus and Aberdeenshire, the handsome town of Montrose, Dunnottar Castle, the Maritime Museum and Marischal College in Aberdeen.

Traffic-free sections over 3 miles:

- From Dalmeny across the Forth Road Bridge (NCN 1)
- Tentsmuir Forest, Fife (NCN 1)

Aberdeen to John o'Groats

501 miles from Aberdeen to John o'Groats, Orkney and Shetland via Banff, Elgin, Inverness, Tain, Tongue and Thurso. Highlights include the traffic-free Formartine & Buchan railway path, the coast of the Moray Firth, Elgin Cathedral, the ancient town of Forres, the north coast of Scotland, the Norse heritage of Orkney and Shetland.

Traffic-free sections over 3 miles:

- Formartine & Buchan Way, north of Aberdeen (NCN 1)

Clyde to Forth Cycle Route

171 miles of cycle route around Glasgow and Edinburgh, covering the route between the two cities plus Glasgow to Loch Lomond, Glasgow to Gourock, Glasgow to Ardrossan & Kilmarnock, Edinburgh to Musselburgh and Edinburgh to the Forth Road Bridge. Highlights include the ancient city of Edinburgh, the Union Canal and Water of Leith, the Clyde Walkway into Glasgow, views of the Firth of Clyde from above Greenock.

Traffic-free sections over 3 miles:

- Union Canal, Edinburgh (NCN 75)
- Water of Leith, Edinburgh (NCN 75)
- Airdrie to Bathgate Railway Path (NCN 75)
- Clyde Walkway, Glasgow (NCN 75)
- Johnstone to Greenock (NCN 75)
- Johnstone to Kilbirnie (NCN 75)
- Glasgow to Loch Lomond (NCN 75)

Other areas for lane cycling

Unsurprisingly for such a vast area, Scotland offers a wide variety of cycling from easy rolling country up the east coast to expedition-style trips linking the various islands of the **Outer Hebrides** on

the west coast. Almost all the population of Scotland is concentrated in the Central Belt from the Clyde to the Forth around the two hubs of Glasgow and Edinburgh. To the south of the Central Belt there are thousands of miles of quiet lanes through **Dumfries & Galloway** and the **Scottish Borders** with any number of fine little towns which could be good bases for a few days: big enough to offer a variety of accommodation and refreshments but small enough for you to be in the countryside in less than 10 minutes cycling. North of the Central Belt there is a big east / west divide: the **west coast** is more spectacular, mountainous, wetter and broken into hundreds of islands linked by ferries to the mainland; the **east coast** is less mountainous, drier, with a much more extensive lane network but less extraordinary by Scottish standards. Take your pick! The other warning is about midges: less troublesome for cyclists than for walkers they are nevertheless pretty unpleasant during the summer months. Late spring or early autumn may be better times of year to appreciate the beauty of Scotland.

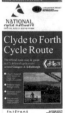

Sustrans

Listed below are the Sustrans maps that cover the National Cycle Network within the region. Some of the maps may describe routes that continue on into adjacent regions: these maps are mentioned in both chapters. The maps are not only useful for people wishing to ride the the whole route over several days they also show all the traffic-free sections which make good day rides. The maps cost £5.99 each and are available from Sustrans.

Sustrans Order Line:
Call **0845 113 0065** or visit their website at
www.sustrans.org.uk

Scotland Trails

1 GALLOWAY FORESTRY PARK

CATEGORY

Waymarked forest trails.

DISTANCE

7 - 19 miles.

ROUTES / CENTRES

8 routes / 4 centres.

This is the first of several entries in this section where a group of waymarked forestry routes are brought together under one heading: this is because all the routes are described in one leaflet which you will need to obtain to make the most of your day(s) out. In this instance the leaflet is *Cycling in the Forest - Galloway Forest Park*. In almost cases these leaflets are available from the nearest Tourist Information Centre, the nearest Forest Visitor Centre or from the local Forest District Office. See below under **Useful publications** for more details. For the Forest District Offices see page 331. There are three Forest Visitor Centres in the Galloway Forestry Park: at Kirroughtree, Glentrool and Clatteringshaws, each of which have routes starting from them enabling you to explore the surrounding woodland and return to the centre for something to eat and drink.

Kirroughtree Forest (2 routes)

Kirroughtree Visitor Centre tells the story of the development of modern forestry. The forest offers a wide range of habitats and spectacular views of Bargaly Glen and the massif of Cairnsmore of Fleet. There are two waymarked trails.

STARTING POINT FOR 2 TRAILS BELOW

Kirroughtree Visitor Centre, off the A75 about 4 miles east of Newton Stewart (grid reference 452644 / Ordnance Survey Landranger Map 83).

Dallash

DISTANCE	GRADE / WAYMARKS
18.7 miles	Moderate / Green

Heads north up the Bargaly Glen following the course of the Palnure Burn, using the A712 for 2 miles on its return to the visitor centre.

Larg Hill

DISTANCE	GRADE / WAYMARKS
6.8 miles	Moderate / Brown

A shorter route exploring Auclannochy Hill and Larg Hill.

Clatteringshaws (2 routes)

The cycle routes of Clattteringshaws have the loch as their focal point and the hills of Galloway as their backdrop. The visitor centre, as well as offering light refreshments, tells the story of the wildlife of the Galloway Forest Park.

STARTING POINT FOR 2 TRAILS BELOW

Clatteringshaws Forest Wildlife Centre on the A712 about 6 miles west of New Galloway (grid reference 551763 / Ordnance Survey Landranger Map 77).

Clatteringshaws Loch

DISTANCE	GRADE / WAYMARKS
13.8 miles	Easy / Purple

An easy route along the north side of Clatteringshaws Loch, crossing Black Water of Dee further west.

Craignell Hill

DISTANCE	GRADE / WAYMARKS
14.4 miles	Moderate / Pink

One major climb from the Black Loch to the top of the pass rewarded by excellent views.

Glentrool Forest (3 routes)

Glentrool Visitor Centre by the Water of Minnoch tells the story of the glen and offers light refreshments.

STARTING POINT FOR 3 TRAILS BELOW

Glentrool Visitor Centre, off the A714 about 10 miles north of Newton Stewart (grid reference 372786 / OS Landranger Map 77).

Palgowan

DISTANCE	GRADE / WAYMARKS
8.2 miles	Easy / Red

A circular route to the north of the visitor centre linking forest roads and National Cycle Network Route 7 (the Lochs & Glens Cycle Route). An undulating route with no big climbs.

Garwall Hill

DISTANCE	GRADE / WAYMARKS
15.6 miles	Moderate / Blue

The ride starts and finishes as per the Palgowan Route but goes further north with a circuit around Balunton Hill, from where the Merrick, the highest peak in South Scotland, is seen.

Water of Minnoch

DISTANCE	GRADE / WAYMARKS
10.2 miles	Moderate / White

The ride leaves the visitor centre on National Cycle Network Route 7 then turns south crossing Water of Trool, Ferrach Burn and Water of Minnoch on its way through the woodland.

Carrick Forest

Carrick is one of several named woodlands that forms parts of Galloway Forest Park and lies at the northern end of the area.

STARTING POINT FOR LOCH BRADEN ROUTE

Picnic site and car park on the minor road

between Glentrool village and Straiton (B741) halfway between Ayr and Newton Stewart (grid reference 398985 / OS Landranger Map 77).

Loch Braden

DISTANCE	GRADE / WAYMARKS
14.4 miles	Moderate / Green

A double loop around Loch Braden and Tairlaw Plantation with an optional spur east to Loch Finlas and Loch Doon.

Station: Dumfries or Girvan.
TIC: Dumfries, 01387 253862.
Other nearby trails: The Lochs & Glens Cycle Route (National Cycle Network Route 7) passes through the forest. There are other forestry routes in Southern Scotland include Mabie, Dalbeattie, Craik and Glentress.
Useful publications: OS Landranger Maps 77, 78 & 83. The leaflet *Cycling in the Forest - Galloway Forest Park,* is available from Dumfries Tourist Information Centre, from Kirroughtree, Glentrool and Clatteringshaws Forest Visitor Centres or from Galloway Forest District Office (01671 402420).
Website: www.forestry.gov.uk/recreation
Refreshments: At the Clatteringshaws Forest Wildlife Centre, Glentrool Visitor Centre and the Kirroughtree Visitor Centre.

2 Glentrool to Gatehouse Station along the Lochs & Glens Cycle Route

CATEGORY
Minor roads and forestry tracks.

DISTANCE
Up to 25 miles each way.

Dumfries & Galloway is one of the least populated and most densely forested regions in the whole of Great Britain. This is excellent news for every kind of cyclist with a fine network of quiet roads and hundreds of miles of

forestry tracks. This route uses a section of the Lochs & Glens Cycle Route (National Cycle Network Route 7) through forest and past lochs, with two climbs, the first through Glen Trool between Loch Trool and Loch Dee and the second to the south of Clatteringshaws. The route runs from Glentrool Village east to Gatehouse Station (northwest of Gatehouse of Fleet) via Loch Dee, Clatteringshaws Loch and Meikle Cullendoch Moss. It is an alternative to the main Lochs & Glens Cycle Route which stays closer to the coast, passing through Creetown and Newton Stewart.
NB Care should be taken crossing the A712 near Clatteringshaws Loch.

STARTING POINTS & PARKING
→ In **Glentrool** village, off the A714 between Newton Stewart and Girvan (grid reference 371786 / OS Landranger Map 77).
→ At **Clatteringshaws Loch** Visitor Centre, on the A712 between Newton Stewart and New Galloway (grid reference 551763 / OS Landranger Map 77).
→ **Dromore** Visitor Centre, off the northern end of the B796, and the old Gatehouse Station, 7 miles northwest of Gatehouse of Fleet (grid reference 554638 / OS Landranger Map 83).

Station: Barhill (Cairnlea) south of Girvan.
TIC: Newton Stewart, 01671 402431.
Other nearby trails: There are plenty of forestry routes in Galloway Forest Park; other forestry routes in Southern Scotland include Mabie, Dalbeattie, Craik and Glentress.
Useful publications: OS Landranger Map 77. Sustrans *Lochs & Glens Cycle Route* map (£5.99) includes many traffic-free sections between Glasgow and the Ayrshire Coast as well as this trail. It is available from Sustrans Information Service (0845 113 0065) or www.sustrans.org.uk
Refreshments: Tea room in the Clatteringshaws Loch Visitor Centre.

3 Dalbeattie Forest (3 routes)

CATEGORY

Waymarked forest routes.

DISTANCE

2.4 - 10.6 miles.

ROUTES / CENTRES

3 routes / 1 centre.

Dalbeattie has been developed as one of the sites for the Seven Stanes project, a visionary plan to create a series of mountain biking centres of excellence throughout Southern Scotland. As well as the challenging Hardrock Trail, Dalbeattie has a choice of easier rides including the Ironhash Trail and the Moyle Hill Trail. The Forestry Commission leaflet describes the Hardrock Trail in the following terms: 'This amazing new route offers a riding style unlike anything else in the UK. The Seven Stanes trailbuilders have carved out feature-filled singletrack that seems to go on forever undulating up and down, weaving in and out of trees and over and around Dalbeattie's famous granite rock. It is a physically long and challenging ride but all the tricky rock features include easier options - always ride within your ability'.

STARTING POINT FOR 3 TRAILS BELOW

Richorn car park on the A710 about 2 miles south of **Dalbeattie**, to the southwest of Dumfries (grid reference 836592 / OS Landranger Map 84).

Ironhash Trail

DISTANCE	GRADE / WAYMARKS
7.1 miles	Easy / Green

Moyle Hill Trail

DISTANCE	GRADE / WAYMARKS
8.7 miles	Moderate / Blue

Hardrock Trail

DISTANCE	GRADE / WAYMARKS
16.8 miles	Difficult / Red

Station: Dumfries.

TIC: Dumfries, 01387 253862.

Other nearby trails: There are other forest trails at Mabie and in Galloway Forest Park. The Lochs & Glens Cycle Route (National Cycle Network Route 7) passes through the forest.

Useful publications: OS Landranger Map 84. A Forestry Commission leaflet, *7 Stanes Dalbeattie,* is available from Dumfries Tourist Information Centre.

Websites: www.forestry.gov.uk/recreation and www.7stanes.gov.uk

Refreshments: Dalbeattie.

4 Mabie Forest, south of Dumfries (5 routes)

CATEGORY

Waymarked forest routes.

DISTANCE

2.4 - 10.6 miles.

ROUTES / CENTRES

5 routes / 1 centre.

Lying to the south of Dumfries, Mabie, as with Dalbeattie, has been chosen as one of the sites for the Seven Stanes project, a visionary plan to create a series of mountain biking centres of excellence throughout Southern Scotland. As well as the challenging routes, Mabie has a choice of easier rides including the Big Views

Loop and the Woodhead and Lochbank Loops. With plenty of ups and downs they will give a great introduction to mountain biking and to Mabie Forest.

STARTING POINT FOR 5 TRAILS BELOW

→ The car park by Mabie House Hotel, off the A710 about 4 miles southwest of **Dumfries** (grid reference 950708 / OS Landranger Map 84).

Big Views Loop

DISTANCE	GRADE / WAYMARKS
5.1 miles	Easy / Green

Woodhead Loop

DISTANCE	GRADE / WAYMARKS
6.2 miles	Moderate / Blue

Lochbank Loop

DISTANCE	GRADE / WAYMARKS
7.8 miles	Moderate / Blue

The Phoenix Trail

DISTANCE	GRADE / WAYMARKS
10.6 miles	Difficult / Red

Mabie's Dark Side

DISTANCE	GRADE / WAYMARKS
2.4 miles	Severe / Black

NB There is also a 10-mile family trail called the Windy Hill Route, with green waymarks, at the Forest of Ae, starting from Glen Ae car park about 11 miles north of Dumfries, off the A701 Moffat road (grid reference 986895 / OS Landranger Map 78).

Station: Dumfries.
TIC: Dumfries, 01387 253862.
Other nearby trails: There are other forest trails at Dalbeattie and in Galloway Forest Park. The Lochs & Glens Cycle Route (National Cycle Network Route 7) passes through the forest.
Useful publications: OS Landranger Map 84. A Forestry Commission leaflet, *7 Stanes Mabie,* is available from Dumfries Tourist Information Centre.
Websites: www.forestry.gov.uk/recreation and www.7stanes.gov.uk
Refreshments: Only in Dumfries.

339

5 Craik Forest, southwest of Hawick (2 routes)

CATEGORY

Waymarked forest trails.

DISTANCE

7.5 or 11.2 miles.

CENTRES / ROUTES

2 routes / 1 centre.

Craik Forest covers 10,000 acres and rises to almost 1500 feet on the boundary of Dumfries & Galloway and the Scottish Borders, with two waymarked forest trails. Riders of all standards will find the narrow paths fast and fun. Both routes head west from Craik Village on forest roads and tracks before swinging north across Wolfcleuch Burn and onto Crib Law. Here you choose between the stiff cyclepath climbs and flowing single track of the Red Route or an easy spin alongside Aithouse Burn on the Blue Route. The trails converge south of Hunter Holes and share a grassy hill track back to base.

STARTING POINT FOR 2 TRAILS BELOW

The hamlet of **Craik**, at the end of the minor road that leads southwest from the B711 Hawick to Ettrick road, 12 miles west of Hawick in the Scottish Borders.

Wolfcleuch Loop

DISTANCE	GRADE / WAYMARKS
7.5 miles	Easy-Moderate / Blue

Crib Law Trail

DISTANCE	GRADE / WAYMARKS
11.2 miles	Moderate-Hard / Red

Station: Lockerbie.

TIC: Hawick, 01450 372547.

Other nearby trails: There are plenty more forest trails in Southern Scotland: see Glentress, Galloway Forest Park, Dalbeattie and Mabie.

Useful publications: OS Landranger Map 79. A Forest Enterprise map, *A Guide to the Walks and Cycle Trails in Craik Forest* is available from Hawick TIC or from the Scottish Borders Forest District Office (01750 721120).

Website: www.forestry.gov.uk/recreation

Refreshments: None on the route, the nearest are in Hawick.

6   Galashiels to Melrose Black Path, Scottish Borders

CATEGORY
Railway path.

DISTANCE
3 miles each way.

The Scottish Borders is one of the few regions in the country that no longer has a railway station - they have all been closed down and the nearest are at Carlisle, Berwick-on-Tweed or Edinburgh. Unfortunately none of the hundreds of miles of disused railways have been converted to use for cyclists with the exception of this short, mainly urban section from the centre of Galashiels east to the edge of the historic town of Melrose. However, as population density in the Scottish Borders is about one twentieth that of the South-East of England there is plenty of wonderful cycling on the network of quiet lanes throughout the region. The trail forms part of the Coast & Castles Cycle Route (National Cycle Network Route 1) from Edinburgh to Newcastle, which largely follows the course of the lovely River Tweed to the coast at Berwick. It is well worth visiting the abbey and Priorwood Gardens in Melrose and, if you are feeling fit, to climb to the top of Eildon Hills for a panoramic view of the whole region.

STARTING POINT & PARKING
The route starts near to the clocktower in the centre of **Galashiels**, on the north side of the river (grid reference 495362) and ends on the western edges of Melrose at the roundabout where the road from the Tweedbank Industrial Estate joins the A6091 (grid reference 528345).

Station: None near by.
TIC: Galashiels, 01896 755551.
Other nearby trails: There are several forestry trails in nearby Glentress and Craik Forests.
Useful publications: OS Landranger Map 73. *Cycling in the Scottish Borders* is a free 48-page booklet available from TICs.
Refreshments: Lots of choice in Galashiels.

7   GLENTRESS FOREST NEAR PEEBLES

CATEGORY
Waymarked forest routes.

DISTANCE
3 - 18 miles.

ROUTES /CENTRE
5 routes / 1 centre.

There are many miles of forest trails in this lovely part of Scotland, looking down on the magnificent River Tweed as it winds its majestic course down to the sea at Berwick. Glentress Forest is one of the locations of the Seven Stanes Project which is creating a series of

centres of mountain biking excellence throughout Southern Scotland. Visit the website www.7stanes.gov.uk for the latest developments.

Glentress Forest Trailquest (3 routes)

There are two Trailquest routes in Glentress Forest, aimed at novices, and one easier mountain bike ride. They start from the upper car park, reducing the amount of climbing. The Trailquest routes encourage you to explore the history of the forest and the mountain bike route gives a taster of harder challenges.

STARTING POINT FOR 3 TRAILS BELOW

Buzzard's Nest car park, Glentress Forest, off the A72, about 3 miles east of **Peebles** *in the Scottish Borders, south of Edinburgh. This is the upper of the two car parks (grid reference 277412 / OS Landranger Map 73).*

Janet's Brae

DISTANCE	GRADE / WAYMARKS
3 miles	Easy / Green

Green Hill

DISTANCE	GRADE / WAYMARKS
6 miles	Moderate / Blue with a dog!

Blue MTB

DISTANCE	GRADE / WAYMARKS
5.6 miles	Moderate / Blue

Glentress Forest Mountain bike trails (2 routes)

The trails are the first in Scotland to be designed and built by enthusiasts. The trails are directional and all the singletrack is segregated for cycling use only. The Black Route is very strenuous, highly technical and for experts only!

STARTING POINT FOR 2 TRAILS BELOW

→ *The Hub car park, Glentress Forest, off the A72, about 3 miles east of* **Peebles** *in the Scottish Borders, south of Edinburgh. This is the lower of the two car parks (grid reference 287402 / OS Landranger Map 73).*

Red Route

DISTANCE	GRADE / WAYMARKS
10.6 miles	Demanding / Red

Black Route

DISTANCE	GRADE / WAYMARKS
18.6 miles	V. Demanding / Black

Station: No nearby railway.
TIC: Peebles, 01721 720138.
Other nearby trails: Black Path between Galashiels and Melrose. Craik Forest, west of Hawick.
Useful publications: OS Landranger Map 73. *Glentress Forest Trailquest - Orienteering on a Bicycle* describes the two Trailquest routes. The free booklet, *Cycling in the Scottish Borders* describes all the forestry routes and many other routes on quiet lanes in this fine cycling region. Both are available from Peebles TIC (01721 720138).
Website: www.forestry.gov.uk/recreation
Refreshments: In Peebles and Innerleithen.

8   Dalkieth to Penicuik, south of Edinburgh

CATEGORY
Railway path.

DISTANCE
8 miles each way.

This is the longest of the dismantled railways near to Edinburgh and the most scenic, passing through many beautiful wooded cuttings. Starting at Eskbank on the southwest edge of Dalkieth, the trail climbs steadily through Bonnyrigg and Lasswade to Penicuik (pronounced 'Pennycook'). Away to the right lie the Pentland Hills*. The most scenic section of the trail runs alongside the tumbling waters of the River North Esk. After passing through two short tunnels you emerge at the A701 in Penicuik near to the distinctive octagonal church tower. Roslin Mills was the biggest gunpowder mill in the country until it closed in 1954 due to mining subsidence. It supplied munitions from Napoleonic times right through to the Second World War as well as explosives for mining and quarrying. When the gunpowder mill was manufacturing, the railway ran through a 200yd corrugated iron tunnel built to ensure no sparks from trains would reach and ignite the gunpowder!

NB The busy B704 needs to be crossed in Lasswade.

* *How & Where to Mountain Bike in the Pentland Hills* is a leaflet with an excellent colour-coded map showing you exactly where cycling is allowed in these hills to the southwest of Edinburgh. Available from Dalkieth TIC (0131 660 6818).

STARTING POINTS & PARKING

→ The Eskbank Post Office, Lasswade Road, on the southwest edge of **Dalkieth**, just off the 6-road roundabout at the junction of the A768 and A6094 (grid reference 324664).

→ The octagonal church at the junction of the A701 and B6372 on the southeast edge of **Penicuik** (grid reference 236596).

Station: Musselburgh.
TIC: Dalkieth, 0131 660 6818.
Other nearby trails: The Pencaitland Railway Walk starts 3 miles northeast of Dalkieth. The Water of Leith runs southwest from Edinburgh through Balerno.
Useful publications: OS Landranger Map 66. An excellent map of Edinburgh and surrounds can be purchased from SPOKES, The Lothian Cycle Campaign, St Martin's Church, 232 Dalry Road, Edinburgh EH1 2JG (0131 313 2114).
Refreshments: Lots of choice in Dalkieth and Penicuik.

9   Pencaitland Railway Walk, east of Edinburgh

CATEGORY
Railway path.
DISTANCE
6 miles each way.

One of several railway paths lying to the south and east of Edinburgh, the Pencaitland Railway Walk runs from West Saltoun past Pencaitland and Ormiston to Crossgatehall across predominantly arable land where there were once open cast coal mines. Passenger services ceased in 1933 and the line closed in 1964 when the last mine in the area closed. The trail could easily be linked at its western end to the railway path from Dalkieth to Penicuik or to form part of a longer ride using the network of quiet lanes that abound to the north of the Lammermuirs. If you want to find out more about the coal mining history of the area it is worth visiting the Scottish Mining Museum near Prestonpans, set in the Lady Victoria and Prestongrange collieries.

STARTING POINT & PARKING

→ The car park in **Pencaitland**, just off the A6093 between Haddington and Dalkieth (grid reference 437686). This is about two-thirds of the way along the trail so you can do two rides, one southeast to the West Saltoun Road and one northwest to Crossgatehall.

Station: Prestonpans.
TIC: Edinburgh, 0131 473 3800.
Other nearby trails: The Dalkieth to Penicuik Trail starts 3 miles to the west of the end of the Pencaitland Walk. There is another railway path between Haddington and Longniddry.
Useful publications: OS Landranger Map 66. The *Edinburgh Cycle Map* (£4.95) shows all the cycle routes in and around Edinburgh. It is available from SPOKES, The Lothian Cycle

Campaign, St Martin's Church, 232 Dalry Road, Edinburgh EH1 12JG (0131 313 2114) (ansaphone).

Refreshments: None on the route.

10 Haddington to Longniddry, east of Edinburgh

CATEGORY
Railway path.

DISTANCE
4 1/2 miles each way.

This is just one of several railway paths lying close to Edinburgh. East Lothian is a very progressive authority and there will eventually be a safe link for cyclists from Longniddry, along the coast to Musselburgh and thence into the centre of Edinburgh. This trail runs from the west side of Haddington (Alderston Road) to Longniddry railway station. Haddington is a handsome town with wide streets, dating from the 12th century. The Town House was built in 1748 and the church in the 15th century. The town was the home of the reformer John Knox and also Thomas Carlyle, whose house has a fine façade. Longniddry was a mining village for 500 years until the 1920s. Gosford House, the seat of the Earl of Wemyss, was designed by Robert Adam.

STARTING POINTS & PARKING
→Alderston Road, on the west side of **Haddington**, near to the hospital. From the centre of Haddington follow signs for Edinburgh. Alderston Road is a street on your right towards the end of the village (grid reference 502740).

→**Longniddry** railway station (grid reference 446762).

Station: Longniddry.
TIC: Musselburgh, 0131 665 6597.

Other nearby trails: The Pencaitland Railway Walk lies 7 miles to the southwest. The Dalkieth to Penicuik Cycleway is a little further west.
Useful publications: OS Landranger Map 66. An excellent publication, *The Edinburgh Cycle Map* (£4.95) showing all the traffic-free routes in and around Edinburgh is produced by SPOKES, the Lothian Cycle Campain Group. Available from SPOKES, St Martin's Church, 232 Dalry Road, Edinburgh EH11 2JG (0131 313 2114) (ansaphone).
Refreshments: Haddington and Longniddry.

11 Innocent Railway, Edinburgh

CATEGORY
Railway path.

DISTANCE
4 miles each way.

The Innocent Railway offers a good exit from the heart of Edinburgh out to the east, passing beneath the towering mound of Arthur's Seat which rises to over 800ft. The trail starts from St Leonard's Bank, on the western edge of the magnificent Holyrood Park in the centre of this beautiful city and heads through a tunnel near the start towards Duddingston Loch, Bingham and Brunstane. Holyrood Park itself is shut to traffic on Sundays from 1000 - 1600 hrs. The Innocent Railway lies at the start of the Coast & Castles Cycle Route (National Cycle Network Route 1) that links Edinburgh to Newcastle via the Scottish Borders and the Northumbrian Coast. There are long term plans to create a traffic-free route from the end of the Innocent Railway path through Dalkieth Country Park and along another disused railway to Gorebridge and North Middleton.

STARTING POINT & PARKING

→ St Leonard's Bank, Newington, near the Royal Commonwealth Pool, at the southwest edge of **Holyrood Park** (grid reference 266727).

Station: Waverley Station, Edinburgh or Musselburgh.
TIC: Edinburgh, 0131 473 3800.
Other nearby trails: There are several trails in or near Edinburgh ie Water of Leith, Union Canal, Newbridge & Forth Road Bridge, Dalkieth to Penicuik and the Pencaitland Railway Walk.
Useful publications: OS Landranger Map 66. Much better the SPOKES *Edinburgh Cycle Map* (£4.95) which can be purchased from SPOKES, St Martin's Church, 232 Dalry Road, Edinburgh EH11 2JG (0131 313 2114) (ansaphone).
Refreshments: Lots of choice at the Edinburgh end.

12 Water of Leith, East of Edinburgh

CATEGORY
Canal towpath.
DISTANCE
6 miles each way.

Although the Water of Leith wends its way right through the heart of Edinburgh to the Docks, the inner city stretch is not easy to follow on a bike and there are frequent road sections. The best part for cyclists runs from Kingsknowe, southwest of the city centre (off the Lanark Road), to Balerno, passing the many old mills which used the water from the river as a source of power. There were over 70 mills in its heyday, producing flour, paper, spices and snuff. The famous Scotts Porage Oats were made in Colinton from 1909 to 1947. If you wish to cycle from the centre of Edinburgh, you can follow National Cycle Network Route 75 from the Meadows, soon joining the Union Canal towpath. Shortly after crossing the aqueduct carrying the canal over the Water of

13

Leith you turn off to the left onto a continuation of Route 75. The traffic-free trail stops at Bridge Road, Balerno, just off the A70 Lanark Road.

STARTING POINTS & PARKING

→ The Union Canal Bridge, on the Lanark Road (A70) just to the east of **Kingsknowe** Railway Station on the west side of Edinburgh.

→ Bridge Road, **Balerno**, just off the A70 on the north side of the village (grid reference 164670).

Stations: Edinburgh, Currie.

TIC: Edinburgh, 0131 473 3881.

Other nearby trails: The Union Canal also runs into the west side of Edinburgh. There is a cyclepath between Newbridge and the Forth Road Bridge.

Useful publications: OS Landranger Map 66. *The Edinburgh Cycle Map* (£4.95) is an excellent map which can be purchased from SPOKES, The Lothian Cycle Campaign, St Martin's Church, 232 Dalry Road, Edinburgh, EH1 2JG (0131 313 2114) (ansafone).

Refreshments: Lots of choice all along the route.

13 Newbridge and the Forth Road Bridge, west of Edinburgh

CATEGORY

Railway path and bridge over Firth of Forth.

DISTANCE

7 miles each way.

Riding across the Forth Road Bridge is one of the most extraordinary cycling experiences in Scotland. You cross from South Queensferry to North Queensferry in complete traffic-free safety along the cycle lanes that run either side of the bridge, hundreds of feet above the waters of the Firth of Forth, with views to the east of the magnificent Forth Rail Bridge (the one where, as the saying goes, they start painting at one end the moment they have stopped at the other!) Starting from Newbridge, on the A8 to the west of Edinburgh, you follow a dismantled railway north through Kirkliston and Dalmeny to pass under the Forth Rail Bridge before climbing through Queensferry, named after Queen Margaret who used the ferry to cross the Forth in the 11th century. After crossing the bridge you have the choice of returning on the other side or dropping down into North Queensferry for refreshments, a visit to Deep Sea World and a train trip back to Edinburgh across the Forth Bridge.

NB There is a cyclepath alongside the A89 and A8 enabling you to get safely from Newbridge onto the footbridge over the M9 to the start of the railway path.

STARTING POINT & PARKING

East of **Newbridge**, just off the A8 to the west of Edinburgh (grid reference 125726). You can cycle along both sides of the Forth Road Bridge.

Station: North Queensferry or Dalmeny.
TIC: Edinburgh, 0131 4733800.
Other nearby trails: The Water of Leith Walkway from Balerno to Edinburgh.
Useful publications: OS Landranger Map 65. Much better is the *West Lothian Cycle Map* (£4.95) which can be purchased from SPOKES, St Martin's Church, 232 Dalry Road, Edinburgh EH11 2JG (0131 313 2114) (ansaphone).
Refreshments: In Kirkliston, Queensferry and North Queensferry.

14 Airdrie to Bathgate Railway Path, east of Glasgow

CATEGORY
Railway path.
DISTANCE
15 miles each way.

One of several long sections of dismantled railway path in the Glasgow area (the others lie to the west of the city), the Airdrie to Bathgate path forms part of the Clyde to Forth Cycle Route (National Cycle Network Route 75). There is a gentle climb from both Bathgate and Airdrie up to Hillend Reservoir, which is at the highest point, in the middle of the ride. Originally built in the 1850s, the Airdrie to Bathgate Junction Railway carried coal, ironstone and limestone to the numerous works in the Monklands district. Closed to passengers in 1956 and to freight in the mid 1980s, the railway still gives you the chance to feel what this part of Scotland may have been like in its heyday. All along the route there are remains of these old industries: quarries, coalmines and

14

mining villages. The route is accompanied by a sculpture trail which closely identifies with communities through which it passes.

STARTING POINTS & PARKING

→ Drumgelloch railway station, on the east side of **Airdrie**, just off the A89 Armadale Road to the east of the roundabout with the A73 (grid reference 776654).

→ Guildiehaugh, south of **Bathgate**, at the roundabout on the B792 (grid reference 987677).

Station: Airdrie or Bathgate.
TIC: Glasgow, 0141 204 4400.
Other nearby trails: The new town of Livingston has a fine network of traffic-free cycleways. The Union Canal and Forth & Clyde Canal lie to the north.
Useful publications: OS Landranger Maps 64 & 65. This trail plus many others in Central Scotland is covered by the *Clyde to Forth Cycle Route* map (£5.99) available from Sustrans.
Sustrans Order Line: Call 0845 113 0065 or visit their website at www.sustrans.org.uk
Refreshments: Airdrie, Caldercruix, Blackridge and Bathgate.

15 Johnstone to Kilbirnie, west of Glasgow

CATEGORY
Railway path.
DISTANCE
11 miles each way.

There are two dismantled railways that run west from Johnstone: the trail to Greenock is described below. This one takes a more southerly direction, passing Castle Semple Loch, Barr Loch and Kilbirnie Loch along its course. The colour-washed houses in Lochwinnoch date from the early 19th century. The village was a centre for cask and barrel making. The trail is part of the Lochs & Glens Cycle Route (National Cycle Network Route 7) that runs from Glasgow to Carlisle. There are long term plans to extend the traffic-free section along the valley of the River Garnock from Kilbirnie to Kilwinning, thus bringing the dream one step closer of creating a traffic-free path all the way from Glasgow to the Ayrshire Coast.

STARTING POINT & PARKING

→ Johnstone, 1 mile to the west of the B789 / A761 roundabout at the point where Old Road passes beneath the railway (grid reference 444635).

→ Castle Semple Visitor Centre in **Lochwinnoch** (grid reference 363595).

→ **Kilbirnie** (grid reference 319537).

Station: Johnstone, Kilbirnie.
TIC: Glasgow, 0141 204 4400.
Other nearby trails: The trail links with the Johnstone to Greenock Route.
Useful publications: OS Landranger Maps 63 & 64. Sustrans *Clyde to Forth Cycle Route* map (£5.99) contains details of this and many other traffic-free trails in the Glasgow and Edinburgh area.
Sustrans Order Line: Call 0845 113 0065 or visit their website at www.sustrans.org.uk
Refreshments: Johnstone, Lochwinnoch, Kilbirnie.

16 Johnstone to Greenock, west of Glasgow

CATEGORY
Railway path.

DISTANCE
14 miles each way.

Although there is a waymarked National Cycle Network route starting right in the heart of Glasgow it is very bitty between Bells Bridge and Johnstone and uses several sections of roads. By contrast the Johnstone to Greenock route is almost entirely on the course of an old railway line. It runs from Johnstone via the Bridge of Weir, Kilmacolm and Port Glasgow to the Lady Octavia Recreation Centre above Greenock. There are splendid views across the Firth of Clyde to the hills above Helensburgh on the north shore. Greenock is famous for ships, sugar and as the birthplace of James Watt, improver of the steam engine. The Comet, Britain's first passenger steamboat, was built at nearby Port Glasgow in 1812. A replica is on show at Port Glasgow Railway Station. The ride forms part of the Clyde to Forth Cycle Route (National Cycle Network Route 75) which runs from Gourock through Glasgow and Edinburgh to Leith Docks.

STARTING POINTS & PARKING

→ The ride starts in **Johnstone**, 1 mile to the west of the B789 / A761 roundabout at the point where Old Road passes beneath the railway (grid reference 444635).

→ You could also start in **Bridge of Weir**, **Kilmacolm** and **Port Glasgow**.

→ The western start / finish is at the Lady Octavia Recreation Centre in **Greenock**, off the B788 Kilmacolm Road up to the southeast of town (grid reference 295747).

Station: Johnstone or Whinhill Station, Greenock.
TIC: Glasgow, 0141 204 4400.
Other nearby trails: Links with the Johnstone to Kilbirnie Route.
Useful publications: OS Landranger Maps 63 & 64. Sustrans *Clyde & Forth Cycle Route* map (£5.99), contains details of this and many other traffic-free trails in the Glasgow and Edinburgh area.
Sustrans Order Line: Call 0845 113 0065 or visit their website at www.sustrans.org.uk
Refreshments: Johnstone, Bridge of Weir, Kilmacolm, Port Glasgow, Greenock.

17 Glasgow to the banks of Loch Lomond

CATEGORY

Railway path, canal towpath, riverside path.

DISTANCE

Up to 19 miles each way.

One of several traffic-free routes in and near Glasgow, this one links the Lowlands with the start of the Highlands on the banks of Loch Lomond. Starting at Bell's Bridge in central Glasgow you pass John Brown's shipyard in the centre of Clydebank, where the great ships the Queen Mary, Queen Elizabeth and Queen Elizabeth II were built. Beyond Clydebank the route joins the Forth & Clyde Canal on a broad, well-maintained towpath. The canal, built in 1790, was the main route across Scotland linking the Clyde at Bowling, west of Glasgow with the Forth near to Falkirk / Grangemouth. The ride becomes more open with green views of the Kilpatrick Hills behind Erskine Bridge. A second railway path starting at the end of the canal takes you through woodland and between rocky outcrops to the outkirts of Dumbarton, the ancient fortress-capital of the Kingdom of Strathclyde. The route through Dumbarton is on quiet roads and soon you join the waterside path alongside the River Leven which leads to Balloch and the bonny banks of Loch Lomond. It is worth stopping to read the information boards along the river with interesting background detail about the history and wildlife of the riverside.

NB Short sections of road are used through Dumbarton.

STARTING POINT & PARKING

The path starts at **Bell's Bridge** in central Glasgow, near to the Scottish Exhibition & Conference Centre, just west of the M8 Jct 20.

Station: Railway stations all along the way.
TIC: Glasgow, 0141 204 4400.
Other nearby trails: This is part of the Lochs &

17

Glens Cycle Route (National Cycle Network Route 7). At Bell's Bridge in Glasgow, you can link to the Johnstone to Greenock and Johnstone to Kilbirnie Routes.

Useful publications:

OS Landranger Maps 63 & 64.

Sustrans *Clyde to Forth Cycle Route* map (£5.99) shows this and many other traffic-free trails in the Glasgow / Edinburgh area. CycleCity produce the *Glasgow Cycling Map* which shows the traffic-free paths and advisory routes around the city. Available from CycleCity Guides, Wallbridge Mill, The Retreat, Frome BA11 5JU (01373 453533). E-mail: info@cyclecityguides.co.uk

Sustrans Order Line: Call 0845 113 0065 or visit their website at www.sustrans.org.uk

Refreshments: Lots of choice along the way.

18 Strathblane - Kirkintilloch (Strathkelvin Walkway), north of Glasgow

CATEGORY
Railway path.
DISTANCE
8 miles each way.

There are a plethora of traffic-free tracks in and around Glasgow, some use riverside paths, some use canal towpaths and others, like this trail, use dismantled railways. This is one of the most spectacular, running parallel with the dramatic Campsie Fells, which rise to almost 2000 ft on Earl's Seat, to the north of Strathblane. The tree-lined trail uses the course of the old Kirkintilloch to Gartness Railway. It is worth diverting 1/2 mile off the railway path to visit the Clachan of Campsie where there is a craft village, a coffee shop and a bike shop. Kirkintilloch was originally Caerpentulach, meaning the 'fort on the ridge', the fort being part of the Roman Antonine Wall. It developed

dramatically after the arrival of the Forth & Clyde Canal in 1773 and was soon operating as Scotland's first inland port, linked to the Forth by the canal.

STARTING POINTS & PARKING
→ **Strathblane**, 10 miles north of Glasgow on the A81. The trail starts just to the east of the junction with the A891 (grid reference 565794).
→ **Kirkintilloch**, 8 miles northeast of Glasgow on the A803. The trail starts on the north side of town on the B757 towards Milton of Campsie (grid reference 655746).

Station: Milngavie, south of Strathblane or Auchinloch, south of Kirkintilloch.
TIC: Glasgow, 0141 848 4440.
Other nearby trails: The Forth & Clyde Canal runs through Kirkintilloch. There is another long railway path between Airdrie and Bathgate.
Useful publications: OS Landranger Map 64.
Refreshments: Strathblane, Lennoxtown, Milton of Campsie and Kirkintilloch.

19 Forth & Clyde Canal, between Glasgow and Edinburgh

CATEGORY
Canal towpath.
DISTANCE
Up to 32 miles each way.

With the opening of Sustrans Clyde to Forth Cycle Route (which uses a mixture of railway paths and other canal towpaths) there are two ways of cycling between Scotland's major cities on largely traffic-free routes. The Forth & Clyde Canal towpath starts to the west of Glasgow and ends just beyond Falkirk. It was one of the great engineering projects of the late 18th century: construction of a canal to create an east-west shortcut through Central Scotland had been

16

suggested as early as the reign of Charles II but a route was not properly surveyed until the early 1760s. Work began at the Grangemouth end in 1768 and Kirkintilloch was operating as Scotland's first inland port by 1773. It was a further 17 years before it was completed in 1790. It was open for over 170 years until it was finally abandoned in 1962. There are now plans to restore the canal, together with the Union Canal, near to Edinburgh. However, as a result of many years of neglect the towpath is no longer continuous so it is wise to carry a map and / or street atlas of Glasgow with you, in order to negotiate those sections where the towpath has disappeared. The full course of the route is from Bowling and Clydebank along the northern edge of Glasgow passing Kirkintilloch, Kilsyth and Bonnybridge to Falkirk and Grangemouth. The Union Canal links Falkirk to Edinburgh.

STARTING POINT & PARKING

The canal joins the Clyde at **Bowling**, just off the A82 between Clydebank and Dumbarton, 1 1/2 miles west of the Erskine Bridge (A898). It follows the route described above and ends between Falkirk and Grangemouth, just to the west of the M9 Jct 6.

Stations: There are railway stations on or close to the route along its entire length.
TIC: Falkirk, 01324 620244.
Other nearby trails: The towpath links with the Glasgow to Loch Lomond Trail at its western end, crosses the Strathblane to Kirkintilloch Path (Strathkelvin Railway Walkway) in Kirkintilloch, and runs very close to the Union Canal in Falkirk.
Useful publications: OS Landranger Maps 64 & 65. A Glasgow street atlas will be useful where the course of the canal has been built over and you need to find street alternatives.
Refreshments: All along the way.

20 Union Canal, west of Edinburgh

CATEGORY

Canal towpath.

DISTANCE

Up to 30 miles one way.

The Union Canal is one of two waterways that enters Edinburgh from the west, the other being the Water of Leith. The canal was opened in 1822 to link Edinburgh and Falkirk. It was built to follow the 240ft contour so it needed no locks except a flight of 11 to join it to the Forth & Clyde Canal at Falkirk. The contour method increased the distance but saved the time and water needed for lock operation. The Millennium Link is a project to regenerate the Forth & Clyde and Union Canals, re-opening them to navigation via the dramatic Falkirk Wheel that raises and lowers boats almost 80 ft between the two canals. The regeneration includes the upgrading and improvement of the towpath. The canal runs from the centre of Edinburgh through Ratho, Broxburn, Winchburgh and Linlithgow to Falkirk.

NB You will need to use some road sections if you intend to cover the whole length of the canal.

STARTING POINT & PARKING

→ The towpath starts in Edinburgh at the junction of Gilmore Park and Dundee Street, Fountainbridge (southwest of the castle).

Stations: Edinburgh, Slateford, Kingsknowe, Linlithgow, Polmont, Falkirk.
TIC: Edinburgh, 0131 473 3800.
Other nearby trails: The Water of Leith also has a towpath. There is a cyclepath between Newbridge and the Forth Bridge.
Useful publications: OS Landranger Maps 65 & 66. The excellent *Edinburgh Cycle Map* (£4.95) can be purchased from SPOKES, The Lothian Cycle Campaign, St Martin's Church, 232 Dalry Road, Edinburgh EH1 2JG (0131 313 2114) (ansafone).
Refreshments: All along the way.

20

21 West Fife Cycleway: Dunfermline to Clackmannan

CATEGORY

Railway path

DISTANCE

11 miles each way

Forming part of the Kingdom of Fife Millennium Cycleways, the old railway path between Dunfermline and Clackmannan is the longest unbroken stretch of traffic-free trail in the whole project. Dunfermline was a favourite residence of Queen Margaret who married King Malcolm III of Scotland in 1070. The town's 19th-century church contains the grave of Robert Bruce, the 14th-century king of Scotland. The railway was opened in 1850 linking Dunfermline to Alloa and the Stirling line. It closed in 1968.

STARTING POINT & PARKING

The car park at the junction of William Street and Baldridgeburn, the A907 Alloa Road, on the west side of **Dunfermline** (grid reference 081881).

Station: Dunfermline Town.

TIC: Dunfermline, 01383 720999.

Other nearby trails: Forestry routes in Fife's forests - Blairadam, Devilla, Tentsmuir and Pitmedden

Useful publications: OS Landranger Maps 65 & 58. The *West Fife Cycle Route Map* shows the whole of the Kingdom of Fife Millennium Cycleways network in the southwest corner of Fife.

Website: www.fife-cycleways.co.uk

Refreshments: Plenty of choice in Dunfermline. Pubs just off the route in Carnock, Oakley, Comrie and Blairhall.

22-25 FIFE FORESTS

CATEGORY

Waymarked forest trails

DISTANCE

2 - 9 miles

ROUTES / CENTRES

12 routes / 4 centres

As part of the Kingdom of Fife Millennium Cycleways Project three short routes have been waymarked in each of the four small forests that lie within the boundaries of Fife, namely Tentsmuir to the north of St Andrews, Pitmedden to the southwest of Newburgh, Blairadam to the north of Dunfermline and Devilla Forest to the east of Kincardine.

22 Devilla Forest (3 routes)

The forest has a long history of occupation and use. Prehistoric coffins, stone circles and Roman urns have been found in different parts of the forest. In 1038, King Duncan fought the Danes, who were camped at Moor Loch, at the Battle of Bordie near the Bordie Loch.

STARTING POINT FOR 3 TRAILS BELOW

*Devilla Forest car park, just off the A985 about 9 miles **west of Dunfermline** (grid reference 964872 / OS Landranger Map 65).*

WAYMARK	GRADE	DISTANCE
Yellow	Easy	2.7 miles
Blue	Easy / Moderate	3 miles
Purple	Moderate	5.5 miles

Station: Dunfermline.

TIC: Dunfermline, 01383 720999.

Refreshments: Kincardine

23 Blairadam Forest (3 routes)

The Scottish architect, Sir William Adam, planted Blairadam in the early 18th century. Most of the

23

original forest was felled during the two World Wars and the Forestry Commission replanted with Sitka and Norway spruce. One of the ways to tell the difference between a spruce and a pine is to remember that S is for spruce and single needles and P is for pine and paired needles!

STARTING POINT FOR 3 TRAILS BELOW

*Blairadam Forest car park, 7 miles **north of Dunfermline**. Leave the M90 at junction 4, follow the B914 towards Saline for 1/4 mile then turn right onto the forest road for almost 1 mile to the car park (grid reference 130947 / OS Landranger Map 58).*

WAYMARK	GRADE	DISTANCE
Yellow	Easy / Moderate	2.2 miles
Blue	Moderate	3 miles
Purple	Moderate	6.5 miles

Station: Cowdenbeath.
TIC: Dunfermline, 01383 720999.
Refreshments: In Kelty.

24 Pitmedden Forest (3 routes)

Nearby Auchtermuchty was part of the hunting ground for the Kings and Queens of Scotland when they stayed at Falkland Palace. It is likely that Pitmedden was part of this hunting land too. In 1917 large parts of the forest were felled to supply wood for the war effort. It was replanted with the spruce trees like those you can see today.

STARTING POINT FOR 3 TRAILS BELOW

*Pitmedden Forest car park, 4 miles southwest of **Newburgh**. From the A913 between Abernethy and the A912 / 913 roundabout (southeast of M90 Jct 9) take the minor road towards Strathmiglo. Go through Glenfoot, climb steeply for 1.5 miles and the forest car park is on your left (grid reference 188139 / OS Landranger Map 58).*

WAYMARK	GRADE	DISTANCE
Yellow	Moderate	2.2 miles
Blue	Moderate	4.2 miles
Purple	Moderate / Hard	9 miles

25

Station: Ladybank.
TIC: Kinross, 01577 863680.
Refreshments: In Abernethy.

25 Tentsmuir Forest (3 routes)

This is the flattest Forestry Commission holding in all of Scotland with many miles of easy tracks. During Malcolm Canmore's reign (1058-93) courtiers from Leuchars Castle hunted in the forest. Medieval chroniclers believed that it was a marshy area inhabited by *diaboli* (devils) and at one time there was even a colony of shipwrecked sailors living in the forest.

STARTING POINT FOR 3 TRAILS BELOW

Kinshaldy Beach car park, **Tentsmuir,** *at the end of the minor road to the northeast of Leuchars (grid reference 499242 / OS Landranger Map 59).*

WAYMARK	GRADE	DISTANCE
Yellow	Easy	2.7 miles
Blue	Easy	4.5 miles
Purple	Easy	5.2 miles

Station: Leuchars.
TIC: St Andrews, 01334 472021.
Refreshments: In Leuchars or Tayport.

OTHER INFORMATION

Other nearby trails: Dunfermline to Clackmannan railway path. Forth Road Bridge cycle path.
Useful publications: OS Landranger Maps 58, 59 & 65. *Kingdom of Fife Millennium Cycleways Forest Routes* is available from TICs.
Websites: www.forestry.gov.uk/recreation and www.fife-cycleways.co.uk

26 Aberfoyle to Callander in the Trossachs, north of Glasgow

CATEGORY

Forest trails, specially-built lochside route, quiet lane.

DISTANCE

14 miles each way.

Aberfoyle is an ideal base for exploring the Trossachs and is located on the National Cycle Network Route 7 (Lochs & Glens Cycle Route) from Glasgow to Inverness which runs north and south from Aberfoyle on forestry roads. This ride follows the route north from Aberfoyle, climbing steeply on the waymarked trail through Achray Forest, dropping down to the track along the south side of beautiful Loch Venachar with views across the water to the towering bulk of Ben Ledi, rising to almost 2900ft. A quiet lane east from Invertrossachs takes you into Callander, an attractive and popular tourist destination with the option of extending your ride northwards on a traffic-free path past the Falls of Leny and Loch Lubnaig to Strathyre.

NB There is a 1/2-mile section on the A81 at the northern end of the ride and a longer section on a minor road west of Callander.

STARTING POINT & PARKING

The Queen Elizabeth Forest Park Visitor Centre, on the A821 just to the **north of Aberfoyle**, north of Glasgow (grid reference 520014).

Station: Dunblane, east of Callander.
TIC: Aberfoyle, 01877 382352.
Other nearby trails: National Cycle Network Route 7 continues north from Callander to Strathyre. There are two waymarked trails in Queen Elizabeth Forest Park in Loch Ard Forest to the west of Aberfoyle.
Useful publications: OS Landranger Map 57. A better map is produced by the Forestry Commission and can be purchased from Forest Enterprise, Aberfoyle (01877 382383). Sustrans *Lochs & Glens Cycle Route* map (£5.99) shows this and several other traffic-free sections on

26

27

National Cycle Network Route 7.
Sustrans Order Line: Call 0845 113 0065 or visit their website at www.sustrans.org.uk
Refreshments: Lots of choice in Aberfoyle and Callander. Pub just off the route in Brig o' Turk.

27 Queen Elizabeth Forest Park in the Trossachs

CATEGORY
Waymarked forest routes.

DISTANCE
10 - 25 miles.

ROUTES / CENTRES
2 routes / 1 centre.

First designated as a Forest Park by the Forestry Commission in 1953 to mark the coronation of Queen Elizabeth II, the park attracts over a million visitors a year. From the east shore of Loch Lomond to the rugged terrain of Strathyre, the park encompasses mountain and moorland, forest and woodland, rivers and lochs. It is home to a rich variety of animal and plant life. The park covers three forests in the Aberfoyle

and Callander area - Strathyre, Achray and Loch Ard. The Lochs & Glens Cycle Route (National Cycle Network Route 7) uses tracks through Achray Forest and alongside Loch Lubnaig in Strathyre Forest on its way north to Callander and Killin. In Loch Ard Forest there are two waymarked circular routes.

STARTING POINTS & PARKING
→ The **Yellow Route** (up to 25 miles) starts from Manse Road, near the Tourist Information Centre in Aberfoyle on the A81 north of Glasgow (grid reference 520010)
→ The **Red Route** (10 miles) starts at Milton, about 1 1/2 miles west of Aberfoyle along the B829 (grid reference 503014).

Station: Balloch, Milngavie or Dunblane.
TIC: Aberfoyle, 01877 382352.
Other nearby trails: The Lochs & Glens Cycle Route (National Cycle Network Route 7) passes through Aberfoyle and Callander. There is a traffic-free road along the north side of Loch Katrine.
Useful publications: OS Landranger Map 57. A leaflet, *A Guide to Queen Elizabeth Forest Park*, produced by the Forestry Commission shows

the routes. It is available from the visitor centres and Tourist Information Centres or from the Forestry Commission (01877 382383).
Website: www.forestry.gov.uk/recreation
Refreshments: In Aberfoyle, Callander and Strathyre.

28 Loch Katrine, the Trossachs, north of Glasgow

CATEGORY
Route along shoreline of loch.
DISTANCE
10 miles each way (ie this is **not** a circuit).

This exploration of Loch Katrine is one of the loveliest in the whole book - there is a delightful tarmac track which is shut to traffic but open to walkers and cyclists along the north side of the loch and part of the south side as far as Stronachlachar. There is **not** a complete circuit of the lake. If you wish to go on from Stronachlachar to Loch Lomond and the Inversnaid Hotel for refreshments you will need to use a road which carries some traffic, particularly in the high season as it is a popular day trip for vehicles from Aberfoyle to Loch Lomond. There has been some talk of completing the circuit by building the missing 2-3 miles at the southeast corner of the loch on the northern slopes of Ben Venue although this is probably some years away. It would create one of the best and most spectacular lakeside circuits in the whole of Great Britain.

STARTING POINT & PARKING
The pier car park at the **eastern end of Loch Katrine** at the terminus of the A821, to the west of Callander and to the north of Aberfoyle (grid reference 496073).

Station: Nowhere nearby - Glasgow and Dunblane are both more than 20 miles distant.
TIC: Aberfoyle, 01877 382352.

28

Other nearby trails: There are two waymarked forestry tracks in the Queen Elizabeth Forest Park southwest of Aberfoyle. There are two traffic-free sections of the Lochs & Glens Cycle Route from Aberfoyle to Callander and from Callander to Strathyre.

Useful publications: OS Landranger Maps 56 & 57.

Refreshments: At the Captain's Rest Cafe at the start. The Inversnaid Hotel, on the east shore of Loch Lomond, lies 5 miles to the west of Stronachlachar (ie this would add another 10 miles to the trip).

29 Callander to Strathyre, northwest of Stirling

CATEGORY

Railway path and forest tracks.

DISTANCE

10 miles each way.

You should enjoy spectacular views of Ben Ledi and Loch Lubnaig along the course of this dismantled railway linking Callander with Strathyre via the Falls of Leny and the west side of Loch Lubnaig. This forms part of the Lochs & Glens Cycle Route from Glasgow to Inverness (National Cycle Network Route 7). There are several short climbs where the route leaves the course of the railway path to join forestry tracks. Strathyre is 200ft higher than Callander. The trail uses the course of the old Caledonian railway line which until 1965 used to run from Stirling to Oban. Passing through broadleaf woodland alongside the swift waters of the River Leny the ride runs a parallel course to the A84 through the Pass of Leny, known as the entrance to the Highlands. It is said that 2000 years ago the Druids lit fires at the top of Ben Ledi to celebrate the changing of the seasons.

STARTING POINTS & PARKING

→ The central car park in **Callander**. The route starts at the western end of the car park. Follow signs for Strathyre and Balquhidder or for National Cycle Network Route 7.

→ There is also car parking off the A84 at the **Falls of Leny** and in **Strathyre**.

Station: Dunblane.

TIC: Callander, 01877 330342.

Other nearby trails: South to Aberfoyle from Callander along the banks of Loch Venachar. Two waymarked routes in Queen Elizabeth Forest Park southwest of Aberfoyle. North from Kingshouse along National Cycle Network Route 7 through Glen Ogle to Killin.

Useful publications: OS Landranger Map 57. Sustrans *Lochs & Glens Cycle Route* map (£5.99) shows this and several other traffic-free sections on National Cycle Network Route 7.

Sustrans Order Line: Call 0845 113 0065 or visit their website at www.sustrans.org.uk

Refreshments: Lots of choice in Callander and Strathyre.

30 Killin to Kingshouse via Glen Ogle, north of Callander and the Trossachs

CATEGORY

Railway path, woodland path and an old military road.

DISTANCE

9 miles each way.

The route through Glen Ogle on a mixture of old military road, woodland paths and a disused railway has been one of Sustrans greatest triumphs in the creation of the National Cycle Network in Scotland, as the alternative was a very unpleasant ride along the busy A84 and A85. There is a climb of over 500ft from Killin south along the railway line and up through the forestry to reach the highpoint and the pass just to the south of Lochan Lairig Cheile. The spectacular Glen Ogle Viaduct is crossed then you can enjoy a 500ft descent down to Kingshouse where there are refreshments at the hotel. Glen Ogle has over the centuries been used by Roman and English armies as the easiest way to get to and from the Highlands. Queen Victoria even called it the 'Khyber Pass of Scotland'!

NB Care should be taken crossing the A85 near Glen Ogle Cottages.

STARTING POINT & PARKING

The Breadalbane Folklore Centre in **Killin**, on the A827 about 20 miles to the north of Callander (grid reference 570322).

Station: Pitlochry.
TIC: Killin, 01567 820254.
Other nearby trails: The continuation of the Scottish National Route southwards has traffic-free sections between Strathyre and Callander then south of Callander via Loch Venachar and Achray Forest to Aberfoyle.
Useful publications: OS Landranger Map 51. Sustrans *Lochs & Glens Cycle Route* map (£5.99) shows this and several other traffic-free sections on National Cycle Network Route 7.
Sustrans Order Line: Call 0845 113 0065 or visit their website at www.sustrans.org.uk
Refreshments: In Killin, Lochearnhead and Kingshouse.

30

31

31 ARGYLL FOREST PARK, COWAL PENINSULA

CATEGORY

Waymarked forestry routes.

DISTANCE

5 - 20 miles.

ROUTES / CENTRES

5 routes / 2 centres.

The park lies on the Cowal Peninsula to the west of the Firth of Clyde and Loch Long and is approached either by ferry from Gourock to Dunoon or the A82 / A83 via Arrochar. There are five waymarked trails through this spectacular part of Scotland, two from Ardgartan and three from Glenbranter.

Routes from Ardgartan Visitor Centre (2 routes)

STARTING POINT FOR 2 TRAILS BELOW

Ardgartan Visitor Centre, A83 west of Arrochar (grid reference 269038 / OS Landranger Map 56).

Cat Craig Loop

DISTANCE	GRADE / WAYMARKS
5 miles	Medium / Green

A circular trail which includes some spectacular views over Loch Long and Arrochar.

Ardgartan Peninsula Circuit

DISTANCE	GRADE / WAYMARKS
20 miles	Difficult / Red

A grand tour of the wild, rugged and remote Ardgartan Peninsula with excellent views of the Clyde and surrounding mountains. Best done clockwise.

Routes from Glenbranter (3 routes)

STARTING POINTS FOR 3 TRAILS BELOW

Glenbranter, A815, south of Loch Fyne (grid reference 112979 / OS Landranger Map 56).

Glenbranter Splash

DISTANCE	GRADE / WAYMARKS
6 miles	Difficult / Red

A circular route that is demanding and provides a variation in terrain and challenges, with two fords to be crossed. Expect to get muddy!

Glenshellish Loop

DISTANCE	GRADE / WAYMARKS
8 miles	Easy / Blue

The ride gives a good introduction to the delights of offroad cycling for the family and novice riders.

Loch Eck Shore Trail (linear)

DISTANCE	GRADE / WAYMARKS
9 miles	Easy / Green

The trail uses forest roads which stay close to the west shore giving attractive views across the hills of Cowal. The tearoom at Benmore makes a welcome destination.

Station: Tarbet.

TIC: Inveraray, 01499 302063.

Other nearby trails: There are waymarked forest trails in Queen Elizabeth Forest Park southwest of Aberfoyle.

Useful publications: OS Landranger Map 56. An excellent leaflet, *Cycling in the Forest - Argyll Forest Park,* is produced by the Forestry Commission can be purchased from Ardgartan Visitor Centre or from Forest Enterprise, Cowal Forest District, Kilmun, By Dunoon, Argyll PA23 8SE (01369 840666).

Website: www.forestry.gov.uk/recreation

Refreshments: At Ardgartan Visitor Centre. Hotel at Lochgoilhead. Tea rooms at Benmore, south of Glenbranter.

32-36 WEST OF SCOTLAND FORESTRY

CATEGORY
Waymarked forestry routes
DISTANCE
4 - 19 miles
ROUTES / CENTRES
20 routes / 12 centres

A leaflet produced by the Forestry Commission, *Cycling in the Forest - West of Scotland* describes a whole series of waymarked forestry routes in holdings lying to the west of a line from Glasgow to Fort William. Many have spectacular views of the lochs, coastline and islands in this magnificent part of Scotland.

32 Routes near Lochgilphead (3 routes)

STARTING POINT FOR 2 TRAILS BELOW

Druim-an-Duin *car park, off the B8025 Tayvallich road, 20 miles south of Oban, off the A816 (grid reference 784906 / OS Landranger Map 55).*

Ardnoe

DISTANCE	GRADE / WAYMARKS
12 miles	Hard / Blue

Excellent views across the Sound of Jura and Loch Sween.

Faery Isles (linear route)

DISTANCE	GRADE / WAYMARKS
6 miles	Easy / Red

Ride through broadleaf woodland of the Faery Isles Caledonian Forest Reserve with stunning views of Loch Sween.

STARTING POINT FOR TRAIL BELOW

*Dunardry car park, near **Cairnbaan** on the B841, about 20 miles south of Oban, off the A816 (grid reference 824908 / OS Landranger Map 55).*

Lochan Buic

DISTANCE	GRADE / WAYMARKS
10 miles	Hard / Green

There are views over Kilmartin Glen and Knapdale National Scenic Area on your way to Achnamara and Dunardry.

33 Routes east of Oban (3 routes)

STARTING POINT FOR 3 TRAILS BELOW

Barnaline car park, on the minor road on the west side of Loch Awe, at the road junction east of Loch Avich, southeast of Oban (grid reference 971141 / OS Landranger Map 55).

Two Lochs*

DISTANCE	GRADE / WAYMARKS
9 miles	Easy / Red

There are magnificent views of Loch Avich and Loch Awe on this route.

Loch Avich Trail*

DISTANCE	GRADE / WAYMARKS
14 miles	Moderate / Green

A circuit of Loch Avich. Dorlin Point, on the north shore of the loch is a great place to have a picnic.

Kilmaha & New York*

DISTANCE	GRADE / WAYMARKS
10.5 miles	Moderate / Blue

This ride runs along the shore of Loch Awe and climbs into the heart of Inverliever Forest
*These 3 routes are shown on a separate leaflet, *Loch Awe Up Close*, available from Forestry Commission, Lochgilphead (01546 602518).

Glen Orchy (linear)

STARTING POINT

*Car park at **Bridge of Orchy**, on the A82 between Crianlarich and Fort William (grid reference 296397 / OS Landranger Map 50).*

DISTANCE	GRADE / WAYMARKS
8 miles	Hard / Red

A demanding route through some of Scotland's wildest scenery. Two of the westernmost outposts of Caledonian pine forest are located in the area.

Fearnoch & Glen Lonan

STARTING POINT

Quarry car park in the forest east of Fearnoch village on the A85 between Connell and Taynuilt, northeast of Oban (grid reference 968324 / OS Landranger Map 49).

DISTANCE	GRADE / WAYMARKS
5 miles	Easy / Red & Green

A circular route within the forest (green waymarks) and a through route into Glen Lonan (red waymarks). Glow worms can be seen at the right season in the dusk just before reaching the village of Fearnoch.

Mill Farm & Barcaldine

STARTING POINT

Forest car park 1 mile south of Barcaldine, on the B845, northeast of Oban (grid reference 964404 / OS Landranger Map 49).

DISTANCE	GRADE / WAYMARKS
8 miles	Easy / Red & Purple

A through route from Barcaldine to Mill Farm (red waymarks) and a circular route within the forest (purple waymarks).

Glen Dubh

STARTING POINT

Sutherland's Grove car park, 1/2 mile northeast of Barcaldine on the A828 northeast of Oban (grid reference 967426 / OS Landranger Map 49).

DISTANCE	GRADE / WAYMARKS
5 miles	Easy / Blue
8 miles	Medium / Green

Two routes, one shorter, for families (blue waymarks), one longer and more challenging (green waymarks). The reservoir provides water for the alginate factory which processes seaweed into valuable food compounds.

34 Routes near Tobermory, on the Isle of Mull (2 routes)

Lettermore & Loch Frisa

STARTING POINT

Aros Forest Office, on the A848, about 10 miles southeast of Tobermory, Isle of Mull (grid reference 564452 / OS Landranger Map 48).

DISTANCE	GRADE / WAYMARKS
5 (loop)	Easy / Blue
8 (linear)	Easy / Red

The Ledmore Circular Route (5 miles / blue) goes through woodland and fields, passing the traditional burying place of the Clan MacQuarrie. The Ledmore to Lettermore Through Route (8 miles one way / red) runs along the east side of Loch Frisa to the B8073.

Ardmore & Glengorm

STARTING POINT

Forest car park 2 miles along the minor road from Tobermory towards Glengorm (grid reference 486557 / OS Landranger Map 47).

DISTANCE	GRADE / WAYMARKS
4 miles	Easy / Red

A route through the forest and along the coast, returning by the county road. Fine views of the Ardnamurchan Peninsula. The fastest growing Sitka spruce trees in Britain are here, near the shore at Penalbanach.

32

36

35 Routes near Lochaline, Morvern (2 routes)

Head of Loch Aline & Savary
STARTING POINT

Lochaline, at the end of the A884, about 40 miles southwest of Fort William (grid reference 679445 / OS Landranger Map 49).

DISTANCE	GRADE / WAYMARKS
9 miles	Medium / Red

A long climb on forest roads takes you up to a viewpoint with panoramic vistas followed by a descent on an old drove road. Soaring Golden eagles and sea eagles are very occasionally seen here.

Head of Loch Aline & Arienas
STARTING POINT

*Loch Arienas, off the A884, about 4 miles **north of Locahaline**, 40 miles southwest of Fort William (grid reference 683504 / OS Landranger Map 49).*

DISTANCE	GRADE / WAYMARKS
3.5 miles	Easy / Blue

Linking Loch Aline and Loch Arienas with an easy climb. Pine martens can often be seen running along the roadside. They are dark brown and about the size of a small cat.

36 Routes north of Oban & near Fort William (2 routes)

Glenachulish & St Johns
STARTING POINT

*Car park in **Glenachulish**, 1/4 mile west of the Ballachulish Bridge on the A82 Oban road, east of the A82 / A828 junction (grid reference 047589 / OS Landranger Map 41).*

DISTANCE	GRADE / WAYMARKS
6 miles	Easy / Blue & Red

A steep circular route in the forest (blue waymarks) and a through route to St John's (red waymarks). The scars of a large landslide can be seen on the hillside.

Leanachan Forest

STARTING POINT

*Aonach Mor ski facility, 6 miles **north of Fort
William** (grid reference 172773 / OS Landranger
Map 41).*

DISTANCE	GRADE / WAYMARKS
Lots!	All grades

There are over 25 miles of tracks to explore
with spectacular views of Ben Nevis and the
Great Glen throughout. There are also two
Trailquest routes, the Torlundy Trail and the
Cour Trail, aimed at families, covered by a
separate leaflet, *Leanachan Forest Trailquest*
(see below under **Useful publications**).

Useful publications: OS Landranger Maps 41,
47, 48, 49, 50, 55 & 56.
Much better are the leaflets produced by the
Forestry Commission, available from Lochaber
Forest District, Torlundy, Fort William,
Inverness-shire PH33 6SW (01397 702184) -

- *Cycling in the Forest - West of Scotland*
- *Leanachan Forest Trailquest - Orienteering on
  a Bicycle*
- *Loch Awe Up Close*

Website: www.forestry.gov.uk/recreation

37 Tay Forest Park, near Aberfeldy (2 routes)

CATEGORY

Waymarked forest routes

DISTANCE

6 and 9 miles

ROUTES / CENTRES

2 routes / 2 centres

Tay Forest Park includes some of the most
scenic areas in Highland Perthshire, where a
favourable climate and rich soil have nurtured
Scotland's finest forests. The story of Perthshire's
place at the heart of the great resurgence in
Scottish forestry in the 17th and 18th centuries

is evident at Drummond Hill and Craigvinean
Forests. Following centuries of over-
exploitation, the 'planting lairds' of Breadalbane
and Atholl created fine new forests and tested
newly discovered species from overseas.
Craigvinean was created from larch seed that
was brought back from the Alps for the Second
Duke of Atholl. Several innovative techniques
were employed in planting the trees including
scattering thousands of seeds by cannon onto
the dramatic crags of Craig Barns just across the
River Tay.

Drummond Hill

STARTING POINT

*Forest car park to the **west of Aberfeldy** along
the A287 to Kenmore then east along the minor
road to the Mains of Taymouth (grid reference
772460 / OS Landranger Map 52).*

DISTANCE	GRADE / WAYMARKS
6 miles	Moderate / Green

Craigvinean

STARTING POINT

*forest car park west of Dunkeld off the A9 on
the minor road leading to the Hermitage (grid
reference 006418 / OS Landranger Map 52).*

DISTANCE	GRADE / WAYMARKS
9 miles	Moderate / Blue

Station: Dunkeld.

TIC: Dunkeld, 01350 727688; Aberfeldy, 01887
820276.

Other nearby trails: The traffic-free sections of
the Lochs & Glens Cycle Route between Killin
and Aberfoyle lie about 20 miles to the
southwest of Aberfeldy.

Useful publications: OS Landranger Map 52.
Leaflet available from Aberfeldy Tourist
Information Centre.

Website: www.forestry.gov.uk/recreation

Refreshments: Only in Aberfeldy and Dunkeld.

38 Great Glen Cycle Route from Banavie / Fort William to Gairlochy

CATEGORY
Canal towpath.

DISTANCE
7 miles each way.

The Great Glen Cycle Route is one of the most spectacular long distance routes in the country using a mixture of canal towpath, minor roads and forestry tracks, passing alongside several lochs. The route is broken down into the traffic-free sections. This section follows the Caledonian Canal northwest from Banavie, near Fort William, to Gairlochy. There is one short climb, alongside the locks of Neptune's Staircase, where on fine days you will see Ben Nevis to your right. The route is waymarked with a series of white on brown 'Great Glen Cycle Route' signs. Beyond Gairlochy the route follows the relatively quiet B8005 for 4 miles to Clunes before joining the next traffic-free section alongside Loch Lochy.

STARTING POINT & PARKING
The car park at Neptune's Staircase off the A830 to the **northeast of Fort William** (grid reference 113768). The towpath runs along the south side of the canal ie keep the water to your left as you head away from Fort William.

Station: Fort William.
TIC: Fort William, 01397 703781.
Other nearby trails: See Northern Highlands Forestry and Northeast Scotland Forestry.
Useful publications: OS Landranger Map 41.
The Great Glen - Cycling in the Forest leaflet is available from: Forest Enterprise, Strathoich, Fort Augustus, Inverness-shire PH32 4BT (01320 366322).
Refreshments: Lots of choice in Banavie and Gairlochy.

38

39

from: Forest Enterprise, Strathoich, Fort Augustus,
Inverness-shire PH32 4BT (01320 366322).
Refreshments: None on route, lots of choice in
Invergarry.

40 Great Glen Cycle Route from Oich Bridge to Fort Augustus

CATEGORY
Canal towpath.

DISTANCE
5 miles each way.

This easy section of the Great Glen Cycle Route
follows the Caledonian Canal from the Bridge of
Oich to Fort Augustus where there is a wide
choice of refreshments. The canal joins Loch
Oich to Loch Ness. The scenic Kytra lock lies in
the shadow of the ancient Torr Dhuin hill fort.
Fort Augustus was built after the 1715 Jacobite
uprising and named after Prince William
Augustus, the Duke of Cumberland. Local
history is covered in the Great Glen Heritage
Centre. The link to the section alongside Loch
Lochy is via a steep climb through forestry,
passing through Invergarry.

STARTING POINTS & PARKING
→ **Bridge of Oich on** the A82 southwest of Fort
Augustus (grid reference 338035).
→ **Fort Augustus** on the A82 half way between
Fort William and Inverness.

Station: Fort William or Inverness.
TIC: Fort Augustus, 01320 366367.
Other nearby trails: See Northern Highlands
Forestry and Northeast Scotland Forestry.
Useful publications: OS Landranger Map 34. *The
Great Glen - Cycling in the Forest* leaflet is available
from: Forest Enterprise, Strathoich, Fort Augustus,
Inverness-shire PH32 4BT (01320 366322).
Refreshments: Lots of choice in Fort Augustus.

39 Great Glen Cycle Route from Clunes to Kilfinnan (Laggan)

CATEGORY
Forestry track alongside loch.

DISTANCE
10 miles each way.

The second traffic-free section of the Great Glen
Route follows the north shore of Loch Lochy
from Clunes northeast to the historic Kilfinnan
graveyard, passing the ruins of Glas Dhoire.
This section of the trail involves some climbs
with great views across to the hills on the east
side of Loch Lochy. If you are lucky you may
glimpse red deer and even a golden eagle. A
minor road continues beyond Kilfinnan towards
Invergarry. Steep forest roads lead on to the next
easy section.

STARTING POINT & PARKING
The car park at **Clunes** on the B8005, off the
A82 / B8004 to the northeast of Fort William
(grid reference 205885).

Station: Fort William.
TIC: Fort William, 01397 703781.
Other nearby trails: See Northern Highlands
Forestry and Northeast Scotland Forestry.
Useful publications: OS Landranger Map 34. *The
Great Glen - Cycling in the Forest* leaflet is available

41 Great Glen Cycle Route from Fort Augustus to Drumnadrochit

CATEGORY

Challenging forestry roads.

DISTANCE

Up to 19 miles each way.

This final traffic-free section of the Great Glen is the hardest of the four sections described, with several demanding climbs, rewarded by wide-ranging views over woodland, water and mountains. Who knows, you may be rewarded with a wave from the Loch Ness monster! Starting at Allt na Criche car park to the northeast of Fort Augustus the trail goes through Invermoriston along the north side of Loch Ness. The final 4 miles are on a minor lane dropping you steeply right down into Drumnadrochit where you have a chance of refreshment. From Drumnadrochit to Inverness the Great Glen Cycle Route is all on road, albeit quiet lanes until almost reaching Inverness where you have to join the busy A82.

NB Quiet lanes take you into and out of Invermoriston but the busy A82 is joined for a few hundred yards through the village.

STARTING POINTS & PARKING

→ The Allt na Criche car park and picnic site, about 1 mile **northeast of Fort Augustus** along the A82 (grid reference 391107).

→ **Invermoriston** at the junction of the A887 and A82 (grid reference 419165). By starting here you could break the route up into two: a south and north section.

→ **Drumnadrochit** on the A82 between Fort Augustus and Inverness (grid reference 513290).

Station: Inverness.

TIC: Inverness, 01463 234353.

Other nearby trails: See Northern Highlands Forestry and Northeast Scotland Forestry.

Useful publications: OS Landranger Maps 26 & 34. *The Great Glen - Cycling in the Forest* leaflet is available from: Forest Enterprise, Strathoich, Fort Augustus, Inverness-shire PH32 4BT (01320 366322).

Refreshments: Invermoriston.

42 AVIEMORE: ROUTES IN GLENMORE AND INSHRIACH FORESTS

CATEGORY

Waymarked forest routes.

DISTANCE

4 - 8 miles.

ROUTES / CENTRES

4 routes / 2 centres.

Aviemore has become a centre for offroad cycling: there are routes in Glenmore and Inshriach Forests; the Speyside Way can be followed north towards Boat of Garten and Nethy Bridge; there are trails in Rothiemurchus and Glenlivet Estates; and the Lochs & Glens Cycle Route (National Cycle Network Route 7) passes through the resort on its way north from Pitlochry to Inverness.

Glenmore Forest, east of Aviemore (2 routes)

STARTING POINT FOR 2 TRAILS BELOW

Glenmore Visitor Centre on the minor road east of Aviemore towards Cairngorm (grid reference 976098 / OS Landranger Map 36).

Sluggan & Badaguish

DISTANCE	GRADE / WAYMARKS
6 miles	Easy / Yellow

Heading northwest from the Glenmore shop, the route climbs gently through woodland then levels out before reaching the Badaguish Outdoor Centre. Beyond here you cross open

42

ground with good views of the distant hills before turning back towards the start. The ride could easily be extended by linking to the blue trail on the south side of Loch Morlich.

Serpents' Loch

DISTANCE	GRADE / WAYMARKS
4 miles	Moderate / Blue

The ride follows the south shore of Loch Morlich before climbing steadily past Serpents' Loch to the summit with good views of Ryvoan Pass and the Cairngorms.

Inshriach Forest, south of Aviemore (various routes)

There are a series of short routes to the north and south of Feshiebridge that can be linked to provide satisfying trails through the forest:

→ To the north, link the blue waymarked trails of **Insh Marshes** and **Creag Chone** to create a 7 mile trail.

→ To the south link **The Ord Trail** (yellow waymarks) to the **Kinvunicack** and **Drumguish Trails** (both blue waymarks) to create a linear 8-mile route from Feshiebridge to Drumguish with alternative options for your return.

STARTING POINT

*For both routes: **Feshiebridge** on the B970 south of Aviemore towards Kingussie (grid reference 853045 / OS Landranger Map 35).*

Station: Aviemore or Kingussie.
TIC: Aviemore, 01479 810363.
Other nearby trails: Rothiemurchus Estate, the Speyside Way,
Useful publications: OS Landranger Maps 35 & 36. More useful is *Cycling & Skiing in the Forest - Strathspey,* available from Glenmore Visitor Centre (01479 861220).
Website: www.forestry.gov.uk/recreation
Refreshments: None on the route. There is an inn in Kincraig.

43 Rothiemurchus Estate, southeast of Aviemore.

CATEGORY

Minor roads and estate tracks.

DISTANCE

7 or 11 miles.

There are two trails which start from
Rothiemurchus Visitor Centre to the southeast of
Aviemore. Both start by using the road that
heads east towards Loch Morlich and Glenmore
then climb up on estate roads into the forested
hills at the foot of the mighty Cairngorm
mountains. The main types of tree you will see
are Scots pine, birch and the shrub juniper. This
is a typical Caledonian forest habitat, important
as a home to a wide variety of wildlife such as
capercaillie, crossbill, crested tit, red squirrel
and pine marten.

NB There are more, similar trails in the
Glenlivet Estate centred around Tomintoul and
Tomnavoulin to the northeast of Aviemore. Call
the Glenlivet Estate Office (01807 580283) for
more details or visit the website:
www.crownestate.co.uk/glenlivet

STARTING POINT & PARKING

Rothiemurchus Visitor Centre on the B970
about 1 mile to the southeast of Aviemore (grid
reference 902109).

Station: Aviemore.
TIC: Aviemore, 01877 382352.
Other nearby trails: The Lochs & Glens Cycle
Route (National Cycle Network Route 7) passes
through Aviemore with a traffic-free section
north to the Boat of Garten. There are trails from
Glenmore Visitor Centre and in Inshriach Forest.
Useful publications: OS Landranger Map 36. A
leaflet, *Rothiemurchus Mountain Bike Trails*, has
a map showing both routes.
Website: www.rothiemurchus.net
Refreshments: At the Rothiemurchus Visitor Centre.

44 Speyside Way, east of Inverness.

CATEGORY

Riverside path and railway trail.

DISTANCE

16 miles each way.

The Speyside Way is predominantly a walking
route that follows the River Spey, famous for its
fishing and whisky distilleries, from Aviemore to
the coast at Spey Bay. From a cyclist's point of
view there is a long rideable middle section
largely on the course of an old railway line
between Ballindalloch (Cragganmore) and
Craigellachie with a spur to Dufftown. You can
also continue north along the Speyside Way for
a further 13 miles from Craigellachie to
Fochabers but be warned that it contains some
hillier and rougher sections through the forest.
The trail described runs close to the river for
much of its length, passing the famous
distilleries of Tamdhu and Knockando.

NB There is a short section from the end of the
railway path on A941 to get right into Dufftown.

STARTING POINTS & PARKING

→ The visitor centre in **Craigellachie**, at the
junction of the A95 and A941, southeast of
Elgin (grid reference 292454).

→ **Cragganmore**, at the end of the B9137, off
the A95 between Grantown and Aberlour (grid
reference 167367).

Station: Elgin or Keith.

TIC: Elgin, 01343 542666.

Other nearby trails: There are waymarked trails in the Wood of Ordiequish, to the south of Fochabers. See North East Scotland Forestry.

Useful publications: OS Landranger Map 28. More information about the trail can be obtained by calling the Ranger Service on 01340 881266 or visit the website: www.speysideway.org

Refreshments: In Fochabers, Craigellachie and Ballindalloch.

45 The Old Deeside Line (Aberdeen to Peterculter)

CATEGORY

Railway path.

DISTANCE

7 miles each way.

The Old Deeside Line offers an attractive wooded exit from the centre of Aberdeen west to Peterculter with occasional views across the wide valley of the River Dee. There are two road crossings near to the start where bridges are missing and a short section on quiet streets at the end of the railway path to get to the refreshments in Peterculter. Aberdeen is known as 'Granite City' because of the speckled grey stone used in so many of the city's buildings.

Duthie Park has floral displays in all seasons including the spectacular 'rose mountain'. The Winter Gardens house exotic plants, flowers, birds, fish and turtles!

STARTING POINT & PARKING

Duthie Park Gardens, to the south of **Aberdeen** city centre.

Station: Aberdeen.

TIC: Aberdeen, 01224 632727.

Other nearby trails: The Formartine & Buchan Way (Aberdeen & Peterhead Lines). See also: North East Scotland Forestry.

Useful publications: OS Landranger Map 38. A photocopy of the Old Deeside Line leaflet is available in person from Aberdeen Tourist Information Centre.

Refreshments: Lots of choice in Aberdeen and Peterculter.

46 Formartine and Buchan Way (Aberdeen and Peterhead Lines)

CATEGORY

Railway path.

DISTANCE

Up to 25 miles each way. A further 15 miles to Fraserburgh or 13 miles to Peterhead.

The longest railway path in the whole country, stretching north for 40 miles from Aberdeen to the coast at either Fraserburgh or Peterhead. It can easily be broken down into much shorter sections. The closer you are to Aberdeen, the better the surface. From Dyce railway station (next to Aberdeen Airport) the trail heads north past Newmachar, Ellon and Auchnagatt to Maud, with spurs beyond to Fraserburgh and Peterhead. There is a gentle 300 ft climb north from Dyce to Newmachar. Just south of Newmachar is the highest embankment and one

46

of the deepest cutings of the line. In the 1940s a train was stuck in the snow here for many weeks. Beyond Newmachar you will see the distinctive outline of Bennachie, far to the west. **NB** Care should be taken crossing the A920 near Ellon and the A948 in Auchnagatt.

STARTING POINT & PARKING
The railway station at **Dyce**, 6 miles north of Aberdeen on the A947 (grid reference 885127).

Station: The route starts at Dyce railway station to the north of Aberdeen.
TIC: Aberdeen, 01224 632727
Other nearby trails: There are several forestry routes in the Aberdeen area. See 'North East Scotland Forestry'.
Useful publications: OS Landranger Map 38. A leaflet *The Formartine and Buchan Way* is available from Aberdeen Tourist Information Centre (01224 632727).
Refreshments: In Dyce, Newmachar, Udny Station, Ellon, Auchnagatt and Maud (and at Strichen / Fraserburgh or Mintlaw / Peterhead).

47-53 NORTH EAST SCOTLAND FORESTRY

CATEGORY
Waymarked forestry routes
DISTANCE
4 - 10 miles
ROUTES / CENTRES
24 routes / 12 centres

The area covered here lies to the north and east of a line drawn from Inverness to Aberdeen. See also Northern Highlands Forestry.

47 Forestry southwest of Aberdeen: Durris, Drumtochy, Fetteresso and Blackhall (8 routes)

STARTING POINTS FOR 2 DURRIS ROUTES
Inchloan car park, on the minor road towards Inchloan, off the A957, south of its junction

with the A93, about 15 miles southwest of Aberdeen (grid reference 853113 / OS Landranger Map 38). Also Slug Road car park on the A957 Stonehaven to Banchory road (grid reference 781909 / OS Landranger Map 38).

White route

DISTANCE	GRADE / WAYMARKS
8 miles	Moderate / White

Circular route with moderate gradients at each end and mostly level ground for the middle section. This is used for accessing the Red Route, below.

Red route

DISTANCE	GRADE / WAYMARKS
1 mile	Hard / Red

A more arduous climb is rewarded with spectacular views from the summit of Cairn-mon-earn Hill to lower Deeside and surrounding areas.

STARTING POINTS FOR DRUMTOCHY ROUTES

Drumtochy Glen car park, 25 miles southwest of Aberdeen, on the minor road between the B794 Banchory to Montrose road and the village of Auchenblae (grid reference 698799 / OS Landranger Map 45)

White

DISTANCE	GRADE / WAYMARKS
12.4 miles	Moderate / White

The route offers the options of a circular route or a long link to Fetteresso Forest. There are extensive views over the Mearns and surrounding areas.

STARTING POINTS FOR FETTERESSO ROUTES

Blue / white route

Use Swanley car park, on the minor road between Stonehaven and the A957 (grid reference 830873 / OS Landranger Map 45).

DISTANCE	GRADE / WAYMARKS
9.3 miles	Easy / White & Blue

Follow the white waymarked trail linking into the blue route which loops around the Hill of Trusta and gives good open views to the south and west.

Yellow route

Use Slug Road car park on the A957 Stonehaven to Banchory road (grid reference 791894 / OS Landranger Map 45).

DISTANCE	GRADE / WAYMARKS
6.8 miles	Easy / Yellow

The trail circles Hill of Three Stones and and gives views to the southeast over the basin of the River Cowie

Red route

Use Quithel car park, on the minor road west of Stonehaven towards Auchenblae (grid reference 774856 / OS Landranger Map 45).

DISTANCE	GRADE / WAYMARKS
5.5 miles	Moderate / Red

A circuit around the picturesque basin of the Finglennie Burn.

STARTING POINTS FOR BLACKHALL ROUTES

White route

Use Shooting Greens car park, on the minor road between Potarch (A93, west of Banchory) and Waulkmill (B796, west of Strachan) (grid reference 633944 / OS Landranger Map 37 & 38).

DISTANCE	GRADE / WAYMARKS
5.5 miles	Easy / White

The route provides fine far reaching views over Deeside and the gradients are moderate throughout.

Red route

Park your car in Banchory, on the A93 west of Aberdeen, as there is no parking in the forest. The trail starts from the minor road on the south side of the River Dee, to the west of the Bridge of Dee (grid reference 685955 / OS Landranger Map 45).

DISTANCE	GRADE / WAYMARKS
7 miles	Easy / Red

A linear route that can be linked to the white route described above.

48

48 Forestry west of Aberdeen: Pitfichie and Kirkhill (4 routes)

STARTING POINT FOR 2 TRAILS BELOW

For Pitfichie routes: Pitfichie car park, southwest of Monymusk, 16 miles west of Aberdeen, near the junction of the B993 & A944 (grid reference 656133 / OS Landranger Map 38).

Blue

DISTANCE	GRADE / WAYMARKS
9 miles	Moderate / Blue

The ride uses steeper and harder sections on the western side of the forest, rewarded with panoramic views over the Vale of Alford.

Red Route

DISTANCE	GRADE / WAYMARKS
4 miles	Hard / Red

Largely on open ground with some very difficult sections. Magnificent views from the hill tops.

STARTING POINT FOR KIRKHILL ROUTES

Mountjoy car park, at the junction of the B979 and A96, about 6 miles west of Aberdeen (grid reference 853113 / OS Landranger Map 38).

Red / White Routes

DISTANCE	GRADE / WAYMARKS
9 miles	Moderate / Red & White

A circular route waymarked red goes around Tyrebagger Hill and Hill of Marcus and provides open views to Bennachie to the west. This is accessed by a linear route waymarked white running north from Mountjoy (grid reference 853113) or south from East Woodland (grid reference 855145).

49 East of Strathdon (3 routes)

STARTING POINTS FOR GREEN, BLUE & RED ROUTES

- *Bellabeg village car park or Semeil car park, near Bunzeach (Strathdon), 40 miles west of Aberdeen, near the junction of the A944 & A939.*
- *Semeil car park- grid reference 392117 / OS Landranger Map 37.*
- *Bellabeg car park - grid reference 354130 / OS Landranger Map 37.*

Green Route

DISTANCE	GRADE / WAYMARKS
4 miles	Easy / Green

This route offers a choice of direction with both options leading onto minor roads, offering you a choice of return. Fine views over the River Don.

Blue Route

DISTANCE	GRADE / WAYMARKS
5 miles	Easy / Blue

Wide views onto the rolling countryside of Strathdon.

Red Route

DISTANCE	GRADE / WAYMARKS
8 miles	Moderate / Red

One short difficult section rewarded with spectacular views over the Grampian foothills and valleys.

50   Southeast of Huntly in Gartly Moor Forest (3 routes)

STARTING POINTS FOR BLUE, RED & BROWN ROUTES

Gartly Moor car park, 6 miles southeast of Huntly, off the A96 Aberdeen to Elgin road on the minor road towards Insch (grid reference 580327 / OS Landranger Map 29).

Blue Route

DISTANCE	GRADE / WAYMARKS
3 miles	Moderate / Blue

Using a mixture of forest track and road, this trail is mostly easy to moderate but has short sections which are difficult.

Red Route

DISTANCE	GRADE / WAYMARKS
5 miles	Moderate / Red

Fine views over the surrounding countryside from the high points on the forest roads.

Brown Route

DISTANCE	GRADE / WAYMARKS
6 miles	Easy / Brown

The trail runs along the lower edge of the forest with views on to the farmland below.

51   East of Rothes in Ben Aigan Forest (2 routes)

STARTING POINTS FOR RED AND BLUE ROUTES

The car park 12 miles southeast of Elgin, on the A95 southwest of Mulben (grid reference 333492 / OS Landranger Map 28).

Red Route

DISTANCE	GRADE / WAYMARKS
4.5 miles	Moderate / Red

The easier of the two Ben Aigan routes with excellent views over the Spey Valley.

Blue Route

DISTANCE	GRADE / WAYMARKS
6 miles	Moderate / Blue

This route is for the real mountain bike enthusiast with some very demanding terrain. The whole of Moray can be seen from the top of the climb.

52   East of Fochabers in Whiteash & Ordiequish Forest (3 routes)

STARTING POINTS FOR ORANGE AND BLUE ROUTES

Winding Walks car park, 1 mile south of Fochabers on the A96, about 10 miles east of Elgin (grid reference 358586 / OS Landranger Map 28).

Orange Route

DISTANCE	GRADE / WAYMARKS
7.7 miles	Moderate / Orange

This route tours Whiteash Forest culminating in the breathtaking views from the top of Whiteash Hill at the monument to the Duchess of Richmond.

Blue Route

DISTANCE	GRADE / WAYMARKS
6.2 miles	Moderate / Blue

This route is essentially a link between Whiteash and Ordiequish Forests with the pleasing reward of extensive panoramic views from the highest point.

STARTING POINT FOR RED ROUTE

*Slorach's Wood car park, on the minor road
south from Fochabers parallel with the River
Spey (grid reference 341562 / OS Landranger
Map 28).*

Red Route

DISTANCE	GRADE / WAYMARKS
5.5 miles	Moderate / Red

This ride takes you through a contrasting pattern
of attractive mature forest, young plantation and
also open moorland.

53   East of Nairn in Culbin Forest (2 routes)

These two easy routes through the pines and
sand dunes of the remarkable Culbin Forest
are covered by a separate leaflet *A Guide to
Forest Walks and Trails in Culbin Forest*, which
is available from Moray Forest District
(01343 820223).

STARTING POINTS FOR YELLOW AND RED ROUTES

*Either Nairn East Beach car park on the minor
road leading northeast out of Nairn towards
Kingsteps (grid reference 903576 / OS
Landranger Map 27) or Cloddymoss car park,
further east, in the forest itself (grid reference
981600 / OS Landranger Map 27).*

Yellow Route

DISTANCE	GRADE / WAYMARKS
11 miles	Easy / Yellow

Red Route

DISTANCE	GRADE / WAYMARKS
9 miles	Easy / Red

Useful publications: OS Landranger Maps 28,
29, 30, 37, 38, 44 & 45. Much more useful is
the leaflet produced by the Forestry
Commission: *Cycling in the Forest - North East
Scotland*, available from Forest Enterprise, North
Scotland, 21 Church Street, Inverness IV1 1EL
(01463 232811).
Website: www.forestry.gov.uk/recreation

54-58   NORTHERN HIGHLANDS FORESTRY

CATEGORY
Waymarked forestry routes

DISTANCE
4 - 22 miles

ROUTES / CENTRES
7 routes / 6 centres

This region lies to the north of a line between
Inverness and Ullapool. See also pg.374. The
routes are listed south to north ie they start with
the routes on the Black Isle, close to Inverness
and end up with the routes close to Wick.

54   Black Isle
Black Isle Route
STARTING POINT

*on Black Isle, 10 miles north of Inverness, on
the minor road parallel with the A832, next to
the Mount Eagle Mast on the Munlochy to
Culbokie Road (grid reference 640578 / OS
Landranger Map 21 & 26).*

DISTANCE	GRADE / WAYMARKS
10 miles	Moderate / White

The ride offers splendid views across the
Cromarty and Moray Firths.

55   Strathpeffer Route
Torrachilty (linear)
STARTING POINT

*Contin Car Park, 20 miles northwest of
Inverness, on the A835 (grid reference 452571 /
OS Landranger Map 26).*

DISTANCE	GRADE / WAYMARKS
16 miles	Moderate / White

The ride follows the River Blackwater with views
towards Ben Wyvis (3400ft). It ends near the
Inchbae Lodge Hotel on the A835 Ullapool road
(grid reference 406689 / OS Landranger Map 20).

56 Near Tain (2 routes)

STARTING POINT FOR 2 TRAILS BELOW

Lamington car park on the minor road southwest of Tain, 35 miles north of Inverness, off the A9 (grid reference 755793 / OS Landranger Map 21).

Morangie

DISTANCE	GRADE / WAYMARKS
12 miles	Moderate / Green

Strathrory

DISTANCE	GRADE / WAYMARKS
24 miles	Moderate / Purple

The Morangie route offers fine views across the Dornoch Firth and up the Sutherland coast. It has some demanding offroad sections with 1300ft height gain. The Strathrory route climbs to a viewpoint over the Cromarty Firth, the Moray Coast and Ben Wyvis with a 1950 ft height gain.

57 East of Tongue (2 routes)

Truderscraig

STARTING POINT

Rosal Village car park, 35 miles southwest of Thurso, at the junction of the B871 and the B873 (grid reference 691427 / OS Landranger Map 10 & 16).

DISTANCE	GRADE / WAYMARKS
13 miles	Moderate / Red

This there-and-back ride runs parallel to the River Naver, a famous salmon fishing river, to reach the fascinating pre-clearance village of Truderscraig. Total height gain: 650 feet.

Borgie

STARTING POINT

Car park on the A836 to the south of Borgie, 30 miles west of Thurso on the A836, west of the junction with the B871 (grid reference 679579 / OS Landranger Map 10).

DISTANCE	GRADE / WAYMARKS
10 miles	Moderate / Blue

This ride uses a gently undulating forest road passing magnificent sitka spruce over 100ft tall,

groves of old Scots pine and pleasant open riverside areas with fine views north towards the coast and south towards Ben Stumanadh and Ben Loyal. Total height gain: 780 feet.

58 Route near Wick

Camster

STARTING POINT

car park 12 miles southwest of Wick, on the minor road running north from the A99 towards Watten (the Cairns of Camster road), starting just east of Lybster (grid reference 264429 / OS Landranger Map 11).

DISTANCE	GRADE / WAYMARKS
16 miles	Moderate / Red

The route rises to a fine viewpoint that makes the climb worth the effort. To the north and west lie the open peatland expanses of central Caithness and to the south and east there is a good view over the coast to the oil rigs that now dot the North Sea. On a clear day you can see from Hoy in the Orkney Islands to the Moray Coast on the other side of the Firth. Total height gain: 650 feet.

Useful publications: OS Landranger Maps 10, 11, 16, 17, 19, 20, 21 & 26. Much better is the leaflet produced by the Forestry Commission - *Cycling in the Forest - Northern Highlands* available from Forest Enterprise, North Scotland, 21 Church Street, Inverness IV1 1EL (01463 232811). **Website:** www.forestry.gov.uk/recreation.

Index